Connect, compete and change for inclusive growth

ABSTRACT

ID=43161   2015   F-06.08.01   SME

International Trade Centre (ITC)
SME Competitiveness Outlook 2015: Connect, Compete and Change for Inclusive Growth
Geneva: ITC, 2015. XXX, 235 pages.

The first annual flagship report of ITC on the topic of SME internationalization. The report highlights the fundamental role SMEs have in addressing global income inequality and presents a new analytical framework to measure, identify and enhance SME competitiveness. It introduces a working definition of firm competitiveness and introduces the SME Competitiveness Grid as a tool to classify determinants of firm competitiveness according to how they affect competitiveness and according to the layer of the economy at which this determinant intervenes. The report provides 25 country profiles containing SME competitiveness pilot assessments. It informs ITC's work in strengthening SMEs and trade and investment support institutions (TISIs). The case studies illustrate how ITC assistance fits within the wider evidence on SME competitiveness and describe practical steps to strengthen SME competitiveness at the firm level. Includes bibliographical references (p. 217-235).

Descriptors: **SMEs, Competitiveness, Statistics, Economic Indicators, Global Value Chains, Case Studies, Country Profiles.**

English, French, Spanish, Arabic (separate editions)

ITC, Palais des Nations, 1211 Geneva 10, Switzerland (www.intracen.org)

Digital image on the cover: © shutterstock

Doc. P258.E/DMD/OCE/15-X

ISBN 978-92-9137-428-1
United Nations Sales Number E.15.III.T.3

International Trade Centre, Palais des Nations, 1211 Geneva 10, Switzerland
(http://www.intracen.org)

Contents

Thought leaders

Case studies

Figures

Tables

Boxes

Acronyms

ACP	African, Caribbean and Pacific
ADB	Asian Development Bank
ASEAN	Association of Southeast Asian Nations
B20	Business 20 (business leaders from the G20 countries)
BRICM	Brazil, the Russian Federation, India, China, and Mexico
EOS	Executive Opinion Survey
EPA	Export Potential Assessment
EPI	Export Potential Indicator
EU	European Union
FAMEX	Fonds d'Accès aux Marchés d'Exportation
FDI	Foreign Direct Investment
G20	Group of Twenty
G2C	Government to citizen
G2G	Government to government
G7	Group of Seven
GCC	Gulf Cooperation Council
GCI	Global Competitiveness Index
GDP	Gross domestic product
GEM	Global Entrepreneur Monitor
GNI	Gross national income
IADB	Inter-American Development Bank
ICC	International Chamber of Commerce
ICT	Information and communications technology
IFC	International Finance Corporation
ILO	International Labour Organization
IMF	International Monetary Fund
ISO	International Organization for Standardization
IT	Information technology
ITC	International Trade Centre
ITU	International Telecommunications Union
IVC	International value chain
LAC	Latin America and Caribbean
LDC	Least developed country
LLDC	Landlocked developing country
LMIC	Lower-middle income country
LPI	Logistics Performance Index
MDG	Millennium Development Goal
MENA	Middle East and North Africa
MIGA	Multilateral Investment Guarantee Agency

MSME	Micro, small and medium-sized enterprise
NGO	Non-governmental organization
NTM	Non-tariff measure
OECD	Organisation for Economic Co-operation and Development
PDI	Product Diversification Indicator
PPP	Purchasing power parity
R&D	Research and development
SIDS	Small island developing States
SME	Small and medium-sized enterprise
SPS	Sanitary and phytosanitary
TBT	Technical barriers to trade
TFA	Trade Facilitation Agreement
TISI	Trade and investment support institution
TPO	Trade promotion organization
UN	United Nations
UNCTAD	United Nations Conference on Trade and Development
UNDP	United Nations Development Programme
UN-ECLAC	United Nations Economic Commission for Latin America and the Caribbean
UN-ESCAP	United Nations Economic and Social Commission for Asia and the Pacific
UNESCO	United Nations Educational, Scientific and Cultural Organization
UNIDO	United Nations Industrial Development Organization
UNPAN	United Nations Public Administration Network
USITC	United States International Trade Commission
WB	World Bank
WEF	World Economic Forum
WIPO	World Intellectual Property Organization
WTO	World Trade Organization
WTPO	TPO Network World Conference and Awards

Foreword

The year 2015 is particularly important for the global community. The United Nations Financing for Development Conference in Addis Ababa in July underscored the need for official development assistance, private sector investment and domestic resource mobilization to work in partnership for development.

The United Nations Global Goals (this refers to the 2030 Agenda for Sustainable Development), adopted by the UN in New York in September, will serve as the international community's compass in achieving sustainable and inclusive growth over the next fifteen years. And the end of 2015 sees key efforts to make progress on climate change at the COP in Paris and on trade at the World Trade Organization (WTO) Ministerial Conference in Nairobi.

Taken together, these prepare the groundwork for a global development agenda. A compact with ourselves.

As we move from the encouraging but uneven implementation of the Millennium Development Goals (MDGs), we have much to learn on how to make this next phase yet more successful. Collectively, we have the opportunity to engender a generational shift.

The International Trade Centre (ITC), the joint agency of the UN and WTO, will focus on helping to achieve this new agenda for sustainable development and growth.

The past fifteen years have witnessed unprecedented levels of international trade and investment flows, but have also shown how global crises can derail the trade agenda. But trade is resilient. And trade must be a centrepiece of the global growth effort being charted from now until 2030.

To achieve this sustainable and equitable growth, we have to care about what happens between and across economies, but also within economies. There must be greater attention paid to the actors that have the most potential to harness and share the power of trade. Crucial among these are small and medium-sized enterprises (SMEs).

SMEs make up the bulk of the economic tissue of the economy. In developing countries they represent the majority of employment, including female employment. Investing in SMEs is a long-term and smart strategy, with sustainable returns that multiply across regions, countries and societies.

There is a pressing need for active participation in trade to go beyond the wealthiest 5% of the global economy. This is all the more important because political consensus in favour of open trade and investment ultimately relies on the perception that these policies benefit the majority of voters.

In all economies of this world, the majority of voters is employed in SMEs. Although SMEs account for the vast majority of businesses, they generate only about half of GDP. For the gains from trade to be distributed equitably and benefit the economically vulnerable – and the majority of average voters – SMEs have to be at the heart of the story.

This first annual flagship report of ITC considers how this can be achieved. With its cursor placed firmly on evidence-based practical solutions, it is an immediate contribution towards implementing the UN Global Goals. It also contributes to a nascent discussion at the WTO on how to better leverage trade policies for SMEs.

The report's focus on the private sector reflects one of the strong messages of the UN Global Goals: the value of working with the private sector to achieve sustainable development.

This report highlights one simple but very striking fact: small enterprises are on average less productive than large ones, but the productivity gaps are much larger in developing economies than in industrialized countries. This suggests that many opportunities to generate wealth are wasted because too many firms do not take advantage of chances to move up the productivity value chain.

It also suggests that a majority of workers could benefit from higher wages and better working conditions if their employers were able to catch up with larger counterparts.

Last but not least, this report suggests that many economies are less vibrant than their potential, given the lack of clear policy direction from within SMEs.

The report examines the causes for lagging productivity and unrealized competitiveness gains among SMEs. The analysis goes beyond the overall macroeconomic business environment to identify factors, both outside and within firms, which can serve as a lever to accelerate participation in trade.

Together, these forces and factors define whether firms manage to connect, compete and change to be competitive in regional and global markets and contribute to inclusive growth in their home country.

With the comprehensive data analysis presented in this and forthcoming reports, the SME Competitiveness Outlook will contribute to understanding better how SME competitiveness compares across countries. It will also allow:

■ SMEs to assess their strategic position within their lines of business.

■ Foreign investors to identify SMEs that can become useful partners in international value chains.

■ Governments and trade and investment support institutions (TISIs) to identify where action is needed to increase SME competitiveness.

The report will inform ITC's work in strengthening SMEs and TISIs. The report's case studies illustrate how ITC assistance fits within the wider evidence on SME competitiveness and describe practical steps to strengthen SME competitiveness at the firm level and in the immediate and macroeconomic environments.

ITC is not the only agency active in the area of SMEs. This report builds on and complements the many efforts by national, regional and global institutions to understand the world of SMEs. Significantly, the report also builds on the experience of entrepreneurs, who actively experience what it means to be an SME competing in global markets or to work with SMEs across borders.

My particular thanks go to the academic experts who provided background studies and above all to the five global thought leaders who contributed personally by outlining their vision for SMEs and their role in regional and global markets.

While none of us knows precisely what the coming fifteen years will bring, it is clear that there will continue to be change. With the SME Competitiveness Outlook, ITC provides a tool that puts SMEs in a position to be drivers and beneficiaries of that change and to contribute to shaping the world that we want in 2030.

Arancha González
Executive Director, ITC

Executive Summary

SMEs are the missing link to inclusive growth. SMEs account for approximately 60-70% of total employment. The wages paid by SMEs are significantly lower than those paid by large firms. This is largely because their productivity lags behind large firm productivity. Addressing the 'productivity gap' is crucial for inclusive growth. This report argues that to increase productivity, firms must connect, compete and change.

Part I. SMEs and global markets: The missing link for inclusive growth

1. Understanding SMEs

SMEs contribute significantly to employment, GDP and exports

SMEs constitute the overwhelming majority of firms. Globally, SMEs make up over 95% of all firms, account for approximately 50% of GDP and 60%–70% of total employment, when both formal and informal SMEs are taken into account. This amounts to between 420 million and 510 million SMEs, 310 million of which are in emerging markets.

Many shapes and sizes

The term 'SME' encompasses a broad range of definitions, which differ according to factors such as country, geographic region, level of development and business culture. Even within countries, definitions may vary or be non-existent. In addition, the definition itself is often linked to national support programmes and other regulations, making the adoption of a single definition difficult.

Firm size and the structural make-up of economies

The importance of the SME sector has changed over time, reflecting the impact of technological change, changing market conditions and rising standards of living.

Before the industrial revolution, production was dominated by what today we might call SMEs. Small workshops and self-employed farmers employed few people and produced bespoke specifications. As the industrial revolution picked up steam, firm sizes began to increase steadily. For example, the median number of workers in cotton firms in Manchester, England more than tripled between 1815 and 1841. This increase was linked to the integration and emergence of national markets, which functioned as important sources of demand, encouraging production of large volumes of goods. Technological innovation and mechanization contributed to radical changes in modes of production. The advent of factories often required high levels of fixed investment, forcing firms to expand to benefit from economies of scale. This reorganization of production, alongside the expansion of firm sizes, grew apace well into the 20th century.

Since the 1970s, the trend has been changing. Increased concentration of employment and value added in large firms reversed in a number of OECD countries, and SMEs began to be viewed as sources of nimble innovation and job creation. Partly fuelled by a desire to outsource non-core competencies, the trend allowed firms to focus on their core competencies – resulting in horizontal (cluster) and vertical (value chain) production systems.

While the historical experience is interesting, it may also be of relevance for the near future. With increased market integration and expansion in recent decades, conditions may once again be in favour of large firms. On the other hand, factors like information and communications technology (ICT) create an environment that may be conducive for the re-emergence of SMEs. The spread of ICTs has led to the phenomenon of 'born globals': SMEs which, from day one of operations, sell or intend to sell to a global client base via e-platforms, blurring the traditional picture of the internationalization process.

2. Why the 'middle' matters

It is hard to grow up

The overwhelming majority of SMEs in the developing world are micro enterprises with fewer than ten employees. In many economies, the private sector is split into two segments: small – often micro – enterprises on the one hand, and a few very large enterprises on the other hand. This phenomenon is called the 'missing middle'. Among the explanations for the 'missing middle' is the central tenet that small firms have few incentives to growth, because they are adversely affected by taxes and access to finance policies once they are medium-sized.

A balanced firm size distribution stimulates competition

Domination by a few large players with significant market power tends to make economies less dynamic, in particular if small firms are too small to challenge the big players in the market and when lobbying for policy reforms. A balanced firm size distribution instead, stimulates competition within the economy and puts more firms in a position to also compete internationally.

3. SMEs, the missing link for inclusive growth

SMEs tend to be less productive than large firms...

It is well known from the trade literature – both theoretical and empirical – that larger firms are more productive, more likely to export and pay higher wages. What is less well known is that the productivity gap between small and large firms tends to be much more pronounced in developing countries than in industrialized countries. In Germany, productivity of small firms is some 70% that of large firms. In Argentina, by contrast, the productivity of small firms is less than 40% that of large firms; in Brazil, the figure is below 30% (OECD-ECLAC, 2013). In some countries, the productivity gap between small and large companies is even greater: in India, for instance, enterprises with more than 200 employees have been found to be ten times more productive than enterprises with five to 49 employees.

…and as a result pay lower wages

SMEs account for a considerable share of total employment. They employ an even larger share of the most vulnerable sections of the workforce, namely less experienced and less educated workers belonging to poorer households. Due to their lower productivity, SMEs also tend to pay lower wages. This is partly a reflection of the sectors SMEs tend to operate in: low value-added, labour intensive, low productivity sectors.

Significant inclusive growth opportunities are possible if the productivity gap can be closed …

Closing the productivity gap between SMEs and larger firms in developing countries is likely to have two direct effects: it would contribute to GDP growth, because of increased SME productivity; and lead to higher wages in the low-wage segment of the economy, with positive and equitable distributional effects.

This latter effect points to the inclusiveness of the growth potential generated by the rise in SME productivity. Those effects are likely to go beyond the immediate income effect on poor households. Higher wages for female employees are likely to have knock-on effects on the wider economy, as women in developing countries are known to have a higher propensity than men to invest in their families and in the community at large, leading to a positive impact for the country as a whole.

… for example via internationalization, as international firms are more productive

It has long been clear that internationally active firms tend to pay higher wages, employ more people and have higher productivity levels. Only the most productive and large firms are able to internationalize, as they are the firms able to afford the costs involved, such as fixed costs related to regulatory compliance or to identifying profitable markets and reliable partners. At the same time, internationalization can increase competitiveness through learning by doing and exposure to increased quality standards, superior technology and superior competition. There are significant gains to be made from internationalization – once firms have the capacity to do so.

4. Being part of international value chains

Stepping stones to internationalization

The potential advantages for SMEs to participate in international value chains (IVCs) are numerous, with some authors writing of a 'laundry list of benefits'. On the macro level, there are opportunities to create jobs, increase income, improve working conditions and diversify production and exports. On the micro level, IVCs can help increase access to finance, shorten lead times, reduce operational disruptions, cut inventory, improve quality and customer service, speed innovation and reduce risk.

SME chances to begin exporting increase when they participate in both local and international production chains. A study on Italian firms found that the probability of exporting for firms employing 1–9, 10–49 and 50–249 persons, increased by 98%, 34% and 34%, respectively, if they were part of a supply chain. This suggests that especially small firms can benefit from the reduced costs of entry and economies of scales by engaging in IVCs.

Importing intermediates also contributes to productivity increases

Furthermore, firms already exporting can benefit from engaging in IVCs, as the access to superior imported intermediate inputs can upgrade the production of outputs and increase the effectiveness of exports. It has, for instance, been shown that the effect of exports on the productivity and profitability of Tunisian firms was magnified if the firms also imported intermediates. This finding is in line with growing empirical firm level evidence: importing intermediates increases the quality and quantity of exports, and therefore magnifies its effect on productivity. Indeed, such imported inputs can be a strong channel for technology diffusion and particularly stimulate product and process innovation. The global lead firms of the chain have an incentive to improve their supplier products and processes.

Engaging with IVCs does not guarantee increased economic performance

Engaging with IVCs is by no means a guarantee for increased economic performance. The extent to which firms can reap these benefits will largely depend on their position within the value chain and their potential to move up the value chain. It is conceivable that firms can get stuck in the low value-added activities of the production chain, such as basic assembly activities or the extraction of resources, capturing only a limited fraction of the chains' rents and profits. SMEs in developing countries naturally enter IVCs via such activities. While this can lead to initial static gains in areas such as employment and productivity, it may hinder dynamic gains if firms are unable to move into higher-value added activities. This can be caused by power asymmetries between the chain's global buyers and local suppliers and incentives for the former to maintain the status quo. In other words, global lead firms may obstruct their suppliers from functional upgrading if this interferes with the lead firms' core activities such as marketing, R&D or sales.

How SMEs engage in IVCs depends on their competitiveness

As the inability to move up the value chain is largely due to these power asymmetries, the governance structure of the chain plays a key role in local firms' abilities to move up the chain. In the literature, the distinction between four types of governance structures can be found, which increase in their level of power asymmetry: arm's length relationships, networks, quasi-hierarchy and full hierarchy, or vertical integration. Under the first type of structure, the relationship among firms is not strong enough to facilitate technological spillovers. In fully hierarchical structures, lead firms will try to impede suppliers' upgrading. Relational networks and quasi-hierarchical structures have been found to be most conducive for upgrading, although for developing country suppliers it is difficult to enter relational networks, as they often require significant up front investments and high levels of capacity on the side of suppliers.

5. Internationalizing the elegant way: Competitiveness is critical

What determines whether SMEs manage to export directly or indirectly? What determines the governance structure within a value chain? What determines whether they manage to move up the value chain or gain a profitable and interesting position within a value chain, possibly with potential for upgrading?

Much depends on whether they are globally competitive in their chosen business activity. The recipe for successful SME internationalization is therefore likely to boil down to the determinants of SME competitiveness.

Competitiveness is often expressed in relation to selected 'lines of business'...

Defining competitiveness is complex. Dimensions involved include time (punctual or sustainable), scale (optimal firm size), space (e.g. national or international) and scope (focus only on firm level resources or also on capabilities).

This report expresses competitiveness in relation to 'lines of business', takes a dynamic approach and uses a definition that is applicable to firms acting in an international context:

> *Competitiveness is the demonstrated ability to design, produce and commercialize an offer which fully, uniquely and continuously fulfils the needs of targeted market segments, while connecting with and drawing resources from the business environment, and achieving a sustainable return to the resources employed.*

...with smaller firms having a tendency to be active in fewer lines of business

The 'scale' dimension is not explicit in this definition, which is meant to apply to firms of all size. Firms active in a wider portfolio of businesses tend to be larger and firms transiting from small to medium-sized to large have to remain competitive during the entire process if they wish to survive. SMEs have the particularity that they often are only active in one business, especially the smaller firms in the SME category.

In fast moving, global markets, the dynamic aspect of competitiveness is crucial

The term 'continuously' in this definition reflects the use of a dynamic concept of competitiveness (the time dimension). What is sufficient today to achieve adequate returns for the resources employed may not be sufficient tomorrow if the competitive environment changes. Firms operating in a global environment are constantly exposed to change, and adequate returns can only be achieved in a sustained manner if the firm is able to adjust to, or to embrace change.

Being connected is key for being competitive today

External factors change very rapidly. Competitiveness implies adaptation and resilience. Industry phases, breakthrough or disruptive innovations, increased competition, exchange-rate fluctuations and numerous other events require strategies to adapt. Firms that adapt successfully pre-empt change before external events strike, or follow with changes immediately afterwards, so that change is rapid.

Successful firms are directed by strong managers...

The quality of a company's business strategy is a major determinant of its success. The firm's leadership defines the business strategy and is responsible for executing it. A strong strategy leads to the configuration of an offer that allows the firm to position its goods or services successfully in a specific market segment. A successful offer typically consists of the appropriate combination of a number of aspects: quality and product characteristics, quantity, costs, and timeliness of delivery.

… who base their business strategy on up-to-date market intelligence

Firms do not design their business strategy in a void. They design it in the context of the competitive environment they are operating in. A prerequisite for designing a successful business strategy is therefore to be aware of, and familiar with, the competitive forces shaping a firm's environment. Information about consumer trends, compliance requirements, demographics, trade size and flows, trade agreements, preferential status, barriers to trade, or competition intensity, among others, is highly relevant to determine what can be a successful business strategy.

Meeting quality and sustainability standards is becoming a competitive 'must'

The rise of IVCs has been accompanied by a proliferation of mandatory/regulatory, voluntary and firm-specific standards. Investing in operations that comply with these standards – many of which are private standards – is no longer just an option; it is a major determinant of firms' competitiveness. The successful certification of products and services may facilitate firms' access to finance and new markets, as well as promote higher quality products and services in a sustainable way.

Access to finance determines daily operational efficiency and the ability to make investments for the future

Financing is essential for the implementation of business strategies and is an essential part of operating any business. Different stages of the business life cycle have varying needs for cash, with the start-up, growth and transition stages being particularly important. A firm's ability to grow and strengthen its competitiveness depends highly on its potential to invest in new ventures, innovation, improvements and diversification over time. All of these investments need short- and long-term capital; therefore, access to finance – including for female entrepreneurs – is a central issue. The implementation of transparent financial planning and record-keeping on budgets, purchases, sales, assets and liabilities in combination with a comprehensive business plan does not only promote firms' access to finance but also their potential to integrate into export markets and strengthen their competitiveness.

Access to talent is required at all levels of operations

Skilled employees are not only more likely to deliver high quality inputs into the production process; they are also more likely to be flexible enough to adjust, triggered by changes in the market environment. Access to skilled labour has been shown to increase SMEs' technical efficiency, their capacity to absorb foreign technologies, and enter into more knowledge-intensive activities. Access to skills – including soft skills – increases capabilities to communicate with clients abroad and makes it easier to meet international standards. SMEs that remain below a certain threshold level in terms of their employees' skills are therefore more likely to end up in the low value-added segment of IVCs.

Access to inputs and customers abroad matters for competitiveness...

While firms can do much to improve their competitive position, certain factors remain outside of their control. One major factor affecting firms' ability to access customers abroad is their market access as determined by their home country's or destination country's trade policy. Firms engaged in IVCs are particularly susceptible to the costs imposed by trade policy, as they may be taxed twice if they both import intermediate goods and subsequently export them again after processing. As tariffs have fallen over the last three decades, non-tariff measures (NTMs) are now widely seen to be an equal or bigger impediment to trade than tariffs. Research by OECD indicates that NTM-related costs add up to an average of 15% of total production costs.

... and is notably determined by trade policy and logistics

Serving customers can be a costly undertaking, and depends on the availability and quality of transport infrastructure as well as on the presence of relevant logistics service providers. In particular for time-sensitive products – like perishable goods – logistical aspects are crucial for competitiveness. Increasingly, SMEs follow the examples given by large counterparts and apply sophisticated supply side management and strategic logistic approaches. Yet, as much as SMEs are willing to do so, they will always be subject to their immediate and macro environment, including the nature and quality of processes imposed by border authorities.

Innovative firms are more productive and more likely to export

Innovative firms tend to experience higher levels of productivity and economic growth and are more likely to export – and do this successfully. At the firm level, innovation implies undertaking a series of concrete activities that may improve their innovative capabilities, such as R&D, patenting, spin-offs, incremental innovations, niche market segmentation, standardization, quality up-grading, differentiation, lean manufacturing (the elimination of waste), corporate re-engineering (downsizing, rightsizing, outsourcing, and offshoring). In this context, marketing research and product R&D are critical.

6. Addressing the challenges of internationalization

SMEs face challenges directly related to their size. Many of these challenges are amplified when set in a global context, and as a result, contribute to SME low survival rates. Although these rates vary widely between countries and sectors, studies suggest that around 20% of new firms go out of business after their first year, rising to just over 50% after five years. High failure rates are not in and of themselves a problem. The extent to which market failures cause SMEs to go out of business, when they might have otherwise grown to become export champions, is a cause for concern.

SMEs struggle to gain access to information on export opportunities...

In a recent monitoring survey carried out by ITC for the Fifth Global Review of Aid for Trade, 'access to information about export opportunities' was ranked first out of nine areas in which SMEs would value improvement: 64% of the surveyed SMEs mentioned this factor as one of their top three priorities, while for large firms the figure was 44%. Inadequate provision of business information by public or private associations is a well-recognized market failure, which increases costs and barriers to entry for SMEs.

...adding to other challenges to meet mandatory and voluntary standards...

The need to meet voluntary or mandatory standards and other regulatory requirements affects SME operations at all stages of production and delivery:

- Information: SMEs need to become informed on the details of the requirements.

- Implementation: SMEs may need to adapt products and processes to comply with these requirements.

- Certification: SMEs are required to demonstrate compliance, which typically entails certification of products or processes by recognized bodies.

- Recognition: The final step necessary for exporting SMEs is the recognition of the certificate by customs authorities at home and abroad.

Recent business surveys on NTMs undertaken by ITC reveal that compliance with technical regulations and standards, be it at the implementation or at the demonstration stage, are considered as the dominant problem, especially for smaller firms. On average, 49% of exporting SMEs in 23 surveyed countries report that their business suffers from at least one NTM. This percentage stands at 42.5% for large firms.

...calling for stakeholders to facilitate SME implementation and verification of standards

Various stakeholders play an important role in disseminating information on standards and NTMs, e.g. through the creation of global or national data platforms by international organizations or national trade and investment support institutions; in building capacity to conform to requirements (e.g. training institutes); and in facilitating the verification of standards (e.g. customs authorities). At the national level, government efforts have been oriented towards building quality technical infrastructure in developing countries, including accredited laboratories and certification bodies.

SMEs still suffer from a lack of funding for working capital and investment needs...

SMEs consistently cite lack of access to finance as a severe constraint. Often, the costs and risks of serving SMEs are perceived to be too high by banks. Because of information asymmetries and the high costs of gathering adequate information to assess the creditworthiness of typical SME borrowers, banks are usually reluctant to extend them unsecured credit, even at high interest rates. Subsequently, many SMEs with economically viable projects, but inadequate collateral, cannot obtain the most needed financing from traditional lenders. Female entrepreneurs are particularly exposed to this problem as lack of collateral, inadequate financial infrastructure and other barriers involving gender-based social and cultural barriers restrict the potential of women-owned SMEs.

The International Finance Corporation (IFC) reports that top banks serving SMEs in non-OECD countries reach only 20% of formal micro enterprises and SMEs, and just 5% in sub-Saharan Africa. Underscoring the scale of problems with access to finance, the Asian Development Bank (ADB) estimates that there is a global gap of US$ 1.9 trillion between the supply and need for trade finance alone. This gap widens especially at the 'lower end of the market', where almost half of SMEs requests for trade finance are estimated to be rejected, compared to only 7% for multinational corporations.

... but private and public initiatives can go a long way in closing the SME financing gap

Credit information systems, as well as movable collateral frameworks and registries, can prove particularly effective to facilitate access to finance for SMEs. Other promising solutions include direct assistance to SMEs to meet the requirements of formal financing. These include educating and training SMEs to prepare effective requests for financing and ensuring they have the relevant information to navigate complex loan application procedures. As commercial banks increasingly recognize the untapped and profitable opportunities the SME segment represents, there could be value in supporting the adoption of international best practices to successfully serve this strategic sector. There is scope to encourage cooperation between banks and providers of business development services. Finally, policymakers have placed increasing attention on enabling SMEs to diversify their funding sources beyond conventional bank credit to the non-financial private sector, including trade credit among firms, or through crowdfunding and investing platforms.

SMEs struggle to attract high quality workers due to inadequate market supply…

National skills policies are a major determinant of access to skills for SMEs. The capacity of SMEs to attract good talent with prior education/training and experience will depend on the ability of both relevant education and vocational education and training systems to provide young people with a comprehensive set of readily applicable, job-relevant skills.

… as well as their own limited ability to train their own employees

Skill mismatches are frequently observed in labour markets in both developed and developing countries. They are likely to affect SMEs disproportionately, which do not have the means (both financial and human resources) to invest in training their own workforce. Policy options to facilitate SMEs' access to skilled labour include training subsidies and support to employer networks that foster SME participation in training initiatives. Such networks can be horizontal networks – with SMEs jointly purchasing training services – as well as vertical – by taking advantage of buyer-supplier linkages.

Limited skills availability extends to the managerial and entrepreneurial level…

Furthermore, the lack of skills at the managerial level may be at the heart of (small) firm failure. Research suggests that firms in emerging markets tend to have poorer management practices than those in developed economies, and has been found to be a significant explanation for low firm productivity. This lack of managerial skills feeds negatively into entrepreneurial capacities, which are further constrained by socio-cultural factors, such as the fear of failure, especially pronounced for young and women entrepreneurs.

… and can be tackled by fostering a strong entrepreneurial culture

Shaping a strong entrepreneurial culture and fostering entrepreneurial skills hinge upon the quality and quantity of entrepreneurship education and training provided. In this context, it seems essential to start entrepreneurship education at young age, encouraging young people to become entrepreneurs driven by opportunity rather than by necessity. There is evidence that policymakers are indeed devoting more resources to stepping up cooperation with the business community, for example by developing entrepreneurship teaching materials and in providing training, incentives and support to teachers involved in entrepreneurship activities.

Technology adoption and scope for innovation are often weak among SMEs

A shortage of skilled labour has further implications: it can impede investments in technology. The benefits of technology are undisputed, and yet many SMEs are not realizing the full potential technology can bring. Their low level of technology engagement is recognized as a serious barrier to improved competitiveness, and they suffer the consequences in terms of inefficiencies and increased costs. In addition to a shortage of skilled manpower (e.g. of technical skills), four other key bottlenecks have been identified that could explain SMEs reluctance to invest in and adopt technology: the high costs of technology, a low awareness of the benefits of technology, data security and privacy issues, and an inadequate core infrastructure.

Finally, logistics costs relative to sales are significantly higher for SMEs than for large firms...

Studies on firms' logistics costs show that they tend to be significantly higher for SMEs than for large firms. For example, logistics costs in Latin America and the Caribbean (LAC) represent 18% to 35% of the final value of goods, compared to 8% in OECD countries. There is evidence that for SMEs this percentage may be over 40%, mainly as a result of high inventory and warehousing costs.

... and to reduce them, both hard and soft aspects of logistics, matter

For a country's logistics operations to function properly there needs to be a modern and efficient transport infrastructure. According to recent research by McKinsey & Company, US$ 57.3 trillion of investments in infrastructure development is needed by 2030. Besides these hard infrastructure investments, soft aspects of logistics are critical to make best use of the existing infrastructure. For instance, trade facilitation measures can assist in creating the right conditions for SMEs to internationalize by seeking to cut red tape related to trade, such as the cost of clearing goods, documentary costs, and border delays.

7. Small but numerous: Pooling resources, creating linkages

Due to small sizes, SMEs have limited political bargaining power...

Small firms are at a disadvantage with their limited ability to influence decision-making processes, market outcomes and defend their own interests. Small firms often have less bargaining power than large firms and may therefore only receive a limited portion of the chain's profits. Difficulties of being heard due to their size, extends to policymaking processes, which can end up favouring those with a louder voice. The result is a regulatory environment that systematically disadvantages SMEs.

One way of overcoming small size and isolation is to join forces. Two mechanisms are frequently used: the first consists of institutions that represent SME interests and provide relevant services; the second mechanism facilitates linkages among SMEs through clusters.

...for which they can compensate by working with trade and investment support institutions...

Whether general, sector- or function-specific, trade and investment support institutions (TISIs) cover all aspects of global trade: exporting, importing and investment. Recent economic literature has shown that the impact on trade of TISIs, in particular trade promotion organizations (TPOs), can be significant. According to one study, a US$ 1 increase in TPO budgets can result in an up to US$ 200 increase in exports. Another study showed that assistance directly targeted to individual enterprises is most effective for export generation when targeted to medium-sized firms.

...or by forming clusters...

Clusters can help SMEs to improve their productivity, innovation and overall competitiveness. What makes clusters potentially beneficial to SME competitiveness are the opportunities of 'collective efficiency', derived from both positive external economies and joint actions. For policymakers, clusters offer the opportunity to better streamline strategic intervention by providing an essential lever for policymakers to design and implement policies to improve SME competitiveness and their upgrading prospects, and help them overcome some of the barriers to internationalization.

...that can facilitate innovation spillovers

To help overcome coordination failures and support collective actions, cluster development policies can help to develop local competitive factors and strengthen linkages. It has been argued in the literature that cluster policies can address, inter alia, skilled labour shortages, facilitate innovation spillovers (dynamic efficiency), contribute to addressing first-mover-externalities (learning by exporting), and facilitate access to high quality business services.

Yet, although numerous successful clusters exist, it is probably the case that unsuccessful attempts to create sustainable clusters are even more numerous. Cluster policies can be conducive to the creation and sustainability of clusters, but they need to be well designed and are not a panacea for all economic development problems.

8. SMEs and global policy initiatives

Creating conditions in which SMEs can perform better in global markets and contribute to inclusive growth depends on action within countries, as well as international policies and measures.

The role of SMEs is increasingly recognized in global policy debates, especially those taking place in the context of the UN Global Goals, as well as the G20 and B20. The World Trade Organization's Trade Facilitation Agreement (TFA) is also of high relevance for SMEs.

The United Nations Global Goals call for a better leveraging of SMEs

The UN Global Goals established this year by UN Member States is notable for its ambitious reach and cross-cutting approach. In contrast to the Millennium Development Goals (MDGs), the post 2015 UN Global Goals make specific mention of micro, small and medium-sized enterprises (MSMEs).

In particular, Goal 8 promotes '...development-oriented policies that support productive activities, decent job creation, entrepreneurship, creativity and innovation, and encourage the formalization and growth of MSMEs, including through access to financial services'. Goal 8 also acknowledges the need to reduce trade-related costs and red tape for exporters by calling for increased Aid for Trade support for developing countries.

UN Global Goal 9, meanwhile, encompasses two other themes that are key to improving SME competitiveness – getting products to the consumer through improved logistics and being forward-looking through innovation. Goal 9 includes a target to 'increase the access of small-scale industrial and other enterprises, in particular in developing countries, to financial services, including affordable credit, and their integration into value chains and markets.'

The agreement adopted by the Third International Conference on Financing for Development (Addis Ababa, July 2015) is part of the UN Global Goals. It sets out principles and policies needed to deliver the UN Global Goals, with the focus on mobilizing resources and looking in depth at MSMEs.

The agreement's opening overview 'A global framework for financing development post-2015' notes that MSMEs, 'which create the vast majority of jobs in many countries, often lack access to finance'. It commits countries to work 'with private actors and development banks' to promote 'appropriate, affordable and stable access to credit to MSMEs, as well as adequate skills development training for all, including youth and entrepreneurs'. To address constraints in obtaining finance, especially for women entrepreneurs, the accord makes concrete suggestions regarding the design of financial regulations.

SMEs and the B20/G20: a spotlight on SMEs and inclusive growth

In its role as G20 president during 2015, Turkey established three overarching themes: Inclusiveness, Implementation, and Investment for Growth. Within these, Turkey views SMEs as a cross-cutting subject, emphasizing in particular the connection between SMEs and ensuring that 'the benefits of growth and prosperity are shared by all segments of the society' (Turkey's G20 Priorities, 2015).

In designating SMEs as a cross-cutting issue, Turkey has given prominence to SMEs in G20 discussions. Moreover, Turkey launched the World SME Forum in May 2015 to drive the contribution of SMEs to global economic growth, trade and employment.

In tandem with the Turkish presidency, the B20 group of G20 business leaders has sought to highlight the role of SMEs in growth and job creation, reflected in the creation of a B20 SME and Entrepreneurship Taskforce. The Taskforce's report pinpoints five barriers to growth faced by SMEs and entrepreneurs and makes five recommendations: access to international markets; access to finance; access to skills and talent; access to innovation ecosystems and the digital economy; and the ability to comply with business regulations.

The WTO Trade Facilitation Agreement helps SMEs

The WTO TFA establishes binding obligations to improve customs procedures, transparency, predictability, efficiency, and cooperation among border regulatory agencies and the private sector. The TFA can contribute to integrating SMEs into global markets. SMEs suffer disproportionately from fixed trade-related costs, because they cannot offset costs as easily as large firms. They also often lack capacity to comply with complex rules, customs and border procedures. Trade facilitation can cut costs and result in smoother, simpler export and import processes.

The WTO Trade Facilitation Agreement can help foster SME participation in public-private dialogue

Public-private dialogue is particularly suited for identifying policy priorities in the area of reducing trade costs and for building consensus on reforms. The TFA's measures for involving private sector representatives in trade policy formulation offer opportunities for organizations representing SMEs to be active in trade facilitation reforms and implementation. National efforts to include SMEs in public-private dialogue mechanisms should be encouraged.

Trade facilitation can help reduce discrimination against SMEs

The TFA contributes to reducing discrimination against SMEs in trade-related procedures, such as customs clearance. The Agreement specifically forbids the use of criteria that may be discriminatory against SMEs, such as the size of a company or quantity of goods shipped. By looking at areas where SMEs currently suffer discrimination, it is possible to use the process of implementing the TFA to improve trading conditions for SMEs.

Part II. SME competitiveness: A pilot assessment

SME competitiveness matters for SME success in export markets, for the competitiveness of their country, for GDP growth and the inclusiveness of this growth.

Understanding how SME competitiveness compares across countries is interesting for multiple reasons:

■ SMEs can assess their strategic position within the lines of business for which they compete.

■ Foreign investors can identify SMEs that may become useful partners within IVCs.

■ Governments and TISIs will be able to identify where action is needed in order to increase SME competitiveness.

This report presents the 'SME Competitiveness Grid' as basis for conducting a pilot statistical assessment of SME competitiveness.

The SME Competitiveness Grid

Based on three competitiveness pillars – to Connect, Compete and Change – the SME Competitiveness Grid makes it easier to spot strengths and weaknesses of enterprises. It determines whether these are from within the firm, the immediate business environment or the macro level national environment. This helps countries understand their trade potential and address what is stopping them.

FIGURE   The SME Competitiveness Grid

		Pillars		
		Capacity to Compete	Capacity to Connect	Capacity to Change
Layers	FIRM LEVEL CAPABILITIES			
	IMMEDIATE BUSINESS ENVIRONMENT			
	NATIONAL ENVIRONMENT			

Source: ITC.

Connect, Compete, Change

The three pillars in the SME Competitiveness Grid capture the time-sensitive nature of competitiveness: Connect, Compete, Change. The quick pace of innovation, the rise of IVCs and the dynamic nature of many markets require a high level of adjustability and flexibility from firms, and SMEs in particular. Firms that are competitive today, need to connect effectively to information channels and world markets to sustain their competitiveness, while retaining the capability to adapt to the new market conditions of tomorrow.

The Capacity to Compete refers to the static dimension of competitiveness. It centres on present operations of firms and their efficiency in terms of cost, time, quality and quantity. The Capacity to Change refers to firms' capacity to execute change in response to, or in anticipation of, dynamic market forces. The Capacity to Connect refers to the capacity to gather and exploit business relevant information and knowledge, including information about consumer trends, compliance requirements, demographics, trade size and flows, trade agreements, preferential status, barriers to trade and competition intensity.

On average, high-income economies perform better along all pillars and layers of SME competiveness

A total of 38 indicators from well-known sources are used as proxies for different determinants of competitiveness within each pillar/layer combination, including 17 indicators with data by firm size. These indicators are normalized and transformed into scores comparable across indicators and countries.

The data shows that, as expected, competitiveness scores are correlated with income group. The higher the GDP per capita in US$, the higher the score. A detailed analysis of different determinants of competitiveness is presented in the profiles of 25 countries (Part III). Geographic and development stage groupings are based on data gathered for 111 countries, and suggest that there are significant cross-country differences regarding the composition of the SME Competitiveness Grid.

Least developed countries and landlocked developing countries perform particularly poorly in the connectivity pillar

Least Developed Countries (LDCs) perform particularly poorly in the Capacity to Connect pillar, reflecting low ICT and cluster development scores. The SME Competitiveness Grid reveals that landlocked developing countries (LLDCs) have more than just a physical challenge with roads and ports. They also have a virtual challenge: e-connectivity rates are among the world's lowest.

Small firms systematically perform worse than large firms …

Large firms systematically outperform medium-sized firms, and medium-sized firms systematically outperform small firms. This holds for all income groups and for all regional groupings examined in this report.

… with the size of the gap being significantly larger in poorer economies

The gap between large and small firm performance is lower in high-income countries than in low-income countries. Taking the score of large firms as a baseline, in low income countries, small firms achieve 42% of the baseline, compared to 67% in high-income countries, based on SME Competitiveness Grid data. This suggests that the determinants used in the pilot assessment correlate well with the productivity differences identified and discussed in Part I.

The biggest gap between small and large firms is in connectivity

The gap between SMEs and large firms is most pronounced in the Capacity to Connect pillar. Small firms and medium-sized firms in developed countries score 64% and 86% of the large firm baseline in with regard to Capacity to Connect. In the same pillar, small firms and medium-sized firms in LDCs only score 22% and 54%, respectively. In three world regions – East Asia and the Pacific, sub-Saharan Africa, and South Asia – the gap between small and large firms is biggest in the connectivity pillar.

In LDCs, access to finance drags down small firms' capacity to compete and to change

In the Capacity to Compete pillar small firms in LDCs score 57% of the score attained by large firms, compared to 74% in developed countries. Dragging LDCs' scores down are the low rates of firms with bank accounts (25% for small firms and 40% for medium-sized firms). The low proportion of investment financed by banks also lowers the Capacity to Change of small firms in LDCs.

In South Asia, small firms' Capacity to Compete suffers due to difficulties to meet quality certifications

Large firms' Capacity to Compete in South Asia is comparable to that of large firms in LAC, and in Europe and Central Asia. Yet, small firms in South Asia are behind on the Capacity to Compete of their counterparts in the other two regions, mainly because they score poorly on quality certification.

In LAC, and in Europe and Central Asia, medium-sized firms outperform the median global firm

When taking the 'median global firm' as the benchmark for competitiveness, medium-sized firms are found to outperform the median global firm in LAC, and in Europe and Central Asia. Small firm performance is also relatively strong in these regions.

Small firm capabilities are strong in Europe and Central Asia, LAC, but weak in South Asia and sub-Saharan Africa

When comparing firm level capabilities across regions, the data reveal that small firm performance is relatively strong in LAC, and in Europe and Central Asia. In contrast, in sub-Saharan Africa and South Asia, small firms' capabilities are very weak. In South Asia, the low use of company e-mail addresses and websites by small firms is particularly striking.

SMEs in LAC: A model for entrepreneurship?

SMEs in LAC are strong entrepreneurial performers. When focusing on firm level capabilities, they outpace average performance in other regions. As assessed in this report, this includes East Asia and the Pacific, and the Middle East and North Africa (MENA). In their capacity to change, they also outperform SMEs in Europe and Central Asia.

Yet, when all layers of determinants are taken into account, LAC SME competitiveness is lower than SME competitiveness in Europe and Central Asia across all three pillars of competitiveness. It is on par with competitiveness in MENA, reflecting that firms in LAC have to struggle with a significantly weaker national environment.

The catch-up potential for SMEs is considerable

The analysis suggests that the 'catch-up' potential for SMEs is considerable. If SMEs in developing countries can increase their productivity and therefore competitiveness in relative terms to the level seen in developed countries, the gain from growth, particularly to vulnerable groups SMEs employ, would be significant. The country profiles in this SME Outlook give a first indication of how this can be accomplished.

Acknowledgements

The SME Competitiveness Outlook 2015 was prepared by a team led by Marion Jansen and under the general supervision of Anders Aeroe. The team members included Daniela Benavente, Loe Franssen, Sebastian Klotz, Alexandre Lauwers, Olga Solleder and Jasmeer Virdee.

Data and statistical assistance was provided by Abdellatif Benzakri, Lisa Bogler, Yvan Decreux, Ursula Hermelink, Xavier Pichot and Julia Spies. Research assistance was provided by Virginie Trachsel. Josephine Stott provided editorial and administrative support. Julie Wolf contributed to this report as a writer and editorial consultant.

The report benefited from background papers prepared by Leila Baghdadi, Charles Harvie, Ashraf A. Mahate, Dorothy McCormick, Gerald A. McDermott, Carlo Pietrobelli, Longxiang Shi, Herbert Wamalwa, Yaroslav A. Zhalilo, Hang Zhang and Lei Zhang.

Special thanks go to the thought leaders who contributed personal columns to this report: Minister Axel M. Addy, Carmen Castillo, Victor K. Fung, Anabel Gonzalez and Rifat Hisarcıklıoğlu.

The report benefited from comments from Alberto Amurgo Pacheco, Trineesh Biswas, Stefania Casappa, Giorgia Giovanetti, Charles Harvie, Iris Hauswirth, Leonardo Iebra Aizpurúa, Hernan Manson, Dorothy McCormick, Gultekin Ozaltinordu, Carlo Pietrobelli, Christian Planchette, José Prunello, Robert Teh, Marcos Vaena and Matthew Wilson. It also benefited from comments received from participants and panellists in the following events: SMEs and Global Markets: The Missing Link for Inclusive Growth (WTO, Geneva, 23 March 2015), Third CEPR-Modena Conference on Growth in Mature Economies: Revisiting the Contribution of Openness (Modena, 11–12 May, 2015) and 1st MENA Trade Workshop (Carthage, 3 June 2015).

The production and editing of the report was managed by Natalie Domeisen in cooperation with Mixtli de la Pena Gimenez, Evelyn Seltier and Olga Solleder. Kristina Golubic and Iva Stastny Brosig were responsible for design and layout. The report benefited from advice from Touchline during the conceptualization phase. Serge Adeagbo and Franco Iacovino provided digital printing services.

PART I.

SMEs and global markets: The missing link for inclusive growth

CHAPTER 1

Understanding SMEs

The influence of small and medium-sized enterprises (SMEs) on the structure, performance and future prospects of a nation's economy is the subject of increasing interest among policymakers at the national, regional and global level.

This reflects the fact that in most countries, SMEs constitute the overwhelming majority of firms and are major sources of employment. Add to this evidence that SMEs, and in particular young small firms, have been net contributors to employment growth since the 2008 financial crisis, and the rationale behind the greater focus on SME performance becomes clear (Haltiwanger et al., 2011; Criscuolo et al., 2014).

This section outlines firm size distribution in various parts of the world and key factors that have affected this distribution. It also discusses what constitutes an SME and provides an introduction to their performance in international markets.

SMEs contribute significantly to employment, GDP and exports

SMEs constitute the overwhelming majority of firms. Globally SMEs make up over 95% of all firms, account for approximately 50% of value added and 60%–70% of total employment, when both formal and informal SMEs are taken into account (ACCA, 2010; Ayyagari et al., 2011; Edinburgh Group, 2013). This amounts to between 420 million and 510 million SMEs, 310 million of which are in emerging markets (IFC, 2013).

Numbers by region

In the European Union (EU), SMEs constitute 99.8% of all businesses, 66.9% of employment and 58.1% of value added (EC, 2013; EC, 2014). This translates into 88.8

million jobs and over €3.6 trillion in value added, with SME exporters contributing 34% of total EU exports, or €1.54 trillion (Cernat et al., 2014).

In the United States of America, SMEs account for 99% of all firms, employ 50% of the private sector workforce, account for over half of non-farm gross domestic product (GDP), and represent 34% of total export revenue (USITC, 2014; Grover and Suominen, 2014).

Evidence for 10 South-East Asian countries shows that, on average, SMEs account for 98% of all enterprises and employ 66% of the labour force (Harvie, 2015; ADB, 2013). These SMEs contribute approximately 38% of GDP and about 30% of total export value (ADB, 2013). In China, the world's biggest exporter, SMEs represent 41.5% of total exports by value, clearly underlining their importance to the Chinese economy (ADB, 2013).

In Gulf Cooperation Council (GCC) countries, SMEs are estimated to account for 22% of GDP, a relatively low share when compared with other parts of the world (Mahate, 2015). This trend extends to employment, with SMEs accounting for only about 40% of employment.

In Latin America and the Caribbean (LAC) region, SMEs account for 99% of firms and 67% of employment. However, their contribution to GDP is relatively low. This is because in LAC countries, large firms are six times more productive than SMEs, compared with 2.4 times in countries belonging to the Organisation for Economic Co-operation and Development (OECD) (OECD-UNECLAC, 2013). If SMEs in LAC countries were to narrow this productivity difference to levels found in the developed world, they could achieve massive economic gains.

While few pan-African SME statistics are available, SMEs in Africa are known to dominate the means of production to a greater extent than in other regions. For example, in

Ghana, SMEs represent 92% of Ghanaian businesses and contribute about 70% of GDP (Abor and Quartey, 2010).

Clearly, SMEs comprise a large segment of the global economic structure. In developing countries, there is a substantial productivity gap between SMEs and large firms, raising the question of whether anything should and can be done to help SMEs bridge this divide.

One caveat in comparing these statistics involves the definition of an SME. Unfortunately, there is no uniform definition. The regional statistics mentioned above assume regional definitions for SMEs, where applicable. It is clear that what constitutes an SME merits a closer look.

Many shapes and sizes

The term 'SME' encompasses a broad range of definitions, which differ according to factors such as country, geographic region, level of development and business culture. Even within countries, definitions may vary or be non-existent. In addition, the definition itself is often linked to national support programmes and other regulations, making the adoption of a single definition difficult.

Adding to the plethora of country definitions for SMEs are those created by international organizations and non-governmental organizations (NGOs). The specific needs and environment of their project portfolios often drive such definitions. For instance, for the World Bank's Enterprise Surveys, an SME is a firm with 99 employees or fewer, whereas for the Asian and African development banks, an SME is a firm with 50 or fewer employees. This probably reflects the firm size distribution of the regions in which the latter institutions operate, and thus the level of economic development.

From under 20 to 300 employees

Richer countries generally apply higher employee thresholds than poorer ones. However, there are plenty of exceptions. Table 1 shows 12 country definitions of SMEs, by the number of employees. The left side shows countries in descending order according to per capita gross national income (GNI). Countries on the right are ordered according to the size of their definition of SME by number of employees. This shows that Viet Nam applies a significantly higher maximum employee limit than Norway.

For the purposes of this report, ITC uses the definitions adopted in the source material (Table 1).

Small, but 'born global'

A traditional way of viewing firm activity according to firm size would be as follows:

- **Small firms** tend to employ twenty or fewer people, are more likely to serve the local or national economy, use basic production technologies and possess limited fixed assets. Turnover and assets are expected to be about US$ 100,000.

- **Medium-sized companies** may employ 20 to 50 people, and are likely to be focused on serving the national economy. Turnover and assets are expected to be in millions of dollars. These companies likely will use competitive production methods and be relatively well equipped to join existing international value chains (IVCs), either by direct exports or by serving large or foreign firms in the domestic market.

- **Large firms** will have well over a hundred employees and have revenues in the tens of millions of dollars or more. They are likely to be internationally active (possibly at the head of an IVC) or export significant amounts of their production to international markets.

The above view is in line with recent economic modelling of trade (such as Melitz, 2003). Yet many companies will not fit into this characterization. This is partly due to the specific features of different economic sectors, but also reflects the levelling effect of new technologies.

TABLE 1   National SME definitions in 12 countries

Country ranked by per capita GNI	Max # employees	Country ranked by SME size	Max # employees
Norway	100	Viet Nam	300
Switzerland	250	Moldova	250
Australia	200	Switzerland	250
Brazil	100	Australia	200
Thailand	200	Thailand	200
Moldova	250	Bangladesh	100
Egypt	50	Brazil	100
Pakistan	50	Ghana	100
Viet Nam	300	Norway	100
Bangladesh	100	Malawi	50
Tanzania, United Republic of	20	Pakistan	50
Malawi	50	Tanzania, United Republic of	20

Source: Gibson, Tom and Hubertus Jan van der Vaart (2008).
Note: GNI: Gross National Income

New online platforms have made it possible for firms administered by relatively few people, ostensibly in small or even micro enterprises, to sell to a global client base. These trends tie into the rise of new types of firms such as '**born globals**'.

These firms are highly active in international markets from their founding; have managers with a strong international outlook; place a big emphasis on superior product quality; and use advanced information and communications technology (ICT) in a sophisticated manner. Even in manufacturing, innovations that lower the cost of entry, such as 3-D printers, may encourage the formation of SMEs to supply bespoke products to global markets.

Most developing country SMEs are informal

Adding to the complexity of describing the world of SMEs is the distinction between formal and informal SMEs. The formal-informal divide has multiple dimensions, and can be seen as a continuum (McCormick, 1987, 1993). One key dimension is official registration. Registration brings the 'inconvenience' of being subject to taxation as well as health, labour and environmental standards, but it also improves access to finance and other services. Globally, 74% of SMEs are informal, rising to 77% for developing countries (IFC, 2013).

Firm size and the structural make-up of economies

The distribution of various firm sizes within various economies has developed over time. This section provides a brief overview of the effects of industrialization, servicification, and internationalization on firm size distribution, with a focus on developing countries.

With industrialization, firms grew in size

The importance of the SME sector has changed over time, reflecting the impact of technological innovation, changing market conditions and rising living standards.

Before the industrial revolution, production was dominated by what today we might call SMEs. Small workshops and self-employed farmers employed few people and produced to bespoke specifications. Large firms did exist; almost all of their employment was domestic labour. The firm owned the raw materials, the goods in production and often the tools and equipment, and outsourced physical production to home workers (Mokyr, 2001).

As the industrial revolution picked up steam, firm sizes began to increase steadily. For example, the median number of workers in cotton firms in Manchester, England more than tripled between 1815 and 1841 (Lloyd-Jones and Le Roux, 1980). This increase was linked with the integration and emergence of national markets, which functioned as important sources of demand, encouraging production of large volumes of goods (Sokoloff, 1984).

Technological innovation and mechanization contributed to radical changes in modes of production. The advent of factories often required high levels of fixed investment, forcing firms to expand to benefit from economies of scale. This reorganization of production, alongside the expansion of firm sizes, grew apace well into the 20th century.

Since the 1970s, the trend has been changing. Increased concentration of employment and value added in large firms reversed in a number of OECD countries, and SMEs began to be viewed as sources of nimble innovation and job creation (Van Ark and Monnikhof, 1996). Partly fuelled by a desire to outsource non-core competencies, the trend allowed firms to focus on their core competencies – resulting in horizontal (cluster) and vertical (value chain) production systems.

The role of SMEs in the industrialization process has varied significantly across countries. Some countries experienced internationally competitive clusters of SMEs as a core of the industrialization process, such as Italy, Germany and Denmark. In other countries such as France, large companies primarily drove industrialization. Interest in the challenges and opportunities facing SMEs has been developing in this context over subsequent decades.

The historical experience may be relevant for the near future. With increased market integration and expansion in recent decades, conditions may once again be in favour of large firms. Yet other factors, such as ICTs, create an environment that may be conducive to the re-emergence of SMEs. These new types of SMEs are very different from their historical counterparts.

Highlighting some of the central drivers of this structural change is instructive. In short, in many sectors, fixed costs have fallen dramatically, lowering the overall barrier to entry for small firms; at the same time, the emergence of global demand, easily accessed via new information technology (IT) platforms, has allowed SMEs to expand dramatically their potential client base.

Services reversed the trend

The rise of the services sector may be the most significant example of this shift.

'Servicification' – the process of services becoming a major part of the production process and a major source of value added in an economy – is thought to be driven by changing consumer demand. As incomes rise, material wants are more or less satisfied and demand for services, such as health, education and ICT services, increases. These trends have led to a blurring of the distinction between 'goods' and 'services'.

Now, services are often integral parts of the production process itself, contributing to product design, assembly, marketing and logistics. There are also optional services with which final products can be bought.

What's more, increasing complexity of production has led to a strong demand for coordination services. Within IVCs, services tasks are often the links that create the most value, and define the competitiveness of the value chain as a whole – such as coordination services logistics, information management, and product branding. Often, these companies only require an office, IT equipment and highly skilled employees to begin operations, foregoing the huge fixed investment costs associated with building factories.

Small services firms have higher turnover per employee than small manufacturing firms. Large services firms have smaller turnover per employee than large manufacturing firms.

To look at the relationship between firm size and turnover, Figure 1 plots the number of full-time employees against turnover (in purchasing power parity terms; hereafter PPP) for a sample of about 50,000 firms from 123 countries. PPP US-dollars are used to control for differences in GDP per capita.[1]

Data from the World Bank's Enterprise Surveys have been used to generate Figure 1. The Enterprise Surveys primarily cover developing countries, although a few developed countries have been surveyed. These developed countries mainly consist of Eastern European countries, which are not fully representative of the developed country grouping as a whole. Nevertheless, it can be instructive to compare countries at different development levels.

Firms are classified by sector, allowing comparisons of profitability, productivity and turnover between sectors. For manufacturing firms, there is a strong relation between the number of employees and turnover. A possible explanation revolves around the benefits of economies of scale.

For services firms, the distribution is rather different, with a strong concentration around small sized firms. Nevertheless, at small sizes, per employee turnover is somewhat higher for services firms than for manufacturing firms. Interestingly, this trend reverses as enterprises expand. Manufacturing firms with more than a few hundred employees tend to have higher per employee turnover than large services firms reflecting the possible presence of economies of scale in manufacturing that are not present in the services sector.

FIGURE 1 Manufacturing vs services: No. of employees vs turnover

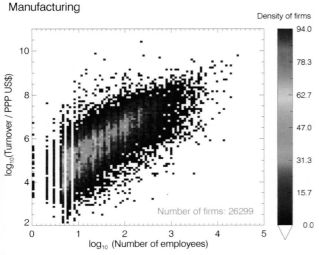

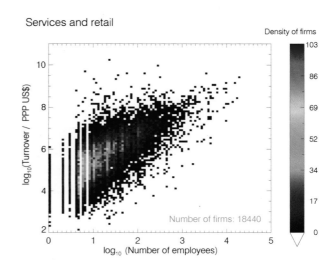

Source: ITC calculations from World Bank Enterprise Survey dataset.

It is possible to break this down further into specific sectors. Company data for the African, Caribbean and Pacific (ACP) group of countries reveal that service sectors, such as wholesale and retail trade, auxiliary transport activities, hotels and restaurants, and other services, comprise a large proportion of SMEs.

The manufacture of textiles, food products and beverages, and chemical products, meanwhile, relies more on large companies (Figure 2). This underscores that SMEs tend to gravitate towards the delivery of services. This likely is related to the high fixed costs associated with entry in many manufacturing industries. Such entry barriers tend to be lower in the services sector and in agriculture.

New horizons, thanks to technology

The globalization of demand also has created new niche markets that SMEs are well placed to serve. Technological advances and reduced trade barriers have provided SMEs with opportunities to internationalize, directly or indirectly, via international value chains.

For example, online platforms such as eBay have enabled SMEs from around the world to sell their goods and services to customers who might traditionally have been ignored by larger firms. This is the case for born globals – SMEs that sell, or intend to sell, to a global client base from the start – contrary to the traditional process of internationalization (Knight and Cavusgil, 1996; Madsen and Servais, 1997; Cavusgil and Knight, 2009).

A large firm level survey by DHL (2013) found that 24% of all SMEs in Brazil, the Russian Federation, India, China and Mexico (BRICM) countries and 13% of SMEs in G7 countries are born global.

In the future, large productive firms are expected to start as SMEs, in contrast to many legacy firms, which were effectively 'born large' after state-owned companies were privatized. Therefore, ensuring that policy addresses the concerns of SMEs will lead to a more dynamic and productive SME sector and also to more SMEs becoming large, improving national productivity and competitiveness.

Finally, falling communication costs combined with speedier Internet connections have enabled SMEs to overcome information-related barriers to entry and market failures. For example, learning about international quality standards and gathering market information is much easier than it was two or three decades ago.[2]

Unlocking the dynamic energy within SMEs by addressing market failures that disproportionately affect SMEs will help boost national productivity, and help ensure that the gains from growth are more evenly distributed. In later sections, this report elaborates on the effects of internationalization for the productivity, employment and wages of SMEs.

FIGURE 2 Firm size by sector in ACP countries

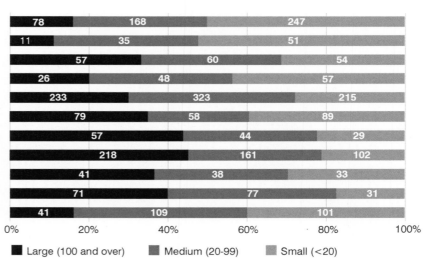

Source: ITC (2014).

CHAPTER 2
Why the 'middle' matters

If the vast majority of businesses are SMEs, they account for a significant portion of an economy's employment and GDP. The concept of the 'missing middle' shows that in many developing countries most SMEs are micro or small rather than medium-sized. Addressing this gap is a key to sustainable, inclusive growth.

Strong SMEs are exporters

It is well known that firms which export tend to be larger, both in terms of number of employees and turnover, than non-exporting firms (for example, Bernard et al., 2007; DHL, 2013). When plotted, the difference is remarkable (Figure 3). Exporters have significantly higher turnover and employee counts than firms that do not export. The maximum density for exporting firms is centred on 100 employees and approximately US$ 10 million (PPP adjusted). For firms that do not export, the maximum density is centred on firms with fewer than 10 employees and with turnover of about US$ 100,000 (PPP adjusted), although there is significantly more spread among non-exporters.

Most striking is the relatively tight elliptical distribution upon which exporting firms lie. This is all the more remarkable given the wide variety of countries (and hence business and regulatory environments) included in this sample of exporting firms. Indeed, the tightness of the distribution resembles that of individual countries. Irrespective of the country of origin, once a firm begins to export in earnest it enters a new market with its own set of rules and competitive pressures.

FIGURE 3 Densities according to export status: No. of employees vs turnover

Non-exporters

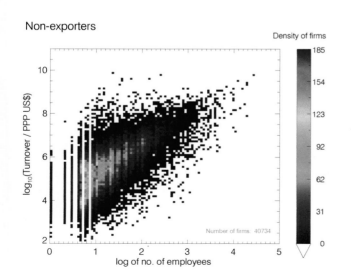

Exporters

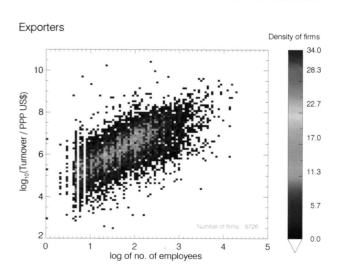

Note: Here, exporters are defined as firms that export, either directly or indirectly, at least 10% of their total sales.
Source: ITC calculations from World Bank Enterprise Survey dataset.

These findings are in line with broader research literature. For example, DHL (2013) found that international SMEs tend to perform better than average SMEs, with 26% of the international SMEs ranked as high performers, compared with only 13% of the purely domestic firms. A large proportion of respondents viewed internationalization as a way to improve long-term business growth by acquiring know-how and diversifying products.

SMEs export directly and indirectly

Firms can serve global markets in various ways. They can decide to export directly or indirectly by providing goods to firms within their national borders, which then export these goods. While large firms predominate in global trade, SMEs are major contributors to total exports.

In India, for example, SMEs accounted for 38%–40% of exports from 1998 to 2008 (Tambunan, 2009). In Viet Nam, SMEs contributed 20% of exports; in Thailand, the figure was 46% (Tambunan, 2009). These statistics do not include the significant contribution made by 'indirect exporters'.

Figure 4 provides firm level statistics on ACP exporters. Indirect exporters generally account for about 20% of total SME exporters, and sometimes this increases to 50%. Thus, SME exporters' contributions to employment and value added would likely figure significantly higher if indirect exporters were included.

SMEs have also had another option to internationalize over the past two or three decades. With production fragmented across borders due to fewer trade barriers and technological progress, firms in different countries can specialize in a specific stage of the production chain, and trade these intermediate goods internationally.

This report elaborates later on opportunities and challenges of IVCs, as well as the conditions for SMEs to reap benefits.

Medium-sized firms for healthy economies

A balanced spread in firm sizes is highly important for an economy. Medium-sized firms contain unique beneficial characteristics. For example, a recent study on Viet Nam found that its firm size distribution harms its economy because 'labour productivity is highest among firms in the middle of the distribution, yet such firms account for a very small share of total employment and their rate of growth is the lowest of all firm size categories' (Shaffer and Le, 2014).

Smaller firms do tend to employ more vulnerable groups within a society, such as women, youth and the poor (ANDE, 2012). This way, SMEs ensure that growth emerging from trade is sustainable and equally distributed, as opposed to the gains achieved by large firms.

FIGURE 4 Company size by export status

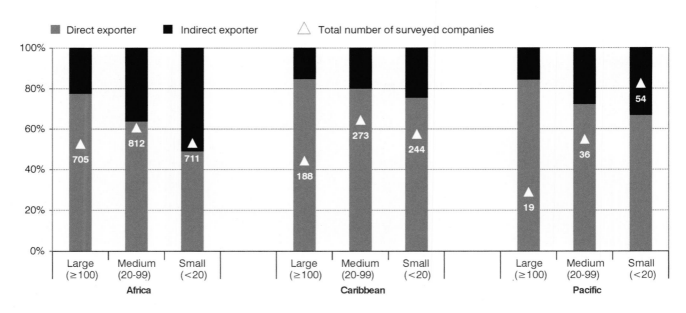

Source: ITC (2014).

Once the firm size drops to the micro level, however, various problems emerge. For instance, employment created by micro enterprises is confined within families for two reasons. First, they do not tend to create jobs for people outside of the family. Second, they do not train their employees in a way which would allow them to find employment outside of the firm.

These firms are often born out of necessity and for subsistence, making it unlikely that they will grow and create jobs for the local community (Banerjee and Duflo, 2007; Collins et al., 2009; Schoar, 2009). The informal nature of jobs within micro enterprises also limits their potential to contribute to economic development.

Countries require a substantial strata of mid-sized firms. They combine the best of two worlds. Firms in this segment offer diversified and local employment opportunities, including for vulnerable groups. At the same time, they provide an indispensable contribution to growth in the formal economy. While small firms mainly employ or engage the poor, the growing firms can help them out of poverty with higher, more stable wages (ANDE, 2012).

Economies with a healthy 'middle' are likely to be more dynamic and competitive. Domination by a few, large global players that use their market power to maintain the status quo tends to make economies less dynamic. Meanwhile, small firms that often serve as agents of change (Audretsch, 2002) are too small to challenge the big players and lobby for policy reforms (Gelb, Meyer and Ramachandran, 2014).

A balanced firm size distribution stimulates competition within an economy. This helps firms to improve productivity and, in turn, export competitiveness (World Bank Group, 2015). The United States is sometimes taken as an example of how firm size distribution can stimulate an economy's dynamism and competitiveness. For example, with a 10% entry and exit rate of new businesses, its dynamism is higher than that of many other economies (UN-ESCAP, 2012).

It's hard to grow up

Industrialization, servicification and internationalization have had a significant impact on firm size distribution over the years. This is notably reflected in the large differences in the distribution of firm size among countries according to levels of economic development, even with PPP adjustments (Figure 5). In least developed countries (LDCs), there is a high concentration of very small firms with fewer than 10 employees. In addition, the area of

FIGURE 5 Densities of firms by country group: No. of employees vs turnover

Developed

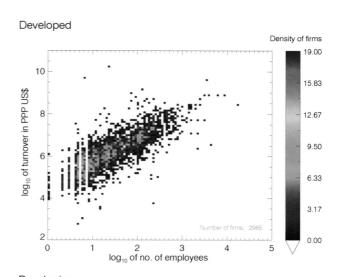

Developing

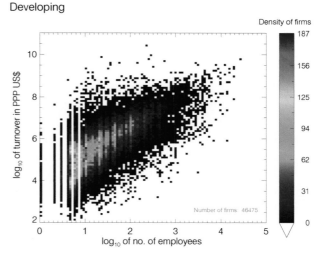

LDCs

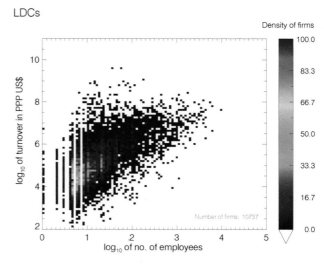

Note: Here, 'developed countries' are mostly made up of Eastern European countries.
Source: ITC calculations from World Bank Enterprise Survey dataset.

highest density seems to be roughly circular, with the density falling rapidly as the number of employees increases. This suggests that small firms in LDCs find it hard to make the transition to medium-sized enterprises, a phenomenon known as the 'missing middle'.

For developing countries as a whole, there is a similar high concentration of very small firms. However, density drops much less as the number of employees increases, indicating that progression to medium and large-sized companies is easier. In addition, the tail of the distribution (e.g. the high employee and turnover quadrant) is better populated than for LDCs, even when taking into account that the sample size is roughly four times bigger.

For developed countries, the relationship between the number of employees and turnover is much tighter. This may be due to the fact that the developed countries group is mostly composed of former communist Eastern European countries (Figure 5).

In addition, firm turnover is systematically shifted upwards, implying higher per employee turnover. These results are broadly in line with development research observations: LDCs and developing countries have a very high number of micro and small firms, while developed countries have a more even distribution of firms.

Most SMEs are small, if not micro

The overwhelming majority of SMEs are micro enterprises with fewer than ten employees, as seen in Figure 6.[3] This suggests that the private sector is split into two segments: the small, often micro and informal enterprises on the one

hand; and a handful of very large enterprises on the other hand. This clearly displays the phenomenon of the 'missing middle'.

Country level evidence is mounting for the 'missing middle' at country level. In Tunisia, for instance, micro firms with up to five employees are estimated to account for 96.6% of private firms (Baghdadi, 2015). Small firms with 6–49 employees account for 2.7% of private firms, while medium-sized firms with 50–199 employees and large firms with over 200 employees account for 0.5% and 0.15% of Tunisian private firms, respectively.

A country study on Ukraine identifies a similar firm size distribution (Zhalilo, 2015). According to the study, 80.9% of Ukrainian firms employ fewer than 10 people, and 14.1% employ between 11 and 50 workers. Medium-sized firms (50–250 employees) account for 4.8% of total firms while only 0.2% of firms employ more than 250 workers.

In the Association of Southeast Asian Nations (ASEAN), meanwhile, more than 75% of firms employ fewer than five people and only 10%–20% of firms employ between five and 19 workers. Medium-sized firms (20–99 employees) account for just 5% (Harvie, 2015).

Firm size distribution in LAC is even more skewed towards small enterprises than in the ASEAN region (McDermott and Pietrobelli, 2015). As illustrated in Table 2, micro firms that employ fewer than 10 people account on average for almost 90% of total firms. About 9% of firms employ between 11 and 50 workers, while medium (51–250 employees) and large (more than 250 employees) firms account for only 1.3% and 0.4% of LAC firms, respectively.

FIGURE 6 The 'missing middle':
Most SMEs are small, if not micro

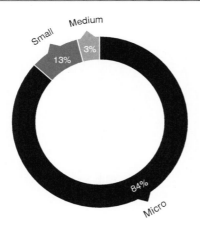

Source: ITC calculations, based on the International Finance Corporation (IFC) MSME Country Indicators.

TABLE 2 Firm size distribution in selected LAC countries

Country	Micro (0–10)	Small (11–50)	Medium (51–250)	Large (250+)
Argentina	81.6	16.1	1.9	0.4
Brazil	85.4	12.1	1.4	1.0
Chile	90.4	7.8	1.2	0.6
Colombia	93.2	5.5	1.0	0.3
Ecuador	95.4	3.8	0.6	0.2
Peru	98.1	1.5	0.3	0.02
Uruguay	83.8	13.4	3.1	0.6

Note: Figures reflect percentage of firm size category for each country.
Source: OECD - ECLAC (2013).

Tax and access to finance policies penalize medium-sized firms

Among the explanations for the 'missing middle' is the central tenet that small firms have few incentives to grow, because medium-sized enterprises are very adversely affected by tax and access to finance policies (Harvard CID, 2015, The Economist, 2015).

Medium-sized firms are often just large enough to be taxed, but too large to be eligible for microfinance schemes.

Small enterprises, in contrast, often choose to stay small and 'under the radar' to avoid regulations and taxes (Joumard, Sila and Morgavi, 2015) and remain entitled to microfinance.

Large firms have the capacities to develop sophisticated business models that maximize their access to capital and minimize fiscal obligations. A recent study on France shows (Figure 7) that most firms stay small, as firms with 50 or more employees face considerably more regulation (Gourio and Roys, 2014).

FIGURE 7 Firm size distribution in France

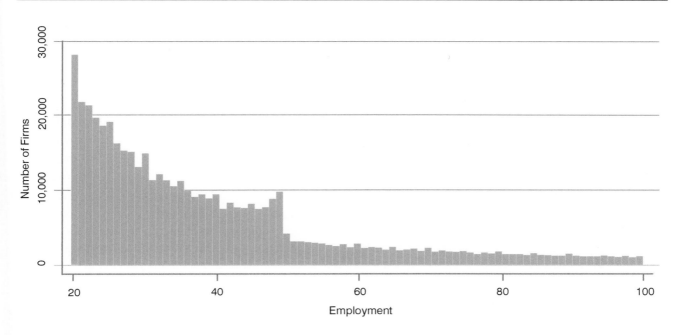

Source: Gourio, François and Nicolas Roys (2014).

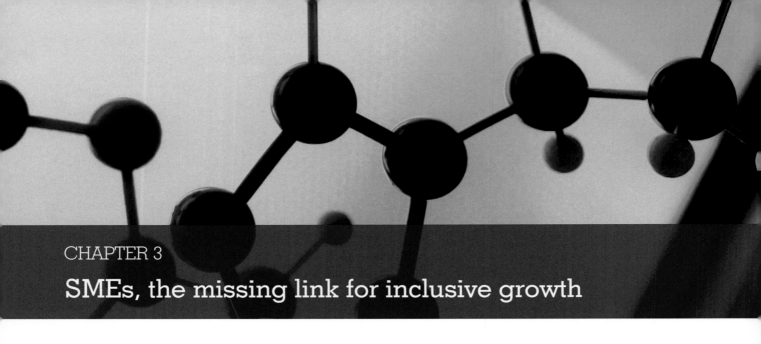

CHAPTER 3

SMEs, the missing link for inclusive growth

Large firms are more productive and pay higher wages than small firms. In Ukraine, for instance, large firms sell 2.2 times more products per employee than small firms, and 2.7 times more than micro enterprises (Zhalilo, 2015). The average wage in large Ukrainian firms was 1.5 times that of medium-sized firms and 2.7 times that of micro enterprises.

It is less well known that productivity differences between micro/small and large firms are much more pronounced in developing countries than in industrialized ones.

Evidence on LAC and OECD firms illustrates that productivity and wage gaps between micro/small and large enterprises are more pronounced in developing than in industrial countries (McDermott and Pietrobelli, 2015, Figure 8). This confirms evidence for a size productivity

premium and a development productivity premium (Gönenç et al., 2014, Figure 9, as well as Chang and van Marrewijk, 2013).

Given that SMEs employ the most workers in most economies, closing the productivity gap likely would have two direct effects. It would contribute to GDP growth because of increased SME productivity. It would also lead to higher wages in the low-wage segment of the economy, improving income distribution.

The indirect effects of stronger SME productivity are important, too. The indirect impact on demand, with increased wages for low-wage workers, would likely change the structure of demand. This would expand the market for higher value-added products (OECD, 2010a).

FIGURE 8 Productivity and wage gaps in selected LAC and OECD countries (Large firms=100)

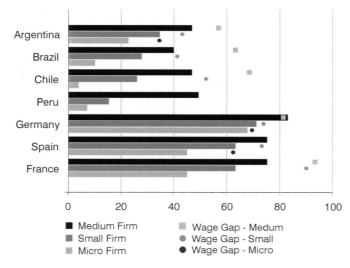

Source: OECD - ECLAC (2013).

FIGURE 9 Labour productivity ratio: Largest to smallest enterprise size class (2010)

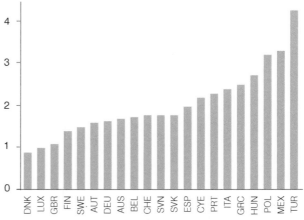

Source: Gönenç, Rauf, Oliver Röhn, Vincent Koen and Fethi Öğünç (2014).

Spillover and competition effects could also affect the supply side of the economy (van Stel, de Vries and de Kok, 2014). Knowledge embedded in higher quality intermediate inputs supplied by more productive SMEs may spill over to large firms and lead to higher productivity there. Higher productivity in SMEs may also lead SMEs to compete in the same segment as larger firms. The authors find that a 1% increase in SME labour productivity raises the productivity of large firms by about 0.2% and economy-wide productivity growth by about 0.7%. This effect is particularly strong for countries with lower levels of economic development.

SMEs account for nearly 70% of employment

The wage increases triggered by productivity growth in SMEs can significantly affect overall income distribution. This is because SMEs employ a large share of the overall labour force and because they tend to employ a relatively high share of the more vulnerable groups of society, notably women and youth.

SMEs account on average for about 60%–70% of employment in developing and developed economies alike (e.g. Ayyagari, Demirguc-Kunt and Maksimovic, 2011, 2014; ERIA, 2014; De Kok et al., 2011).

This figure, however, only represents an approximation and is possibly an underestimation. SME employment is difficult to measure because many micro and small enterprises are part of the 'informal' economy, for which detailed data is rarely available. Studies on the effect of firm size heterogeneity on employment creation tend to be based on formally registered SMEs. This likely leads to an underestimation of the real contribution of SMEs to employment and GDP (Li and Rama, 2015). The IFC database, for instance, contains information on 1.6 million registered SMEs in India. Yet the country has an estimated 26 million unregistered SMEs (Kushnir, Mirmulstein and Ramalho, 2010).

Although some research is sceptical about the role of SMEs in job creation (for instance, Page and Söderbom, 2012), a significant number of studies find SMEs to be important drivers of employment growth (see overview in De Kok, Deijl and Veldhuis-Van Essen, 2013). Studies by Neumark, Wall and Zhang (2011), De Kok et al. (2011) and Ayyagari, Demirguc-Kunt and Maksimovic (2014) provide strong evidence on the positive contribution of SMEs to employment growth. De Kok et al. (2011) calculate that SMEs accounted for 80% of the increase in total employment in the European non-financial economy between 2002 and 2010.

In developing and emerging countries, SMEs have been found to account for as much as 95% of job creation (Ayyagari, Demirguc-Kunt and Maksimovic, 2014).

A study in Turkey underlines the significant contribution of SMEs to employment growth. Between 2003 and 2010, employment in firms with 20 to 40 employees grew from half a million to over 1.2 million and employment in firms with 50 to 249 employees from 0.9 million to over 1.7 million (Gönençe et al., 2014). A slightly different research branch focuses on the firm level and compares employment growth across firms of different size. Relevant studies have found that in developing countries, SMEs create jobs at a faster pace than large firms (Aterido, Hallward-Driemeier and Pagés, 2011; Jung, Plottier and Francia, 2011; Ayyagari, Demirguc-Kunt and Maksimovic, 2014).

Firm age also matters when it comes to job creation. Successful young SMEs are the most important creators of jobs. In OECD countries, young SMEs are on average responsible for 42% of job creation, and only contribute 22% to job destruction (Criscuolo, Gal and Menon, 2014). Older SMEs, instead, are net job destroyers in some countries. As a result, firm age has been found to be the main determinant of job creation in selected countries.

In the United States, once firm age is controlled for, firm size does not matter anymore for net job creation (Haltiwanger, Jarmin and Miranda, 2013). The findings of Ayyagari et al. (2014), however, suggest that this is not the case for the majority of developing and emerging economies as they find that even after controlling for firm age, SMEs are characterized by higher employment growth.

International SMEs: More employment, earnings, profits

It is not just size and age that affect how much enterprises contribute to employment growth. SMEs vary in their contributions to employment growth based on productivity, ability to export and import, and other firm characteristics.

Theoretical and empirical studies show that larger firms are more productive, more likely to export and pay higher wages (Bernard et al., 2007). One analysis using data from five African countries finds that exporting SMEs employ up to 56% more people than non-exporting SMEs (Boermans, 2013). The employment of exporting SMEs also grows 12% faster than that of non-exporting SMEs, according to this research.

Productivity gains depend on export destinations, but export participation is associated with faster growth in employment, earnings and profits, regardless of destination. Exporting helps firms become more innovative when it comes to organizing production processes (Damijan, Kostev and Polanec, 2010).

Importing as well as exporting improves productivity, signalling that firms learn by importing (Vogel and Wagner, 2010). Internationally active SMEs demonstrate higher employment growth; 7% growth for exporters, and 3% for non-exporters – with a larger difference between importers and non-importers, of 8% and 2%, respectively (Edinburgh Group, 2013). Recent country studies commissioned by ITC have drawn similar conclusions (China: Zhang, Shi and Zhang, 2015; Tunisia: Baghadi, 2015).

In Tunisia, firms which export, import, or import and export, are responsible for 55% of the share of waged jobs, even though they only make up approximately 18% of total firms (Rijkers et al., 2014; Jaud and Freund, 2015). Even after controlling for factors such as firm size and age, firms that both import and export are associated with strong, positive job creation.

Interestingly, the potential gains from trade are not confined to the most productive firms. Powell and Wagner (2014) test the seminal Melitz (2003) model and find that the export premium is positive at all productivity levels, but highest at the lowest segments of the productivity distribution.

Gains for women

SMEs provide employment and empowerment opportunities for women. The logic for supporting women is not purely social. Successful women in developing countries have a higher propensity to invest in their offspring and in the community at large, leading to positive outcomes for the country as a whole.

Scope for more female SME owners

Some nine million women-owned SMEs are formally registered worldwide, or 34% of total SMEs (IFC 2014). Women-owned SMEs are underrepresented in all stages of economic development (World Bank, 2011b), as shown in Figure 10.

TABLE 3   Employee size in formal SMEs, by gender of ownership, 2011–2012

	Women-owned	Men-owned	Total
Mean	40 employees	44 employees	44 employees
Median	14 employees	15 employees	15 employees

Source: IFC (2014).

FIGURE 10 SME ownership by gender and country group

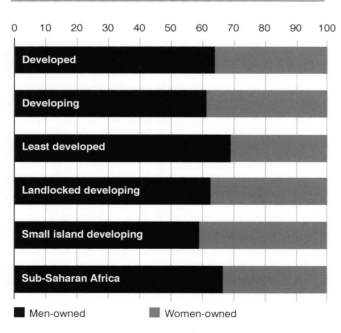

Source: ITC calculations, based on IFC Enterprise Finance Gap Assessment database.

FIGURE 11 Women in SME management, by gender of ownership, 2011–2012

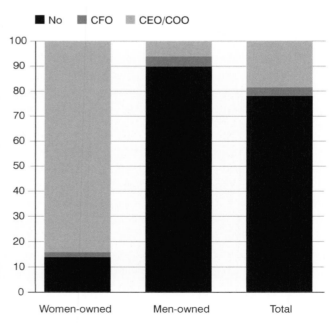

Source: IFC (2014).

More women in senior management

Existing data allow for comparisons between women-owned and men-owned SMEs regarding scale of employment, sector of operation and performance (measured by annual sales). Table 3 shows women-owned SMEs operate only on a marginally smaller scale than their men-owned counterparts.

However, the gender composition of the senior management differs significantly (Figure 11).

Only 10% of men-owned SMEs have women in their senior management, while almost 85% of women-owned SMEs have female chief executives, chief operating or chief financial officers.

Underrepresentation of women in top management can negatively affect business performance (Dezsö and Ross, 2012). An earlier study (McKinsey & Company, 2008) corroborates this. Women in senior management score higher in business characteristics such as leadership, coordination and control. These, in turn, are positively associated with higher operating margins.

Fewer women-owned SMEs in high value-added sectors

The gap between male and female owners is most pronounced in the retail and wholesale sector – 41% of women-owned SMEs vs 30% of men-owned SMEs. Healthcare, beauty and cosmetics is the only other sector in which the concentration of women-owned SMEs, at 2%, is larger than that of men-owned SMEs, at 1% (Figure 12).

In Viet Nam, female economic activity in these low-skill sectors may have long-term consequences (Thoburn, Sutherland and Hoa, 2007). Unlike high-skill activities, the associated skills are less easily transferable to other sectors and therefore women remain trapped in the low value-added sector. The underrepresentation of women-owned SMEs in sectors that are more likely to export further limits the opportunity for women to learn from exporting.

FIGURE 12 Sectors of formal SMEs, by gender of ownership, 2011–2012

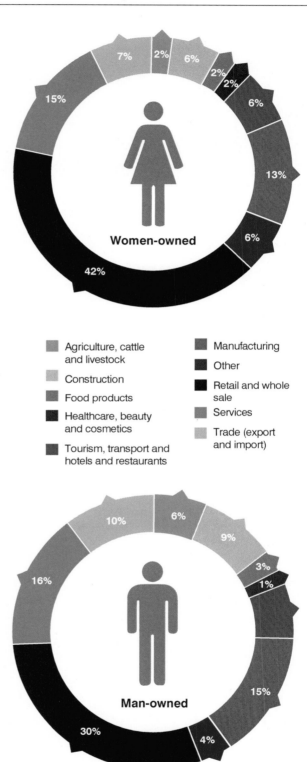

Source: IFC (2014).

First-ever woman coffee exporter in Papua New Guinea secures premium price from major international buyer

'*It's real. I am now an exporter.*'

Marey Yogiyo, coffee farmer, Bauka Women Coffee

Coffee farmer Marey Yogiyo has been selling coffee to buyers in her native Papua New Guinea for 16 years. Earlier this year, she became the first ever woman in the coffee sector to receive an export licence – and promptly saw the price she received rise 63% above the local rate.

Olam International, one of the world's leading agribusiness companies, bought 60 bags of coffee from her company for US$ 18,000.

'It's real. I am now an exporter,' said the 56-year-old mother of five, who lives in the Eastern Highlands Province, the centre of the country's coffee production industry.

Yogiyo's export success appears set to continue: Olam is considering an even bigger purchase in 2015.

Before she could sell abroad, however, Yogiyo needed a permit, not to mention clients. In 2014, she got both. In July, her company, Yogiyo Coffee Ltd, became the first women-owned coffee company in

the country to receive a government licence to export. The first bags of Bauka Blue were shipped to the United States shortly after. 'After ten years of consistently working on perfecting the quality and looking for markets, the first order from Olam re-energized Bauka Women Coffee to see it through the next ten years', she said.

'*After ten years of consistently working on perfecting the quality and looking for markets, the first order from Olam re-energized Bauka Women Coffee to see it through the next ten years.*'

Marey Yogiyo

With ITC to international markets

Yogiyo made the initial contact with her new buyers at a buyer mentor group organized by ITC and the International Women Coffee Alliance (IWCA) on the margins of the Specialty Coffee Association of America's annual conference in Seattle in April 2014. The training provided participants with knowledge and skills to meet the demands of international

> '*2015 will be an exciting year for Bauka Women Coffee and we are looking forward to that.*'
>
> Marey Yogiyo, coffee farmer, Bauka Women Coffee

buyers, enabling them to position their coffee to be more competitive in international markets and fetch higher prices. Following her return, ITC liaised with the Papua New Guinea Investment Promotion Agency to facilitate the issuance of her export licence.

Increase in price received by Yogiyo after getting **export licence**

63%

Olam International is one of the world's largest food buyers, with annual sales of US$ 15 billion and operations in 65 countries. On its website for its industrial buyers, Olam emphasizes Yogiyo's story and vision for creating a distinctive product. 'She founded the group to encourage women to make coffee a way of life so that they can support themselves and their families,' the site says.

Empowered women powering trade

Yogiyo, who herself has a mid-size farm with 20 acres of coffee, will also buy coffee from nine other farmers as of the coffee year 2015. She hopes to build an export business supporting many of the 645 coffee growing households in the area. 'This is a great avenue to support women in coffee groups, maximizing their net return on their coffee,' she said.

Papua New Guinea's coffee, while making up only 1% of global production, is known in specialty coffee circles for a unique aura and for the brightness and complexity of its flavours. The Aiyura Valley, where Bauka Women Coffee is situated, first saw coffee grown in the 1940s; its plantations and smallholder gardens are known for the varied berry and citrus flavours of the coffee they produce.

Source: ITC (2015a).

Differences in operating sectors also account for the disparity in annual sales value and total assets between women-owned and men-owned SMEs. The median value of annual sales and total assets for women-owned SMEs is about 30% lower than for their men-owned counterparts (IFC, 2014). Men-owned SMEs are dominant in higher value-added sectors in which sales and assets are generally higher. However, in a number of sectors, notably services and trade, the IFC (2014) finds that median sales and median assets for women-owned and men-owned SMEs are similar.

In summary, women-owned SMEs are almost equally as productive as men-owned SMEs, operate at a similar employment scale and promote women in senior management. A study on South Africa, meanwhile, finds that female traders in charge of their own informal or formal SME are more educated than their male counterparts (Bossuroy et al., 2013). Despite such characteristics, women-owned SMEs account for only a third of SMEs globally.

Unequal distribution has severe consequences for empowerment of women as well as for economic prosperity. Gender gaps in entrepreneurship and labour force participation are detrimental to aggregate productivity and may cause total income losses of up to nearly 30%, according to a study across several countries (Teignier and Cuberes, 2014).

Women are more likely to share the rewards of economic returns with their children, benefiting their health and education and consequently society as a whole (Klasen and Wink, 2002; Klasen, 2005; Klasen and Lamanna, 2008). More women in the workforce could result in higher expenditure on school enrolment for children, including girls, potentially triggering a virtuous cycle, with educated women becoming female role models (Aguirre et al., 2012).

Start-up barriers for women-owned firms

Why are there so few women who own SMEs? Financial and non-financial barriers at the start-up stage of the business cycle particularly affect women-owned SMEs (Blackden and Hallward-Driemeier, 2013). Lack of collateral, inadequate financial infrastructure and other barriers involving gender-based social and cultural barriers restrict the potential of women-owned SMEs (Harvie, 2015, ITC video interview).

Non-tariff barriers also contribute to pushing female producers and traders into the informal sector, where they lack finance, information and networks. They may also disappear from the data, given that data collection is mostly restricted to the formal sector (Brenton and Gamberoni, 2013).

An interesting side observation: while medium-sized enterprises owned by women in sub-Saharan Africa face barriers such as those described above, small women-owned enterprises actually tend to be less credit constrained than their male counterparts, due to female favouritism in lending to micro and small-sized firms (Hansen and Rand, 2014).

FIGURE 13 Youth unemployment

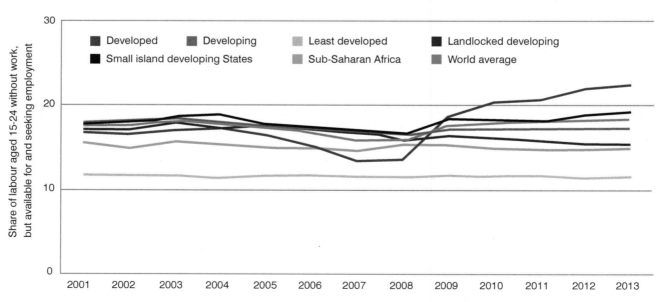

Source: ITC calculations, based on the modelled ILO estimate taken from the World Bank's World Development Indicators.

Gains for youth

Youth unemployment is a challenge of our times. It is of great concern to policymakers everywhere, especially since the 2008 crisis.

Of the world's 1.3 billion young people, more than one billion live in developing countries. Worldwide, youth unemployment is estimated at about 74 million, and an even more staggering 500 million young people are underemployed. In 2013, the world's average youth unemployment rate was 18%. Figure 13 illustrates the evolution of global youth unemployment since 2001.

Tackling youth unemployment and underemployment is crucial as they limit long-term growth and productivity and contribute to undesirable social outcomes. The SME sector can help improve the fortunes of young people.

Developed countries differ considerably in levels of youth unemployment. Austria, Germany, Japan, Korea, Norway and Switzerland registered youth unemployment rates of between 7% and 9% in 2013; Italy and Cyprus recorded rates of almost 40%; and Greece and Spain almost 60%.

Similar disparities were also found among other country groups in 2013. LDC youth unemployment ranged from 0.7% in Cambodia to 43% in Mauritania. In landlocked developing countries the rates went from 0.7% in Rwanda to 52% in the former Yugoslav Republic of Macedonia. Developing small island states had a range of 5% in Papua New Guinea to 36% in Jamaica, while sub-Saharan countries ranged between 2% in Guinea and 54% in South Africa.

Sensitive to business cycles

Despite wide variations in youth unemployment, all countries have a concentration of youth unemployment in sectors that are sensitive to business cycles, such as retail and services. As a result, variations in youth unemployment are closely related to variations in output.

A recent study on Europe, for example, estimates that youth unemployment rates are, on average, almost three times as sensitive to output growth as adult unemployment rates (Banerji et al., 2014). As many SMEs tend to be in cyclical sectors, youth unemployment changes are likely to be linked to changes in SME performance.

Long-lasting effects

High youth unemployment causes skills attrition and human capital depreciation, known as hysteresis. This depresses young people's employment and earnings prospects for decades to come (Banerji et al., 2014).

In the face of the problem's seriousness, governments have started to introduce programmes to place young people in decent jobs. Some of these, such as the European Union's Youth Guarantee, also recognize SMEs as an engine for growth and employment. The Youth Guarantee scheme, for instance, is coupled with the Competitiveness of Enterprises and Small and Medium-sized Enterprises (COSME) scheme, which

TABLE 4 SME contributions to employment, GDP, and exports in South-East Asia, 2005–2011

Country	SME share of total establishments		SME share of total employment		SME share of GDP		SME share of total exports		Youth unemployment (%, 2005–2011)
	Share (%)	Year	Share (%)	Year	Share (%)	Year	Share (%)	Year	
Cambodia	99.8	2011	72.9	2011	-	-	-	-	3.5
Indonesia	99.9	2011	97.2	2011	58.0	2011	16.4	2011	23.0
Malaysia	97.3	2011	57.4	2012	32.7	2012	19.0	2010	11.3
Philippines	99.6	2011	61.0	2011	36.0	2006	10.0	2010	19.3
Singapore	99.4	2012	68.0	2012	45.0	2012	-	-	6.7
Thailand	99.8	2012	76.7	2011	37.0	2011	29.9	2011	3.0

Source: Harvie, Charles (2015).

Axel M. Addy

Minister of Commerce and
Industry, Liberia

*In Liberia, 60% of the
population is under 25
years old.*

*SMEs dominate
Liberian employment.*

Why SMEs are the bedrock of the Liberian transformation agenda

Slowly but surely, Liberia is rising. Since 2003, the country has enjoyed peace, two democratic elections, and the economic recovery has been progressing steadily in the past decade. For a country traumatized by years of conflict and instability, these are important achievements. With the Ebola crisis behind us, we are now looking to the future.

In 2013, we launched a five-year development strategy called the Agenda for Transformation (AfT). The aim of AfT is to lay the foundation for Liberia to become a middle income country by 2030, while ensuring the gains from growth are distributed in an equal and inclusive manner. This was backed up in 2014 when we launched Liberia's national export strategy and a national trade policy, which were both developed in partnership with ITC.

SME development is critical to achieving the goal of the transformation agenda. Nearly 80% of all formal Liberian firms employ fewer than 20 people, with only a further 13% employing between 20 and 100 people. We should also keep in mind that Liberia is comprised of mostly young people: 60% of the population is under the age of 25 and 70% of people in employment are found in the informal sector. As such, it is safe to say that SMEs dominate Liberian employment.

The challenge for Liberia, and in particular for us in government, is how to structure programmes to best support the development of SMEs. Currently, the economy is dominated by extractive industries, which are highly dependent on volatile commodity prices. These are capital-intensive operations that do not create the kinds of jobs that will transform the economy and encourage a creative environment for inclusive growth. For example, Liberia's tourism sector has a huge potential to deliver jobs and growth for the young, and SMEs in other sectors would be well positioned to exploit downstream linkages and supply services to the tourism sector.

To facilitate this transformation, we must address the challenges that exist within firms, the business environment and the national environment.

In Liberia, the average SME has three major challenges: access to training, access to markets, and access to finance. And through our SME policy we are trying to address those issues – one by one – with a view to strengthen the capacity of service providers to develop training programmes that will meet the specific needs of SMEs.

For example, how do you train a woman who has been managing her operations from her purse to manage a business from her bank account, and enable her to understand clearly what belongs to her and what belongs to the business? To meet such challenges we are working with a range of providers to meet different demands; from basic marketing skills, to financial management, and book-keeping practices.

To further back up the AfT, the annual National SME Conference and Trade Fair has been set up to promote innovation among SMEs. Through the conference, we identify SME champions and let those champions tell their stories to inspire others. And the SMEs with the most innovative solutions are presented with awards.

We are aware that linkages and the business environment are critical to our growth agenda. We are in the process of creating linkages for SMEs in the agro-processing industry through our Food and Agriculture Policy and Strategy programme. To back up this effort, we are also facilitating the creation of a packaging company, as we've identified packaging as the missing link to increase the export of Liberian products.

At the national level, we are actively seeking to improve the business climate by making it more predictable and transparent. Recently, President Ellen Sirleaf Johnson signed into law the Small Business Empowerment Act (SBEA), which obliges the government to award 25% of public procurement to SMEs. The government procurement system is specifically designed to encourage SMEs to register, to become regular tax payers, and therefore come into the formal sector. The SBEA is also designed to boost competition, innovation, and access to finance so that SMEs become an integral part of the transformation that we aspire to see in our country.

We believe in the potential of our youth to be major drivers of our transformation story.

The AfT is ambitious, but ambition on its own is not enough. Serious long-term commitment and leadership are needed for the reform process to succeed. In Liberia, such leadership is provided by our President. Since she was first elected, she has ensured that the government is engaged with the private sector, including meeting in person private sector representatives about the challenges they face. This focus on creating a public-private dialogue has been crucial for the government in identifying how it can help mitigate challenges faced by the private sector, and keep the AfT on track.

Liberia is also in the process of acceding to the WTO. The domestic reform process is forcing us to upgrade our laws and has led to the development of new laws in areas where we previously had no legislation. This process is literally forcing us to rethink what we mean when we say we want Liberia to be an 'investment-friendly destination'. In trying to answer these questions, we are putting in place programmes to ensure that the country becomes an attractive and competitive destination – for Liberians and foreign investors.

We strongly believe in our potential and the potential of our youth to be major drivers of our transformation story, as they are arriving every day on the job market with the audacity of hope to live fulfilled lives in self dignity.

FIGURE 14 Youth entrepreneurship

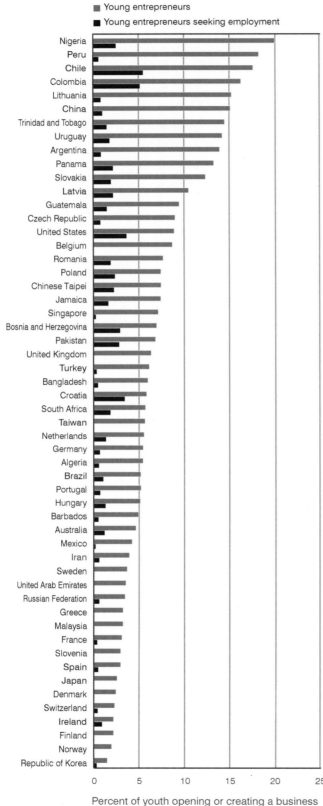

Source: ITC calculations, based on GEM 2011 APS Global Individual Level Data.

supports SMEs with access to finance for employing young people and vocational training schemes.

In Asia, youth unemployment may also be related to SME export performance. Table 4 shows that youth unemployment is lowest in Thailand at 3%, and highest in Indonesia at 23%, with Thailand being the country with the most successful SMEs in terms of exports. The share of SMEs in GDP, however, is relatively low in Thailand, which may mean that highly productive exporting SMEs coexist with large numbers of SMEs with extremely low productivity.

Young SME owners hire youth

A significant strategy to boost youth employment and job creation is to promote young entrepreneurs. They are more likely to hire fellow youths, and pay them higher wages than older firms (Ouimet and Zarutskie, 2013). They are also more active in high growth sectors. By encouraging young entrepreneurs, it could help to reduce the concentration of SMEs in cyclically sensitive, low value-added sectors, and promote the accumulation of SMEs in the 'missing middle' (GEM, 2013).

While young entrepreneurs may have much to contribute to economic prosperity, their numbers could be higher. On average, only 7% of youth aged 18–24 are engaged in creating or owning their own business, compared to 11% of 25–34 year olds, 10% of 35–44 year olds and 8% of 45–54 year olds, according to the 2013 Global Entrepreneur Monitor (GEM). This figure, however, differs considerably across countries and stages of economic development.

Figure 14 ranks 54 countries according to the percentage of youth in the process of creating, or already owning, a business. In Nigeria, 20% of young people own their own business; the Republic of Korea, with 1.6%, is at the other extreme.

To provide an indication of the scale of necessity vs opportunity-based entrepreneurship, Figure 14 also includes the percentage of youth that are founding or already own their business, while actively seeking other employment. This percentage is strongly correlated (coefficient of 0.56) with the percentage of youth owning or creating a business.

For more insight, Figure 15 shows the age distribution of entrepreneurs by country, and ranks their share of young entrepreneurs. On average, young entrepreneurs aged 18–24 only account for

FIGURE 15 Entrepreneurs by age group and country

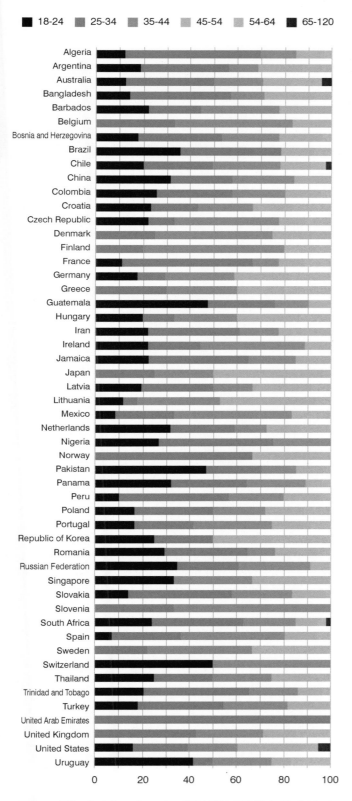

■ 18-24   ■ 25-34   ■ 35-44   ■ 45-54   ■ 54-64   ■ 65-120

Source: ITC calculations, based on GEM 2011 APS Global Individual Level Data.

15% of total entrepreneurs. The largest share of entrepreneurs is among 25–34 year olds (29%), followed by 35–44 year olds (27%) and 45–54 years olds (19%)[4].

No clear pattern emerges for the age group of entrepreneurs. In Belgium, for instance, more than a quarter of entrepreneurs are under 25 years old. In other developed countries such as Switzerland, Republic of Korea, Sweden, Norway, Ireland and Japan, fewer than 9% of entrepreneurs are aged 18–24.

This low share of young people in entrepreneurship impedes the rise of innovative SMEs that would help to reduce youth unemployment, as well as promote the migration of SMEs to higher value-added, less cyclically-sensitive sectors.

The challenges of women and youth reinforce the need to create supportive environments for SMEs. Promoting ownership of SMEs by women and young people and strengthening their capacity to overcome bottlenecks faced when internationalizing, can play a vital role in generating inclusive economic growth and spreading gains across all strata of society.

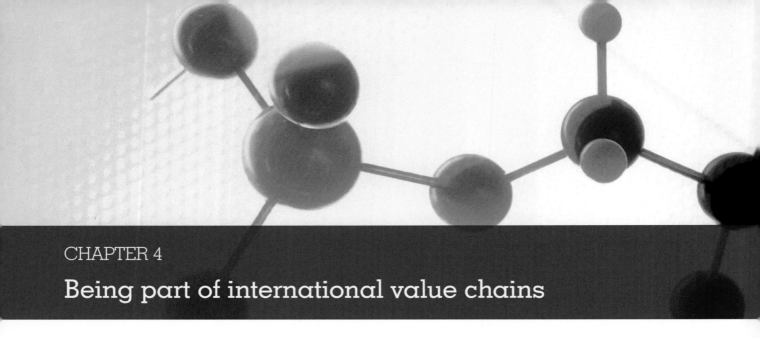

CHAPTER 4

Being part of international value chains

Firms that are integrated in global markets are more productive, pay higher wages and create more jobs (Wagner, 2005, 2011).

The exact nature of the relationship remains a topic of debate. On the one hand, more productive firms tend to transfer into international markets, as they are the only firms that can afford the associated entry costs, such as transportation, production and marketing (Helpman, Melitz and Yeaple, 2003). On the other hand, there is the hypothesis that internationalization leads to increased productivity through learning by doing and exposure to increased quality standards, superior technology and greater competition.

Despite the significance of SMEs in national economies, research on internationalization strategies and outcomes mainly focuses on large firms, and the evidence on SMEs is scarce. Therefore, studying the opportunities for SMEs to internationalize is not only relevant but also of immediate policy interest (Giovannetti, Marvasi and Sanfilippo, 2014).

Stepping stones to internationalization

Firms must decide which mode of internationalization to pursue. Traditionally, firms could choose between serving foreign markets by exporting or by acquiring a foreign firm in the target area (through horizontal FDI), with the proximity-concentration trade-off[5] (Brainard, 1997) guiding firms' decisions.

Recent technological advances and reductions in trade costs, however, have made it possible to fragment production into individual tasks, allowing firms to specialize in parts of a supply chain. Once fragmentation occurs across national borders, this specialization can stimulate firms' internationalization and leads to the creation of regional or global IVCs.

As result of this fragmentation, trade in intermediate, as opposed to final, goods has increased massively over the past two decades, and is estimated to account for two-thirds of all trade (Johnson and Noguera, 2012).

Firms can now opt to import or export intermediate goods, directly or indirectly. Engaging in IVCs can increase SME productivity, wages and employment, and serve as a stepping stone to more advanced modes of internationalization. These include direct exporting or FDI, facilitated by decreasing the entry and search costs of internationalization. It also allows firms to specialize and play to their strength more than was possible in the past.

Whereas firms and countries previously specialized in producing certain goods, they now can specialize in specific tasks within a value chain. A recent study, for example, on the experience of African SMEs engaging in regional and international value chains found that this integration expands their markets, improves their productivity, and helps them attain financial stability (Wamalwa and McCormick, 2015).

At the same time, participation in IVCs has to be properly managed and is by no means a guarantee for improved economic performance (Morrison, Pietrobelli and Rabellotti, 2007).

The impact of IVCs is so significant that a number of economists argue that globalization has entered a new paradigm (Baldwin, 2006), offering opportunities and challenges for SMEs that can have wider effects on countries' development paths. Indeed, a recent WTO-OECD survey (2013) showed that lack of integration of low-income countries into IVCs is a major obstacle to their development.

Supply chains lower entry costs

The potential advantages for SMEs to participate in IVCs are numerous, with some authors writing of a 'laundry list of benefits' (Park, Nayyar and Low, 2013).

On the macro level, there are opportunities to create jobs, increase income, improve working conditions (Shingal, 2015) and diversify production and exports (WTO, 2014).

On the micro level, IVCs can help increase access to finance (Box 1), shorten lead times, reduce operational disruptions, cut inventory, improve quality and customer service, speed innovation and reduce risk (Arend and Wisner, 2005; Fawcett et al., 2008; Vaaland and Heide, 2007).

SMEs' chances to begin exporting increase when participating in both local and international production chains. A recent study of over 7,500 Italian SMEs, for example, indicated that even small and less

productive firms involved in production chains could take advantage of reduced costs of entry and economies of scale that enhanced their probability of becoming exporters (Giovannetti et al., 2014). For firms employing 1–9, 10–49 and 50–249 persons, the probability of being an exporter increased by 98%, 34% and 34%, respectively, when the firms were part of a supply chain.

Supply chains can assist SMEs by establishing well-defined contractual arrangements with other companies along the chain. This may facilitate access to cheaper or higher quality intermediate inputs. Being part of a supply chain may be the preferred strategy when capital and research and development intensity are relatively low. Such inputs are more likely to be controlled by downstream firms improving their capacity to internationalize. This way, SMEs can tap into international markets without taking on all the tasks along the value chain, lowering the requirements for internationalization associated with exports (OECD, 2008).

BOX 1: Financing supply chains

One financial challenge exporting SMEs face is the time period between selling and shipping items and receiving payment.

Often, there can be a delay of 60–90 days, significantly reducing the working capital of small and medium-sized suppliers. This in turn can impede SMEs from making necessary investments in equipment, machinery, technology or future contracts, thus reducing productivity (Avendaño, Daude and Perea, 2013),

Supply chain finance can address this challenge. It is considered as one of the innovations most likely to change the trade finance industry in the future by the ICC Global Survey (2014).

Supply chain finance has recently introduced the practice of reverse factoring. This provides for the lead firm within a production chain, i.e. the multinational buyer, to sell its accounts payable to a financial intermediary known as the factor or financier, which pays the small or medium-sized supplier immediately.

Reverse factoring marks a significant improvement from the more traditional form of factoring – where the supplier, not the buyer, sells accounts receivable to the intermediary. Factoring incurs higher intermediation costs than reverse factoring, because the discount rate (equal to interest plus service fees) is higher if creditworthiness is based on the supplier rather than the buyer.

This way, supply chain finance can unlock working capital previously caught up along the supply chain. For the high-risk SME supplier, it boosts cash flow and secures liquidity at lower cost; for the high-credit quality buyer, it offers an elongated period to make the payment and it reduces risk by making suppliers more resilient and reliable.

The mechanism of reverse factoring is particularly attractive for SMEs in countries with underdeveloped contract enforcement regimes, inefficient bankruptcy systems and opaque credit information infrastructures. These include developing countries in South Asia and Africa (Klapper, 2005).

A good example of reverse factoring is found in Mexico, where the state-owned development bank, Nacional Financiera (NAFIN) offers online reverse factoring services to SME suppliers through its Cadenas Productivas (productive chains) programme. This leverages the links between small suppliers and large buyers in productive chains, providing immediate liquidity to approximately 80,000 SME suppliers for receivables from about 445 big buyers through an electronic discount on their invoices before the due date.

Source: Klapper, Leora (2006); IFC (2010).

Carmen Castillo

President and CEO,
SDI International Corp.

*SMEs have the ability
to adapt quickly.*

In business, David and Goliath should sometimes work together

Competition has been the engine behind business and supply chains since the two sprung into existence. Even back when the first people swapped goods and bartered for services – and when the term 'supply chain' was millennia away from being coined – competition was a driving force.

With competition playing such a critical role in the business realm, one might underestimate the smaller players. How can a regional hotel brand compete with hospitality giants like Marriott and Hilton? How can the small or mid-sized retailer go toe-to-toe with Walmart?

True, the smaller players are sometimes struggling to emerge from their larger competitors' shadows. Indeed, titans like Amazon have proved ruthless adversaries to the traditional, brick-and-mortar stores on main street.

But that doesn't mean SMEs aren't a force to be reckoned – or partnered – with. While they may not have the deep pockets or name-recognition of the big guys, they possess their own proficiencies: like the ability to adapt quickly, to be nimble, and to change at a moment's notice. They are also hungry for growth and, unable to afford customer attrition, intensely loyal.

Often, these proficiencies outstrip the bloated bureaucracies and lumbering pace of the giants. For proof, look to the world of online payments and transactions. It's a landscape that has grown explosively over the past few decades, and still manages to change and grow rapidly. Paying online with credit cards has been supplanted by services and applications like PayPal and Venmo. And now, the currency we're accustomed to – dollars, euros, pounds and yen – is quickly becoming passé: it's now all about Bitcoin.

In this tumultuous payment landscape, the smaller guys can have a clear and distinct advantage. Smaller companies, especially tech start-ups out in colorful and innovative Silicon Valley, have been quick to adopt Bitcoin payments. But the industry giants, not so much. Even presidential campaigns – those mammoth undertakings that require hundreds of millions of dollars to operate – have been slow to adapt. Rand Paul is the first-ever candidate to accept Bitcoin donations.

Smaller teams, globally interconnected, may be better placed to bring fresh concepts to market.

Bitcoin usage is merely a single example of pioneering practices. Arguably, smaller companies may well have an edge in swiftly delivering new designs or products. Agile, smaller teams that are globally interconnected with fewer echelons of hierarchy and less bureaucracy may be in a better position to bring fresh concepts to market. Even the slightest change management can progress at a lumbering pace.

Combining strengths

In the world of supply chain process outsourcing, this struggle behind big and small doesn't need to exist. Indeed, the two can come together to favorably complement one another.

The Marriotts and Walmarts of the world have their own core competencies, and they perform them spectacularly: housing guests around the globe, and retailing a vast variety of goods. Why, then, would they concentrate their energies on repeatedly retooling or re-engineering an untold quantity of corporate processes? Undeniably, for efficiency: but, should they?

Consider SDI, the medium-sized supply chain process outsourcing business that works with Fortune 500 companies. SDI can partner with companies and perform the tasks that are not strategic for the larger company to carry out. These tasks, for example, include managing independent contractors and non-strategic (tail-end) corporate spend. Often, an enterprise lacks the time, resources and proficiency to execute nonessential processes efficiently. Enter a capable partner. SMEs – through rapid innovation, closer contact to customers and a menu of evolving skills such as data analytics and visual modelling – keep their larger competitors on their toes and are precisely the associates with whom to partner.

SDI – or comparable, competent outsourcing businesses – can be particularly essential during difficult times, when there may be, for example, a constraint on commodities and services, such as plant closings, tariff changes, and supply shortages. Not to mention the ability to offer a more intimate customer experience.

Competitiveness and collaboration offer the marketplace a potent combination.

In fact, examples of industry giants working with smaller global experts are swiftly becoming popular, if not the norm. The Huffington Post (2015) recently noted: 'As entrepreneurs, leaders, business owners of organizations small and large to succeed in the new world we need a new operating system; one that sees us move from a 'competitive' way of doing business to that of a "collaborative" workspace'. Who would have thought that NASA would join forces with Danish company Lego to form a multi-year partnership? The intent of the association has been to encourage children to increasingly take part in STEM (science, technology, engineering and math) subjects.

Ultimately, competitiveness and collaboration offer the marketplace a potent combination. Emerging and established SMEs may offer flexibility, independence and perhaps even a greater appetite for growth, but when coupled with their larger, veteran counterparts, the global market offers an array of quality goods and services.

FIGURE 16 Productivity and internationalization

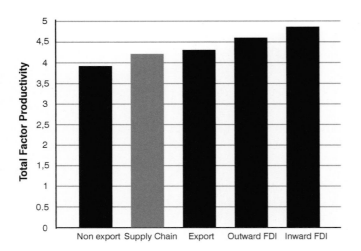

Source: Giovannetti, Giorgia, Enrico Marvasi and Marco Sanfilippo (2014).

Firms that engage in IVCs have a productivity level between that of purely domestic firms and exporters, indicating again that smaller, less productive firms may use IVCs to internationalize (Figure 16). Larger firms on the other hand, might internationalize regardless of supply chain integration due to different structural characteristics (Giovannetti et al, 2014; OECD, 2008).

Importing

The link between exporting and increased economic performance is well established. That importing can also spur such gains is less well known. Traditionally, under mercantilism, imports were seen as substituting domestic production and so adversely affecting SMEs. However, when it comes to importing intermediate goods, there are considerable benefits.

Indeed, success in international markets today depends to a large extent on the capacity to import world-class inputs (OECD, 2013). One benefit from importing intermediates, especially for firms in developing countries, is that such products can embody superior technology that is more productive than found in domestic inputs. This can encourage firms to reallocate resources and specialize, leading to greater efficiency and stimulating SME performance (Miroudot, Lanz and Ragoussis, 2009).

For firms that sell only on the domestic market, importing intermediates for further processing offers one way to engage with IVCs. Following the logic in Melitz (2003) this engagement with IVCs can, in turn, act as a stepping-stone for more advanced forms of

internationalization by breaking down the fixed costs, such as regulatory compliance, and costs of searching to identify profitable markets and reliable partners (Giovannetti et al., 2014).

Even for firms that already export, findings increasingly show that importing intermediates can increase the effectiveness of exports (Freund and Jaud, 2015). There is empirical evidence at firm level that importing intermediates improves the quality (Freund and Jaud, 2015; Bas, 2012) and quantity (Feng, Li and Swenson, 2012) of exports and therefore magnifies its effect on productivity.

There is even evidence that importing intermediates increase firm productivity more so than exporting does (Amiti and Konings, 2007; Goldberg et al., 2015). For example, Amiti and Konings (2007) found that while a 10 percentage point fall in output tariffs increased Indonesian firms' productivity by about 1%, an equivalent fall in input tariffs led to a 3% productivity gain for all firms and an 11% productivity gain for importing firms.

Looking at the Middle East and North Africa (MENA) region for further evidence, Cruz and Bussolo (2015) found that 'firms that are relatively more exposed to input tariff perform better in those sectors with the largest input tariff reduction with better access to markets, higher probability to survive when exporting new products in those sectors and higher export value growth'.

In Tunisia, for instance, firms engaging in trade are more productive, more profitable and create more jobs than firms that do not engage in any form of trade (Baghdadi, 2015). Firms with different trade status differ in terms of productivity from purely domestic firms (Table 5). It shows that all forms of trade are related to increased productivity.

The table also shows the importance of imported intermediates. Comparing importing and non-importing firms, both onshore and offshore, we see that the marginal effect of importing on productivity is very large for both types of firms. It is also interesting to see that firms only importing are more productive than firms only exporting.

Similar findings arise when only examining trade status premiums for exporting and importing firms without distinguishing whether they are onshore or offshore (Baghdadi, 2015). The trade status premium reflects percentage differences in firm characteristics between firms that do not trade and firms that trade.

TABLE 5 Tunisian firm productivity and trade status, 2000–2010

	Firms with more than one employee			
	All	Manufacturing	Non-manufacturing	Services
Non-exporting and importing firms	0.519*	0.750*	0.687*	0.388*
Onshore firms exporting and non-importing	0.261*	0.491*	0.451*	−0.010
Onshore firms exporting and importing	0.899*	1.122*	1.042*	0.662*
Offshore firms exporting and non-importing	0.732*	0.313*	1.851*	1.213*
Offshore firms exporting and importing	1.000*	1.077*	1.199*	1.013*
N	458473	111023	35296	304047
R2	0.3476	0.2606	0.1502	0.3640

Note 1: This analysis takes firm level, sector and time fixed effects into account
Note 2: * refer to 1% statistical significance level
Note 3: Onshore (offshore) firms sell the majority of their production domestically (internationally)

Source: Baghdadi, Leila (2015).

Tunisian firms that only export are found to be 34% more productive than non-traders (non-exporters and non-importers). Firms that only import are 105% more productive than non-traders. Finally, two-way traders are 162% more productive than non-traders.

For these reasons, Jaud and Freund (2015) state that governments should break from their traditional logic of 'export, do not import' and instead facilitate all firms' access to imported inputs. In the case of MENA, they argue that a lot of gains could be made if governments were to reduce tariffs on intermediate goods as rapidly as the rest of the world.

Technology fuels innovation

IVCs have another advantage, especially for firms in developing countries: the capacity to act as a channel for technology diffusion, which can stimulate innovation (Pietrobelli and Rabellotti, 2011). This can happen in various ways.

First, if a firm engages with IVCs by exporting intermediate goods, it must satisfy the chain's requirements regarding product quality, delivery time, process efficiency – as well as potential environmental, labour and social standards (Pietrobelli and Raballotti, 2011). These demands may require SMEs to upgrade their production or delivery methods, as well as their actual product, for which they need to acquire foreign technology via licensing arrangements. For this reason, Humphrey and Schmitz (2002) conclude that engaging in IVCs is especially good for encouraging product and process upgrading.

Second, importing intermediate goods can lead to a direct diffusion of technology if the imports are technologically superior. This, in turn, can stimulate improvements in human capital if the imports require training. Especially for small LDC firms, participation in value chains is crucial to obtain information about the type and quality of products and technologies required by global markets and to gain access to those markets (Pietrobelli, 2008).

Leaders in the chain have a key role in transferring knowledge to their suppliers. Multinationals or other large integrated industrial enterprises are central in controlling the production system (Gereffi, 1994). Foreign firms typically make their technologies widely available to their local suppliers to avoid delays in the delivery process (Blalock and Gertler, 2008). For instance, Volvo provides its suppliers in Brazil, China, India and Mexico with technological assistance to improve their operations (Ivarsson and Alvstam, 2005). In Chinese Taipei, local manufacturers in the computer industry benefited strongly from an intensive collaboration with IBM, including through training of local engineers (Kishimoto, 2004).

Even without direct support, foreign buyers can stimulate innovation. For example, firms in Chinese Taipei developed a triangle manufacturing system in response to pressure from their foreign buyers to reduce delivery time (Gereffi, 1994 and 1999). This system enhanced these firms' capabilities to coordinate, search for and procure external goods and services (Kishimoto, 2004).

Other case studies on the role of multinationals in disseminating knowledge through production chains include the seminal work by Gereffi (1994, 1999) about East Asia. This argues that for the East Asian apparel industry, leading firms, or buyers, play a prominent role in providing primary sources of material input, technology transfer and knowledge.

Further empirical proof comes from Poon (2004), who looks at global leaders and first-tier suppliers in the Chinese Taipei ICT industry. The suppliers have been able to upgrade gradually their technological

capabilities through technology transfer and knowledge diffusion in the industry and the supply chain, resulting in the upgrade of all manufacturers operating within the IT global production network.

Other researchers find productivity gains, greater competition, and lower prices among local Indonesian firms upstream from foreign entrants. They also find that the technology transfer leads to increases in value added and output for firms that are suppliers as well as for firms that are buyers (Blalock and Gertler, 2008).

BOX 2: Value chains help SMEs upgrade

Value chains open new doors to suppliers for knowledge and technology transfers, which stimulate innovation and lead to various forms of upgrading.

Process upgrades bring better or more innovative production methods, for more efficient conversion of inputs into outputs.

Product upgrades involve producing better or higher quality products.

Functional upgrades enable firms to move from low value-added tasks, such as assembly or extraction of minerals, to higher value-added activities, such as marketing or R&D (Humphrey and Schmitz, 2000).

Chain upgrades allow firms to tap into value chains that represent more value added as a whole – moving from a textile chain to an electronics chain. Such chain upgrading is thought to have been key in Chinese Taipei's development path (Humphrey and Schmitz, 2002).

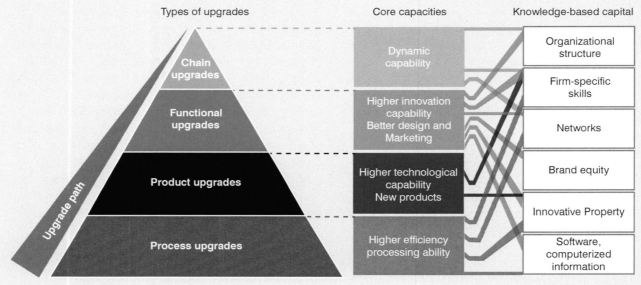

Source: Avendaño, Daude & Perea (2013).

IVCs offer especially favourable conditions for product and process upgrades. The international buyer has an incentive to stimulate suppliers' production and delivery methods, as well as product quality.

It is more complicated for firms to upgrade functionally. The lead firm has little incentive to assist its suppliers, as such upgrades can be a threat to the buyer's activities (Humphrey and Schmitz, 2002).

Firms in the Central and East European automotive industry managed to increase their production of passenger cars and components (Fortwengel, 2011; Pavlínek, Domanski, and Guzik, 2009). They raised their share of value creation, providing evidence of functional upgrading. This is moving up the value chain (Fortwengel, 2011). What's more, in countries that are well integrated into IVCs, such as Hungary and Slovakia, the automotive industry exhibits higher labour productivity than in other countries (Pavlínek, Domanski and Guzik 2009).

Moving up

SMEs do not automatically reap the benefits of participating in value chains. The extent to which SMEs successfully link to IVCs largely depends on their internal level of competitiveness, addressed later in this report (Box 2).

The danger, however, exists that SMEs can get stuck in low value-added activities, such as assembly or provision of raw materials. In such instances, firms absorb little, if any, of the profits, technology and extra returns generated by the value chain.

A closer look at the gains created along a typical value chain for jeans is indicative. From the harvesting of raw materials and initial manufacturing in China to the sale of jeans in France, for each €50 dollar pair of jeans, only €3.20 remains in China (Ruffier, 2008). Table 6 provides a breakdown of the costs along the value chain.

Firms have many reasons why they may be unable to upgrade functionally. Some of these may be external to the firm, such as regulatory and infrastructural problems or limited access to finance. Others may be internal to the firm, such as being unable to meet increased quality or delivery standards. Internal factors are closely tied in with a firm's existing level of competitiveness, which to a large extent determines its ability to benefit from internationalization. A more IVC-specific factor, however, has to do with the governance of the value chain, where power asymmetries between buyers and sellers determine much of the gains SMEs can realize.

Power asymmetries

Global firms may keep SMEs from functional upgrades, if this threatens their own core activities, such as marketing, research and development or sales. Therefore, large firms are crucial in determining

TABLE 6 Distributing value:
€50 jeans produced in China, sold in France

Country	Function	Cost in Euro	Cumulating
Chinese farmers	Raw material	1	1
Chinese factory	Manufacturing costs	2	3
Chinese factory boss	Margin boss	0.2	3.2
French brand	Design	0.1	3.3
	Boat	0.2	3.5
	Customs	0.5	4
Chinese state plant	Quotas	0–0.5	
French brand	Distribution	20	24
French brand	Market research	5	29
French brand	Advertising	15	44
French brand	Margins	6	50

Source: Ruffier, Jean (2008).

the extent of SME upgrades. Large firms are responsible for the inter-firm division of labour, and hence for the capacities of particular participants to upgrade their activities (Kaplinsky and Morris, 2001).

Chain leaders coordinate and govern the IVC. Healthy, stable profits depend fundamentally on the power relationships within the chain. Lead firms often hold considerable bargaining power, which is based on three key factors (Gereffi, Humphrey and Sturgeon, 2005):

- capabilities of the supplier base;
- degree to which a job can be codified;
- complexity of the job.

If a job can be relatively easily codified and is not too complex – often the case for standard manufacturing and assembly – a supplier can be easily replaced. Suppliers with these functions have reduced bargaining power.

A further factor is the cost to suppliers of switching to another buyer, which effectively can lock them into a single buyer. For the mobile phone IVC, intense competition has driven out most lead firms, with Apple and Samsung dominating the market (Lee and Gereffi, 2013).

Sturgeon and Memedovic (2011) identify an additional dynamic: the ability of lead firms to play suppliers off one another as they select and place orders.

From an economic perspective, such power dynamics may lead to lower economic growth and greater volatility, as firms with low margins will find it hard to increase their productivity and will be especially sensitive to outside economic shocks, such as environmental disasters or financial crises. In addition, persistently low wages among the poorest will inhibit them from increasing their productivity by investing in their own skills and education.

From a development perspective this is especially troubling, as aid programmes such as Aid for Trade are often targeted at firms lower down the value chain, which tend to employ economically vulnerable people (Mayer and Milberg, 2013). For this reason, value chain governance is of critical importance in determining the potential direct and indirect benefits from technology.

A case study of how IVCs can stimulate product and process upgrading, but impede functional upgrading is provided by Humphrey and Schmitz (2002).

A footwear production chain extended from large United States buyers to small Brazilian suppliers during the late 1960s. Initially, the lead firms assisted their suppliers in choosing technology and organizing transport and payment, upgrading their product and process standards. This technical assistance, together with increased market access, allowed local firms to grow considerably.

Problems began when Chinese producers joined international markets and were able to undercut Brazilian firms on price. This sparked a need among Brazilian firms to upgrade into higher value-added activities. There was no support for such upgrading from the lead firms, which feared that it would infringe on their core competences, leaving suppliers stuck in low value-added activities.

Reaping the benefits from IVCs through upgrading and enhanced industrial performance in developing countries is therefore not an automatic and riskless process (Morrison et al, 2006). A number of forces, internal and external to the company, come into play.

Value chain governance and firm competitiveness are among the factors that influence SMEs' gains from participating in IVCs.

Value chain governance matters

Value chain governance – the power structure between the lead buyer firm and local suppliers – is critical to determining how much knowledge and profits are shared throughout the chain. While IVCs provide fertile ground for product and process upgrading, the ability to upgrade functionally and engage in higher value-added activities is limited. Fortunately, this is not a necessary outcome, with much depending on the way the value chain is governed.

Four types of value chain governance (Humphrey and Schmitz, 2000, 2002), in increasing order of power asymmetry, are:

- arm's length relationships;
- networks;
- quasi-hierarchy;
- full hierarchy, also known as vertical integration.

These offer different opportunities for upgrading.

As there is no strong relationship between firms engaging in arm's-length transactions, there will be no problems from power asymmetries, but also no fertile ground for technology sharing.

Networks have stronger relationships and reciprocal independence. In other words, not only does the supplier depend on the buyer in terms of its sales, but the buyer also depends on the seller to deliver high quality products, which in turn gives the buyer an incentive to stimulate its supplier's product quality where possible.

In a quasi-hierarchical relationship, one firm exercises a high degree of control over other firms, characterized by significant quality standards.

In a fully hierarchical role, the lead firm takes direct ownership of some operations of the chain (Humphrey and Schmitz, 2002).

Networks offer ideal conditions for all forms of upgrading (Pietrobelli, 2008), but are least likely to occur with producers in developing countries. The lead firm will not have sufficient confidence in the suppliers' capabilities. Networks require significant investment by local producers and support from local institutions, and that process and product upgrading typically is slow.

Quasi-hierarchical chains, therefore, potentially offer the most favourable conditions for process and product upgrading, but hinder functional upgrading (Humphrey and Schmitz, 2000). Suppliers' capabilities greatly influence the governance structure chosen by lead firms – and thus the bargaining power and probability of upgrading that suppliers will encounter (Gereffi, Humphrey and Sturgeon, 2005).

What can firms lower down the value chain, often SMEs, do to increase their bargaining clout and capture a higher proportion of profits and economic benefits? One solution is to form or join sector associations or producer organizations. This can reduce transaction costs; provide some market power; increase representation in national and international policy forums (World Bank, 2008); and help the SME to diversify its customer or product base, thus reducing dependence on the fortunes of one product. All in all, these associations increase the competitiveness of the SME, which in turn boosts its bargaining power in the value chain.

One example of such an alliance is the Confederação dos Trabalhadores na Agricultura (CONTAG) in Brazil, which brings together trade unions and small farmers' organizations to strengthen the bargaining position of vulnerable populations in rural areas (ILO, 2008 and WTO, 2014). Wignaraja (2015) finds that the positive impact of larger firm size on IVC participation is not automatic. While economies of scale and fixed costs are significant in the early stages of joining IVCs, they are less relevant in the longer term, as SMEs may form clusters or focus on niche markets to overcome the disadvantage of their small size.

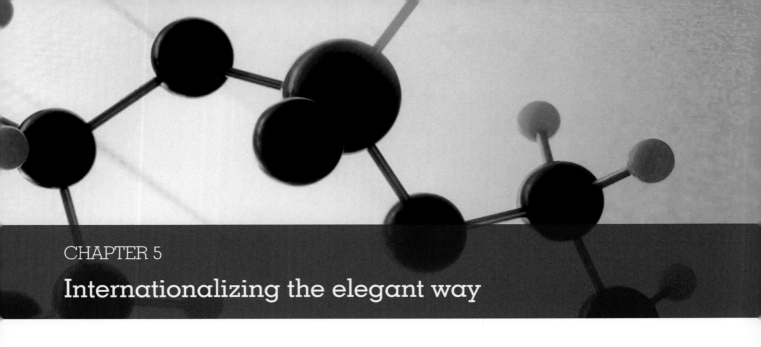

CHAPTER 5

Internationalizing the elegant way

What determines whether SMEs manage to export directly or indirectly? What determines the governance structure within a value chain? What determines whether they manage to move up the value chain or gain a profitable and interesting position within a value chain, possibly with potential for upgrading?

Much depends on whether they are globally competitive in their chosen business activity. The recipe for successful SME internationalization is therefore likely to boil down to the determinants of SME competitiveness.

What makes an SME competitive?

Defining competitiveness is complex. Dimensions involved include time (punctual or sustainable), scale (optimal firm size), space (e.g. national or international) and scope (focus only on firm level resources or also on capabilities).

This report expresses competitiveness in relation to 'lines of business', takes a dynamic approach and uses a definition that is applicable to firms acting in an international context:

Competitiveness is the demonstrated ability to design, produce and commercialize an offer that fully, uniquely and continuously fulfils the needs of targeted market segments, while connecting with and drawing resources from the business environment, and achieving a sustainable return on the resources employed.

The 'scale' dimension is not explicit in this definition, which is meant to apply to firms of all sizes. Firms active in a wider portfolio of businesses tend to be larger and firms transiting from small to medium-sized to large have to remain competitive during the entire process if they wish to

survive. SMEs have the particularity that they often are only active in one business, especially the smaller firms in the SME category.

The term 'continuously' in this definition reflects the use of a dynamic concept of competitiveness (the time dimension). What is sufficient today to achieve adequate returns for the resources employed may not be sufficient tomorrow if the competitive environment changes. Firms operating in a global environment are constantly exposed to change, and adequate returns can only be achieved in a sustained manner if the firm is able to adjust to, or to embrace, change.

While this definition does not explicitly mention the term 'international', it applies to firms operating in a global context. Given that foreign firms are likely to be present in an open national economy, even for purely domestic firms, competitiveness implies generating adequate returns in light of foreign competition. For exporting firms, the relevant market segment is 'the international market'.

Be connected to be competitive

External factors change very rapidly. Competitiveness implies adaptation and resilience. Industry phases, breakthrough or disruptive innovations, increased competition, exchange-rate fluctuations and numerous other events require strategies to adapt.

Firms that adapt successfully pre-empt change before external events strike, or follow with changes immediately afterwards, so that change is rapid.

The key to adaptability is to be constantly connected to major sources of information. By accessing and exploiting information about consumer demand, competitors and technological developments, firms stay efficient and enable future change.

The concept of competitiveness in this report is in line with that used in other publications focusing on SMEs (e.g. UNESCAP, 2009; UNCTAD, 2005) that stress dynamic aspects of competitiveness. Connectivity is about access to information, which allows firms to be dynamic. This reflects the view that access to information and the ability to exploit information is absolutely crucial in modern economies characterized by constantly changing environments.

The definition is also in line with standard competitiveness concepts applied to countries, including that used in the World Economic Forum's Global Competitiveness Indicators (WEF, 2008). This report's focus is complementary, in that it looks at firm level rather than national competitiveness. That said, WEF (2008) considers that nations' competitiveness ultimately depends on both macroeconomic and microeconomic competitiveness, with the latter being determined by the sophistication of companies' operations and strategies.

The quality of a company's business strategy is a major determinant of its success in one or several business lines. Up-to-date information is key to having strategies that can be implemented.

The following section describes a number of core capabilities that are necessary for firms to be competitive in international markets. While they are probably relevant for all firms, the focus will be on firms that export directly or are suppliers within a larger supply chain. In other words, the focus is on capabilities SMEs need rather than those required by lead firms within IVCs.

Leadership and management

Management has long been recognized as important to success in business literature. Master of Business Administration students typically dedicate a significant amount of time to understanding what makes a good manager or business leader. In economics research, a growing number of publications emphasize managerial human capital and management practices for improving productivity, given their impact on marginal productivity of inputs and resource constraints (e.g. Syverson, 2011).

Management practices are strongly associated with enterprise productivity, growth and longevity, according to a study of nearly 6000 medium-sized firms in developed and fast-growing countries,

including Brazil, China and India (Bloom and Van Reenen, 2010), even with significant variations in management practices across enterprises in the same industry and country.

Profile of a successful entrepreneur

A solid command of management skills covering marketing, cost control and cash flow, along with some legal knowledge, are common traits of successful entrepreneurs.

Such entrepreneurs also tend to possess adequate education, relevant experience, deep market knowledge, professional networks, a marketable idea, adequate resources (financial, technological and human) and a solid business plan (UNESCAP, 2012).

Largely beyond the control of entrepreneurs is the external environment in which they operate. Entrepreneurs fare best in a policy and regulatory environment that keeps barriers low, rewards innovation and protects private property. Finally, entrepreneurs need to be highly aware of the wider political, social and cultural contexts in which they function.

Entrepreneurial activity is not based on a heroic act of an individual. Rather, it brings together an individual's intentions, capabilities (motivation and skills) and all the distinct conditions of the environment in which the individual is located, from cultural factors to various aspects of the business environment (GEM, 2015).

Not every business model suits SMEs

Business literature offers tools to help enterprises plan and execute their strategies. Information on strategy design can be found in popular references on the design of business models (e.g. Osterwalder and Pigneur, 2010) or design of value propositions (Osterwalder et al., 2014).

Classical management references for strategy execution include research in areas such as total quality management (Deming, 1982); lean manufacturing and innovation (Ohno, 1988); employee multitasking and corporate re-engineering (Hammer and Champy, 1993); the turn-key franchise for small businesses (Gerber, 1995); or statistical methods in quality management, as expressed in the Six Sigma Method (Pande, Neuman and Cavanagh, 2000), to name a few.

The time dimension is important. Techniques that worked well in the past are not necessarily suited to

Victor K. Fung

Group Chairman
of the Fung Group

Risk management and readiness to change within international value chains

In the last three to four decades, advances in technology and an enabling policy environment have allowed businesses to internationalize their operations across multiple locations in order to increase efficiency, lower costs, speed up production, and provide new opportunities to millions of workers.

Through international supply chains, businesses today seek to add value in production where it makes most sense to do so. Indeed, this has become a key element of corporate competitiveness. For their part, some governments – though not all – recognize that participating in international supply chains will bring value and opportunities to their workers and economies; they have thus sought to foster friendly policy frameworks.

These production relationships embody the interdependence among nations that characterizes our world today. They also embody the interdependence among firms of different sizes, with different strengths and weaknesses and based in different locations. While there are many advantages to these international supply chains, they also bring with them new or intensified risks, endangering their sustainability. Those risks need to be properly managed by businesses themselves and national governments, as well as the international community as a whole.

Different types of risk can disrupt supply chains.

Different types of risk can disrupt supply chains. Some of those risks are chain specific, like those linked to technological disruptions (innovation; changes in business model) or disruptions related to changes in consumer tastes or in product reputation. Other risks are rather location-specific in nature like social disruptions (strikes, armed conflict, terrorism) or natural disruptions (earthquake, ash cloud).

Disruptions related to policy changes (e.g. trade policy, regulation) can belong to either category. Macroeconomic disruptions – like financial crisis – can be systemic in nature and have global impacts that act across supply chains. Last but not least, there are risks that have the potential to trigger fundamental changes in the set-up of supply chains. This may be the case with the rise of 3D printing – that has the potential to fundamentally change the role of

Policymakers need to be aware that international firms manage location-specific risks by adapting their sourcing strategy.

manufacturing and logistics within supply chains – or of long term trends in the global distribution of wealth that may affect where supply chains begin and where they end.

Any of these disruptions tends to affect all private sector players within a value chain. But the extent of the impact is likely to differ depending on the position of individual firms both literally (location) and figuratively (role within the supply chain). The extent of the impact will depend on how risk is managed in an anticipatory sense, as well as the availability of mitigation strategies within a given position in the chain. The availability of mitigation strategies will also very much depend on the nature and foreseeability of risks.

Consumption and R&D are shifting to emerging economies.

Location-specific disruptions can be highly disruptive for actors that are bound to the location. For international lead firms, instead, location-specific risks are often manageable as they tend to source inputs from several locations or can shift their sourcing strategy. Policymakers need to be aware of this. Political instability can have major consequences for the potential of local firms to connect to value chains. Even minor changes in the design or administration of policies can have major local economic effects if they affect sourcing decisions of lead firms. Countries that build up a reputation of instability and unpredictability will be avoided by major players in global supply chains and may find it hard to reverse such reputations.

Sometimes external factors change slowly, and the risk they entail for supply chains are in principle foreseeable. Yet such foreseeable risks do not always trigger reactions, maybe because they are not felt to represent an immediate threat. The rise of the middle class in Asia, for instance, has been changing the configuration and design of supply chains in a process that already started a number of years ago. More and more supply chains are ending with consumption in emerging economies. This is affecting where distribution and marketing takes place. With a significant part of R&D being dedicated to adapting products or services to consumer needs, R&D is also increasingly shifting towards emerging markets. Yet, university text books still tell us that R&D takes place in the 'industrialized' world.

Product life cycles are shorter, change is faster and more international.

Foreseeing and managing value-chain specific risks should really be part of daily business for any actor within a value chain. Product life cycles are becoming shorter, change has become more rapid and more 'international' in nature. Foreseeing and managing risk has therefore become more challenging, but it has also become more important than ever for being successful in business. Being ready to change and adjust to changes in the market should be enshrined in every entrepreneur's DNA and, to the extent possible, the policy environment should make it easy for entrepreneurs to foresee and manage change.

SMEs depend more on the quality of the business environment to manage risk.

SMEs depend more than their larger counterparts on the quality of the business environment in order to manage risk and change within supply chains. True, smaller-sized players are sometimes more agile, which is an advantage in a changing environment. Yet, the costs of risk management strategies also represent a higher burden for smaller firms.

SMEs therefore find it easier to survive and prosper within regional or global supply chains if they are operating within a stable and predictable policy environment and have ready access to high quality and up-to-date information about developments in the markets of relevance for them. Timely awareness of threats will make it possible to avert crisis and identify new opportunities instead.

current imperatives and contexts. Lessons are extracted from cases of success (Collins, 2001) and failure (Christensen, 1997). What works for large firms does not necessarily work for SMEs. Handbooks and guides with SME-specific information exist (Box 3 and ISO, ITC, and UNIDO, 2015).

Elements of a successful business strategy

Leadership defines a firm's competitive strategy. Low prices usually lead to high volumes at low margins. A select customer segment can be targeted with upper-end high quality goods and services. The firm might bet on diversification by offering a large selection of products or it might offer a singular product not offered by competitors due to proprietary technology. It might build a competitive edge by proposing better customer or after-sale services, etc.

Designing a business strategy – including the business model, the business plan, and the value proposition – involves several steps:

- Ideally, the enterprise starts by generating a reasonable amount of business ideas, analysing their feasibility to choose which ones to pursue, and transforming them into a workable and profitable concept. In this process, the enterprise has to make sure the business ideas are sufficiently unique and innovative to become successful.
- Then comes the stage of identifying the market, in which the enterprise selects potential markets or geographical destinations on the basis of research on compliance requirements, demographics, etc.
- Market segmentation is next. This involves identifying potential customers with similar needs, wants, expectations, and buying patterns and habits; and estimating the potential market size, taking due account of the level of satisfaction with current offers, and potential moves by competitors, new entrants and substitutes.
- Segment validation is achieved only when the firm can be assured of having selected a potential customer base that is large enough to generate substantial profitability and small enough for the enterprise to command substantial market power.

A well-implemented business strategy leads to the configuration of an offer that allows the firm to position its goods or services successfully in a specific market segment. A successful offer typically consists of the appropriate combination of a number of aspects: quality and product characteristics, quantity, costs and timeliness of delivery (Box 3).

Accessing and interpreting information

Firms do not design their business strategy in a void, but within the context of their competitive environment.

Porter's pioneering book on competitive strategy in 1985 established what has become the predominant view regarding the competitive forces at play in the micro-environment of a firm. Porter distinguished five forces:

- threat of new competitors (entrants);
- threat of substitute products;
- bargaining power of customers (buyers);
- bargaining power of suppliers;
- intensity of industry rivalry.

The competitive environment goes beyond the boundaries of the industry – suppliers, customers, and substitutes matter as much as competitors.

A prerequisite to design a successful business strategy is to be aware of the competitive forces shaping a firm's environment. Information about consumer trends, compliance requirements, demographics, trade size and flows, trade agreements, preferential status, barriers to trade and competition intensity is highly relevant for a successful business strategy. In modern, open economies, competitive forces are constantly changing. Being connected, in the sense of being informed about the nature of and changes in the competitive environment, is therefore a crucial ingredient for firm competitiveness.

When a firm is able to 'connect' it can gather information about customers, suppliers, competitors, products, technologies and government policies. Sometimes connectivity also involves actively reaching out to provide information about the firm or its products. Examples include marketing efforts towards potential clients or outreach efforts towards actors within a value chain (Box 4).

Until recently, the access to information was often restricted or expensive; with decreasing telecommunication costs, the Internet, and the proliferation of open platforms and technology-bridging institutions, access to information has been vastly democratized (OECD, 2010b). Availability of ICT capabilities, and the competences to use them, has since become a prerequisite for success.

Firms or firm managers can also gather information by linking up to relevant institutions or private sector

BOX 3: Product positioning for a market segment

In its strategy, the firm specifies its 'offer', a product aimed at a specific market segment. In an ideal case, purchases, production and delivery tasks will be clearly defined to fulfil pre-established objectives regarding quantities produced, quality and characteristics of the product, costs/price, time of production and delivery:

- **Quality and product characteristics.** An enterprise may offer a customized good or service, a standardized one, or a combination of the two.

  It might establish its own standard, or follow a voluntary national or international quality standard. It might have a particular standard imposed by its forward-linkage in the supply chain (a multinational for example); and it might need to comply with one or several technical regulations imposed in domestic or foreign markets (for safety reasons for example).

  The enterprise might use quality control methods, such as third-party certification of conformity, to verify that its outputs meet the specifications, and to anticipate any future failure to do so.

  Finally, the enterprise might also propose after-sale services, such as offering right to return, warranty servicing, repairs, recalls, updates or upgrades.

- **Quantity.** The firm's capacity to meet its volume requirements implies that it identifies the required equipment and process inputs, allocates resources accordingly, designs the sequence of tasks and operations and installs facilities and workshops.

- **Cost.** The firm needs optimal planning of its organization and systems. Implementing a programme for improvements and cost reductions might imply balancing production to meet cost targets. The enterprise might practice preventive diagnostic and maintenance to avoid production downtime and unplanned costs.

- **Time.** Production and delivery time requirements need to be clearly established at each level of the value chain.

  The enterprise has to identify and select suppliers, and negotiate and process purchase orders and incoming deliveries.

  The enterprise needs to plan for and keep track of its stocks. It must move supplies and materials to ensure their timely availability and avoid spoilage and waste.

  While nearby suppliers are often perceived as a first best situation, dealing with a reliable foreign supplier might provide a competitive edge. To meet delivery targets, the enterprise needs to schedule a production and dispatching plan, assign production tasks accordingly, and control freight operations (select the means of transportation and prepare documentation).

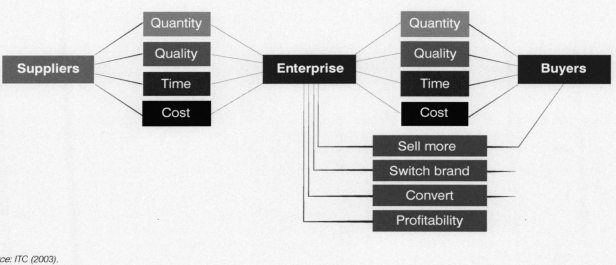

Source: ITC (2003).

counterparts. The firm develops its linkages by making an effective and efficient use of the external facilities at its disposal.

Signalling quality and sustainability with standards

Firms need information about product or service specifications demanded by customers, be they final consumers or firms in charge of distribution at the next stage in a production chain.

Those specifications are often set out in national or international standards to sell in relevant market segments. Such specifications may simply make a product compatible with other consumer goods (e.g.

plug and socket) or with other parts of a final product (seat fits into car). The specifications may signal quality, possibly related to safety (e.g. fire resistance of doors).

Increasingly, those specifications are meant to provide signals about the social or environmental sustainability of goods or services.

Navigating the standards maze

In recent years there has been a proliferation of standards, codes of conduct and other sustainability initiatives. These create challenges for consumers, multinational enterprises, NGOs, government and particularly SMEs.

Prominent standard marks such as Fairtrade International, CE, Halal, Global GAP and USDA

BOX 4: Acquiring customer information

The catchy concept of the 'marketing mix' (Borden, 1964) has been widely used in management literature to describe the craft of the marketing executive – a 'mixer of ingredients', one who is constantly engaged in fashioning creatively a mix of marketing procedures and policies in his efforts to produce a profitable enterprise' (Borden, 1964).

As often, business literature caught up with Borden and reduced the alchemy of the marketing mixer to each of its basic ingredients. McCarthy's 4Ps classification – product, price, promotion and place – was the first and most influential (McCarthy, 1960). When this was deemed too product-centric, a customer-centric approach was proposed, the 4Cs – consumer, cost, convenience, and communication (Lauterborn, 1990).

The two frameworks are closely related.

- Product/consumer addresses the needs and wants of the user and includes elements such as branding, packaging, warranties, guarantees, after-sale support, etc.

- Pricing/cost includes quotes, pricing, sales, discounts, preferential pricing schemes, price negotiations, and activities to reduce indirect costs incurred by buyers in purchasing the good or services (time, effort, search costs).

- Place/convenience refers to distribution channels, points of sale, retail vs e-commerce, postal service, intensive vs selective or exclusive distribution, geographic and market segmentation, etc.

- Promotion/communication includes advertising, personal selling, publicity, catalogues, flyers, sales promotion, public relations, direct marketing, digital marketing and sponsorship.

At the beginning of the 1990s, Shimizu tinkered with the framework. He added the firm, consumers and the immediate business environment to the mix,[6] deriving two marketing strategies. The first focused on promotion, with the goal of increasing profits, while the other focused on communication, with the goal of increasing confidence (Shimizu, 2009).

Customer linkages address the different dimensions of the marketing mix. Each enterprise defines the mix that is appropriate to achieve its marketing objectives: reach the selected customer segment, stimulate sales enquiries, handle responses to enquiries, build purchase intentions and lead to transactions.

Small and larger firms do not necessarily use the same methods, as some are more effective in certain contexts or for certain products.

In marketing, assumptions are often challenged. For example, 30 years ago, the now-classic book Guerrilla Marketing (Levinson, 1984) started promoting networking, disruptive and unconventional marketing tactics among small businesses. In an era where social media and smartphone applications are ubiquitous, these methods are also used by large businesses.

Organic are only the tip of the iceberg. Generally, standards provide assurance on product aspects to help consumers choose among seemingly similar goods. This extensive use of sustainability standards may reflect the predominance of a business approach centred on corporate social responsibility rather than 'creating shared value' (Porter and Kramer, 2011).

Standards can be grouped into mandatory and regulatory standards; voluntary standards; and company-specific codes.

Mandatory standards are set by public institutions responsible for ensuring the safety and quality of products and services. These standards, such as technical regulations and sanitary or phytosanitary (SPS) standards, generally present the very minimum requirements for a firm to trade internationally.

Voluntary standards are developed by the private sector and civil society to address issues not covered by mandatory standards. By definition, these standards are not legally binding. In practice, suppliers must nevertheless often fulfil 'voluntary' standards specified by private buyers to participate in specific value chains. Company-specific codes of conduct are notably often relevant for suppliers of given brands to communicate the quality attributes of a company's products that are not directly observable.

Standards open doors for SMEs

Investing in operations to comply with the relevant standards is not just an option for firms; it is a major component of their business and a determinant of their competitiveness.

Respecting standards can strengthen SME competitiveness in four areas:

- finance;
- management;
- quality;
- sustainability.

Certified products and services allow SMEs to charge a higher price premium and increase profits, and can facilitate access to credit. Voluntary standards require good organizational and managerial skills, which also increase credibility with investors. SMEs may even receive technical and financial support from the standard organizations to assist them in implementing the standard requirements and ensuring full compliance. Thus, standards can signal creditworthiness to financial intermediaries, improving access to finance.

Certification opens new business and market opportunities. Recently, voluntary certified markets have displayed double-digit growth rates, often surpassing conventional market growth rates.

SMEs can move from niche to mainstream markets and gain the status of a preferred supplier for multinational brands. Such medium to long-term relationships are particularly positive for both buyers (often multinational enterprises) and suppliers (often SMEs).

Mexican suppliers, for example, have an advantage in linking up with the retailer Walmart. The retailer requests that suppliers meet certain product and process standards and accept very competitive market prices. In return, the retailer significantly decreases transaction costs for the suppliers and makes it possible for them to supply markets nationally while producing locally. This arrangement is very profitable for suppliers that are relatively productive and find it relatively easy to meet standards (Iacovone et al., 2011).

The direct link to the retailer contributes to a process that ultimately leads to increased productivity in the relevant market segment. Standards introduced through investment in developing countries by multinational enterprises can thus stimulate these countries' international trade activities and help to reduce poverty (Maertens et al., 2011).

Financing working capital and investments

Different stages of the business life cycle have varying needs for finance. Start-up, growth and transition stages are critical. Competitiveness depends greatly on its potential to invest in new ventures, innovation, improvements and diversification over time. All of these investments need short and long-term capital; therefore, access to finance is a central issue.

In the early stages, firms often depend on internal financial resources, including an entrepreneur's own savings, retained earnings and funding through the sale of assets. Alternatively, they seek finance from informal sources such as family and friends.

As firms expand, external sources become more essential. Their availability plays a prime role in the capacity of firms to grow and change. The external sources of finance can be informal (family and friends or supplier finance) and formal (debt, equity, trade financing and grants or government aids).

Bank financing, such as loans, credit cards or overdrafts, is a major source of funding for companies' working capital and investment needs, no matter how small the firm (Figure 17; IFC, 2010a). Supplier credit, in the time period between when businesses receive goods and services from their suppliers and pay for these, is commonly used to meet short-term working capital needs. Factoring is another source of working capital. Leasing is an important complementary source of investment finance. Fast-growing companies with high potential can also fund their long-term investment needs through equity financing, especially from venture capitalists and 'business angels'.

Availability of external finance is positive for new firm entry into export markets as well as for post-entry firm growth. For instance, access to external finance has a positive effect on firm performance in terms of sales, capital stock and employment in France (Musso and Schiavo, 2008).

Better access to finance is associated with more innovation by firms, too. A study of firm innovation in over 19,000 firms across 47 developing economies (Ayyagari, Demirgüç-Kunt, and Maksimovic, 2011) found that external finance was associated with greater innovation by all private firms. Firm level and cross-country evidence are unambiguous (Demirgüç-Kunt, Beck, and Honohan 2008): access

to and use of finance are positively associated with firm performance along a number of distinct aspects, including investment, growth, innovation and firm size distribution.

Finance shapes firms' capacity to enter export markets and expand abroad. Trade is a capital-intensive endeavour, with high up-front costs, such as creating overseas distributor networks; and higher variable costs, such as shipping, logistics and trade compliance.

Quick access to working capital and sufficient cash flow is essential to cushion risks, such as customer non-payment and exchange-rate volatility. The cash conversion cycle is usually longer than in domestic trade, affecting the liquidity necessary to fill firms' next contracts. For example, better access to external finance increases the probability of starting to export and shortens the time before firms decide to serve foreign customers (Bellone et al., 2010).

Credible finance proposals

Firms' financing choices are influenced by managers' preferences and, more importantly, the options that are available. The instruments, providers and cost of financing chosen depend on a wide range of factors, both internal and external to the company (Demirgüç-Kunt, Beck, and Honohan 2008).

Leveraging finance from outsiders depends on the firm manager's own ability to project a credible financing proposal. Credibility depends on the nature

---

FIGURE 17 External financing sources, by firm size

External financing sources for fixed investment

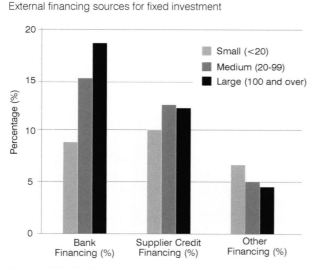

External financing sources for working capital

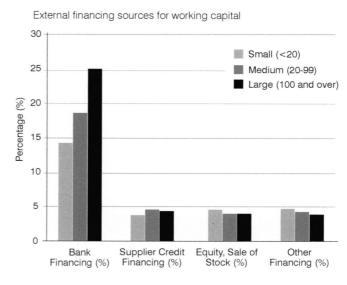

Source: IFC (2010).

and substance of the business plan, and the uncertainties and risks involved in implementing it, how the firm is governed and the transparency of operations and financial health.

Financial planning and record keeping on budgets, purchases, sales, assets and liabilities are expected. The enterprise also has to manage its cash flows proficiently to pay its suppliers, employees and other dues on time. In addition, it is required to check that customers have good credit references, follow up to ensure their timely payment, and take measures to collect payments when needed. In other words, firm capability in the area of financial management is likely to be a significant determinant of access to finance.

Access to skills for competitive edge

A skilled workforce is central to the ability of firms to pre-empt change or to adjust to it.

Economic globalization, coupled with rapid changes in technology, is changing the landscape for many SMEs. In this dynamic environment, successful firms need to be flexible enough to adapt and take advantage of opportunities while handling challenges.

Skills are a determinant of individuals' adaptability to new settings and have been found to be an important determinant of economic growth (Woessman, 2011). Cadot, Carrère and Strauss-Kahn (2011) find that education increases export diversification.

In developing economies, firms need workers with education and training to absorb foreign technologies, and to innovate in adapting these, as they enter more knowledge-intensive activities. A skilled workforce can also determine the capabilities of SMEs in dealing with foreign clients' quality standards (Jansen and Lanz, 2013). Moreover, internationalization can require soft skills such as presentation, communication and language skills (CEDEFOP, 2012).

Skill upgrading attracts more skill-intensive activities via IVCs, resulting in a higher distribution of rents and profits, according to Khalifa and Mengova (2012). Their study identifies a threshold level, where firms in countries with relatively low skill levels receive low skill-intensive tasks and firms in countries with high skill levels receive higher skill-intensive tasks. For example, in order to deal with competition from low-wage countries, Belgian textile producers were able to increase the skill content of their products and move up the value chain (Montfort, Vandenbussche and Forlani, 2008).

A challenge for policymakers and firms alike is that access to skills often has a geographic or industry specific component. It is, for instance, easier to tap into a skilled labour force in cities than in the countryside.

Access to inputs and customers

Some factors remain outside of a firm's control. One of them is market access, determined by the trade policy of home or destination countries.

Firms in value chains are susceptible to trade policy costs, as they may be taxed twice, if they import intermediate goods and subsequently export them after processing. The increased production costs dampen foreign demand, affect production and investment at all stages of the value chain and ultimately reduce their capability to compete in export markets (OECD, 2013). Not surprisingly, there is ample evidence that trade liberalization (i.e. lower tariffs and fewer barriers to trade) leads to better economic outcomes (Wacziarq and Welch, 2008).

Encouragingly, applied tariffs rates, based on the most favoured nation principle (MFN), have fallen from about 30% in the 1990s to about 10% today (Cadot et al., 2011). Nevertheless, tariff complexity (e.g. number of tariff lines, tariff dispersion, and presence of tariff peaks) still inhibits firm competitiveness and should be reduced or simplified where possible.

Import tariffs are easily understood and visible impediments to trade. Non-tariff measures (NTMs), such as customs procedures and domestic regulations, are less easily understood but no less important. With tariffs having fallen over the last three decades, NTMs are now widely seen as an equal or bigger obstacle to trade than tariffs (Cadot et al., 2011; Fliess and Busquets, 2006). NTM-related costs add up to an average of 15% of total production costs (OECD, 2013).

Non-tariff barriers add 87% to the restrictiveness imposed by tariffs on trade (Kee, Nicita and Olarreaga, 2009). In 34 of the 78 countries in the study's sample, such barriers were a greater burden to trade than tariffs. The average ad-valorem tariff equivalent for NTMs on international trade amounts to about 12%.

When trade liberalization lowers entry costs, and fixed costs more generally, SMEs stand to improve their competitive position. Market access remains an important determinant of competitiveness, especially for SMEs.

Getting goods to the customer with logistics

Serving customers can be costly. The quality of transport infrastructure and relevant logistics service providers are crucial to competitiveness, especially for time-sensitive products, such as perishable goods.

A successful logistics strategy is a 'very important part of the total value chain of a company and a significant source of competitive advantage' (Deloitte, 2014). SMEs consider logistics services as having a strong positive effect on many aspects of their business performance (Table 7), with SMEs in BRICM countries assigning this a higher importance than their G7 peers (DHL Express-IHS, 2013). A study on LAC SMEs goes even further to say that 'the optimization of [logistics and] supply chain management within a firm is an element that will determine the success or failure of its internationalization process' (Kirby and Brosa, 2011).

Logistics matter to successful supply chain management because they guarantee that the right products are channelled to the right customers at the right cost, time, quality and quantity (Deloitte, 2014). Optimizing warehouse capabilities and improving distribution, operations and transportation

TABLE 7   SMEs say that logistics affect business performance

Business performance	G7 SMEs	BRICM SMEs	SMEs
Increasing sales	19%	38%	27%
Opening new markets	17%	38%	26%
Accessing new products, materials or suppliers	13%	31%	21%
Differentiating your product or service offering	14%	28%	20%
Reducing your need for long term capital	13%	21%	16%
Reducing operating costs	12%	19%	15%
Reducing stock obsolescence	11%	18%	14%

Source: DHL Express-IHS Global Insight (2013).

management are some ways in which firms can optimize costs along the supply chain, minimize working capital and mitigate supply chain risks.

For a long time, large companies dominated the use of supply chain management and strategic logistics. It is becoming imperative for SMEs to fit the dynamic supply of their resources to the decision-making processes of their key buyers, often multinational enterprises, and to insert themselves successfully into the higher end of the supply chain (Liotta, 2012). Jain and Leong (2005) provide an example of where an SME was selected as a local supplier for a defence contractor, after it managed to meet requirements and targets by stimulating its logistics capabilities.

Logistics suppliers, transport infrastructure boost performance

To restructure their distribution networks and concentrate on core business, manufacturing and retailing firms are outsourcing all or part of their logistics operations. Logistics service providers are specialized in handling transportation, warehousing, inventory control, packaging, freight forwarding and other tasks. Logistics outsourcing is generally recognized as a direct marker of strong logistics performance and a mature logistics market.

Yet firms will always be subject to their immediate and macro environment. Extensive and efficient transport networks – roads, ports, airports and railway lines – play a vital role, enabling entrepreneurs to get raw materials and intermediate components to production sites and from there to consumption markets in a secure, cost-effective, reliable and timely manner. Extensive research points to transport and logistics infrastructure as an export performance factor (Box 5).

To reduce transport and logistics costs, large-scale aid efforts have addressed transportation infrastructure. The World Bank Group alone (including IFC and the Multilateral Investment Guarantee Agency) have committed close to US$ 50 billion for operations or guarantees in the transport sector, reaching approximately 12% of total expenditure (IEG, 2013). The World Bank's Logistics Performance Index provides countries with a benchmarking tool that identifies the challenges and opportunities in their performance on trade logistics.

Keys to innovation

Innovative firms tend to experience higher levels of productivity and economic growth (Cainelli, Evangelista and Savona, 2004). They are more likely to export, and export successfully (Love and Roper, 2013; Cassiman et al., 2010). There is strong complementarity between exporting and innovation.

Innovation can be depicted in various ways. This description particularly suits an analysis of competitiveness: innovation is the 'implementation of a new or significantly improved product (good or service), a new process, a new marketing method, or a new organizational method in business practices, workplace organization or external relations' (OECD/EC, 2005).

Product innovation is especially important for SMEs (Simon, Houghton and Aquino, 2000). A firm's capacity to innovate – its ability to generate innovative outputs (Neely et al., 2001) or more broadly, its ability to continuously transform knowledge and ideas into new products, processes and systems for the benefit of the firm and its stakeholders (Lawson and Samson, 2001) – is strongly linked with its technological capabilities.

Technology in this instance should be thought of as foundational technologies, such as personal computing and productivity tools; connectivity tools, such as Internet access and the use of mobile technology; online presence and the use of social networks; and enterprise-enabling capabilities, such as cloud-based services. Both globalization and rapid advances in new technologies, notably ICTs, have spurred the innovation capabilities of SMEs (Awazu et al., 2009). The dramatic advance of information technology has helped to strengthen the competitive position of SMEs – the excellent business performance of certain SMEs in Japan can be attributed to their strategies for maximum use of externally available technology information (Tanabe and Watanabe, 2003).

Firms improve their innovative capabilities through R&D expenses, patenting, spin-offs, incremental innovations, niche market segmentation, standardization, quality upgrading, differentiation, lean manufacturing (the elimination of waste) and corporate re-engineering (downsizing, rightsizing, outsourcing and offshoring).

Market research as well as product research and development are critical. The enterprise searches, obtains and interprets information regarding market assumptions, customers' expectations, customers' reactions, and size and profitability, to design and validate the choice of customer groups and the offer. It then performs basic research and development experiments, and innovates by developing new or improved products, services or processes.

Once a firm develops intellectual property, it also must know how to make best use of it, which requires

---

BOX 5: Proof that transport networks boost trade

In developed and developing countries alike, export development plans generally assume that improved transport infrastructure tends to generate increased exports.

To what extent this is actually the case is difficult to establish. It is not always clear which came first – the need for better infrastructure to improve exports or investment in infrastructure as a result of increased exports.

In Latin America, Chile's 2010 earthquake provided researchers with a 'natural experiment' to determine to which extent changes in the internal road transport network cause changes in exports. Volpe Martincus and Blyde (2013) find that between February 2010 and February 2011, Chile's total industrial exports would have been 6.3% larger without domestic road infrastructure re-routings triggered by the earthquake.

A study on the impact of the Peruvian road network's expansion between 2003 and 2010 on firms' exports (Carballo, Volpe Martincus and Cusolito, 2013) estimated that total Peruvian exports would have been roughly 20% smaller in 2010 without the road development programme.

Domestic transport costs (factory-to-port) shape the level and diversification of countries' overall and subnational exports, as well as on the regional distribution of production for export in a number of Latin American countries (IADB, 2013).

Finally, domestic transport infrastructure improvements had a positive effect on the SME probability of exporting, according to a study by Albarran, Carrasco and Holl (2013), using data from a panel of Spanish manufacturing firms.

certain levels of skills and technology. OECD has found that with the exception of high-tech firms, SMEs lack a coherent intellectual property rights strategy and use trade secrets or confidentiality agreements to a greater extent than formal IPRs (OECD, 2011).

Innovation systems

Rather than closed innovation, through sources internal to the firm, enterprises can also engage in open innovation via external sources. In the process of open innovation, the direct business environment involving firm linkages can be a rich source of information (OECD, 2010b).

Firms can be linked geographically in local clusters or through international supply chains. Such links can foster knowledge sharing, not only among firms but also among external actors, such as universities and R&D institutes, stimulating learning and innovation.

SMEs benefit from business-to-business networks (Winters and Stam, 2007) and from public research organizations (Acs, Audretsch and Feldman, 1994). SMEs are increasingly innovating via such linkages, as evident from the rise in joint patent applications (OECD, 2010b). The drive to innovate with others has led to the creation of different types of innovation ecosystems and global innovation networks: science parks, business incubators, research, industrial or services clusters, collaborative research, shared space and facilities, innovation brokers, labour mobility schemes, staff exchange programmes, commercialization of university research and even 'brain circulation'.

Finally, firms' innovative capability also depends on strong innovation systems. These bring together enterprises, universities, governments and research institutes in systemic interactions, and have an effect on the rate and direction of technological change (Lundvall, 1992; Nelson, 1993). In developed countries, such a system focuses on new technology. In developing countries, it focuses on supporting the absorption of technology and improvements in existing capabilities. This is commonly referred to as a national technology system (Lall and Pietrobelli, 2002, 2003, 2005).

CHAPTER 6

Addressing the challenges of internationalization

SMEs face challenges directly related to their size (Dinh, Mavridis and Nguyen, 2010; Cheong, Jansen and Peters, 2013). They find it difficult to enter markets associated with high up-front costs, tend to find it hard to raise capital due to a variety of structural biases in national financial systems, and are often unable to make their voice heard in the policymaking process.

Many of these challenges are amplified when set in a global context, and as a result, contribute to SME low survival rates. Although the failure rate varies depending on the country, sector, economic climate and other factors, studies suggest that about 20% of new firms go out of business after their first year. The figure rises to just over 50% after five years (Dunne, Robertson and Samuelson, 1988; van Praag, 2003; Knaup and Piazza, 2007; Geroski, Mata and Portugal, 2010).

Young SMEs have an increased chance of enduring if they export. For example, in the United Kingdom, SMEs are

11% more likely to survive if they export (CBI, 2015). High failure rates are not in and of themselves a problem. The extent to which market failures cause SMEs to go out of business, when they might have otherwise grown to become export champions, is a cause for concern.

SMEs identify constraints

In developed countries, tax administration and rates, labour regulations, access to an educated workforce, and access to finance are among the largest reported obstacles to current operations of firms. SMEs are approximately 20% more likely than large companies to select tax administration and rates as their primary constraint, suggesting that the rates imposed and compliance costs disproportionately affect SMEs (Figure 18).

FIGURE 18 Bottlenecks faced by SMEs

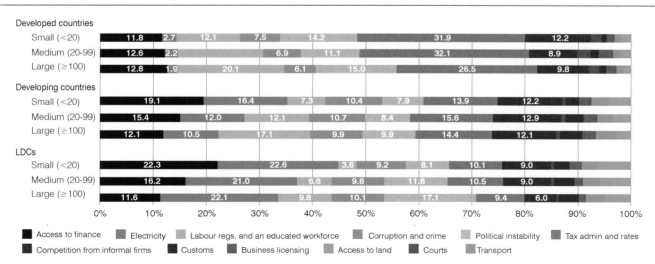

Note: Percentages are broken down according to the frequency firms identified any particular obstacle as the primary obstacle faced. The data contain 60,315 firms from over 100 countries.
Source: ITC calculations based on Enterprise Surveys.

Anabel Gonzalez

Senior Director
World Bank Group Global
Practice on Trade and
Competitivenes

*SMEs employ a large
share of workers in
developing countries
and create more jobs
than larger firms.*

Learning to grow:
Revitalizing the SME Agenda

That SMEs are critical to inclusive growth has become axiomatic. SMEs employ a large share of workers in developing countries – the largest share in lower income countries – and create more jobs than larger firms. The growth and productivity of SMEs has far-reaching implications for quantity and quality of jobs, as well as income levels. Systemic reforms of factor and product markets can reduce the costs and risks that SMEs face, and also expand their opportunities. Targeted efforts that expand access to finance and enhance SME capabilities can also make a difference.

For the greater part of the past decade, the development community committed billions of US-dollars to support SMEs around the world. Over the 2006–2012 period, World Bank Group commitments totalled US$ 10.5 billion in IFC investments, US$ 4.9 billion in World Bank investments, and US$ 2.3 billion in gross exposure of MIGA guarantees. Other major financiers of SME programmes are the European Commission, multilateral development banks, and bilateral agencies. More recently, G20 countries have emphasized the role of SMEs post crisis in promoting economic recovery with jobs. They are joined by the B20 coalition, which represents over 6.7 million businesses and advocates for coordinated efforts to promote competitiveness and jobs.

Even as it takes centre stage, the SME agenda sits at crossroads. Recent research questions the relevance of firm size in and of itself as a special factor in spurring job growth. Recent evaluations by the World Bank's Independent Evaluation Group also point to its mixed track record of targeted SME support. When effective, support programmes that bundle finance, business development services, and technology extension lead to incremental improvements in productivity and job creation. However, most SMEs are not fast growing. Only a small proportion is reflected by the high growth 'gazelles' that contribute to the bulk of job creation of value added. Identifying and cultivating high-potential SMEs remains a significant challenge.

Despite these challenges, policymakers, private sector actors, and the international community continue to have high expectations for SMEs as engines of inclusive growth. To this end, the World Bank Group's Trade and Competitiveness Practice is revitalizing its approach. Our priority is to enable firms of all sizes, in particular SMEs, to be innovation-ready. Integration with global value chains offers new opportunities for innovation-ready firms.

Our priority is to enable firms of all sizes, in particular SMEs, to be innovation-ready. Integration with global value chains offers new opportunities for innovation-ready firms.

This emphasis on 'accelerated organizational learning' in firms – an important but often overlooked aspect of the Asian growth miracles – centres around five lessons:

- **Open and reliable ecosystems for firms of all sizes rest on well-functioning product, labour, and credit markets.** Smaller firms typically experience economic constraints more acutely than larger firms. Hence, they stand to benefit from systemic efforts to reduce the costs and risks of entry and exit for firms regardless of size. Such an economy-wide framework comprises open trade and competition policies, a favourable investment climate, flexible labour market policies, and national innovation systems. Equally important are banking systems that ensure access to credit to increasingly well-managed SMEs at long horizon or manageable interest rates.

- **Integration with global value chains offers new opportunities for innovation-ready firms.** There is growing recognition that SMEs are less likely to be involved in direct exports than larger firms. Integration with global value chains offers opportunities for SMEs to partner with lead firms – whether multinationals or larger domestic exporters – in pursuit of cost-based or quality-based export strategies, and thereby increase growth. A key issue is the capacity of SMEs to learn, to innovate specialized products and processes, and meet lead firm standards. Supplier development programmes, technology extension, and business management training can promote SME readiness.

- **Hands-on technology extension efforts are critical in cultivating high growth firms.** Capabilities and technology spillovers from larger firms or multinational corporations to SMEs are not automatic. Intensive, hands-on initiatives designed to foster technology absorption featured prominently in countries such as Japan and Singapore. Unlike traditional SME support efforts, these initiatives cut across size classes of firms. They emphasize early engagement through low-cost diagnostics, provision of financial resources for R&D and training, and ongoing 'relational support' with the help of both public and private sector institutions.

- **How SME support is delivered matters.** Effective support programmes integrate and sequence delivery of SME finance (lines of credit, partial risk guarantees, private equity schemes and matching grants), business development services and technology extension. They also take a flexible approach to targeting firms based on size classes or other characteristics, while emphasizing continuous improvement.

- **Ensuring SMEs a voice is vital.** Understanding the concerns of SMEs, in particular 'gazelles', is critical to the design of effective public policies. There is scope for public-private dialogue mechanisms to enable this class of firms and entrepreneurs to shape public policies and provide feedback on support efforts.

These lessons offer guideposts for countries seeking to revitalize their SME policies and programmes. Success entails experimenting with new approaches, identifying workable solutions, patiently developing support systems that are fitted to – not limited by – the economic and institutional realities that SMEs inhabit. The ultimate test will be the demonstrable growth and performance of this class of firms, and their contribution to inclusive and dynamic private sector-led growth.

Success entails experimenting with new approaches, identifying workable solutions, patiently developing support systems that are fitted to the economic and institutional realities that SMEs inhabit.

Sources: Ayyagari, Demirgüç-Kunt and Maksimovic (2011); Maloney and Caicedo (2014); Mathews (1996).

Alternatively, this may reflect the stronger voice large firms have in the public domain, combined with better management practices when it comes to taxation. Surprisingly, developed country SMEs do not report access to finance as a constraint more frequently than large companies, which is at odds with other research (Ayyagari, Demirgüç-Kunt and Maksimovic, 2011; IFC, 2010a; IFC, 2013).

The results shown in Figure 18 are limited to countries covered by the World Bank Enterprise Surveys,[7] with the developed country group mostly made up of former communist Eastern European countries. In addition, it does not take into account the relative weight of individual constraints (i.e. tax administration and rates may be the primary obstacle chosen by 30% of firms, but access to finance may have been chosen as the second greatest obstacle by 60% of firms).

The reported obstacles faced by firms in developing countries differ from those in developed countries. Access to finance and access to electricity are among the primary concerns of firms of all sizes. Regarding 'access to finance', the data show that as firm size falls this obstacle grows in importance. SMEs are about 60% and 30%, respectively, more likely than large firms to choose access to finance as their primary obstacle. The same pattern is observed for 'electricity' – small firms seem to suffer disproportionally from lack of access to quality electrical infrastructure. Labour regulations and an inadequately educated workforce are the greatest obstacles for large firms, reflecting that as firms transition from small to medium-sized and medium-sized to large, supportive and flexible labour regulations along with an appropriately skilled workforce are vital.

The obstacles faced by firms in LDCs are an exaggerated version of those found in developing countries. Access to finance follows a similar pattern, with small firms finding it more difficult than their larger counterparts to secure capital. 'Electricity' is by far the biggest constraint in LDCs, however. The effect on productivity and competitiveness caused by weak electricity supply remains unclear. While electrical infrastructure and consumption are generally correlated with productivity growth, causation is difficult to establish once other factors come into play (Fedderke and Bogetic, 2006; Kirubi et al., 2009; Grimm, Hartwig and Lay, 2012). As far as SMEs are concerned, power outages do seem to affect small firms more than large firms (Moyo, 2012) due to limited alternatives, such as generators, for cost reasons.

The next section looks in depth at the seven key constraints faced by SMEs that seek to grow and internationalize. While the list is not exhaustive, it covers some of the most important challenges.

Most of these challenges are not new. They are on the curriculum of undergraduate or graduate programmes for future managers. In many countries they are targeted by specific policies, either through enterprise development programmes or SME-specific elements within the broader policy framework. Ideally such policies create an environment in which small firms can become medium-sized, and medium-sized companies can become large. An environment supportive for start-ups and for entrepreneurship more generally, is also paramount. Young firms that continue to function and grow are the main creators of employment. While governments have a key role to play, there is increasing evidence that initiatives involving the private sector have the highest chances of success.

Business information: Cheap for multinationals, prohibitively expensive for SMEs?

The provision of high quality and up-to-date business information is critical to any business, as it is vital to decision-making processes that determine whether a firm becomes or remains competitive. It is particularly important for SMEs, which often have few means of gathering the array of business information they need. This inhibits their access to markets and ultimately, their economic efficiency. In most developing countries, the SME sector suffers from inadequacies of relevant information usually supplied by public institutions or private associations in developed countries. A study conducted in Northern Uganda shows that SMEs depend mostly on informal institutions for business information, because they lack awareness or the capability to access information from formal trade and investment support institutions (TISIs) (Okello-Obura et al., 2008).

Inadequate provision of business information is a well-recognized market failure that increases costs and barriers to entry for SMEs (Kitching, Hart and Wilson, 2015). When SMEs attempt to internationalize, bottlenecks involving business information are among the first problems they encounter. SMEs' limited ability to acquire information and knowledge about foreign markets and to manage foreign activities is largely responsible for their relatively low level of exporting commitment (Reid, 1984; Seringhaus, 1987; Christensen, 1991).

There are three categories of business information:

- **Market information:** consists of consumer preferences, expectations, habits and the size and profitability of current and future market segments. From an international perspective, it also relates to tariffs, non-tariff measures (NTMs) and border procedures or rules and is crucial for identifying business opportunities. In a recent monitoring survey carried out for the 5th Global Review of Aid for Trade (2015), 'access to information about export opportunities' was ranked first out of nine areas in which exporters would most value improvements (Figure 19).

- **Information relating to the latest forms of business organization or management:** to maintain competitiveness, it is crucial for companies to learn of and implement the latest management and process-related innovations in their industry. Such upgrades begin with becoming aware of innovations, the earlier the better.

- **Information regarding compliance:** there is an excessive amount of advisory services helping firms navigate their local, national and international business environments (e.g. tax laws, registration laws). However, compliance costs in the form of fixed costs hit SMEs particularly hard. Also, many providers of advisory services, such as notaries and lawyers, enjoy high levels of protection, even in developed countries, adding to the costs.

Complying with standards and regulations

The need to meet voluntary or compulsory standards and other technical requirements affects the operations of exporters that are SMEs at all stages of production and delivery. The process of compliance typically involves several stages (Figure 20):

- **Information:** SMEs need to become informed on the details of the requirements.

- **Implementation:** SMEs may need to adapt products and processes to comply with these requirements.

- **Certification:** SMEs are required to demonstrate compliance, which typically entails certification of products or processes by recognized bodies.

- **Recognition:** The final step necessary for exporting SMEs is the recognition of the certificate by custom authorities at home and abroad.

SMEs can face difficulties at each stage, as will be briefly outlined below alongside initiatives aimed at addressing these challenges.

SMEs have difficulties finding and tracing the relevant standards. They are unaware where to look, how to look, and what to look for (EC, 2012). The costs involved in collecting such information are often high, given the high number of private standards and the variety of technical requirements across destination markets. This information-based challenge was highlighted in OECD-WTO (2015) results as the third most important factor in which firms would value improvement (Figure 19).

FIGURE 19 Improvements valued: SMEs vs large firms

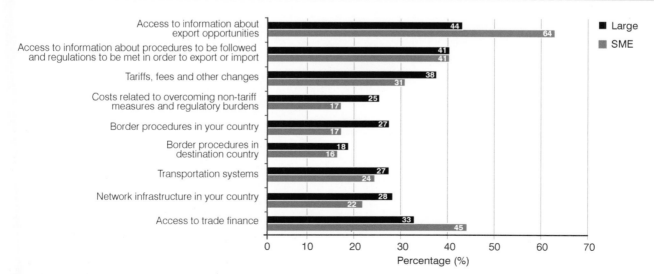

Note: SMEs are defined as firms with fewer than 250 employees. The chart reflects responses of 418 SMEs and 103 large firms to the question 'which are the three factors in which you would most value improvements?'.
Source: WTO and OECD (2015).

Soft to the touch: Cambodian silk producers find new buyers, increase profits

Cambodian silk producers who benefited from an ITC project to boost technical and marketing skills have seen their profits rise by 20% to 30%.

In addition, improved market perceptions of the quality of Cambodian silk have led to new sales opportunities for the producers, according to an independent evaluation of the project conducted for the Enhanced Integrated Framework, a multi-donor programme that helps the world's poorest countries integrate into the world trading system.

'We particularly benefitted from attendance of trade fairs, where I met important buyers and fashion designers, who were very impressed by our products,' says Seng Takakneary, owner of SentoSaSilk, who identified US$ 66,000 in new deals – the equivalent of three months' business – during a two-day Artisans Resources trade fair in New York. 'We also increased the sales at our shop in Phnom Penh by 10% to 20%, and identified eight new weavers' groups in villages to work with, thanks to the project.'

The goal of the project is to alleviate poverty among rural weaving communities by improving technical skills, which in turn enable weavers and exporters to develop new products and designs that meet buyer requirements. It also aims to help them establish new marketing channels.

The direct beneficiaries, 14 women-owned businesses working with weavers in rural areas, have developed export plans, improved their marketing materials, upgraded showrooms and shops, developed new relationships with international buyers and prepared new product collections as part of the project, says Sylvie Bétemps Cochin, ITC project manager. Following training and product upgrading, they attended various trade fairs, signing new contracts and making new contacts, she says. 'The new contracts the group secured represent an important boost to their business,' she adds. 'And the new relationships built are even more key.'

'*The orders we got by participating in the Ambiente trade fair in Germany encouraged us to make the investment, which is a big step for us.*'

Thanan Hok, Director, Kravan House

Sales at VillageWorks, a women-owned handicraft company that is a member of the World Fair Trade Organization, have increased by 40%, and the number of buyers is up by 85%, in the 18-month period since their participation in the project, says Anak Norm, General Manager. 'Learning how to develop an export plan is making our business more professional,' she adds. 'Through monitoring our

export plans, we were able to compare our progress and assess if we are meeting our target.'

VillageWorks has created 20 new jobs thanks to orders from new European buyers. 'We have set up a new sewing workshop, where we provide employment to young handicapped people, mostly victims of polio,' Norm explains. 'We could employ them thanks to the orders we got through the ITC project.'

At Kravan House, Director Thanan Hok hired ten new seamstresses with disabilities. 'The orders we got by participating in the Ambiente trade fair in Germany encouraged us to make the investment, which is a big step for us,' she says.

The Cambodian government identified the silk industry as a strategic sector for poverty reduction. Silk weaving can directly contribute to job creation, particularly in rural communities. Farmers and producers living in rural areas make up 85% of the Cambodian population. Women make up the vast majority of the 20,000 silk weavers.

New designs for new markets

To be competitive in international markets, the companies needed to adapt their designs to the tastes of their buyers, according to Bétemps Cochin. The project supported them in the development of new product lines: silk scarves, fashion accessories, lifestyle and home decoration products, in line with target market requirements and fashion trends.

Lotus silk, based in Phnom Penh, received support to prepare marketing materials, interact with customers and establish its brand, according to the owner,

> '*The additional income is typically invested in the development of small social businesses, training and education, with strong positive effects on both social and economic development.*'
>
> Sylvie Bétemps Cochin, Project Manager, ITC

Vannary San. Even more importantly, she received coaching on running a business, 'We were given more focused one-on-one mentorship about our export plans,' she says. 'We were asked to review and recall our historical performance, and from there, derived our projections.'

Afecip Fair Fashion (AFF), a social enterprise that provides employment to women rescued from trafficking, has a marketing strategy for the first time. 'We always relied on buyers coming to us. When things get tougher, the buyers on whom we rely may disappear and then we have no buyer to turn to,' says the director, Rotha Tep. The company developed five new collections, met seven new contacts and is looking to close a US$ 4,000 deal following its participation at the Maison des Objets trade fair in Paris, its first-ever international exhibition.

The real results of the project lie in the trickle-down effects of the increased profits, Bétemps Cochin says. 'The additional income is typically invested in the development of small social businesses, training and education, with strong positive effects on both social and economic development.'

Source: ITC (2015a).

United States safety certificate could quintuple Peru's exports of indigenous food products

Industry players in Peru expect sales to the United States of sacha inchi, a nutrient-rich traditional plant, to jump to US$ 2.5 million in 2015, following the lifting of a major barrier to trade in their largest export market.

In September 2014, the United States Food and Drug Administration approved a submission prepared on behalf of Peruvian exporters with ITC support, and classified sacha inchi oil as 'generally regarded as safe' (GRAS), a key threshold for exporting large quantities of food products into the United States market. Exports to the United States currently hover around US$ 500,000 annually.

> *'The United States market for ingredients is huge, but the use of ingredients requires GRAS status.'*
>
> Miguel Navarro, Operations Manager, Agroindustrias Osho

'At least five American importers were waiting for the GRAS approval to close contracts with us,' says Juan Manuel Benavides, Director of Amazon Health, an exporter of natural ingredients.

'The United States market for ingredients is huge, but the use of ingredients requires GRAS status,' says Miguel Navarro, Operations Manager at Agroindustrias Osho, another exporter in the region.

> *'Biodiversity trade provides a sustainable means to reduce poverty.'*
>
> Alex Kasterine, Head of the Trade and Environment Programme, ITC

Sacha inchi, sometimes called Inca peanut, is a plant rich in protein and fatty acids, cultivated and harvested in Peru's Amazon region, including in the San Martin area, where it provides cash income to over 1,200 families of producers.

Almost a quarter of Peru's population lives in poverty, and about 90% of them are in areas with high biodiversity. Improving the market position and increasing the sales of biodiversity-based products represents a unique opportunity to improve the living conditions of farmers and harvesters of these products.

In Peru, ITC has provided support to nine exporters of sustainably sourced natural ingredients, including sacha inchi and golden berry, a fruit indigenous to South America. The companies received information about international market conditions and opportunities. 'Comparative and competitive advantages have been established and the market has been quantified. This information is highly valuable,' says Pedro Martinto Housman, CEO of Villandina.

Higher incomes for exporters and farmers

ITC assisted the companies and their farmer suppliers in obtaining fair trade certificates. 'This opens a new market for us: the fair trade market, which we didn't have access to,' Martinto says. 'We can provide higher incomes for the growers,' which in turn improves sustainability of supply, he says. The nine companies working with ITC buy from over 10,000 suppliers in the country's Andes and Amazon regions.

 **2000** Peruvian Sacha Inchi **farmers can** now **access US markets**

'The money from the golden berry that we sell is used to educate children, to pay for health and clothing, as well as to feed ourselves,' says Humberto Durand Chuquimango, one of the 187 golden berry farmers who received training on fair trade and sustainable growing practices.

SMEs also received support to participate in international trade fairs, where they could display their products, demonstrate their nutritional benefits and establish contacts with potential buyers. This was particularly important for sacha inchi, which is little known outside Peru, 'so there is much work to be done and going out to these fairs is a very big opportunity,' says Carolina Sanchez, sales manager at Shanantina.

Next stop: granola bars and mayonnaise

While negotiating with potential customers at these fairs, the exporters realized that convincing buyers about the nutritional qualities of their products was not enough to close deals: without GRAS status, food companies would be unwilling to use their product as an ingredient. In response, ITC, in partnership with government agencies Promperu and Perubiodiverso, agreed to facilitate the preparation of the GRAS submission, which involved both scientific and legal work. Following a seven-month approval process, the certificate was granted in September 2014. Sacha inchi oil may now be used in granola bars, breakfast cereals, chocolates, and fats and oils such as gravies and mayonnaise, among other products.

'This opens the door for widespread use as a mainstream food industry ingredient that can capture the interest of companies like Nestle, Unilever, Procter & Gamble and PepsiCo,' says Guadalupe Amésquita, Sustainable Trade Officer at Promperu.

Source: ITC (2015a).

FIGURE 20 The process of complying with standards

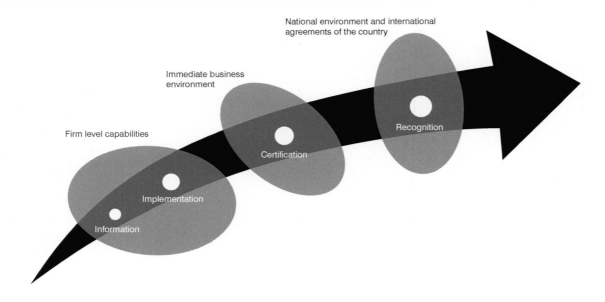

National environment and international
agreements of the country

Immediate business
environment

Firm level capabilities

Recognition

Certification

Implementation

Information

Source: ITC.

Information as a global public good

International organizations play an important role in addressing this information asymmetry by providing information as a global public good. Regarding regulatory measures affecting trade, a significant step in this effort came with the creation of the International Classification of NTMs under the guidance of the Group of Eminent Persons Established by UNCTAD in 2006. The Classification is a detailed taxonomy of all possible types of mandatory regulations affecting trade, including technical requirements. It is updated regularly and part of comprehensive data collection undertaken jointly by several agencies.

ITC, UNCTAD, World Bank and African Development Bank, together with national and regional partners, collect a wide range of legal documents issued by governments and then map them to the harmonized system codes and measure codes from the NTM Classification. The resulting database currently covers 70 countries and represents the largest repository of information on NTMs.

The collected information is harmonized across participating agencies and disseminated as a global public good through ITC's Market Access Map (www.macmap.org), UNCTAD's Trade Analysis and Information System (TRAINS) and the World Bank's World Integrated Trade Solution (WITS). Furthermore, the WTO makes available government notifications

through the Integrated Trade Intelligence Portal (I-TIP). The dissemination of trade-related information reduces transaction costs for businesses and increases compliance, while also assisting governments in taking informed decision on export promotion and trade negotiations.

Voluntary standards are at the core of ITC's Trade for Sustainable Development Programme. It provides comprehensive, verified and transparent information on the increasingly complex market for voluntary sustainability standards through the online Standards Map (www.standardsmap.org). It provides detailed information on over 170 voluntary sustainability standards across several dimensions, including the environment, social aspects, management, quality and ethics – with the objective of strengthening the capacity of producers, exporters, policymakers, and private and public buyers to participate in more sustainable production and trade.

Building the implementation capacity of SMEs

Where relevant information is available and the cost-benefit analysis favours the implementation of a particular standard, SMEs may nevertheless fail to implement it. They frequently lack the absorptive capacity, including the expertise and organizational infrastructure. Moreover, compliance represents a fixed cost that affects SMEs disproportionately compared to larger firms. Quality upgrading, for instance, often involves acquiring new equipment and hiring new staff.

There is evidence that linking up to international value chains can reduce the transaction costs and risks linked with standards. Buyers within the chain often transmit know-how to suppliers and guarantee a certain level of sales if standards are met. Such assistance, however, does not come for free, as suppliers often accept lower prices in return for reduced transaction costs (Iacovone et al., 2015).

In addition to private initiatives, some Aid for Trade projects are working directly with SMEs and their associations to build the capacity to comply with regulations. For example, ISO and ITC have jointly developed a number of publications aimed specifically at SMEs. The ISO 9001 and ISO 14001 Guides for SMEs (ISO, ITC, UNIDO, 2015) help small businesses understand and implement the requirements for quality management and environmental systems. The Standards and Trade Development Facility (STDF) supports developing countries implementing international SPS standards.

Certification can be burdensome

In addition to meeting technical requirements, companies have to be able to prove that they comply with them. Technical requirements define the product characteristics and technical specifications of a product or the production process. Assessing conformity involves determining whether a product or

a process complies with the technical requirement and includes control, inspection, and approval procedures.

Both technical requirements and conformity assessment are a barrier for exporters, with surveys showing that firms often view demonstrating compliance as more difficult than meeting the underlying requirements. For example, among challenges faced by exporters of agricultural products, the primary concern mentioned in 48% of all cases is related to conformity assessment (Figure 21). For manufacturing exports, conformity assessment is the second largest issue, identified as a barrier by 22% of respondents.

Firms also reported reasons for difficulties in compliance, ranging from overly strict requirements to so-called procedural obstacles, which accounted for more than half of all cases. Such procedural problems included administrative burdens; time constraints; informal payments, discriminatory behaviour by officials; limited sector-specific facilities; and the lack of recognition of certificates and other documents.

In addition, certification entails significant costs, especially when target markets have different standards and requirements. Certification and related auditing for Fair Trade International, for example, can cost up to €4,000 annually (ITC Standards Map).

FIGURE 21 NTMs for agriculture and manufacturing exports

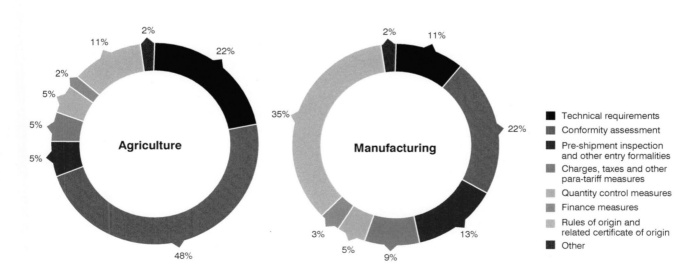

Source: ITC (2015).

Technical infrastructure

Compliance with international standards also depends on a firm's immediate business environment. The 'cold chain', for instance, helps perishable goods to stay fresh and safe for consumption, which needs cooling and storage facilities from the point of slaughter or harvest through to the final consumer. Such infrastructure is key to determine whether firms in this sector are competitive in markets further afield. Supportive local and sectoral business environments are crucial determinants of firm competitiveness, but firms often have limited influence on them.

Accreditation

Two WTO agreements – Technical Barriers to Trade (TBT) and SPS Measures – define the rules under which standards and technical regulations can be formulated and how disputes are resolved. Demonstrating a capacity to conform to standards requires the establishment of mechanisms for efficient testing, certification and accreditation. Countries must be able to prove the reliability of their test data, maintain high-quality certification and inspection procedures and establish conformity to international standards and/or those applied in importing countries. In formulating the agreements, it was recognized that developing countries have significant gaps in national standards infrastructure, and there are specific clauses on the need for technical assistance to be provided.

Recognition

While accreditation is sufficient for recognizing competence at national level, mutual recognition arrangements are necessary when cross-border trade is involved. Accreditation bodies conclude these agreements or arrangements recognizing as equivalent each other's accreditation of laboratories and certification bodies. International collaboration in this area can contribute to facilitating trade and solving problems related to multiple testing, certification and registration for traders and industries – a particularly tough challenge for SMEs. Delegations in the TBT Committee have recently focused on the work of the International Laboratory Accreditation Cooperation (ILAC) and the International Accreditation Forum (IAF) as useful examples of international cooperation in conformity assessment (WTO, 2012).

Making it easier for SMEs to adopt standards

SMEs experience standards and technical requirements very differently than larger firms. To facilitate the adoption of product quality and process standards, the Tokyo Action Statement adopted by OECD countries in 2007 on strengthening the role of SMEs in IVCs made four general recommendations to governments:

- National quality infrastructure should provide information and professional training to implement product quality standards required for exports.

- As standards designed for large companies can be very costly and complicated for SMEs to use effectively, it is crucial to encourage SME participation in the standard-setting process by providing information on standardization and accreditation activities.

- Governments should promote the adoption of harmonized standards by multinational enterprises regarding procurement procedures, as well as the diffusion of that information to SMEs.

- Governments should ensure that national certification systems do not impose excessive burdens in compliance procedures for SMEs. Initiatives such as group certification schemes for SMEs located in the same region could help to reduce the cost of compliance, providing there is trust in the control mechanisms. Promoting labelling initiatives could also allow for low-cost assurance.

In light of the inherent difficulties SMEs face at each step of the standardization process, concerted actions are needed across different levels. It is necessary to recognize, while some of the challenges stem from SME capacities, others are linked to the immediate business environment, national environment and international agreements.

Access to affordable credit and financing

Often, SMEs fail not because of a lack of economic viability and profit potential, but because they lack access to working capital and investment as their business grows. Access to finance is consistently cited as one of the primary obstacles affecting SMEs more than large firms (Ayyagari, Demirgüç-Kunt and Maksimovic, 2012), especially for SMEs in low-income countries (Figure 22). The data reveal that in low-income countries, on average 38% of businesses with 20–99 employees rate access to finance as a major constraint to current operations. In contrast, in high-income countries only 14% of businesses of the same size view access to finance as a constraint. This picture is in line with evidence on access to traditional debt financing instruments.

Credit constraints are typical for SMEs

The provision of debt and equity finance to SMEs is frequently affected by strong market failures, primarily information asymmetries, moral hazard and adverse selection. Lenders view restricting credit as a

FIGURE 22 Financing constraints press smaller firms more

Subjective measure:
Firms viewing access to finance as a major obstacle

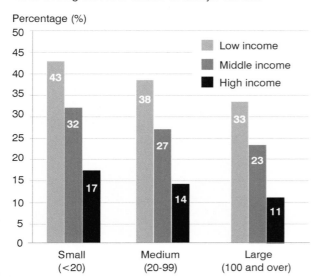

Objective measure:
Firms having access to different types of financing instruments

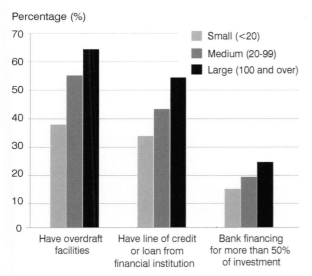

Source: ITC calculation based on World Bank Group Enterprise Surveys (2015) data.

rational screening strategy to select reliable borrowers (Stiglitz and Weiss, 1981). Banks often consider SMEs as 'high risk/high cost' borrowers with opaque financial information due to a lack of credit history, a greater degree of informality in management practices, and inadequate formal documentation and records, such as standardized financial statements. The result is a combination of high interest rates, lending decisions based more on collateral and credit history than on business prospects, and an absence of credit availability.

With banks tending to focus on large and consolidated businesses, credit rationing particularly affects new and small firms. IFC (2011) observes that top banks serving SMEs in non-OECD countries reach only 20% of formal micro enterprises and SMEs. In sub-Saharan Africa this number is even lower, at 5%. These credit constraints are all the more important as SMEs depend largely on private commercial banks to finance business expansion, with about 58% of funding (IFC, 2013) coming from such institutions.

In low and middle-income countries, the World Bank Enterprise Surveys highlight a 'collateral gap', or a mismatch between assets owned by firms and those that most banks accept as collateral. Most private firms, and especially SMEs, have limited fixed assets, such as land or buildings, but possess a wide range of productive, movable assets, goods and machinery, accounts receivable from clients, and receipts from clients and warehouses. While moveable assets typically account for close to three quarters of firms' capital stock, most banks accept only land and buildings as collateral. As a result, movable assets become 'dead capital', in that they lose their capacity to guarantee debt and serve only as inputs in the firms' production process.

In addition, SMEs can exacerbate the problem through their own actions. From the perspective of lenders, SMEs usually lack accounting records, reliable financial statements, or the understanding and skills to prepare a viable business plan to underpin their loan application. This 'opaqueness' renders their risk assessment challenging, and as a result, SMEs generally have to face higher interest rates for any loans they are able to secure, as well as more stringent requirements for collateral.

Furthermore, SMEs often have difficulties in adequately assessing and understanding the increasingly wide range of financial products available. A 2014 survey

Halal certification helps Egyptian dairy group quadruple sales to Malaysia, find new markets

Mohamed Abd El-Wahab had never given a passing thought to halal certification.

'I have worked in the food industry all my life. In Egypt nobody is interested in halal certificates,' says Abd El-Wahab, Export Manager of the Greenland Group for Food Industries. 'Egyptian food is by definition halal.'

> **'***I have worked in the food industry all my life. In Egypt nobody is interested in halal certificates. Egyptian food is by definition halal.***'**
>
> Abd El-Wahab,
> Export Manager of the Greenland Group for Food Industries

That was two years ago (2013). Since Abd El-Wahab's participation in ITC's Enhancing Arab Capacity for Trade (EnACT) programme, Greenland Group has quadrupled its sales to Malaysia, a country that operates one of the strictest halal labelling schemes in the world. It has also found several new markets, including Azerbaijan, Indonesia and Singapore. Sales of halal-labelled products now make up a quarter of the exports of Greenland, which is Egypt's largest dairy company. 'This growth is all thanks to certification,' Abd El-Wahab says.

'Once producers are certified, halal labelling turns from a technical obstacle to a trade enhancer,' says Sadiq Syed, ITC focal point on the halal sector.

ITC and its Egyptian counterparts identified Malaysia as a beachhead in the Asian market for Egypt's processed food exports because of its transparent and rigorous halal labelling and certification regime, which is recognized in many other countries, Syed says.

Egypt had traditionally exported halal products to North American and European markets, which – while growing – are much smaller than markets in South Asia, South-East Asia and the Middle East. It is estimated that there are over 1.7 billion customers for halal products worldwide, an increasing number of them middle class with growing purchasing power.

Yet Egyptian exporters have secured only a small share of the Asian halal market so far, due in part to a lack of halal certification, branding and packaging.

The Egyptian food-processing sector strengthened its presence in the Malaysian market following the ITC project, increasing exports by 30% since 2011, according to figures from the country's Food Export Council.

'This is just the start,' says Manal Karim, the Food Export Council's Executive Director. 'We expect that an

increasing number of food processers will succeed in the market in Malaysia and the wider region following halal certification.'

> '*This is just the start. We expect that an increasing number of food processers will succeed in the market in Malaysia and the wider region following halal certification.*'
>
> Manal Karim, the Food Export Council's Executive Director

Halal certification to the fore

As part of the project, a new halal unit was established at the Egyptian Organization for Standardization and Quality Control, supporting the development of an increased halal-certified export base. The number of halal-certified companies more than doubled from 21 to 52.

In October 2012, ITC brought together over 120 food-processing companies at the Cairo Halal Forum and invited specialists from Malaysia and Turkey to share best practices in audit and certification processes.

Halal dietary guidelines are not limited to meat products. They include other processed foods such as confections, snacks, beverages and chocolates, which might contain non-halal ingredients such as pork-based gelatin. The use of alcohol during the production process also renders products non-halal. 'Certifying and branding their products as halal is an important marketing tool and enables Egyptian companies to capture new markets,' says Syed.

Seven of the enterprises participated in a study tour to Malaysia, where they visited food-processing companies and met with potential clients. Several companies, like Greenland, were able to address issues with labelling, production, storage and distribution that were limiting their sales to Malaysia, and they have subsequently seen their exports grow.

As part of the EnACT programme, ITC also assisted Egypt in identifying burdensome NTMs faced by the country's exporters and importers, developing an electronic commerce strategy and enhancing the competency of a network of TISIs in logistics and export quality management.

Building on the success of the Egyptian project, the new ITC Export Development for Employment Creation, also financed by Canada, is exploring sales opportunities for halal exporters from Morocco. ITC facilitated the conclusion of a cooperation agreement between the Moroccan Exporters Association and the SME Association Malaysia to promote trade between the two countries.

'Malaysia could be a platform for Moroccan products in ASEAN,' says Mohammed Essaber, who heads the Export Support Division at Morocco's Ministry of Foreign Trade. As part of the project, earlier this year Moroccan food exporters participated for the first time in the Malaysia International Halal Showcase (MIHAS), one of the largest international halal food fairs.

Source: ITC (2015a).

by the Asian Development Bank (ADB) on trade finance shows that SMEs are considerably less familiar than multinational enterprises with the many types of trade finance available, which could explain why most did not seek alternatives for rejected transactions.

One of the central problems is providing SMEs with the right level of financing given their size, as their financial requirements are often too large for microfinance, but too small to be effectively served by banking institutions. Figure 23 illustrates how SME finance needs change depending on firm size, and the longevity of the loan they require.

Demand and supply constraints in business financing markets lead to significant gaps in financing for SMEs. According to IFC (2013), there are about 360 to 440 million formal and informal micro, small and medium-sized enterprises (MSMEs) in developing economies. Of these, 45% to 55% are not served or are underserved by the formal financial sector.

MSMEs in developing markets today face an estimated financing gap of US$ 2.1 trillion to US$ 2.6 trillion. About 55% to 68% of formal SMEs (with 5–250 employees) in developing countries, accounting for 13.8 million to 20.4 million firms, are estimated to be unserved or underserved by the financial sector. Today, formal SMEs face an estimated financing gap of US$ 0.9 trillion to US$ 1.1 trillion, nearly half of which involves medium-sized enterprises.

Limited trade finance is a major constraint

For exporters and importers, access to finance includes trade finance. Surveys show that limited access to trade finance is consistently among the primary export constraints for SMEs.

Exporters and importers have different payment possibilities when settling a transaction. Under one option, the exporter produces the good and the importer pays upon receipt (open account); under another, the importer pays before the exporter produces the good (cash-in-advance). In both cases, either the exporter or the importer bears substantial risks.

With cash-in-advance terms, the importer must accept the risk that goods may not be delivered; under open account, the exporter is not assured of payment. Alternatively, trading partners can turn to banks. Acting as a third party, banks mitigate the payment and the supply risk of transactions, while providing the exporter with accelerated receivables and the importer with extended credit (Niepmann and Schmidt-Eisenlohr, 2014). For instance, letters of credit are a dominant trade finance instrument provided by banks in South-South trade[8].

Although one of the safest, most collateralized, and self-liquidating forms of finance, trade finance markets can be very turbulent, as witnessed during the financial crisis of the 1990s and that of 2008–09.

FIGURE 23   Financing by firm size and type

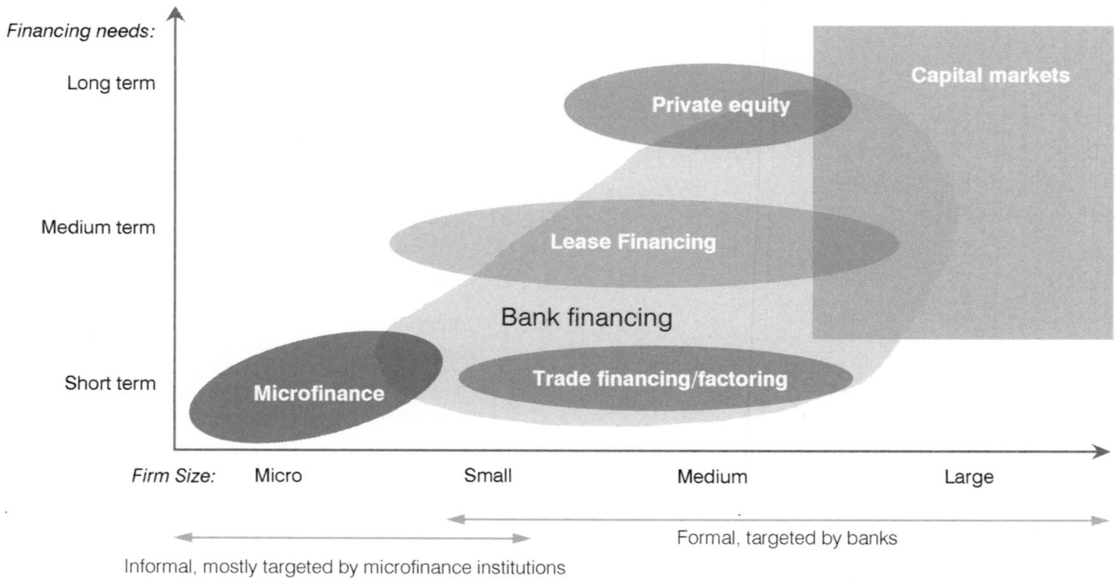

Source: IFC (2010b).

Five years after the last crisis, the ADB (2014) in its second effort to quantify the adequacy of global trade finance estimated that the unmet global demand for trade finance may have reached as much as US$ 1.9 trillion in 2013. This gap is distributed unevenly geographically and among firm types. Shortfalls are widest in emerging markets, notably in Africa and developing Asia. Recently, the African Development Bank (2014) surveyed the trade activities of 276 commercial banks operating in 45 African countries and made a conservative estimate of US$ 120 billion for the value of unmet demand for trade finance in Africa.

Regardless of the region, this gap is wider when it comes to SMEs. About half of requests by SMEs for trade finance are rejected, compared with only 7% for multinational corporations (ADB, 2014). Firms cited price constraints as the key systemic bottleneck to obtaining trade finance. These include the level of interest rates and premiums, insufficient collateral and unacceptable terms of financial institutions. Although specific financing tools such as supply-chain financing and factoring have been created to provide working capital to small suppliers, there is a low uptake in most developing countries.

Enabling access to finance

There is no silver bullet to solve SME financing difficulties given the complexity of this financing gap. Overcoming the financing gap is likely to require a comprehensive policy approach as suggested, for instance, by Kauffmann (2005). Elements contained in such a comprehensive approach are likely to include:

- improving general business conditions;

- helping SMEs to meet formal banking requirements;

- making the financial system more accessible to SMEs;

- diversifying the supply of finance, notably by promoting the involvement of actors from outside the financial sector.[9]

Ensuring a stable macroeconomic environment, a supportive legal and regulatory framework, as well as an effective financial infrastructure are arguably the most important and effective contributions that governments can make to expand the supply of finance to all firms. Such efforts can be particularly valuable to SMEs, which suffer from more severe problems of opacity and information asymmetry than larger companies.

A supportive legal and regulatory framework

Taken together, a country's legal, judicial, and bankruptcy environments make up the legal framework for the extension of credit. In addition, the tax and administrative and regulatory environments affect the entry into a market of various financial institutions – foreign, state-owned, large and small – as well as their market share ability to compete and corporate governance structure.

The government has a fundamental role to play in designing a framework that facilitates alternative sources of working capital and investment finance, such as factoring and leasing. For instance, in the case of the Cadenas Productivas programme run by NAFIN in Mexico, the existence of a supportive legal and regulatory environment – brought by electronic signature and security laws, and favourable taxation treatment – was critical in bringing a secure and Internet-based reverse factoring platform to SME suppliers.

Governments also can play a significant role in setting a sound financial infrastructure. Apart from the need to improve accounting and auditing standards, there is mounting evidence that credit information systems and movable collateral frameworks and registries are crucial features of the financial infrastructure that can ease access to finance for SMEs.

Credit information sharing

By tackling information asymmetry problems between lenders and borrowers, credit information sharing schemes can support the financial inclusion of SMEs. Through a privately held credit bureau or publicly regulated credit registry, lenders are able to share with each other reliable information about the willingness and capacity of their clients to repay. This helps lenders distinguish good borrowers from bad ones and price loans correctly. In general, credit-reporting institutions remain relatively weak in sub-Saharan Africa and in South Asia, but countries such as Jamaica, the United Republic of Tanzania, and Viet Nam have improved their coverage significantly (World Bank, 2014a).

Typically, credit reporting helps borrowers build up a credit history, or 'reputational collateral', which can supplement their need for physical collateral to access formal credit. Research provides extensive evidence that countries with stronger formal information sharing schemes have fewer financing constraints, a higher share of bank financing of SMEs, and lower, but more differentiated, interest rates for SMEs (Djankov, McLiesh and Shleifer, 2007; Love and Mylenko, 2003).

Credit bureau reforms – but not credit registry reforms – are associated with enhanced access to finance for firms, lower interest rates, longer loan maturity and a higher share of working capital financed by banks, as found in a study by Martínez Pería and Singh (2014) using multi-year firm level surveys for 63 countries. These effects seem to benefit smaller, less experienced and more opaque firms in particular.

In countries with no private credit bureaus, the establishment of public credit registries with mandatory participation can jumpstart the development of transparent credit reporting (Jappelli and Pagano, 2002). To be effective, they need to provide relevant, reliable, timely and sufficient data on borrowers.

Credit reporting systems are most effective when their data are electronically accessible. They are likely to provide the most accurate predictions if they contain both positive and negative information, and include information from as many financial intermediaries as possible. These should not only be banks and credit card companies, but also microfinance institutions and a variety of non-financial institutions, such as utility companies and retailers (IFC, 2012a)[10]. As private initiatives spread, the state should ensure fair competition and encourage private bureaus to provide credit-scoring services, which can be effective in improving credit allocation for small business loans.

An effective collateral regime

Effective collateral, or secured transaction, regimes represent another fundamental feature of sound financial infrastructure. The mismatch observed in low and middle-income countries between the assets owned by firms and those that most banks accept as collateral largely stems from non-existent or obsolete secured transaction laws and poorly functioning collateral registries (Fleisig et al., 2006).

Sound collateral laws and registries contribute to SME finance by expanding the variety of assets that can serve as collateral (both immovable and movables), reducing the probability of default, and cutting the losses of lenders when defaults occur. Based on firm level surveys for 73 countries, Love,

Martínez Pería and Singh (2013) found that introducing movable collateral registries had a positive impact on access to credit for firms, especially smaller ones.

Reforming the legal framework for secured transactions can also bolster the adoption of asset-based lending technologies (Berger and Udell, 2006). China, for instance, has successfully established a movable collateral framework since 2004. Thanks to the new regulation, over 50% of SME-owned assets previously considered as dead capital may now actually be used for collateral (IFC Secured Transactions Advisory Project in China). The Pacific island economies, Colombia, Hungary and Jamaica are currently in the process of implementing a functional, integrated and comprehensive secured transaction regime (World Bank, 2014a).

Information and skills: Filling the gaps

Facilitating SME access to formal financing entails filling gaps in the information and skills needed to access external finance, as well as developing financial instruments that mitigate the risk associated with non-transparent SMEs.

It is crucial to run educational and promotional campaigns to ensure SMEs, especially those involved in exports, have an effective knowledge of the array of credit sources, products and services available to them, including alternative financing options from non-bank providers.

SMEs also need to understand how various funding tools can serve different financing needs at specific stages of the firm's lifecycle. This includes understanding the associated advantages and risks, the complementarities and the possibilities for leveraging these sources of finance (OECD, 2015). Supporting SMEs in developing a long-term strategic vision for business financing is therefore a major priority.

There is often a divergence between SMEs complaining about lack of finance on appropriate terms, and prospective lenders complaining SMEs lack bankable proposals supported by sound financial figures and business plans (OECD, 2006).

Efforts to educate and train SMEs to prepare effective requests for financing and ensure they are able to navigate complex loan application procedures can help to bridge the information divide between SMEs and financiers. By offering such support, SME agencies, associations, chambers of commerce and business development service providers (e.g.

Box 6: Turkish bank provides finance and information services, and SMEs gain access to finance

Türk Ekonomi Bankasý (TEB) has been successfully providing Turkish SMEs with tailored financial and non-financial advisory and training services. These address poor access to market information and limited long-term business planning.

The two main pillars of TEB's customer education strategy are the TEB SME Academy and the TEB SME Consultants. Since the strategy began in 2005, the share of SME loans in the bank's total lending grew from 25% in 2006 to 45.33% in 2013, while the non-performing loans ratio declined from 2.8% in 2011 to 2.2% in 2013.

Driven by its success in Turkey, BNP Paribas (one of TEB's larger shareholders) has replicated aspects of this SME banking model in other emerging markets.

Source: IFC (2012).

SEBRAE in Brazil or the capacity-building programme EMPETREC established by UNCTAD) can play an important role in improving SME creditworthiness.

A suitable combination of financial and non-financial services for SMEs is needed most. Creditors could add value to their SME clients by linking up with existing business development providers, or by offering non-financial services directly themselves. Banks in emerging markets are increasingly allocating resources to information sharing, account manager support, training and consulting services to improve their SME clients' management skills and financial reporting (IFC, 2012b; Box 6).

Financial instruments mitigate risks

Apart from the need to build SME capacities, certain financial instruments can help to address the collateral gap. Warehouse receipt financing and leasing are two ways to channel financing to SMEs by shifting the risk to assets. Factoring and Credit Guarantee Schemes, meanwhile, shift risk to more 'credible groups'. While their take-up is lacking in developing countries, these instruments can prove useful in closing the financing gap.

As a collateralized commodity transaction, warehouse receipt finance can be particularly relevant for the pre-export financing needs of small farmers and agriculture producers in food supply chains in emerging economies.[11] Under this mechanism, lenders do not rely on a borrower's balance sheet or credit history, but rather on the value of the commodity itself.

This technique is therefore especially helpful for smaller traders who might struggle to borrow

otherwise. Warehouse receipt is not a new concept – it is already thriving in LAC and parts of Asia, and is progressively gaining a foothold in Africa, including South Africa, Kenya, Ethiopia, and Zambia.

There are a number of prerequisites for a well-functioning warehouse receipt market: legal recognition of warehouse receipts as collateral; government licensing and inspection of warehouses; strong local support from banks and commodity firms; a smoothly functioning commodity exchange that guarantees price transparency; and efficient operations with electronic warehouse receipts.

To promote its use, IFC in late 2010 established its Global Warehouse Finance Program, providing banks with liquidity or risk coverage backed by warehouse receipts. To date, it has backed over US$ 4.6 billion in commodity finance transactions in more than 20 countries, including Liberia, Ghana, Uganda, and the United Republic of Tanzania.

Leasing can help expand the access of SMEs to medium and long-term financing for capital equipment and machinery.[12] Leasing transforms the need for substantial, one-off investments into cash flow management to meet periodic rental payments, improving liquidity and making finance available for other business needs. In addition, the leased asset provides built-in collateral.

Leasing applications are often assessed on the firm's ability to generate sufficient cash flows from business operations to service leasing payments, rather than on its assets, capital base or credit history. This results in lower barriers for young entrepreneurs who are in initial stages of operation and for SMEs that are upgrading existing technologies to modernize production.

Despite the growing significance of leasing, its uptake in emerging markets remains relatively modest. Only about 6% of firms with external financing in low-income countries use leasing, compared with close to 34% in high-income countries (Brown, Chavis and Klapper, 2010).

In many developed and developing countries, Credit Guarantee Schemes have become the policy instrument of choice to facilitate access to formal bank credit for SMEs and start-ups. Unlike interest subsidies or direct credit, the use of Credit Guarantee Schemes limits the burden on public finances (Beck, Demirgüç-Kunt and Martínez Pería, 2008).

The schemes cushion banks from the risks associated with lending to small businesses. Should the SME default, the credit guarantee facility will reimburse a pre-defined share of the outstanding loan to the lender. Because the guarantee outsources part of the lender's risk, these schemes help SMEs to secure both short-term and long-term credits with less collateral, or even without collateral. A side benefit is that by working with SMEs, banks gradually develop expertise in assessing their risk. Another major advantage is that credit guarantees help to leverage substantial loan funding with limited guarantee funding (Levitsky, 1997).

Unlike in high-income countries, where guarantee institutions evolved as private sector initiatives in the form of mutual guarantee schemes, 71% of guarantee funds in middle and low-income countries are publicly operated (Beck, Klapper and Mendoza, 2010). There is, however, growing interest in encouraging the involvement of the private sector, particularly by promoting guarantee societies, as reported in LAC by the OECD-ECLAC (2012).

Regarding trade finance, IFC and all the major regional multilateral development banks have devoted substantial efforts to establishing a global network of trade finance facilitation programmes. These seek to provide risk-mitigation capacity to both issuing and confirming banks to speed endorsement of letters of credit, which are widely used to finance trade transactions among developing countries, and between developed and developing countries (Auboin, 2015).

In addition to the crucial role of export credit agencies, trade finance guarantee programmes of multilateral development banks were particularly important in the wake of the global financial crisis (BIS, 2014). They have continued to grow rapidly in the period since the crisis.

SMEs: A strategic sector for banking

Especially in emerging markets, a growing number of commercial banks are developing strategies and creating specialized units to serve SMEs (IFC, 2010a). Contrary to common wisdom, this trend is not limited to smaller banks with a relationship-based model and includes many large banks. In parallel, a growing number of microfinance institutions have decided to shift their clientele from microbusinesses to SMEs (IFC, 2010b; Dominicé and Minici, 2013).[13]

To serve this new market on a sustainable basis, it is necessary to have a good understanding of SMEs' exposures and needs, as well as the know-how to handle financial innovations and best practices in SME banking. This area has become a significant

FIGURE 24 Success drivers along the banking value chain

Risk managment				
Understand the SME market	**Develop products & services**	**Acquire & screen SME clients**	**Serve SME clients**	**Manage information & knowledge**
◼ Define the SME sector	◼ Design & bundle lending & non-lending products	◼ Market product & services offering to clients	◼ Meet the needs of existing clients	◼ Model & manage risks using portfolio data
◼ Research SME needs & preferences	◼ Ensure profitability of product lending	◼ Build a growing & diversified portfolio	◼ Cultivate new business through cross-selling	◼ Use current customer data to adapt service approaches
◼ Sub-segment the market	◼ Develop SME-specific lending technologies	◼ Distinguish profitable from unprofitable prospective clients	◼ Monitor loans	◼ Analyse & respond to profitability data at segment, product & client level
			◼ Use teams organized for front & back-end servicing	

Source: IFC (2010b).

component in the strategies of international organizations to support SME finance. IFC is particularly active through its Global SME Banking Program. Figure 24 highlights the key success drivers for serving SMEs at each stage of the value chain (IFC, 2010b). In addition, a number of new instruments are being developed to serve this clientele.

Balancing risk management automation with personalized services

Rather than applying the same level of due diligence that goes into issuing a loan to a large company, commercial banks in developed countries have increasingly adopted credit scoring systems to assess accurately SME risk without generating high costs per application.[14] Small business scoring is already well established in the United States and in Western Europe, and is starting to gather momentum in Asia. Studies have found that small business credit scoring has led to an expansion in lending to SMEs in the United States (Berger, Frame and Miller, 2005).

Unlike major financial institutions, smaller banks usually do not have a sufficiently large volume of SME loans to develop customized scorecards and automate credit assessments. The solution for most lenders is to use generic, pooled-data scoring models from an established credit bureau or credit reference agencies.[15]

On the other hand, the automation of risk assessment procedures can be impersonal and have adverse effects on the relationship between lenders and small businesses, given that SME managers value interactions with their local banker and a personalized client service (UNCTAD, 2001). Banks oriented towards the SME sector need to find the right balance.

Alongside extending the portfolio of lending products, remote and technology-based banking approaches – such as Internet banking and mobile phone banking – can be efficient and cost-effective ways to serve SME clients.

A prominent example is the mobile payment services M-Pesa provided by the mobile network operator Safaricom in Kenya since 2007. This can serve as a primary tool for transactions such as the payment of salaries and bills, retail distribution and transport (Lipa Na M-Pesa initiative), and has recently enabled users to save, earn interest, and access microcredit instantly based on their transactions and savings history (M-Shwari).

Cooperation reduces risks and costs

To reduce the risks and costs of lending to SMEs, commercial banks are increasingly cooperating with third parties such as business development service providers or private loan originators. Thanks to their proximity and affinity with their members, business development service providers are better aware of SMEs' problems, needs and financial status, allowing them to ascertain SME creditworthiness better than commercial banks.

Cooperation and partnerships can therefore make up for lack of capacity in commercial banks and help to reduce the transaction costs and information asymmetry of lending to SMEs. For instance, Enterprise Africa, a regional business development service programme of UNDP modelled on EMPRETEC, has developed a joint credit delivery scheme. This provides capacity-building services to SMEs and assumes responsibility for credit appraisal, scoring and monitoring processes of partner financial institutions (UNCTAD, 2001). Such partnerships are generally fruitful for all parties and worth encouraging.

Diversifying the sources of finance

Policymakers have increasingly focused on enabling SMEs to diversify their funding sources beyond conventional bank credit. For example, SMEs can obtain funding from microfinance institutions and non-bank financial institutions. Risk-taking institutions (e.g. venture capitalists, private equity funds, pension funds and mutual funds), capital market organizers (e.g. stock exchanges, and securities dealers and brokers) and specialized financiers (e.g. credit cooperatives, credit unions, leasing companies and factoring companies) can each play an important role by supplementing available bank lending for SMEs. Furthermore, SMEs can tap into the supply of funding from the non-financial private sector, including trade credit between firms, or through crowdfunding and investing platforms.

Funding from the non-financial sector

In nearly every developed and developing economy, trade credit is the most important alternative to bank loans as a source of external funding in the SME sector (Demirgüç-Kunt and Maksimovic, 2001; Allen et al., 2012). Research on the role of trade credit suggests that suppliers can act as 'relationship lenders' thanks to unique proprietary information about their customers (McMillan and Woodruff, 1999; Uchida, Udell and Watanabe, 2011).

Although still in its infancy and small in comparison to traditional funding options, crowdfunding is attracting growing interest, most recently for its potential to raise funds and investment for high-growth entrepreneurs and technology-focused SMEs.

Over the past five years, crowdfunding has experienced unprecedented growth in some regions, including the United Kingdom, the United States, Germany and China.[16] Operating via online web-based platforms, it has evolved from community crowdfunding (i.e. social lending, donations and rewards) to financial return crowdfunding (peer-to-peer lending and equity crowdfunding), where multiple investors provide debt or equity and grow to big players that capture up to 75% of the respective national crowdfunding market. Yet, the regulatory framework has limited the expansion of its use, especially for equity crowdfunding platforms, which are still not legal in some countries and currently comprise the smallest part of the market.

Peer-to-peer lending can be attractive for the underserved SME loans market, offering flexibility, cost-effectiveness and speed, including for small amounts of funds. Equity crowdfunding, in turn, can act as a complement or an alternative to business angels and venture capital for those in the seed and start-up stage (Wilson and Testoni, 2014).

Given the risks for investors, who are often unsophisticated contributors (Kirby and Worner, 2014), a balanced regulatory framework is needed (BBVA research, 2015). In its 2013 Green Paper on Long Term Financing for SMEs, the European Commission indicated its intention to unleash the potential of crowdfunding. At this stage, however, its efforts are mainly directed towards increasing awareness, spreading best practices and building user confidence, notably through the creation of the European Crowdfunding Stakeholders Forum in 2014.

According to a 2013 study by World Bank/InfoDev, Crowdfunding's Potential for the Developing World, developing economies may have the potential to capitalize on this new funding mechanism to finance innovation and growth, with such funding reaching up to US$ 96 billion a year by 2025.

The report identified China in particular, followed by the rest of East Asia, Central Europe, LAC, and the MENA region. Recently, the World Bank launched crowdfunding programmes for SMEs in East Africa. InfoDev's Kenya Climate Innovation Centre is implementing the Crowdfund Investing Pilot, in which six chosen local ventures receive mentorship and training to design and test their crowdfunding strategies.

FIGURE 25 Moving up value chains requires skilled workers

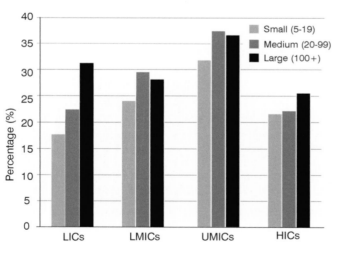

Note: Indicators for income groups are computed using OECD definitions of income groupings and simple averages across countries. Indicators are based on 33 low-income countries (LICs), 38 lower-middle income countries (LMICs), 43 upper-middle income countries (UMICs) and 16 high income countries (HICs).
Source: Jansen, Marion and Rainer Lanz (2013).

FIGURE 26 Suppliers cite workforce skill constraints

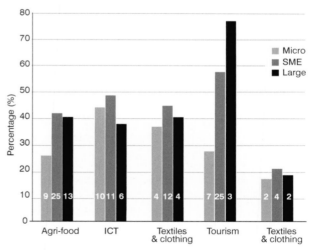

Note: Labels indicate the number of replies mentioning labour force skills as a main national supply side constraint affecting suppliers' ability to enter, establish and move up the value chain. Replies from associations are not included, as no breakdown by size is possible.
Source: Jansen, Marion and Rainer Lanz (2013); WTO and OECD (2015).

Access to skilled labour

Workforce skills are an important asset for both defensive and expansive enterprise strategies in global markets (Jansen and Lanz, 2013). However, in an environment of constant change it is difficult for employers to hire workers with the right skills or to regularly adjust skills through in-house training. These challenges are particularly daunting for SMEs due to their small size.

SMEs: Too busy to train

Figure 25 shows the share of firms by income group identifying an inadequately educated workforce as a major constraint to their operations. About 20% of SMEs in low-income countries identify an inadequately educated workforce as a major constraint. This is low compared to the other categories shown. Joining and moving up value chains often requires a skilled workforce, and it is clear that, as a firm grows, skills shortages become a greater problem.

The 2013 OECD-WTO Aid for Trade monitoring survey confirmed that skills are a major supply side constraint for SMEs (Jansen and Lanz, 2013), notably in the ICT sector, where there is rapid technological change, and in the tourism sector, characterized by frequent employee-client contact (Figure 26).

Mismatches between the skills supplied by countries' education systems and the skills firms seek are a well-known source of economic inefficiency (Jansen and Lanz, 2013). These mismatches often create a paradoxical situation, in which high rates of unemployment among young graduates persist alongside complaints by employers of a shortage of workers with specific skills (Almeida, Behrman and Robalino, 2012). Currently 60% of entrepreneurs name difficulty accessing the right talent as one of their top recruiting concerns, especially scientific, technology, engineering and mathematics (STEM) skills.

Skill mismatches have high economic and social costs, in particular youth unemployment. Weaknesses in the skill mix available in the labour market are likely to affect SMEs disproportionally, as the means to invest in training are non-existent.

For instance, data across OECD countries show that SMEs are two times less likely to be involved in training activities than large firms. World Bank Enterprise Surveys show that on average small firms are approximately 1.6 times less likely to offer formal training to their workers than medium-sized firms, and up to 2.4 times less likely than large firms.

It might be that SMEs do not invest in training simply because their expected rate of return is smaller than the return on other investments (Almeida, Behrman and Robalino, 2012). Several studies, however, have shown that SMEs are likely to face more severe resource constraints than larger firms and, as a result, find it harder to invest in training or retraining (Okada, 2004).

It is also more difficult for small organizations to handle the drop in production that results when an employee is absent for formal training. This is compounded by the lack of resources or the capacity to assess future skills needs (Cedefop, 2012). Others may also not train because of high labour turnover and the fear to lose the investment made in the training of workers (Almeida, Behrman and Robalino,

FIGURE 27 Reasons not to invest in on-the-job training in Central America

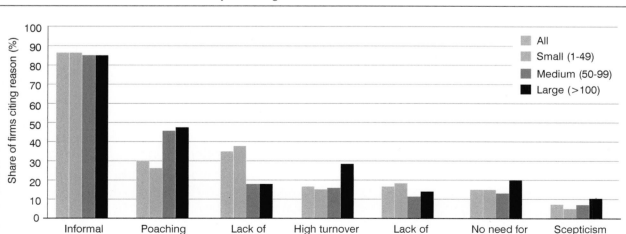

Source: Almeida, Rita, Jere Behrman and David Robalino (2012).

2012). Small firms may be insufficiently aware of the future returns from such training (Adams, 2007). Underinvestment by small firms in knowledge upgrading and the discovery process makes them weaker and more vulnerable in the face of new market challenges.

Figure 27 provides evidence from Enterprise Surveys on the potential constraints to skills development faced by firms in Central America.

Getting the 'skills mix' right

In most countries, it is the education system's responsibility to prepare individuals for jobs with a focus on basic or foundation skills, such as literacy and numeracy. To provide individuals with the right skills for the job[17], it is necessary to raise education levels and provide job-relevant skills and attitudes[18]. In today's globalized economy, employers are increasingly demanding both technical and educational qualifications, as well as certain behavioural qualities in their employees.

Getting the mix of skills right is not an easy task. In numerous countries, high levels of investment in formal education have not succeeded in ensuring that employers find required skills in the labour market (Figure 28). WEF's index includes well-known and accepted metrics for education: secondary and tertiary school enrolment rate statistics. Data on the

FIGURE 28 Higher education vs workforce skills

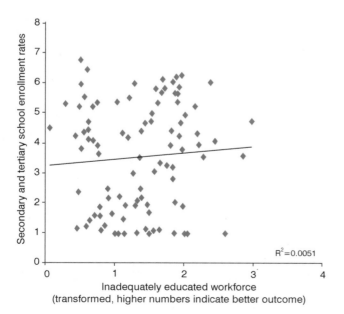

Note: The graph is based on data from 97 countries.
Source: ITC calculation based on data from World Bank and WEF (2015).

SME perspective on workforce skills comes from the World Bank's Enterprise Surveys, which ask firms directly if skills shortages are an obstacle to current operations. It is rather worrying that no correlation between the two variables is found.

Vocational training

In both developed and developing countries vocational education and training can be critical to minimizing mismatches between skills available and those needed in the labour market. Such training helps to integrate young people into the world of work by providing a comprehensive set of readily applicable, job-relevant skills and specialized technical knowledge.

In recent decades, vocational education and training has frequently been a neglected part of initial education, and the widespread skills mismatch suggests that the quality of such training is low in many regions. Attracting young people to vocational training and apprenticeships is therefore crucial.

A well-functioning vocational education and training system needs a high degree of engagement and ownership on the part of social partners (employers and trade unions) and external advisory bodies, such as sector skills councils. For example, the Austrian, German and Swiss models combining part-time apprenticeships in enterprises with part-time education in vocational schools, are deeply embedded in society and have often been considered to be effective in nurturing the skills needed by firms.

The capacity of SMEs to attract good talent with prior education, training and experience will therefore depend on the ability of both relevant national education and vocational training systems to provide young people with knowledge, skills and attitudes in demand (Jansen and Lanz, 2013; Cedefop, 2012). Over the short run, countries also face the challenge of upgrading the skills of those who are already in the labour force, as roughly 80% of the current workforce will still be in the labour market in ten years' time (Cedefop, 2010).

SMEs need continuous training and skills

SMEs are in competition with large firms for a limited number of suitably trained workers and tend to hire a higher proportion of untrained people because they are less likely to pay high wages and benefits. In consequence, these workers need training to raise their

FIGURE 29 Training and skill development choices

Training and Learning Suppliers						
Private-sector trainers & consultants	**Suppliers & other value chain-related business**	**Government agencies**	**Educational institutions**	**Associative networks**	**Unions**	**Other providers**
■ Trainers ■ Consultants	■ Material, machine or equipment suppliers ■ Other value stream related business (distributors, retail) ■ Other branches of the same business	■ Government-funded programmes ■ Economic development centres ■ Municipal organizations ■ Other ministers	■ Schools (vocational or training centres) ■ Colleges ■ Universities ■ Polytechnics	■ Sector-based councils ■ Business association or groups ■ Professional associations ■ Industry associations ■ Non-profit organizations		

Source: Canadian Chamber of Commerce (2013).

basic and technical competence. Yet, most SMEs do not train their employees. In the long-term, this saps their productivity, competitiveness, and staff retention.

Figure 29 shows that the training and skills development ecosystem is complex and the choice of external suppliers wide. This can be confusing for small companies. Another constraint involves the lack of customized and affordable training supply, which is often considered too broad or generic, with a bias towards the needs of large enterprises (Kubitz, 2011; Martinez-Fernandez and Sharpe, 2010). Incentives for training providers to deliver effective and responsive services, and helping SMEs to tap into the range of available training programmes and initiatives can foster SME participation in existing initiatives.

Smaller firms may be reluctant to offer formal training, for fear of losing trained workers to other firms or for issues of cost and affordability. One way to address such reluctance is by subsidizing training, which has characteristics of a 'public good'. Such subsidies can be funded through budget allocations to training institutions; exemptions from employer payroll levies; and grants to firms that undertake certain designated forms of training, both on and off the job (ILO, 2010)[19].

Given the multiple barriers faced by SMEs, even large subsidies and tax breaks may need to be combined with other forms of support. In particular, Stone (2012) identified employer networks and training as the most promising policy measures to upgrade workforce skills in small businesses.

Training networks, value chains, informal channels

Cooperation via horizontal networks, including actors from the public and private sectors, has the potential to strengthen the engagement of SMEs in training. At the same time, such networks can create opportunities for knowledge exchange, resulting in collaborative research and development (Bosworth and Stanfield, 2009). Resources can be pooled, including through the use of collective funds to cover costs of common training programmes. Networks offer SMEs access to services they would otherwise not have, such as appropriately tailored learning and specialist training expertise.

Governments and zone authorities can support such company networks. A prominent example of such collective action is the Penang Skills Development Centre in Malaysia, which acts as a broker between employers and training providers. Networks can also be vertical, linking buyers and suppliers.

International chain leaders stimulate training of their local suppliers, especially if this would benefit product and process quality. However, they may be reluctant to stimulate functional upgrading (i.e. where suppliers can move up the value chain) if this interferes with the leaders' core competencies such as marketing, sales or R&D, for example.

Numerous studies have also underlined the importance of informal learning and training in the workplace for small businesses, although this typically is not reflected in official statistics. A 2013 OECD study based on a survey of SMEs in seven regions found that small employers view informal

FIGURE 30 SMEs have higher logistics costs (example: LAC)

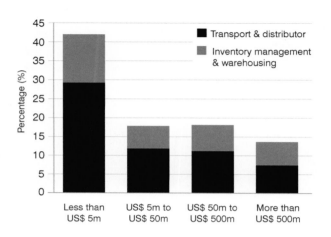

Source: Schwartz, Jordan, José Luis Guasch, Gordon Wilmsmeier and Aiga Stokenberga (2009).

FIGURE 31 Global infrastructure investment needs (in US$ trillion)

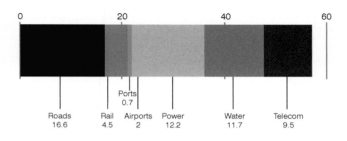

Note: Based on projections of demand equalling 3.5% of global GDP (constant 2010 US$), 2013–2030.
Source: McKinsey Global Institute (2013).

learning through daily activities as a better way to upgrade skills than formal training courses.

Such learning includes mentoring team and staff meetings, co-worker collaboration and project interactions. It is a flexible and cost-effective training approach for SMEs that can be tailored to their needs and conducted as production continues (Martinez-Fernandez and Miles, 2011).

For policymakers this raises questions of whether and how to recognize skills acquired through learning and experience outside formal education (OECD, 2013a). For instance, the European Qualifications Framework for Lifelong Learning uses eight reference levels based on learning outcomes – defined in terms of knowledge, skills and competences – which makes it possible to validate all forms of learning, whether formal or informal (EC, 2008).

Logistics, a higher burden for SMEs

Traditionally, logistics management has been associated with large manufacturing firms, which have pioneered innovations in the field, such as 'just-in-time' production and delivery. Logistics management, however, is an important part of any business, whether large or small. Poor logistics management can render firms uncompetitive, impeding their access to suppliers and buyers, and their participation in international value chains.

Studies on SMEs' logistics costs show that they tend to be significantly higher than for large firms. For

example, according to a study in LAC, the logistics costs for SMEs were two to three times higher than those of large companies (Barbero, 2010). Furthermore, logistics costs in LAC represent 18% to 35% of the final value of goods, compared to 8% in OECD countries. For small companies, the share may be over 42%, mainly due to high inventory and warehousing costs (Schwartz et al., 2009; Figure 30). Why do SMEs face higher costs and more logistics-related difficulties? In the context of international trade, SMEs can find it hard to fill containers with their goods, thus increasing unit costs. In addition, SMEs often do not have a good grasp of logistics management principles or sufficient knowledge of alternative logistics service providers in foreign countries.

They may be subject to excessive controls at the border because they export infrequently and do not benefit from fast-track privileges many large companies acquire. Moreover, SMEs joining complex value chains are sometimes forced to adapt their way of doing business to meet the requirements of the foreign lead firm.

Low transactions costs, predictability and speed are all elements of an optimal logistics system. To achieve this, public entities and the private sector can aim to improve transport infrastructure and services, business logistics practices and trade facilitation procedures.

Public and private sectors: Invest in infrastructure

For a country's logistics operations to function properly, it must have modern and efficient transport infrastructure. There is a mounting need for further and significant investment in infrastructure worldwide, especially in emerging and developing countries.

Research from McKinsey Global Institute (2013) suggests that by 2030, US$ 57.3 trillion will be needed to finance infrastructure development around the world, with roads, airports, ports and rail accounting for 41% of this total (Figure 31).[20] This is likely to be well beyond the means of the public sector acting on its own, making it essential to engage the private sector in infrastructure financing (WTO, 2015).

In many developing countries, private participation via public-private partnerships has provided a viable way to bridge infrastructure spending gaps, but there have also been some significant failures (for best practices, see The Boston Consulting Group, 2013). Another idea under consideration is increasing the percentage devoted to infrastructure from funds managed by pension funds, sovereign-wealth funds, insurance companies and other institutional investors, which stands at just 1% of US$ 79 trillion (World Bank Group, 2014).

SMEs: Participate in infrastructure projects and decisions

Infrastructure development can also provide valuable opportunities for SME development. SMEs may benefit from participating indirectly in infrastructure projects awarded to others, by subcontracting portions of the work, or directly, through involvement in small-scale projects at the local level. Nevertheless, SMEs are often deterred from entering this potentially lucrative market by the procedures and practices used in many tenders, even if they are not specifically excluded.

Common barriers include poor access to information about contract opportunities, excessive bureaucracy, heavy documentation and guarantee requirements, and an overall lack of transparency in the procurement process (Kaspar and Puddephatt, 2012). To promote greater SME engagement, government procurement processes could simplify administrative procedures; reserve a specific percentage of government contracts for SMEs; package large contracts into smaller bids; and put in place preferential financial treatment.

Decisions processes regarding the selection and definition of infrastructure projects can be subject to uneven bargaining power between SMEs and large companies, which can reduce the social returns from transport infrastructure investment. In reality, even in a situation where their needs have equal economic weight, large companies are often better able than

SMEs to leverage their bargaining power in favour of their infrastructure needs. This can further exacerbate the remoteness of SMEs from regional and domestic markets.

It is often hard for SMEs to be heard, with their needs fragmented and dispersed, and a lack of advocacy. To address this, sectoral associations and clustering can contribute to unifying the voice of SMEs and lobbying for government support in attaining strategic infrastructure.

Put existing transport infrastructure to best use

While greater and better investment in transport infrastructure is essential, it is a costly and lengthy process and may not be sufficient on its own to facilitate trade and generate productivity gains for SMEs. For instance, improvements in physical infrastructure may fail to enhance overall trade effectiveness if not accompanied by well-performing, competitive transport and logistics services (Arvis et al., 2007). Thus, there is a need to improve both hard and soft aspects of logistics (OECD, 2013b).

The benefits of high-quality transport infrastructure can only be fully realized when accompanied by appropriate regulations, such as pro-competition policies and laws that encourage affordable and high-quality logistics services auxiliary to transport (World Bank, 2012). OECD (2006) argued that liberalizing such services would bring considerable gains in competitiveness, especially for SMEs, which would benefit from lower costs of entry to the export market and smaller inventory stores at each stage of the production chain.

To encourage efficient use of available transport infrastructure in LAC and thereby minimize logistics costs, the Latin American Economic Outlook 2014 on Logistics and Competitiveness (OECD/UN-ECLAC/CAF, 2013) emphasizes the need for active policies in the short run. These include providing modern storage facilities, efficient customs and certification procedures, using ICT for logistics and implementing standards for appropriate handling and transportation, as well as promoting competition in the transport sector.

Make it easier for goods to cross borders

Improving transparency and predictability of customs, trade procedures and regulations is crucial to help SMEs internationalize. Indeed, burdensome customs and trade regulations are often mentioned in World Bank Enterprise Surveys as significant obstacles to traders, especially to SMEs.

The recent WTO Trade Facilitation Agreement (TFA) addresses these challenges directly, by seeking to cut red tape, such as costs linked to clearing goods, administration and documentation, as well as border delays. The Agreement establishes binding obligations to improve customs procedures, transparency, predictability, efficiency and cooperation among border regulatory agencies and the private sector.

According to the World Trade Report 2015 (WTO, forthcoming), implementation of the TFA is likely to boost SME participation in trade, with some trade facilitation measures particularly benefiting smaller traders. These include information availability, advance ruling and appeal procedures (Fontagné, Orefice and Piermartini, 2015).

Connect SMEs with logistics service providers

The development of logistics platforms, or points in which logistics activities and services are concentrated, can help SMEs overcome difficulties in achieving economies of scale in logistics functions. Another potential source of benefits would be to reinforce ties between SMEs and logistics service providers. Such service providers form the backbone of trading firms, especially larger companies where outsourcing logistics and management of supply chains is widespread.

Many exporting SMEs, however, don't benefit from these services (Barbero, 2010) as large logistics service providers with standard outsourcing solutions often will not work with SMEs (Kirby and Brosa, 2011). This further marginalizes SMEs, as most do not have dedicated shipping departments with experienced personnel.

It is therefore crucial not only to encourage logistics service providers to develop their offerings to better match the needs of SMEs, but also to support logistics training at SMEs so that managers acquire knowledge about designing a logistics chain and making better use of logistics service providers. For instance, DHL Express offers products and services solutions (e.g. Webship, MyDHL) to support SMEs' access to international markets. It also recently embarked on a training programme for SMEs in sub-Saharan Africa, to equip local firms with skills ranging from basic finance to marketing and logistics.

TABLE 8   ICT boosts SME sales growth and profitability

Performance indicator	Enterprises that do not use ICT	Enterprises that use ICT	Improvement
Sales growth (%)	0.4	3.8	3.4
Employment growth (%)	4.5	5.6	1.2
Profitability (%)	4.2	9.3	5.1
Labour productivity (value added per worker US$)	5,288	8,712	3,423

Source: World Bank (2006).

Technology and scope for innovation

Regardless of their size, all companies strive for greater efficiency in controlling production and labour costs, better control of finances, greater responsiveness to new business opportunities, and broader access to information about customers, suppliers and competitors.

Make use of technology

Technology[21] can assist in such efforts and is a strategic resource for sustaining competitiveness. Yet, many SMEs are not realizing the full potential technology can bring. Their low level of technology engagement is recognized as a serious barrier to improved competitiveness, and they suffer the consequences in inefficiencies and increased costs. According to a World Bank study (2006), firms that use ICT effectively boost their sales growth and profitability by 3.4% and 5.1%, respectively (Table 8).

A study by Intuit Inc. (2012) of Indian MSMEs uncovered five key bottlenecks that could explain the reluctance of such companies to invest in and adopt technology:

- costs;
- shortage of skilled manpower (e.g. lack of technical skills);
- low awareness of the benefits of technology;
- data security and privacy;
- inadequate core infrastructure.

Public policy plays a critical role in facilitating technology adoption by SMEs. This means ensuring access to new technologies, supporting the development of a strong skills base, reducing counterproductive government-imposed costs, such as import duties, and promoting a legislative environment that allows SMEs to fully leverage these technologies.

TABLE 9 Share of firms with technological innovation activities engaging in in-house R&D, by size class and sectors (2010–2012, percentage of all firms)

Size class (Number of employees)	Core NACE [24]			Manufacturing[25]			Professional, scientific and technical[26]		
	Permanent in-house R&D	Occasional in-house R&D	Total in-house R&D	Permanent in-house R&D	Occasional in-house R&D	Total in-house R&D	Permanent in-house R&D	Occasional in-house R&D	Total in-house R&D
10 – 49	13.5	8.3	21.8	16.2	13.8	29.9	19.1	8.3	27.5
50 – 249	24.5	11.0	35.5	34.8	15.9	50.7	40.8	8.3	49.1
250 or more	49.8	9.2	59.0	67.6	9.8	77.4	50.5	4.8	55.2
Total	17.5	8.9	26.4	23.6	14.0	37.6	22.4	8.2	30.7

Source: Centre for European Economic Research (ZEW) (2013).

Importantly, SMEs need ICT networks that are accessible, affordable, trusted, and secure. In LDCs, simple ICT solutions, such as obtaining Internet service or creating a website, often represent a significant challenge for SMEs.[22] Cluster policies try to address such challenges by providing access to relevant business services to those located in the cluster. The use of ICT is closely related to the ability of firms to innovate (OECD, 2004a) and with their ability to connect to relevant market information.

Innovation efforts

Both globalization and rapid advances in new technologies, notably ICTs, have put the creation and delivery of innovative products and services at the forefront of competition. Firms need to innovate to strengthen their competitive position. SMEs seem to be better at innovating than their larger counterparts: they frequently operate in niches and have direct contact with customers, enabling them to develop products better suited to market demands. In practice, however, SMEs often face a number of barriers to their innovation efforts due to their restricted resources and capabilities, coupled with market uncertainties (Winch and Bianchi, 2006).

R&D is a major factor in the innovation process of firms, with in-house R&D activities significant in generating technological competence and successful innovations. However, there are systematic differences between small and large firms regarding in-house R&D (Rammer, Czarnitizki and Spielkamp, 2009). Among other barriers, the high fixed costs combined with the large minimum scale of most R&D projects puts pressure on profits and increases the risk of firm failure in the case of R&D failure.[23]

Based on these characteristics, SMEs typically tend to invest in continuous R&D activities (Rammer, Czarnitizki and Spielkamp, 2009). This is backed up by empirical studies based on innovation surveys data, such as the German ZEW Innovation Survey 2013 (Table 9).

Nevertheless, in some studies, small firms were found to be more innovative than large firms, either per dollar of R&D or per employee, especially in high tech manufacturing (Plehn and Dujowich, 2007). Nooteboom and Vossen (1995) revealed that in most industries large firms participate more in R&D than small firms, but when small firms do participate, they tend to do so more intensively and efficiently than large firms – the latter may be at a disadvantage with respect to experimenting and exploring new technological fields.

Even if SMEs are not engaged in continuous R&D activities, they may still perform R&D on an occasional basis, devoting resources only when there is a direct demand from other business functions, such as production or marketing strategy.

Furthermore, Rammer, Czarnitizki and Spielkamp (2009) show that to generate innovations, SMEs can compensate for lack of in-house R&D by applying innovation management practices. These include human resource management, team working and the use of external knowledge. Complementing their own technology resources with knowledge from universities and specialized research institutions widens their opportunities.

Finally, clusters – and their 'coopetition climate' – can facilitate spreading innovation across SMEs. Working together with competitors with similar resources is an effective way to pursue large-scale R&D projects and share risks associated with the technologies.

When SMEs are incubators of new technology, they often face new challenges such as protecting their intellectual property. According to Zhang and Xia (2014), SMEs face difficulties making use of national intellectual property systems as these tend to favour larger and financially stronger enterprises with the resources to navigate their way through 'cumbersome' processes.

To address this challenge, the World Intellectual Property Organization (WIPO) in 2000 created a division focusing on SMEs to increase awareness on issues linked to intellectual property rights, and strengthen the capacity of relevant public and private institutions providing services related to intellectual property.

Management skills and entrepreneurial barriers

Entrepreneurial capacities are a key factor for successful SME development. However, especially in developing countries, entrepreneurship is often constrained, jeopardizing the performance of SMEs. Lack of management skills and a supportive business and national environment that stimulates entrepreneurship are among the main causes.

While some regions offer strong business environments to foster entrepreneurship (e.g. Singapore, Israel, Chile, Republic of Korea, Hong Kong SAR), in other societies, tedious procedures, high monetary costs and poor market access close off entrepreneurial opportunities to many.

Training can tackle lack of management skills

Lack of skills at the managerial level may be at the heart of firm failure, especially of small enterprises. Research suggests that firms in emerging markets tend to have poorer management practices than those in developed economies. This is significant in explaining low firm productivity (Bloom et al., 2010).

A number of experiments in various parts of the developing world have found that the majority of managers – especially in small firms – have inadequate knowledge of basic management, such as the importance of keeping records and how to make business plans, and that rudimentary management training can improve business practices (Sonobe, Higuchi and Otsuka, 2012). Many small self-

employed entrepreneurs do not see the point of investing in management training (Mano et al., 2012), and/or ignore the value of learning about management (Sonobe, Higuchi and Otsuka, 2012).

Entrepreneurs themselves see insufficient education and training as one of the top three constraints to developing their business and many consider entrepreneurship education and training as inadequate in their countries. The outlook and capabilities of an SME owner or manager tend to drive such internal constraints to SME growth (Bruhn, Karlan and Schoar, 2010; Syverson, 2011).

For example, many SMEs are limited by their management's inability to set up and implement strategies for skills development; adopt new strategies and technology; expand into new sectors or venture into new markets; and even prepare effective requests for financing. This impedes their growth and productivity and is reflected in higher failure rates.

As successful management is a key determinant of productivity, researchers have sought to determine whether proper management skills can be taught effectively to entrepreneurs to improve their business performance. Several recent studies conducted experiments to test the effectiveness of training programmes for SME owners in various parts of the developing world[27].

According to a summary review of these programmes, McKenzie and Woodruff (2014) found that most of the interventions had a positive impact on management practices. But the impacts of training on business performance, such as revenue, profit or employment, were often statistically weak[28].

The impact of such training programmes can be increased, however, if they are provided to firm owners in survival-level industrial clusters, where the lack of managerial skills is a major impediment to innovation and growth. Sonobe and Otsuka (2006, 2011) found that elementary management skills in planning, marketing and financial literacy led to an accelerated adoption of improved management practices, increased willingness of owners to pay for follow-up training and reduced likelihood of firms exiting the industry.

These findings suggest that management training programmes could be a valuable form of technical assistance, with the potential for widespread benefits, especially if oriented to 'survival clusters' (Yoshino, 2011).

FIGURE 32   What's stopping youth entrepreneurship?

Key factors and impediments for youth entrepreneurship				
Social/cultural legitimacy & acceptance	**Entrepreneurship education & training**	**Access to finance/ start-up financing**	**Administrative & regulatory framework**	**Business assistance & support**
■ not being taken seriously	■ lack of entrepreneurial education	■ lack of personal savings and resources	■ unsupportive tax regimes	■ lack of business connections: business contacts, suppliers, suitable partners and networks
■ age discrimination	■ wrong curricula or learning methods	■ lack of securities and debt credibility	■ unfavourable bankruptcy laws and property rights	■ lack of business development service
■ lack of family support	■ lack of proper teachers	■ complex credit / financing documentation procedures with long waiting periods for decisions	■ business registration procedures and costs	■ lack of knowledge of available business support services
■ high uncertainty avoidance	■ lack of linkages with business		■ lack of transparency	■ lack of counselling and training
■ fear of failure			■ ineffective competition law	■ lack of mentoring services
■ negative perception of entrepreneurship		■ lack of (successful) micro lending / finance and seed funding	■ often regulatory framework changes	■ lack of exchange networks, forums and meeting places, or lack of workspace
		■ lack of knowledge of financing possibilities		

Source: Based on Schoof, Ulrich (2006).

Youth and women entrepreneurs face specific challenges

Research by Schoof (2006) suggests five key drivers of youth entrepreneurship and presents a range of key constraints and barriers young people face when starting and running a business (Figure 32).

Among the barriers arising from socio-cultural attitudes towards entrepreneurship, the 'fear of failure' in some countries adds to the usual challenges faced by entrepreneurs, especially women (GEM, 2008; Shinnar, Giacomin and Janssen, 2012). Such fear of failure can be aggravated by negative peer pressures, social stigma, lack of confidence due to insufficient knowledge and skills, absence of respectable exit routes without economic penalties and low aspirations (UN-ESCAP, 2012).

Evidence from the 2014 Global Entrepreneurship Monitor Global Report (GEM, 2015) reveals that the fear of failure in some societies can be a strong inhibitor for potential entrepreneurs setting up a business. The highest fear of failure was expressed by respondents in EU economies (40.7%), followed by respondents in Asia and Oceania region (37.5%).

It generally was higher in developed countries with innovation-driven economies than in factor-driven and efficiency-driven economies. Entrepreneurial education can be particularly useful in helping young entrepreneurs overcome fears that accompany starting a business.

Creating a healthy entrepreneurial ecosystem and culture

Promoting entrepreneurship is complex. No single factor alone moves entrepreneurship forward (UN-ESCAP, 2012). As reproduced in Figure 33, the Six + Six Entrepreneurship Ecosystem Model highlights six essential actions required to develop a supportive environment for entrepreneurship, and the six actors/ partners collectively involved in their implementation.[29]

According to GEM (2013), there are basic elements that a government must provide to encourage entrepreneurial activity: macroeconomic stability, a strong regulatory and institutional framework, market

FIGURE 33   Six + Six Entrepreneurship Model

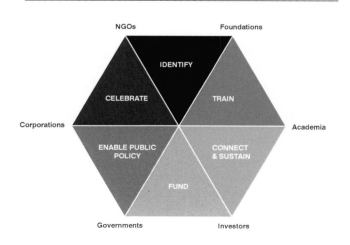

Source: Koltai & Company (2010).

openness, formal education, cultural and social norms, and technological readiness.

Although there is some overlap between SME policies and entrepreneurship policies, Lundström and Stevenson (2005) suggest that SME policy instruments generally focus on enhancing the performance of established firms, while entrepreneurship policy aims to encourage the creation of new firms. It also focuses on the support of individuals rather than firms and seeks to foster a culture that encourages entrepreneurship.

Entrepreneurship is not always viewed positively. To spur and sustain entrepreneurship, a favourable culture needs to be shaped, and progress can sometimes be slow. Entrepreneurial culture is highly sensitive to public policy. Box 7 describes the experience of the GCC countries, where the challenge of youth unemployment has shifted public policy towards supporting entrepreneurship, especially among nationals.

Governments and relevant agencies can promote entrepreneurship through a variety of strategies. These include creating identifiable role models and champions, running awareness campaigns within educational networks and through the media, and establishing confidence-building programmes.

But such programmes need to be rooted in local realities and tailored to the social and cultural norms of each country, especially when addressing the fear of failure among potential entrepreneurs (UN-ESCAP, 2012). This calls for decision makers to engage with the business community in a constructive policy dialogue, so that chambers of commerce and business associations can provide first-hand information on the barriers that entrepreneurs face and offer practical solutions.

Policymakers can also support business incubation programmes. These help start-up and early stage companies to access adequate resources, by linking them to potential funding sources and targeted services, such as accountants and lawyers. They also offer coaching and networking opportunities.

Other policies could include legislative and regulatory reforms that facilitate starting a venture, reward entrepreneurial initiative and reduce the barriers to exit, including financial assistance to rehabilitate or close failed ventures.

Female, youth and rural entrepreneurial programmes also are significant in increasing the diversity of

entrepreneurship and spreading gains to more vulnerable groups. Focus should be on innovative and growth-oriented entrepreneurship rather than entrepreneurs mainly driven by necessity, as the former can have a positive impact on job growth and the development of the economy.

Educating and training entrepreneurs

Generating a critical mass of entrepreneurs hinges upon the quality of education and training. The GEM Model (GEM, 2015) considers entrepreneurship education and training as a framework that affects levels of entrepreneurial attitude, aspirations and activity.

ILO's Recommendation No. 189, adopted in 1998 (ILO, 2001), refers to entrepreneurship education as a way of fostering a positive enterprise culture. In the European Union, entrepreneurial education and training sit at the heart of the Entrepreneurship 2020 Action Plan, adopted in January 2013, alongside two other pillars – removing existing structural barriers and fostering the culture of entrepreneurship in Europe.

Entrepreneurs need to have prerequisite business skills to start up and sustain growth of their SMEs, according to Harvie (2015). Aside from mastering traditional business management skills, such as managing cash flows and developing a business plan, such specific skills include risk assessment and warranting, strategy making, leadership, negotiation, networking, self-confidence and intellectual property protection.

As learning such skills cannot be left to chance, there need to be training-based programmes, ideally at primary and secondary educational levels, to encourage young people to see entrepreneurship as a valid career choice and provide them with the relevant skills.

Schools, vocational training institutions and universities are increasingly incorporating entrepreneurship-focused courses in their curricula (OECD, 2010b). In addition, policymakers are devoting more resources to cooperation with the business community in developing entrepreneurship teaching materials and in providing training, incentives and support to teachers involved in entrepreneurship activities.

An interesting example involves Finland, Denmark and Norway, which have established a 'Nordic model in entrepreneurship education' (Chiu, 2012). Ministries, educational institutions and the business

Box 7: GCC countries foster entrepreneurship to tackle youth unemployment

In the GCC countries – Bahrain, Kuwait, Oman, Qatar, Saudi Arabia and the United Arab Emirates – the rapid growth and relative youth of the population pose both major opportunities and serious challenges. The challenge will be in generating jobs and opportunities in sufficient numbers and quickly. The rate of youth unemployment is already a stumbling block to the region's development, standing at 28% in Saudi Arabia and Bahrain and 25% in Oman. The region needs to create 1.6 million jobs by 2020, especially in Saudi Arabia, just to keep employment close to current levels.

In light of this, GCC governments are increasingly seeking to foster an entrepreneurial culture, especially among nationals, to accelerate job creation and tackle youth unemployment. According to Mahate (2015), entrepreneurship could have a significant impact on economic diversification and on employment opportunities of nationals in the region, which is still heavily dependent on the oil and gas sector and on government spending. Start-ups not only employ their owners, but also can benefit the wider economy – once start-ups mature into SMEs, they become significant contributors to employment and GDP.

The GCC countries have already initiated several entrepreneurial development programmes, such as the Sanad Program in Oman, Qatar's Science and Technology Park and the Intilaaqah Program, or Entrepreneurship Master Class Programs, such as Injaz in Bahrain and Kuwait. In general, these policies and support programmes have focused on providing small levels of loans, training, access to business accelerators and incubators or, on a larger scale, infrastructure investments to create innovation hubs. However, according to Mahate, the GCC countries have not developed a holistic approach that seeks to build a truly entrepreneurial ecosystem.

While entrepreneurship education emerges as an important vehicle to encourage entrepreneurship at a young age and provide young entrepreneurs with skills and knowledge needed to start a business, GCC countries still lack a crucial ingredient to lay the foundations for a positive and dynamic entrepreneurship culture among young men and women.

Containing the growth of public-sector jobs is necessary, but success in this regard has been mixed, as most young people still seem to have a fairly strong preference for public sector jobs. Indeed, for nationals, the continued availability of high-paying and secure public sector jobs creates a strong disincentive to pursue the more risky path of entrepreneurship or seek private sector employment in the tradable sector. In addition to higher pay, the non-wage benefits, working hours, and job security are also more attractive in the public sector.

Thus, measures to alter these incentives by narrowing the wage and benefits differentials between the public and private sectors are critical to spurring entrepreneurship in the region. This was highlighted in a recent report by the IMF (2014), which argued that it is critical for GCC countries to decrease the availability and attractiveness of public-sector employment in order to increase the incentives for nationals to work in the private sector and induce firms to look beyond domestic markets for new export opportunities (IMF, 2014). This missing link needs to go hand in hand with current efforts to strengthen the quality of schools, universities and vocational programmes, to provide young nationals with the skills needed for entrepreneurship and private sector employment

Source: Mahate, Ashraf (2015).

sector are working closely together to equip all pupils and students with knowledge and skills for entrepreneurship, nurture their self-confidence and competencies in self-employment, and promote entrepreneurial values and culture (OECD, 2010b).

These efforts are strongly in line with the recommendation by the GEM 2014 Global Report (2015) that entrepreneurship education should start at a young age so that entrepreneurs become driven by opportunity rather than by necessity.

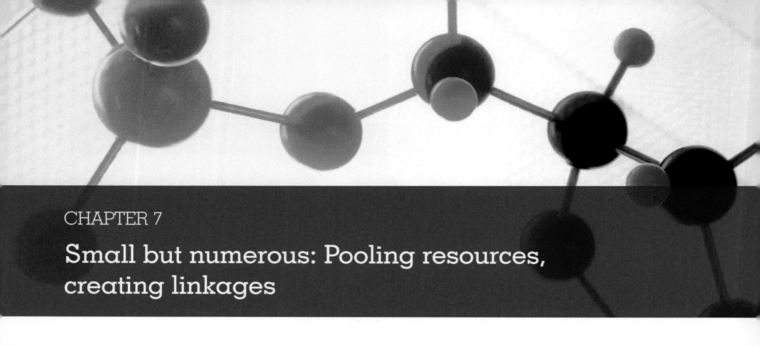

CHAPTER 7

Small but numerous: Pooling resources, creating linkages

Small firms are at a disadvantage with their limited ability to influence decision-making processes, market outcomes and defend their own interests. Small firms often have less bargaining power than large firms and may therefore only receive a limited portion of the chain's profits. Difficulties of being heard due to their size extends to policymaking processes, which can end up favouring those with a louder voice. The result is a regulatory environment that systematically disadvantages SMEs.

In many countries, smallholder farmers influence trade policy indirectly through ministries for agriculture, while large landowners have direct access to the trade minister (WTO, 2014; Cheong, Jansen and Peters, 2013). Smallholder concerns are likely to lose momentum as they progress through the bureaucratic process. This prevents SMEs from efficiently reacting to events or maintaining pressure on ministers.

FIGURE 34 Businesses rank trading concerns

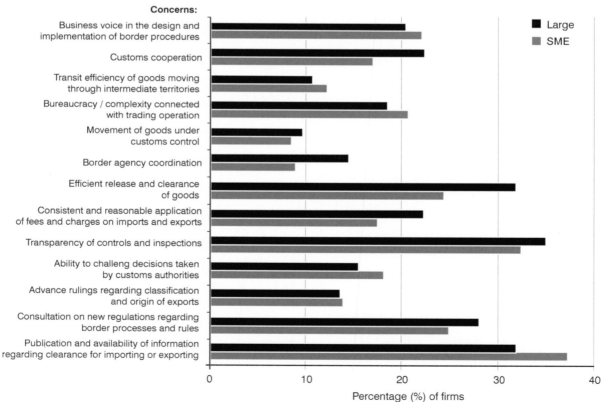

Source: WTO and OECD (2015).

A recent survey of over 750 firms showed that the business voice in policymaking is of more concern to SMEs than to large firms (OECD and WTO, 2015). For SMEs, it ranked 5th in a total list of 13 trade facilitation aspects – for large firms it ranked only 7th (Figure 34). Potential remedies are sector associations or producer organizations that can represent SMEs as one, thus improving their voice and position in policymaking.

SMEs also face the challenge of isolation, which hinders their capacity to scale up production, specialize or exploit economies of scale (OECD-UN-ECLAC, 2012). One way to overcome isolation is to join forces.

Two mechanisms are frequently used: the first consists of institutions that represent SMEs' interests and provide relevant services. They can be public, private or both, and fulfil different combinations of functions. The second mechanism facilitates linkages among SMEs through clusters. Clusters enable policymakers to focus their interventions and serve as a natural springboard to instil SME dynamism.

TISIs pool information and strengthen the voice of SMEs

TISIs enable and encourage SMEs to engage with international markets. They may have a trade support arm, an investment arm, or both. In the past, these services were typically provided by separate agencies. Recently there has been a trend towards merging these service providers.

An ITC study showed that of a sample of 51 merged trade promotion organizations (TPOs), over 70% of the mergers occurred after 2000, in the same period in which the global number of bilateral investment treaties exploded. There are now more TPOs with a dual trade and investment mandate (55%) than a pure trade mandate (45%)[30].

The definition of TISIs covers many institutions, which differ immensely in function, form and funding. However, TISIs can be easily placed into one of three categories: general, sector-specific, or function-specific (Figure 35).

General TISIs include TPOs, investment promotion organizations, trade-related government ministries, chambers of commerce, and economic development agencies. They are some of the largest TISIs, with some of the widest mandates for promoting trade, and often derive their funding from public sources, even if the management of those funds are administered in partnership with the private sector. Such TISIs are often portals for the latest market intelligence and run technical assistance programmes. Chambers of commerce are an important exception, as they tend to be largely membership-funded.

Sector-specific bodies include exporter associations, trade associations, sector chambers and other sector-based bodies. They are typically smaller in size and scope than general TISIs, but often provide highly specialized information and know-how on the sector concerned.

Finally, function-specific TISIs offer services that facilitate the process of importing and exporting for firms, as well as

FIGURE 35 Types of TISIs

General TISIs
- Trade promotion organizations (TPOS)
- Investment promotion agencies (IPAS)
- Ministries (with an interest in export and investment development)
- Chambers of commerce and industry
- Economic development agencies (with a focus on exports or investment)
- Foreign trade representatives
- Regional economic groupings (with a focus on exports/investment)

Spector-specific TISIs
- Exporters associations
- Trade associations
- Investment associations
- Chambers (sector-specific)
- Sector-based bodies (industry and services)

Function-specific TISIs
- Export credit and financing bodies
- Standard and quality agencies
- Export packaging institutes
- International purchasing and supply chain management bodies
- Training institutions
- Trade law and arbitration bodies
- Post-investment after care bodies

Source: WTO and OECD (2015).

guidance and assistance on inward and outward investment. Function-specific TISIs include export and credit financing bodies, standard and quality agencies, export packaging institutes, training institutions, trade and law arbitration bodies, and post-investment after care bodies. In short, these TISIs may be seen as supplying services to the exporter, importer or investor or to act as an intermediary between foreign and domestic firms.

Information to reduce market failures

An ITC survey for the 5th Aid for Trade Global Review asked 24 TISIs in which three areas they would most value improvements for their clients (Figure 36). Access to information about export opportunities came first, followed by access to trade finance and access to information about procedures and regulations.

TISIs surveyed were most concerned about market failures related to the identification of partners, suppliers and distributors.[31] It is striking that the answers provided by TISIs in this survey align well with responses from private enterprises, described earlier in this report. This suggests that TISIs may be a valuable intermediary between the private and the public sectors, especially in facilitating business-to-business contacts and lower trade costs.

TISI services and effectiveness

The economic justification for TISIs rests largely on their role in addressing market failures, including asymmetric information and sunk costs for pioneer exporters. Problems of asymmetric information arise from a firm's need to identify partners, suppliers and distributors. TISIs can help alleviate this problem by facilitating forums and networks in which firms can easily identify suitable counterparts.

Sunk costs in the context of pioneer exporters are costs associated with gathering foreign market information related to consumer preferences, business opportunities, as well as quality and technical requirements, among others. These activities require substantial investment, and the possibility of competitors acquiring the information (directly or indirectly) with little or no investment of their own acts as a deterrent to new entrants into export markets (Roberts and Tybout, 1997). Therefore, TISIs often provide market intelligence as a public good, as well as offering a host of other services (Figure 37).

As TISIs include a wide range of institutions, it is difficult to assess their effectiveness. Over the last decade, a number of studies have investigated the effectiveness of TISIs (e.g. Lederman, Olarreaga and Payton, 2006; Copeland, 2008; Lederman, Olarreaga and Payton, 2009; Volpe Martincus et al., 2010)[32] focusing on TPOs, a subset of TISIs (Figure 35).

The study by Lederman, Olarreaga and Payton (2006) reveals a positive relation between the size of TPO budgets and exports (Figure 38). At the sample median, Lederman, Olarreaga and Payton (2009) finds that a US$ 1 increase in TPO budgets results in a US$ 200 increase in exports.

FIGURE 36   Areas in which TISIs would most value improvements

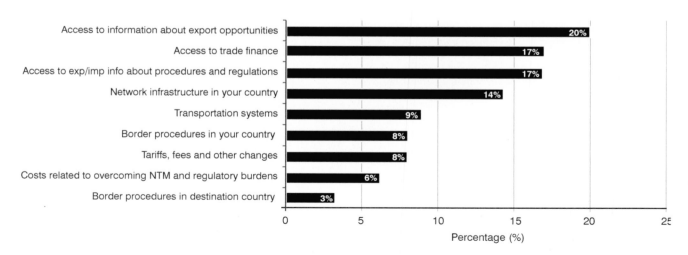

Note: TISIs were asked to identify up to three factors for which they would most value improvements.
Source: WTO and OECD (2015).

FIGURE 37   TISI services for SMEs

Trade intelligence	**Export development**	**Export/investment promotion**	**Enabling business environment**
▪ Trade information ▪ Market analysis ▪ Business contacts ▪ Business opportunities ▪ Market access conditions	▪ Export readiness ▪ Training and counselling ▪ Strategy formulation and development ▪ Value chain optimization	▪ Export promotion ▪ Investment promotion	▪ Facilitating cross-border trade ▪ Lobbying/advocacy ▪ Facilitating access to resources

Source: ITC (2013).

Trade promotion falls into the remit of TPO activities, and may partially explain the relationship found by Lederman, Olarreaga and Payton (2006).

In the United States, state-sponsored trade shows and business-to-business matching programmes contributed positively to SME export performance (Wilkinson and Brouthers, 2006).

Simply opening an export promotion agency office abroad translates into an increase in exports that is approximately 5.5 times larger than enlisting a new embassy or consulate tasked with the same duty, as

reported in a study of six countries in LAC over the 2000–2007 period (Volpe Martincus, 2010). The study also found that TPOs are far more effective when supporting the whole export process (Figure 38).

Which client base, which strategies?

Research has highlighted two key challenges for TPOs – their administrative set-up and their decisions regarding firm level targeting.

TPOs that share a large number of executive board positions with the private sector, but are funded by

FIGURE 38   TISIs abroad: More effective than consulates to increase exports

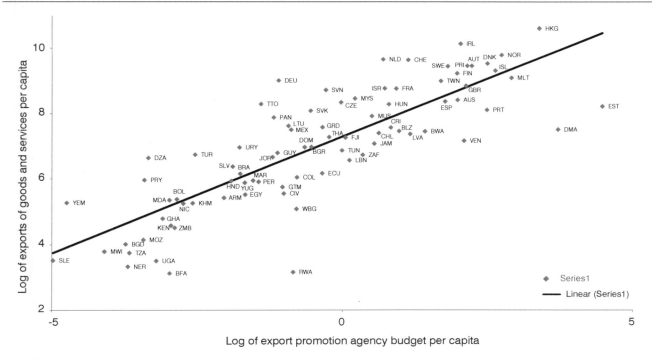

Source: Lederman, Daniel, Marcelo Olarreaga and Lucy Payton (2006).

CASE STUDY

Gaining market intelligence through ITC tools

ITC's suite of market intelligence tools contributed to US$ 126 million in exports in 2014, according to feedback from users. The tools, which are accessible online for free, are particularly instrumental to users in LDCs, where local sources of trade intelligence are often unavailable.

> *'ITC's market analysis tools are of great importance to us as we are a country where there are major issues with the reliability of the statistics available.'*
>
> An exporter from the Democratic Republic of the Congo

'The tools have opened my eyes to new markets I had never considered before,' wrote an exporter from Morocco in a recent anonymous survey. The exporter uses the platform to obtain information on prices and competitors before making a decision to target specific markets.

The tools provide data to help users identify market opportunities. Exporters can use them to gauge the size of potential markets and how fast demand has grown for particular goods and services; which countries supply those markets; which have gained or lost market share; and what tariff and non-tariff barriers they themselves would face compared with competitors based elsewhere. Exporters can also use the tools to identify potential importers and distributors for their products.

'ITC's market analysis tools are of great importance to us, as we are a country where there are major issues with the reliability of the statistics available,' wrote an exporter from the Democratic Republic of the Congo in the recent survey. The user added that with adequate support and training, even more exporters in the country would utilize the tools.

Market analysis improves TISIs service delivery

TISIs use the market analysis tools to create customized market intelligence for their members and clients. In a survey carried out at the end of 2014, 94% of TISIs respondents reported that the tools had a positive or very positive impact on the services they deliver. Of the respondents, about a third came from LAC, just under a fifth each from Africa and Asia-Pacific region, 10% from Eastern Europe and Central Asia, and 9% from Arab States.

Surendra Nath Gongal, Deputy Director of Nepal's Trade and Export Promotion Centre (TEPC), has delivered over 10 training courses in the last five years to groups of SME representatives, chambers of commerce and business associations, both in Nepal and in the wider region.

'The feedback is always very positive,' Gongal says. 'ITC's tools help trade institutions provide timely and targeted trade-related advice to their private sector clients.'

For ITC, trainers at TISIs such as TEPC are invaluable, as they multiply the number of those with access to the online tools.

'Access to trade and market intelligence is critical to international business success,' says Helen Lassen who leads the ITC capacity-building programmes in market analysis. 'We need to find a way to bring this intelligence to exporters.'

Miguel Carrillo, Chief Executive Officer of the Colombian consulting firm Hamkke, first came across ITC's market analysis tools during his university studies in the Republic of Korea - he has used the online platform ever since. He advises companies, mostly SMEs, on business strategies and on ways they can benefit from trade agreements.

'The market analysis tools help us to analyse potential markets for our clients and the production chains into which they could be inserted,' Carrillo says.

ITC tools assist policymaking

Policymakers and government officials use the market analysis tools to monitor national trade performance and collect inputs for the preparation of policy decisions and trade negotiating positions. In the 2014 survey, 92% of policymakers reported that ITC tools helped them to make better-informed trade policy decisions. The policymakers were from across the world, with 28% from LAC, 20% each from Africa and the Asia-Pacific, 12% from Eastern Europe and Central Asia, and 11% from the Arab States.

'The Agency has utilized data from ITC and the market analysis tools to provide input into Zambia's trade negotiations in SADC, COMESA, the COMESA-EAC-SADC tripartite and WTO negotiations,' says Jonathan Simwawa, Acting Director of Export Development at the Zambia Development Agency, referring to talks involving the Southern African Development Community (SADC), the Common Market for Eastern and Southern Africa (COMESA), and the East African Community (EAC).

'The Zambian government also uses ITC market analysis tools in deciding on whether to grant requests for protection from domestic industries,' Simwawa says.

Source: ITC (2015a).

the public sector, are associated with higher national exports than other combinations. A single and strong TPO seems to be more effective than multiple agencies with overlapping responsibilities (Box 8; Lederman, Olarreaga and Payton, 2006).

TPOs have diverging strategies when it comes to targeting the client base. Some TISIs focus on small firms that are most in need of assistance. Others champion large firms to capture large profits. Small, young firms tend to be responsible for the largest share of employment growth in most economies – but may suffer from low productivity and poor product quality. In contrast, large firms are often the most productive. Given that large firms tend to be well-financed and resourced, government support may simply encourage unfair competition rather than address a market failure.

Box 8: Awarding excellence: From export promotion to internationalization

The 10th TPO Network World Conference and Awards (WTPO) was hosted by Dubai Exports in partnership with ITC early November 2014. There was a record turnout of 400 global leaders from government and TISIs. The conference theme – From export promotion to internationalization: The role of TPOs in the global economy – opened the door to in-depth discussions on linking trade and investment promotion; trade facilitation; services; market diversification; women's economic empowerment; branding; and innovation in ICTs for TPOs.

The TPO Network Awards recognize excellence in trade support services, and celebrate TPOs that demonstrate effective, innovative, and efficient performance in their export development initiatives.

'These Awards recognize outstanding TPOs that help firms, especially SMEs, use trade to drive sustainable, inclusive growth. By making modest investments, TPOs and their partners – which include ITC – create impacts that are truly transformational,' said Arancha González, ITC Executive Director. 'Tapping into international production networks can revolutionize prospects for SMEs and their workers. By supporting SMEs to make these connections, TPOs help create jobs and opportunities that lead to growth and development.'

The next WTPO will take place in Morocco in 2016 and will be hosted by Maroc Export.

Winners 2014:

Enterprise Mauritius: Best TPO from a SIDS

Enterprise Mauritius was rewarded for its Go-Export project, which strengthens the export readiness of Mauritian SMEs. The project is addressing trade-related weaknesses and equipping 20 SMEs each year with the skills required to export on a sustainable basis.

Zambia Development Agency: Best TPO from an LDC

The Zambia Export Development was rewarded for its fund, ZEDF, which helps firms meet the challenge of finding pre- and post-shipment export finance. The fund makes low-interest loans to producer associations in traditional export sectors. Since 2011, the fund has issued loans to six exporting associations, supporting exporters in regional markets and beyond.

Proexport Colombia: Best TPO from a Developing Country

Proexport Colombia was awarded for its Selling Methodology 2.0, which aims to increase textile and apparel exports to the United States. The methodology enables Colombian entrepreneurs to boost competitiveness and achieve profitable exports. Significant results have been achieved so far.

Enterprise Lithuania: Special mention

Enterprise Lithuania was awarded for its Wings programme, which is addressing Lithuania's demand for adequately trained, professional export managers. The programme matches talented young people with experienced private sector export project managers. It also provides them with training, thus helping to address both high youth unemployment and bridge the skills gap.

Spain Export and Investment: Special mention

Spain Export and Investment was awarded for its Young Professional Program, which has since 1974 enabled more than 5,500 young graduates to take up work at Spanish companies that are growing internationally.

Source: ITC (2015a).

The long-term impact on exports from Tunisia's FAMEX matching-grant scheme may point to a third way (Cadot et al., 2015). The firms that received assistance were analysed in three categories – small (fewer than 20 employees), medium-sized (20–99), and large (100 or more). After four years, exports of small firms declined by 65%, while exports of large firms were only 6% higher. However, the exports of medium-sized firms increased by 57%. This may be because medium-sized firms are often on the verge of breaking into foreign markets, requiring just a nudge to 'get over the border'.

Investors can connect SMEs to markets

FDI may flow into a country in one of four ways: setting up a company from scratch (i.e. creating a wholly owned subsidiary); purchasing shares in a local company; through mergers; or through an equity joint venture with another investor or enterprise.

Investment promotion agencies (IPAs) provide both general and target-specific assistance. General assistance is mainly information-based, providing potential foreign investors with the market intelligence or regulatory information suited to their specific needs.

Target-specific assistance revolves around the four roles (Figure 39):

- advocacy;
- image building;
- investor servicing;
- investment generation.

Advocacy aims to influence the domestic government to facilitate the entrance of investments, including the removal of possible barriers.

Branding improves the public image of the country as an investment destination. However, according to OECD, 'image building – including advertising, producing promotional materials and attending trade fairs – can be very expensive, as can efforts to target particular investors owing to the high cost of research and incentives to induce the business to invest' (OECD, 2013c).

Investor servicing is the support given to the investor while the project is being established. It facilitates the process by providing information, advice, and guidance.

Finally, investment generation targets foreign investors based on the country's economic plans and strategies via investment campaigns.

FIGURE 39 Investment promotion agency roles

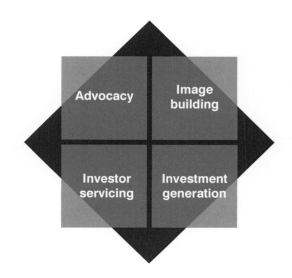

How do SMEs fit into the investment framework? In all cases, companies created or purchased with FDI may be SMEs.

SMEs that gain links to foreign companies through FDI benefit in a number of ways. These include technological transfer, better access to credit via banks or FDI source, extensive training and advisory services, and knowledge of domestic and foreign regulations (OECD, 2013c).

The FDI source tends to bring significant experience of the internationalization process, helping firms to overcome many of the information and management bottlenecks. Thus, SMEs are in a good position to benefit from FDI.

Making the most of clusters

In today's globalized, competition-driven markets, SMEs are under strong pressure to innovate and overcome their size and isolation limitations. They may lack resources to do so. Clusters can help SMEs improve their productivity, innovation and overall competitiveness.

Clusters make it possible for policymakers to focus on interventions and serve as a natural springboard to instil SME dynamism. They allow SMEs to reach a large number of firms, diffusing information rapidly and bringing powerful demonstration effects (UNCTAD, 1998). Clusters also allow for modern, multi-participant and cooperative approaches – embracing the 'triple helix' of university-industry-government interactions.

Benchmarking: Helping TISIs 'AIM' higher

Leadership and Direction

Resources and Processes

Products and Service Delivery

Measurement and Results

Based on the theory that what is not measured cannot easily be improved, ITC has for years been working with TISIs around the world to help them identify their strengths and weaknesses – and see how they match up against their peers.

This comprehensive benchmarking exercise assigns TISIs a score between zero and 100, based on 225 performance indicators covering everything from governance to the services offered. It has helped agencies, especially TPOs, to understand where they need to improve in order to meet global best practices.

Pamela Coke-Hamilton, executive director of the Caribbean Export Development Agency, has worked with five TPOs in the Caribbean region on the benchmarking exercise. 'Not only has it assisted in the identification of areas of strength, but also in pinpointing specific areas for improvement based on international best practices,' she says.

'AIM (Assess, Improve, Measure) for results' goes beyond the benchmarking and helps TPOs to actually address identified weaknesses. Using the findings from the benchmarking exercise, ITC works with the TISI to develop a customized plan, called a performance improvement roadmap that addresses the weaknesses identified. The plan targets managerial and operational issues, as well as the formulation and delivery of each TISI's portfolio of services. It is tailored to respond to the wide differences in the maturity of TISIs across the globe. This 'improvement' phase uses information and technical advisory solutions to deliver sustained improvements.

Finally, a 'measurement' phase quantifies the success the changes have had in enhancing the organization's capabilities. A key priority for this stage is ensuring that the organization shifts towards effectively measuring what is important to help it continuously upgrade their services.

In short, AIM for Results helps TISIs understand their own managerial and operational performance, so they can achieve measurable improvements in their service delivery to clients, especially SMEs that are aspiring to or beginning to connect to IVCs.

By the end of 2014, twelve TISIs were implementing AIM for Results, in Bangladesh, Benin, Burkina Faso, Cambodia, Mauritius, Morocco, Nicaragua, Saudi Arabia, Sri Lanka, Zambia, and Zimbabwe. In addition, five Caribbean countries – Barbados, Belize, Dominican Republic, Jamaica, and Trinidad and Tobago – had been benchmarked, in preparation for a Caribbean-focused AIM initiative.

Costa Rica's agency, PROCOMER, has also been benchmarked and received some of the highest scores across all areas of operation. While PROCOMER's scores make it a model for others around the globe, it is working to implement several ITC recommendations to become even more effective.

> '*Not only has it assisted in the identification of areas of strength, but also in pinpointing specific areas for improvement based on international best practices.*'
>
> Pamela Coke-Hamilton,
> Executive Director, Caribbean Export Development Agency

'We work very hard every day to improve our performance and the quality of services we provide to our clients,' says Jorge Sequeira, who was CEO of PROCOMER during part of the reform process. 'Exporting in a competitive, globalized economy is a challenging task, so they demand our best. The ITC benchmark report is a powerful tool that helps us determine whether we have advanced in the right direction towards becoming a high-performance organization.'

Source: ITC (2015a).

Numerous successful clusters exist, but unsuccessful attempts to create sustainable clusters may be even more numerous. Cluster policies need to be well-designed. They are not a panacea for all economic development problems.

What is a cluster?

There is no agreed definition of what a cluster is. Porter (1998), who made the concept popular in the public policy realm, defines a cluster as 'a geographically proximate group of interconnected companies and associated institutions in a particular field, linked by commonalities and complementarities'.

While there is debate over the merits of individual elements in a cluster, almost all definitions share the ideas of proximity, specialization, networking and knowledge (Figure 40). The principal idea is the agglomeration of firms in one or more sectors of economic activity in a certain geographical space.

Simply being in close proximity is not sufficient to create competitive and innovative clusters. Most definitions emphasize intensive interactions and cooperation among the different actors in a cluster. Firms view each other as competitors as well as potential collaborators, learning from each other both formally and informally. Clusters have a high degree of 'embedded knowledge', based on routines, habits and norms established through collaborative experience (Gertler and Wolfe, 2008).

Clusters provide a constructive and efficient form for dialogue among private businesses, their suppliers and customers, local and national government agencies, and other entities important for competition. These include universities and think tanks, business associations, trade unions and standard-setting agencies, as well as suppliers of key business services.

Many case studies exist on networks and SME clusters that drive the emergence of competitive industries and the revitalization of domestic regions. The process has taken place in both developed and developing countries (Harvie, 2015).

SMEs can benefit in many ways from clusters

Research on IVCs emphasizes the importance of cross-border linkages between firms in global production and distribution. Analysis of industrial clusters focuses on the role of local ties in generating competitive advantage in export industries (Schmitz,

FIGURE 40 Clusters are multi-dimensional

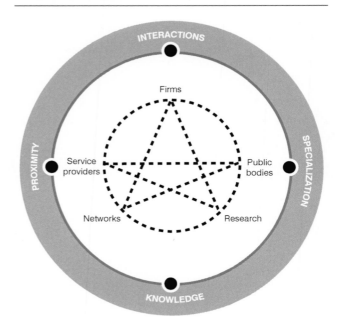

1995 and 1999). Local and international linkages are both essential, each offering different opportunities for SMEs to upgrade.

A main benefit lies in the ability of these networks to improve productivity, generate and spread innovation and entrepreneurship, and thereby enhance the global competitiveness of SMEs.[33] Clusters can nurture specialization and efficiency, creating openings for economies of scale and scope that cannot be achieved by firms acting alone (Ougton and Whittam, 1997). Porter (2011) builds a strong case for developing supportive industry clusters locally as a way to increase productivity and innovation, generating greater 'shared value'.[34]

Opportunities for 'collective efficiency' are derived from either positive, external economies, or the involuntary effects of participating in a cluster; and joint actions, which are the conscious effects of participating to a cluster (Schmitz, 1995).

Clusters offer the chance to consolidate market access, given that the concentration attracts customers. Through clusters, firms have access to a wider pool of specialized and skilled workers and a wide network of suppliers of specialized inputs and services, such as equipment, raw materials, finance and consulting. There is also quick dissemination of new knowledge.

The mutual trust, shared values, and peer pressure that naturally develop within clusters provide the

Box 9: Clusters help SMEs reach new markets

Clusters play a major role in the internationalization of SMEs, as can be seen from the Wenzhou cluster in China. Participating firms had a competitive advantage, thanks to reduced transaction and information costs, integration of resources, and access to a large supply of cheap raw materials and components.

Because they share a 'regional brand,' the cluster helps them to integrate into global production systems, cooperate with multinational companies, and establish multinational joint ventures. Being part of a cluster helped firms in Wenzhou to specialize, absorb new technologies, and procure inputs more easily (Zhang et al., 2015).

Brazil has the most well-developed network of clusters in Latin America covering a wide array of sectors (McDermott and Pietrobelli, 2015). These have helped businesses upgrade technology, modernize their production base, increase training and boost exports, while also reducing the failure rate of SMEs.

Another interesting example is the Nnewi cluster of automotive parts in Nigeria. Despite no infrastructure and weak government support, firms in the cluster have been able to grow, export and upgrade, thanks to local initiatives and learning efforts, as well as close collaboration with foreign technology providers, especially from Chinese Taipei (Abiola, 2008).

Source: ITC (2015).

basis for joint actions, such as bulk purchase of inputs, joint advertising and shared equipment. Such joint efforts also involve firms and their support institutions (e.g. provision of technical assistance by business associations or investments in infrastructure by the public sector).[35]

Participation in a cluster involves both intense competition and close cooperation, sometimes referred as 'coopetition'. Local producers can greatly expand their capacity to learn from their peers via supply chain linkages (i.e. supplier and customer relations), mobility of skilled labour, and spin-off activity. Spreading technology and knowledge is a common by-product (Christopherson, Kitson and Michie, 2008). In addition, when firms inside clusters cooperate with research and development institutions, it leads to synergies and an environment of intense knowledge production.

In this stimulating environment, SMEs upgrade their capabilities, leading progressively to sustainable competitive advantages in sales to distant national and international markets (Porter, 1998). Some of the most spectacular innovations and growth in developing country clusters have involved external linkages with non-local markets and actors (Box 9).

Benefits are not automatic

Not all clusters help firms upgrade technologically or grow to become world competitors. Some are caught in the spiral of stagnation and decline; others never reach their potential, or do not mature past the embryonic stage (Box 10). While geographical

proximity always brings some exchange of information, it does not automatically bring collaboration, positive spillovers or linkages.

While clusters offer remarkable opportunities, they also can have drawbacks, notably because firms within a cluster are also often competitors (Glaeser, Kerr and Ponzetto, 2010). This is known as the 'paradox' of clusters and agglomeration (McDermott and Pietrobelli, 2015).

Coordination failures, information asymmetries, and the ongoing influence of the past (or path dependency) may reduce the effectiveness of clusters or even prevent their creation, according to Ketels (2009).[36]

Box 10: African 'survival clusters'

The vast majority of clusters in Africa survive at the subsistence level. Many of the enterprises in these 'survival clusters' lack the capacity to invest and innovate, mainly because of inadequate access to finance, poor managerial skills, and lack of knowledge (World Bank, 2011a).

Many clusters in Africa stagnate or even regress in their ability to innovate and compete, and are usually left to their own devices (Wamalwa and McCormick, 2015). Many lack access to external sources of knowledge and information, such as universities, science parks, and R&D centres. There is replication and exchange of the same local knowledge, which is viewed as a major constraint to innovation.

Policy options for cluster development

Such market failures have prompted thinking about policies to increase the likelihood that clusters succeed.

Cluster development policies are 'public interventions that foster the beneficial effects of economies of agglomeration by creating a set of incentives to overcome the coordination failures that hamper the development of some industries in specific localities (Maffioli, Carlo Pietrobelli and Stucchi, 2015). These policies recognize the important roles played individually and collectively by stakeholders – firms, business associations, governments, donors, and other support institutions – in helping clusters and networks to grow sustainably (UNCTAD, 1998).

Cluster development has become a policy priority in the past few decades in many developing countries, particularly middle-income countries. Clusters have become both the unit of analysis and a framework for public action in economic development and industrial policies.[37]

Recently, many bilateral and multilateral agencies (including Inter-American Development Bank, OECD, World Bank, International Monetary Fund, United Nations Industrial Development Organization, UNCTAD, ILO, ITC) have begun to recognize the benefits of clustering and are reframing their SME and private sector development programmes to take the role of industrial clusters into account. They have all been major players in sponsoring research, evaluation and development of cluster or cluster policies throughout the world (Glavan, 2008).

While governments need to address systemic or market failure constraints that affect clusters, analysis suggests that public intervention should focus on existing or emergent clusters. The private sector should lead cluster development, and governments should act indirectly as facilitators rather than attempt to create clusters from scratch through direct intervention (Sölvell, Lindqvist and Ketels, 2003).[38] In other words, 'policy should be cooperation positive, but agglomeration neutral' (OECD, 2004b).

A proper cluster development policy should explicitly consider the development of local competitive factors (tangible factors, such as infrastructure; and intangible factors, such as local expertise) and the promotion of networks and linkages (e.g. programmes to upgrade subcontractors, establishment of consortia or business associations), according to Pietrobelli and Rabellotti (2006).

Cluster policy is not always an isolated, independent and well-defined area, and may be at the intersection of more than one policy stream (Figure 41).[39] As such, countries that do not have an officially labelled cluster policy might still have many policies impacting on clusters (EC, 2002).

In practice, according to UNCTAD (2005), most common cluster promotion initiatives are intended to:

- foster inter-firm networks, supply chains and sectoral clusters that reinforce the spread of knowledge, technology and innovation (dynamic efficiency);

- enhance the role for intermediary institutions, such as development promotion agencies and business associations, and facilitate the access to high quality business services;

- stimulate the emergence of institutional networks through regional alliances, formal and informal agreements;

- support the creation of a pool of skilled labour through training; and

- stimulate the emergence of specialized and quality producers through assistance in standardization and certification.

Cluster initiatives are usually defined and implemented with bottom-up involvement of the main local interest groups, both public and private. Here, business associations have an active role to play, as governments are not likely to have the specific information to identify the areas where collective action would be most useful (Rodríguez-Clare, 2005).

According to Maffioli, Carlo Pietrobelli and Stucchi (2015), most cluster development policies involve two stages aimed at promoting interaction and coordination among all stakeholders (private-private and public-private). They typically start by helping local actors to coordinate on prioritizing investment decisions, which may lead to identifying shared objectives and the joint actions required to achieve them. This initial stage in turn provides essential information and helps policymakers understand the key missing inputs that public policies can provide (Hausmann, Rodrik and Sabel, 2008).

Priorities are then implemented in the second stage. Relevant policies can include the co-financing of public infrastructure and public goods that can become a catalyst for new private or public investment projects. These programmes may also

FIGURE 41   A menu for cluster development

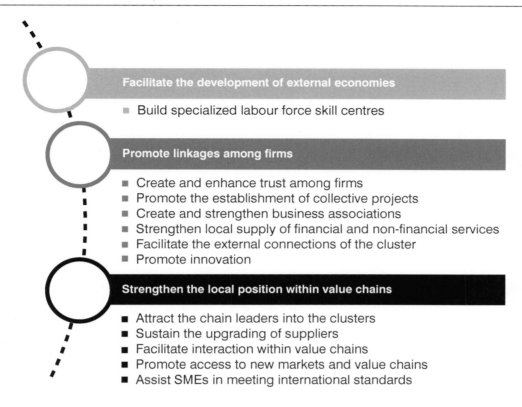

Facilitate the development of external economies

- Build specialized labour force skill centres

Promote linkages among firms

- Create and enhance trust among firms
- Promote the establishment of collective projects
- Create and strengthen business associations
- Strengthen local supply of financial and non-financial services
- Facilitate the external connections of the cluster
- Promote innovation

Strengthen the local position within value chains

- Attract the chain leaders into the clusters
- Sustain the upgrading of suppliers
- Facilitate interaction within value chains
- Promote access to new markets and value chains
- Assist SMEs in meeting international standards

Source: Pietrobelli, Carlo and Roberta Rabellotti (2006).

co-finance machinery and equipment that firms collectively manage and use in co-financed technology centres.

A programme may also include institutional strengthening components and promote overall business cooperation, integration and reforms to enhance the business climate. Some programmes may also include access to finance.

Assessing policy effectiveness

Although many countries have implemented cluster development policies in recent years, evaluations of their effectiveness have been rare, and the evidence is inconclusive. It is difficult to arrive at clear conclusions because most effects of such policies are indirect with many other factors coming into play. This makes it hard to establish clear causal links between cluster policies and their potential impact, and generally requires the application of experimental and quasi-experimental techniques.[40]

Among the existing empirical studies, Figal Garone et al. (2015) presented an evaluation of the impacts on

SMEs of a specific cluster policy in Brazil, Arranjos Produtivos Locais, between 2002 and 2009. They find a positive effect on employment, level of exports and likelihood of exporting, with an increasing pattern over time.

Interestingly, they also look at the indirect effects on firms that do not participate in the programmes, and find positive impacts on their exports, which gain significance in the medium and long term. Their results confirm the need to allow enough of a time horizon when assessing policies, given that some economic and social benefits only materialized in the long term.

A menu for cluster development

Pietrobelli and Rabellotti (2007) present a menu of actions aimed at supporting the upgrading of SMEs located in clusters and integrated into value chains. Their proposed moves are organized according to three complementary goals:

- enhancing the development of external economies;
- encouraging linkages;
- strengthening local positions within a value chain.

The actions must be context-specific, the result of a fruitful public-private dialogue, and implemented so as to reflect the stage of the cluster's life cycle.

Regarding clusters in Africa, Wamalwa and McCormick (2015) recommend that African governments offer support by promoting industry, knowledge providers and government linkages. The World Bank (2011a) identified three core policy areas relevant for upgrading the 'survival clusters' in Africa: building managerial skills, establishing sound spatial and urbanization policies, and supporting market access, regional integration, and linkages with large enterprises.

Based on a rich review of cluster development policies in Latin America, Maffioli and Pietrobelli (2015) derive important insights to design and implement policies that foster upgrading of SMEs in clusters and value chains.

First, they argue in favour of context-specific policies. There is no single blueprint for success or a one-size-fits-all formula. A region's specific industrial and systemic economic strengths and weaknesses need to be taken into account. The level and nature of government involvement, as well as defining and selecting clusters, should reflect specific country and sectoral contexts.

Second, policies need to evolve continuously to reflect cluster evolution and the stage of its life cycle. Public-private dialogue is crucial in designing cluster strategies. Cluster policies and programmes should be assessed more frequently against the expectations of the stakeholders, to minimize gaps between their expectations and the support mechanisms offered. Public policies should also carefully balance policies targeted at clusters with untargeted moves to improve investment climates and provide public goods (Yoshino, 2011)[41].

CHAPTER 8

SMEs and global policy initiatives

Creating conditions in which SMEs can perform better in global markets and contribute to inclusive growth depends on action within countries, as well as international policies and measures.

The role of SMEs is increasingly recognized in global policy debates, notably those taking place in the context of the UN Global Goals, as well as the G20 and B20. WTO's Trade Facilitation Agreement is also of high relevance for SMEs.

The United Nations Global Goals

The United Nations Global Goals is the new set of goals created by UN Member States for 2015 to 2030. Its ambitious, cross-cutting approach is farther-reaching than the Millennium Development Goals (MDGs) adopted 15 years ago, which focused on increasing official development assistance and improving a series of social indicators.

The new agenda sets a wide range of economic and environmental objectives, alongside traditional development priorities such as health, education, food security, and nutrition. Its aim is to create peaceful, better-governed and inclusive societies, with no individuals or groups left behind.

Under the new framework, the eight MDGs are superseded by 17 UN Global Goals with 169 associated targets to address poverty reduction and economic development. Pursued in combination with UN agreements on Financing for Development and combating climate change, the UN Global Goals set the stage to integrate national, regional and international efforts to promote sustainable development.

Supportive international policies

Unlike MDGs, the UN Global Goals specifically mention SMEs, recognizing their role in inclusive development. UN Global Goal 8, 'Promote sustained, inclusive and sustainable economic growth, full and productive employment and decent work for all' contains a target for SMEs. The SME target is to:

'Promote development-oriented policies that support productive activities, decent job creation, entrepreneurship, creativity and innovation, and encourage the formalization and growth of micro-, small- and medium-sized enterprises, including through access to financial services'.

Goal 8 also recognizes the potential role of trade in growth and development with a call to increase Aid for Trade support for developing countries, particularly LDCs. Given that SMEs face difficulties in accessing working capital and investment credits, Goal 8 also calls for strengthening:

'the capacity of domestic financial institutions to encourage and expand access to banking, insurance and financial services for all'.

UN Global Goal 9 encompasses two related themes to improve SME competitiveness – getting products to market through better logistics, and being forward-looking through innovation. Goal 9 is to 'Build resilient infrastructure, promote inclusive and sustainable industrialization and foster innovation'. The SME target is clear:

'Increase the access of small-scale industrial and other enterprises, in particular in developing countries, to financial services, including affordable credit, and their integration into value chains and markets'.

The World SME Forum and the B20 Agenda

Rifat Hisarcıklıoğlu

President of The Union of Chambers and Commodity Exchanges of Turkey (TOBB) and B20 Turkey Chair

Investing in SMEs will encourage growth, development and jobs.

Inclusivity, implementation and investment are the pillars of a healthy global economy.

The Turkish Presidency of the G20 centres on the principles of inclusivity, implementation and investment as the main pillars to re-establish a healthy global economy. These priorities are both pragmatic and far-reaching.

Pragmatism, though, does not have to come at the cost of ambition. By accentuating 'implementation', we focus on a realistic agenda with a long-lasting legacy. Indeed, if all countries put into practice the promises already made, and live up to the trust placed in us, global growth will be 2% more by the end of 2018. That 2% difference is equal to US$ 2 trillion in additional growth. We all have a vested interest in making this happen.

Inclusion is an important theme in Turkey's G20 presidency, as global economic health requires a holistic and comprehensive approach. This year, we have established a new taskforce on SMEs and entrepreneurship to enhance the visibility and impact of SMEs on the B20 platform. We aim to unlock one of the greatest areas of untapped potential in global markets, namely SMEs. SMEs employ two-thirds of the workforce in the global economy.

Our vision for Turkey's G20 legacy is also far-reaching. It stretches far beyond the membership of the G20 to include those nations hardest hit by the 2008 financial crisis and that have found recovery the most difficult. Investing in and enfranchising SMEs in developed countries and LDCs will encourage growth, investment and jobs.

Just as we are continuing the work of Australia's chairmanship, we hope our achievements will extend far beyond 2015, and that China will build upon the edifices and progress of 2015. The successes of Turkey's tenure will be enduring. That is why in May 2015 we set up the World SME Forum to be a permanent structure in global economics. Since the first G20 Business Summit in Seoul in 2010, the B20 has called upon the G20 to address the constraints SMEs face in the global marketplace. Now we are offering a concrete mechanism to level the playing field and deliver the kind of support SMEs have needed for years.

The World SME Forum is a collaboration between the Union of Chambers and Commodity Exchange of Turkey (TOBB), the International Chamber of Commerce (ICC), and ICC's World Chambers Federations. It is designed to be an advocacy arm of SMEs. It will represent them at an international level and serve to influence policy at all levels to ensure the wider economic interests of SMEs, including issues such as financial inclusion, are represented in such international organizations as the G20, ASEAN, APEC, and the UN. To quote ICC Secretary General John Danilovich, the World SME Forum will 'play a key role in helping SMEs tap global markets for the first time, and […] ensure that global policies are designed with the needs of small businesses and entrepreneurs in mind.'

The World SME Forum is a global, independent, non-profit organization that is run by and for the private sector. It looks to identify and address the main difficulties faced by SMEs, and provide greater representation at a global and political level. Its main priority is to be an advocate of and voice for SMEs in political and international circles.

The World SME Forum will also seek to provide advisory services to address one of the biggest difficulties that SMEs face – up-to-date advice and best practice information. It will provide technical expertise, links to potential sources of financing, and specialized assistance to SMEs through virtual means. The lack of digital infrastructure is a significant problem faced by SMEs. As such, the World SME Forum will establish an e-market information services platform to facilitate global connectivity with IVCs, establish networks, and conduct knowledge dissemination/creation. By focusing on these areas, SMEs can be better integrated into global markets.

Small business is the powerhouse of employment, innovation and entrepreneurial spirit.

With the launch of the World SME Forum and its prominence on Turkey's G20 agenda, we hope that 2015 will be the year that the role and value of SMEs is recognized on an international stage. By targeting investment in infrastructure and widening access to information, as well as providing a voice at all levels – regional, national and international – the barriers preventing the growth and full contribution of SMEs can be broken down and their potential in the economy realized.

'The SME sector is vital to the world economy, and small business is the powerhouse of employment, innovation and entrepreneurial spirit,' said Mr. Babacan, then Deputy Prime Minister of Turkey. 'We trade with them; we form partnerships; therefore, we must also be their voice.'

The UN Global Goals recognize that adopting goals is not enough; it is also necessary to spell out ways of achieving them. As a result, the first 16 Global Goals contain targets and policy guidance to spur realization of the goals.

This commitment is then reinforced in UN Global Goal 17 to 'Strengthen the means of implementation and revitalize the global partnership for sustainable development'. Goal 17 underlines the cross-cutting nature of the UN Global Goals with sections on Finance, Technology, Capacity-building, Trade, and Systemic Issues. Under Systemic Issues, targets address policy and institutional coherence, multi-stakeholder partnerships, and data, monitoring and accountability.

The UN Global Goals open the way for governments, international organizations and other institutions to embrace policies and actions that reinforce SME competitiveness and export capacity. Under the Global Goals, UN Member States commit to improving access to finance for companies in developing countries, promoting technology transfer and doubling the share of LDCs in global exports by 2020.

Financing accord focuses on SME needs

Taken together, the UN Global Goals and Financing for Development can play an important role in helping countries, institutions and the international community to create a favourable SME environment in the global economy.

The agreement adopted by the Third International Conference on Financing for Development (Addis Ababa, July 2015) is part of the UN Global Goals. It sets out principles and policies needed to deliver the Global Goals, with the focus on mobilizing resources and looking in depth at MSMEs.

The agreement's opening overview 'A global framework for financing development post-2015' notes that MSMEs, 'which create the vast majority of jobs in many countries, often lack access to finance'. It commits countries to work 'with private actors and development banks' to promote 'appropriate, affordable and stable access to credit to MSMEs, as well as adequate skills development training for all, including youth and entrepreneurs'.

To address constraints in obtaining finance, especially for women entrepreneurs, the accord suggests that financial regulations:

■ permit the use of collateral substitutes;
■ .create appropriate exceptions to capital requirements;
■ reduce entry and exit costs;
■ encourage competition;
■ allow microfinance institutions to mobilize savings by receiving deposits.

The agreement also encourages international and domestic development banks to promote MSME finance, including in industrial transformation, through the creation of targeted credit lines and technical assistance.

In addition to its extensive financing references, the accord links MSMEs to regulatory regimes, trade agreements, Aid for Trade, private-public partnerships and improved infrastructure. The accord highlights trade facilitation as a means to integrate SMEs into regional and global value chains.

SMEs need a higher international profile

The post-2015 picture reflects growing interest in the developmental role of SMEs. This is tied to the need to create more and better jobs in the aftermath of the financial and economic crisis. It also reflects the reality that with many of the world's poorest people working in SMEs, upgrading such jobs helps to combat poverty and economic exclusion.

OECD, World Bank and ILO have ongoing research on SMEs.[42] ILO's work includes consideration of policies that lead to higher productivity and better SME working conditions. For example, the International Labour Conference in June 2015 adopted a Recommendation Concerning the Transition from the Informal to the Formal Economy (ILO, 2015).

OECD and World Bank, meanwhile, are preparing a joint paper for the G20 on SMEs and Low Income Developing Countries in Global Value Chains, to be published in late 2015.

SMEs and the G20/B20

As G20 president for 2015, Turkey established three overarching themes:

■ Inclusiveness;
■ Implementation;
■ Investment for Growth.

By designating SMEs as a cross-cutting issue among these themes, Turkey has given prominence to SMEs in G20 discussions ranging from trade to employment. Turkey views SMEs as essential to ensuring that 'the benefits of growth and prosperity are shared by all segments of the society' (G20, 2015). SMEs are therefore considered by the Turkish presidency as one of the main areas of action in order to address inclusiveness. The other two areas explicitly highlighted under the inclusiveness theme are youth and gender.

This underscores the impact that stronger SMEs can have on income distribution. With SMEs responsible for most employment, especially of workers with lower wages, making SMEs more productive and competitive can increase the wage share of poorer people, as well as boost growth.

Thus, policies that serve to strengthen SMEs also help to tackle inequalities and contribute to Goal 10 of the UN Global Goals: 'Reduce inequality within and among countries'. An associated target focuses on income growth of the bottom 40% of the population, at a rate higher than the national average, by 2030. The work done under Turkey's G20 presidency provides important channels for policymakers to pursue.

Under the Turkish presidency a special B20 SME and Entrepreneurship Taskforce has been created. In addition, the World SME Forum was launched in May 2015 in Turkey, serving as a platform to facilitate the implementation of measures that target the strengthening of SMEs and their contribution to the economy in terms of GDP and employment.

Based in Istanbul, the forum is based on a partnership between the Union of Chambers and Commodity Exchanges of Turkey, the International Chamber of Commerce (ICC) and the ICC's World Chambers Federation. This public-private partnership builds on calls from G20 business leaders to give greater priority to SME constraints. The forum's creation builds on the G20's previous Australian work as well as that of the Global Partnership for Financial Inclusion.

Barriers and solutions

Under Turkish leadership, the B20 group of G20 business leaders is highlighting the role of SMEs in growth and job creation. It presses for SME needs in G20 discussions on trade, finance, infrastructure, and employment and skills development.

The B20 SME and Entrepreneurship Taskforce is made up of senior executives from SMEs and start-ups, as well as representatives of international institutions and business associations. The Taskforce report goes to the heart of SME competitiveness with its analysis and recommendations.

The B20 SME and Entrepreneurship Taskforce outlined the following barriers (B20, 2015a):

- **Access to international markets**. SMEs need to increase productivity to sell intermediate and/or final products; they require support in complying with labour, environmental, social and quality international standards.

- **Access to finance**. Bank lending, the main source of external funding for SMEs, has yet to return to pre-crisis levels in several countries. IFC estimates total unmet demand for credit for micro and SMEs at US$ 3.2 trillion to US$ 3.9 trillion globally. Alternative sources of finance, such as equity, remain limited and volatile.

- **Access to skills and talent**. SMEs are constrained by insufficient managerial skills and specialized talent. Entrepreneurship education and ongoing managerial training are inadequate in most countries.

- **Access to innovation ecosystems and the digital economy**. There is often a lack of a thriving innovation ecosystem whereby government agencies, the private sector, accelerators, universities and R&D centres collaborate to innovate in their products and business processes. For example, Accenture found that in 17 of the G20 countries performance against a Digital Density Index ranged from 28 to 72, with the maximum being 100.

- **Ability to comply with business regulations**. Despite progress in G20 countries, the quality of the business environment is the most critical bottleneck for 70% of SMEs from emerging markets.

To address these targets, the Taskforce agreed on five recommendations and suggested two action points under each recommendation:

1. **Improve SME access to international markets**

   - Provide SME capacity-building programmes and support to comply with international labour, environmental, social, and quality standards. Promote harmonization and consistent application of international standards to ensure level playing field for SMEs.

   - Initiate the development of G20-wide entrepreneurship visa programmes to facilitate international mobility for entrepreneurs and SME executives.

2. **Improve SME access to finance**

   - Broaden and deepen SME access to alternative sources of funding by supporting and harmonizing policies, regulations, and standards.

   - Improve the availability of reliable information on SME performance.

3. **Improve SME access to managerial and entrepreneurial skills**

- Expand skills training programmes, in particular encourage learning agility at different levels of the school and university system and promote entrepreneurship as a desirable career. Support business training programmes focused on development of managerial skills.

- Strengthen entrepreneurship cultures, in particular support development of entrepreneurship networks and centres of excellence.

4. **Improve SME access to the digital economy and innovation ecosystems**

- Commit to improved digital infrastructures, incorporating into the G20 Member Growth Strategies a five-year universal broadband connection target for G20 countries, and provide for continuous investment in next-generation digital networks.

- Promote collaboration between government, business, and stakeholders in education and science.

5. **Ensure business reforms are geared to create a SME-friendly business environment**

- Undertake impact assessments of current and proposed regulations, treaties, and policies to ensure they take SME interests into consideration and commit to measurable improvements in the ease and cost doing business for SMEs.

- Improve digitization of government regulatory processes for speed, ease of access, transparency, and lower costs plus increased access to government procurement for SMEs.

WTO Trade Facilitation Agreement

The WTO TFA establishes binding obligations to improve customs procedures, transparency, predictability, efficiency, and cooperation among border regulatory agencies and private sector. It can contribute to integrating SMEs into global markets. SMEs suffer disproportionately from fixed trade-related costs, because they cannot offset costs as easily as large firms. They also often lack capacity to comply with complex rules, customs and border procedures. Trade facilitation can cut costs and result in smoother, simpler export and import processes.

SMEs in global markets are more productive than those that are not. As a result, implementing the TFA to meet SME needs can have far-reaching economic and developmental implications. The same can be said for related Aid for Trade.

Access to information on export opportunities and access to trade finance are the two areas where SMEs would most value improvements (WTO and OECD, 2015). Close behind is access to information about procedures and regulations.

More transparency

TFA provisions on information availability, advance ruling, and appeal procedures increase transparency and the predictability of the multilateral trading system. Fontagné, Orefice and Piermartini (2015) highlight that these provisions are likely to benefit SMEs.

In today's world of extensive communications, the information gap flagged by SMEs and mentioned above should also not be too difficult to address. This opens possibilities to target Aid for Trade under the TFA to tackle information bottlenecks and improve information quality. A key would be to strengthen the capacity of TISIs to provide tailored information for SMEs.

Lower border costs

The reduction of border costs envisaged by the TFA is likely to benefit SMEs, which suffer disproportionally from fixed costs. The Agreement also contributes to reducing discrimination against SMEs in trade-related procedures, such as customs clearance. Because cross-border transactions by SMEs are less frequent and their payments lower, they can face difficulties. For example, some country regulations bar SMEs from using cross-border fast tracks or other facilities dedicated to larger companies.

The Agreement specifically forbids the use of criteria that may be discriminatory against SMEs, such as company size or quantity of shipped goods. By looking at where SMEs suffer discrimination, the process of implementing the TFA can improve trading conditions for SMEs.

SMEs in public-private dialogue

Public-private dialogue and partnerships are crucial to trade facilitation, as the TFA recognizes. The private sector has an important role to play in reform.

Public-private dialogue is suited to:

- identifying policy priorities;
- reducing regulatory costs;
- building consensus on reforms.

Such dialogue helps to ensure that reforms are demand-driven and in line with priorities of the main stakeholders, including SMEs. Private-sector involvement is necessary at all stages: to assess needs, identify priorities, design solutions, formulate and implement policies, and monitor and evaluate reforms.

TFA measures to involve the private sector in trade policy formulation offer opportunities for organizations representing SMEs. National efforts to include SMEs and organizations which represent them in public-private dialogue mechanisms should be encouraged.

Different policy forums, coherent approaches

The UN Global Goals discussions, B20 and G20 consultations, and TFA negotiations take place in different forums. What they have in common is that they are all global in nature. Interestingly, these three policy initiatives reflect a common view on the role of SMEs in the economy and on policies to address bottlenecks that keep SMEs from contributing to sustainable and inclusive growth. There are, however, differences in focus, some of which stem from differences in mandate.

The TFA has the most specific and restricted thematic coverage. It only deals with issues relevant for the transition of goods and services across borders. SMEs are not explicitly mentioned in the TFA, but some of the Agreement's provisions can have very significant effects on reducing trade costs for SMEs and thus on facilitating their integration in global markets.

The TFA has received explicit support in the outcome document of the B20 Trade Taskforce, and recommendations 1 and 5 of the SME and Entrepreneurship Taskforce regarding the facilitation of

SMEs' access to international markets provide implicit support for the TFA. Ratification and implementation of the TFA is also the first point in the summary of B20 recommendations to the G20 (B20, 2015b).

The issue of access to finance does not fall under the mandate of the TFA, but has been strongly emphasized in the B20, the UN Global Goals discussions, and the finance for development debates. A certain similarity can be found regarding the measures that are advocated to increase SME access to finance. The need to foster innovation among SMEs has also been present in both the UN Global Goals and the B20 debate.

The UN Global Goals discussions have explicitly emphasized infrastructure and logistics for SMEs. This aspect is not high on the agenda in the outcome document of the B20 SME and Entrepreneurship Taskforce; a separate task force was dedicated to the theme of infrastructure. Indeed, the summary document of B20 recommendations to the G20 contains a recommendation for country-specific infrastructure strategies linked to the G20 growth aspirations.

This summary document also emphasizes the need to reach universal broadband connection. This is in line with the SME and Entrepreneurship Taskforce recommendation that SMEs require better access to the digital economy. Broadband is also important to facilitate SME access to information on export opportunities and to information about procedures and regulations.

The recommendations and agreements resulting from these global policy consultations are coherent, and are in line with the overall research, recommendations, focus and title of this report.

Côte d'Ivoire tackles NTMs with trade obstacles alert

Assahouré N'Goran used to wait six months to get the weight certificate required to export cocoa beans to Belgium. Since June 2014, his waiting time has dropped to just two weeks.

'Having the certificates issued quickly makes a huge difference for us,' says N'Goran, Shipping Manager of Outspan Ivoire, a local subsidiary of agribusiness giant Olam International. 'It increases our competitiveness and will lead to higher exports. What is good for our company is good for employment and the growth of Côte d'Ivoire.'

Most such NTMs are very simple to address once they are identified, says Kouakou Germain Yao, Director of Studies and Economic Information at Côte d'Ivoire's Chamber of Commerce and Industry. 'All it takes is to bring in the private sector, so that the problems can be identified,' he says.

N'Goran reported the issue through the country's Trade Obstacles Alert service, an online tool put in place by ITC in 2014 following the completion of the country's first-ever NTM survey. In the survey, nearly three-quarters of the 600 participating companies said they faced non-tariff barriers to trade, significantly higher than the 55% average in the over 25 countries surveyed by ITC.

The companies saw NTMs as barriers particularly in regional markets. One of the biggest challenges identified was the delivery of certificates of origin for export to neighbouring countries. Most procedures are lengthy and susceptible to malpractice, the survey found. Lack of knowledge about the procedures and the agencies in charge of them pose additional challenges for exporting companies, which also complained about a lack of transparency in regulations.

In response to these findings, the government requested that ITC set up the alert service, so officials can learn first-hand about the hurdles faced by the business community and address the concerns.

'This tool is instrumental in helping policymakers to develop programmes and reforms suitable to increase the competitiveness of Ivoirian exporters,' says Gomun Kouya, Director of Export Promotion and Assistance at the Ministry of Trade.

Twenty-four obstacles have been reported since the launch of the service in the summer of 2014, ranging from lack of storage facilities and border points to incorrect customs valuations on exported products. Five had been resolved including the one reported by N'Goran.

Previously, only the president of the Chamber of Commerce was authorized to sign weight certificates, which are required for all exports of cocoa beans, the country's largest export item. Depending on his availability, the certificates can often take a long time to arrive. Following the identification of the problem through the new platform, another official was also given the authority to issue the certificates.

Various government agencies and TISIs are addressing the remaining 19 obstacles identified, Yao says. Following the launch of the tool, the government passed a decree mandating its agencies to use the platform and tackle the reported problems.

'This mechanism will allow us to facilitate our trade by signalling the difficulties we encounter and from which we suffer,' says Daihi Fatoumata, sales manager of the Société de Culture Bananière, a large exporter of bananas and pineapples.

The Trade Obstacles Alert system was put in place in Côte d'Ivoire as part of the ITC Trade Support and Regional Integration Programme (PACIR), financed by the European Union.

Source: ITC (2015a).

ENDNOTES

1. As the majority of firms in the sample do not export, this is a sensible assumption.

2. For instance with platforms such as the ITC Market Access Map and Standards Map providing such information to the private sector.

3. The IFC dataset covers about 1.3 million SMEs from 132 countries and only includes the latest year of a country's available data.

4. 55–64: 9%, 65–120: 1%.

5. The proximity-concentration trade off says that foreign markets should be served by exports rather than FDI if trade frictions and costs are lower or economies of scale are higher.

6. In Shimizu's framework, the 7Ps/7Cs are producer/company, purchaser/consumer, product/commodity, price/cost, promotion/communication, place/channel, and (external) profile/circumstances, with the goals of increasing profits/confidence. In Shimizu's 7Cs Compass Model, consumers are defined by their needs, wants, security and education, and circumstances by national and international, weather, social and cultural, and economic circumstances (both with initials NWSE, like the four points of a compass); while the 'company' element includes awareness of competitors, the organization, and accountability to stakeholders (shareholders and others).

7. Enterprise Surveys is composed of data from 135,000 firms from over 130 countries. The surveys cover a broad range of topics such as access to finance, crime, taxation and various performance measures. Enterprise Surveys primarily covers developing countries, although a few developed countries have been surveyed. In Enterprise Surveys, each firm surveyed was asked to identify the biggest 'obstacle faced by this establishment' from a list of 15 obstacles (see figure 18). Some of the 15 indicators were combined according to thematic similarities. Since data on firm size is also captured, this makes it possible to identify the obstacles which SMEs are more likely to flag when compared to large firms.

8. The importer's bank assists by issuing a letter of credit to the exporter (or the exporter's bank) guaranteeing the payment on presentation of certain documents related to the trade transaction. It usually involves a relatively long and labour-intensive process. The exporter's bank may make a loan to the exporter on the basis of the export contract. To cover the risk that the issuing bank will not pay, an exporter may have a bank in its own country confirm the letter of credit, in which case the confirming bank agrees to pay the exporter if the issuing bank defaults.

9. A major omission in the following discussion regards the potential opportunities and challenges equity financing represents for SMEs. The situation is as, or even more, challenging when considering risk capital. Both debt and equity financing are hampered by information asymmetries as well as high management costs on the side of the financer in order to evaluate and monitor investment into SMEs. Start-up facilities, targeted equity funds, venture funds or angel investors are far from widespread in developing countries. Capital markets also serve developing countries poorly. Institutional weaknesses and complexities hamper appetite for SME risk.

10. Many SMEs are faced with a catch-22 problem as they have had no opportunity to build 'reputational collateral' by way of a proven repayment history. As opposed to information typically sourced from within the formal banking sector, 'non-traditional' credit data, such as energy and water utility payments, phone bills and rental payments, can serve as a good proxy for the willingness and ability to repay. Collecting this alternative data is one of the core strengths of the private credit bureau sector. Also, Commercial Credit Bureaus caters information on the history of trade credit, regularly used by many SMEs, and is considered to be a key component in improving the risk assessment tools for small businesses.

11. Warehouse receipt financing is a lending technique that allows farmers/producers/traders of agricultural commodities to access bank loans by pledging their warehouse receipts issued against commodities deposited in licensed warehouses.

12. With leasing, an enterprise (the lessee) is authorized to use, for a defined period of time, a fixed asset owned by a second party (the lessor) in exchange for periodic payments/rents. Hence, leasing disassociates the legal ownership of an asset from its economic use.

13. This trend is especially present in Latin America, East Asia, the Pacific, and the Russian Federation. A telling example is that of ProCredit Bank, which has cut microfinance from 100% to less than 10% of global assets to focus on the SME sector, and now allocates almost two-thirds of its loan portfolio to SMEs.

14. This automated statistical method involves analysing a large sample of historical data on borrowers to calculate the likelihood that a loan applicant with certain specific characteristics will default in the future. This data can cover both the firm's financial condition and the personal data of the owners.

15. ITC developed LOANCOM, a simple, practical credit scoring software adapted to SMEs, to be used as a standard and systematic credit evaluation procedure when banks receive credit requests. It helps financial service providers to automate their loan application process and make a quick, informed and objective loan decision. The generic Scorecard System is either used as such or further customized to suit specific local conditions. To date, the ITC credit scoring tool is being adapted in 16 financial institutions in Africa and Asia.

16. According to Massolution's industry research report (2015), the industry continues to grow at an incredible rate with global crowdfunding markets (both philanthropic and for financial return) increasing from US$ 1.5 billion in 2011 to US$ 16.2 billion in 2014. By regions, the report indicates that North America captured most of the funding volume (58.4% of the total), followed by the Asian platforms (21%) which experienced recently an astounding growth of crowd-based lending (largely from the Chinese market), and topped the European market (20%).

17. 'The right skills for the job' is the title of a recent World Bank publication (see Almeida, Rita, Jere Behrman and David Robalino (2012). The Right Skills for the Job? Rethinking Training Policies for Workers. Human Development Perspectives, No. 70908. Washington, D.C.: World Bank.

18. Most frameworks identify job-relevant skills as the skills relevant to the specific job of the worker as well as other skills that enhance his or her productivity, including higher-level cognitive skills (problem-solving and analytic reasoning), learning skills, interpersonal and communication skills.

19. For instance, Argentina uses its tax credit regime to provide financial incentives for SMEs to invest in training their workers (see e.g. the Worker and Management Training Tax Credit Programme run by SEPYME and aimed at SMEs as referred to in UN-ECLAC, 2012).

20. Estache (2010) showed that the public sector of developing countries accounts for about 55%–75% of infrastructure financing, while 20%–30% is financed by the private sector and 5%–8% by official development assistance.

21. These include foundational technologies, such as personal computing and productivity tools; connectivity tools, such as Internet access and the use of mobile technology; online presence and the use of social networks; and enterprise-enabling capabilities, such as cloud-based services.

22. While almost 100% of South Koreans, 82% of Germans, and 94% of Norwegians use the Internet, for example, less than 8% of Indians have access.

23. Average R&D intensity (R&D expenditures as percent sales) is particularly high in high-technology sectors such as pharmaceuticals and biotechnology, software and computer services, and technology hardware.

24. Core NACE includes sections B (Mining and quarrying), C (Manufacturing), D (Electricity and gas), E (Water supply and waste management), H (Transportation and storage), J (ICT), K (finance and insurance) and divisions 48, 71, 72, 73.

25. NACE section C.

26. NACE section M.

27. Recent research includes: Karlan and Valdivia (2011), Drexler, Fischer, and Schoar (2014), and Bruhn, Karlan, and Schoar (2010) in their study sites in Latin America for medium-sized enterprises; Berge, Bjorvatn and Tungodden (2012) and Bjorvatn and Tungodden (2010) in Tanzania; Bloom et al. (2013) and Field, Jayachandran and Pande (2010) in India; Bruhn and Zia (2013) in Bosnia and Herzegovina; and Mano et al. (2012) in Ghana.

28. A notable exception is found in Bloom et al. (2013) where the productivity of medium-sized firms in the textile industry in India was enhanced thanks to improved quality and efficiency and reduced inventory. Similarly, Bruhn, Karlan and Schoar (2013) found improvements in productivity, sales and profitability from a group of MSMEs in Mexico after participating in subsidized management consulting.

29. Koltai & Company, 2010.

30. Note that these results were based on a sample of 178 TPOs, 41 of which were excluded from the analysis, as they were part of government ministries.

31. These findings are in line with those of a similar survey conducted by ITC among TISIs during its WTPO-conference in Dubai in October 2014.

32. A related branch of research assesses the effect of foreign embassies and consulates (e.g. Rose, 2005; Creusen and Lejour, 2013) on exports. A study on the link between exports and foreign diplomatic representation found that the presence of embassies and consulates increased bilateral exports (Rose, 2005). The establishment of the first foreign mission in a country is associated with a strong increase in exports of approximately 120%, while the establishment of consulates is associated with a smaller increase of 5%–11%, subject to diminishing returns for additional consulates.

33. This perspective is supported by Porter (1998), who argued that 'being part of a cluster allows companies to operate more productively in sourcing inputs; accessing information, technology, and needed institutions; coordinating with related companies; and measuring and motivating improvement'.

34. Rather than offshoring large parts of production, Porter (2011) argues that firms should focus on their local environment, for example when hiring suppliers or employees. This can stimulate quality and efficiency throughout value chains and also improve the purchasing power of local citizens, creating a positive cycle of economic and social developments. Collective action is further required to enhance infrastructure and institutions, decrease costs and assist in finding the right skills.

35. The joint actions they undertake have significant external effects and may be related, for instance, to generating specialized technology services, setting up testing or measurement laboratories, creating specialized training centres, applied research, establishing product standards or promoting a particular product typical of the cluster.

36. Coordination failures may arise because individual firms consider only the impact on themselves, not others, when making decisions regarding whether to locate in a cluster or what investments to undertake in the cluster. Information asymmetries may exist regarding the steps to be taken for deriving the right 'social' decision, and such information is often dispersed across the many participants of the cluster, especially if there is no interactive dialogue and communication between them. Path dependency may occur because actors in a cluster may ignore future spillovers because of the time lag in reaping the benefits.

37. Under the label of cluster policy, public authorities actively encouraged the establishment of a wide range of initiatives to enhance industrial concentration and cooperation. These have included science parks, business incubators, eco-industrial parks, industrial districts, targeted recruitment, enterprise zones, foreign trade zones, and centres of expertise (Glavan, 2008).

38. There is very little evidence that governments can create clusters and ample examples of where they have failed in such efforts (Porter, 2008). A policy aimed at developing entirely new groups of firms in selected sectors can entail high costs, high risks, serve as a screen for outmoded forms of industrial targeting, and give rise to destructive competition if many regions follow the same policies for the same industries (OECD, 2004b).

39. Many policies labelled under different headings (regional economic development policy, science/technology/innovation policy, industrial/enterprise policy, and even higher education policy) are in fact cluster policies in the sense that they contribute to creating an environment of cooperation among the stakeholders at local and/or regional level (EC, 2007).

40. In this context, Maffioli, Carlo Pietrobelli and Stucchi (2015) have recently proposed a toolkit with a set of complementary quantitative tools in order to build new and solid evidence on the effectiveness of cluster programme development.

41. Examples of spatially blind, sectorally blind are: managerial human capital development, investment in infrastructure to improve connectivity and facilitate cross-border trade, encourage the formation of business associations, facilitate the access to finance among SMEs (Yoshino, 2011).

42. In addition, regional development banks and regional economic commissions regularly produce research on SMEs with a regional focus.

PART II.

SME competitiveness:
A pilot assessment

SME competitiveness: A pilot assessment

SME competitiveness matters for SMEs' success in export markets, for the competitiveness of their country, for GDP growth and the inclusiveness of this growth.

Main findings from Part I

Part I describes SMEs in the global economy, and examines their competitiveness. The following key messages emerged:

SMEs tend to employ 60%–70% of a country's workforce and overproportionately employ vulnerable income groups.

Due to the productivity differences between SMEs and large firms, particularly in developing countries, increasing SME productivity is likely to lead to significant gains in economic growth and inclusiveness, because of resulting wage increases for poor households and vulnerable groups in the labour force.

SMEs that are indirectly or directly connected to global markets, via exports or imports, have higher levels of productivity and job creation. This suggests that increased participation of SMEs in cross-border trade can contribute to inclusive growth.

Economies with a healthy 'middle' are likely to be more dynamic and competitive. SME productivity therefore matters for national competitiveness.

Understanding how SME competitiveness compares across countries is interesting for multiple reasons:

- SMEs will be able to assess their strategic position within the lines of business they compete in.

- Foreign investors will be able to identify (pockets of) SMEs that can become useful partners within IVCs.

- Governments and TISIs will be able to identify where action is needed in order to increase SME competitiveness.

Parts II and III

Part II of this publication provides insights into the approach that has been chosen in order to statistically assess SME competitiveness.

Chapter 9 introduces a working definition of firm competitiveness and introduces the SME Competitiveness Grid as a tool to classify determinants of firm competitiveness according to how they affect competitiveness (using three pillars) and according to the layer of the economy at which this determinant intervenes (using three layers).

Chapter 10 introduces in more detail the variables that have been used in the country profiles to assess SME competitiveness.

Chapter 11 provides a pilot assessment of the SME Competitiveness Grid. Publicly available indicators are used to populate the SME Competitiveness Grid, and give a flavour of how the grid structure could be used to define firm level competitiveness.

This report provides 25 country profiles containing SME competitiveness pilot assessments (Part III).

The SME Competitiveness Grid

A working definition of competitiveness

Defining – or even describing – competitiveness is not straightforward. Different approaches and lines of thought exist. One reason is that the meaning of competitiveness is highly dependent on the context. At the national level, many of the most popular definitions are productivity-based. For instance, WEF defines competitiveness at the country level as 'the set of institutions, policies and factors that determine the level of productivity of a country' (WEF, 2013).

In this report, the focus is on firm level competitiveness. While national competitiveness – as for instance defined by WEF – is highly relevant for firms' competitiveness, a stronger emphasis on micro-evidence is required to understand what is going on at the firm level.

The situation is further complicated by whether the concept of competitiveness is viewed as 'relative' or as the 'application of best practices'. Relative competitiveness is a zero sum game; if one firm becomes more competitive (e.g. gains market share), another firm or group of firms must become less competitive (e.g. lose market share). Best practice competitiveness approaches by one firm do not automatically lead to negative outcomes for other firms.

This report uses a 'relative' definition of competitiveness, in line with the most common business research and analysis approaches. Graphic representations of SME competitiveness, however, take a 'best practice' approach, focusing on determinants of competitiveness.

The concept of competitiveness in this report is expressed in relation to a specific line of business in which firms choose to be active. Lines of business refer to product-to-market combinations, where the product can be a good, a service, or a combination of the two. A firm might have a portfolio of businesses (i.e. product-to-market combinations); it might be more competitive in some than in others.

The competitiveness of the firm will depend therefore on the aggregated performance of all its product-to-market combinations. SMEs, especially the smallest ones, have the particularity of being active in one business line. This is one reason why the size dimension is not explicitly mentioned in the following definition, which applies to firms of all sizes.

Competitiveness is the demonstrated ability to design, produce and commercialize an offer which fully, uniquely and continuously fulfils the needs of targeted market segments, while connecting with and drawing resources from the business environment, and achieving a sustainable return on the resources employed.

This definition is in line with concepts used in other publications focusing on SME competitiveness (e.g. UNESCAP, 2009; UNCTAD, 2005), notably in its emphasis on the role of dynamic aspects of competitiveness. A look at the definition's components provides a more detailed understanding of the competitiveness concept used in this report.

'… demonstrated ability to design, produce and commercialize an offer …'

This refers to the fact that to be competitive, it is crucial for any firm to have a proven track record of delivering a good or service to the market. This track record covers all stages of activity, including design, production and commercialization. This represents the 'supply side' part of the definition. Implicitly, the factors covered here are predominantly under the control of the firm, thus they are firm level factors.

'... fully, uniquely and continuously fulfils the needs of targeted market segments ...'

This refers to the ability of the firm to satisfy the needs of its clients or customers, ideally in a unique and complete manner. This ensures that the firm is producing a product for which there is a market. Thus, this represents the 'demand side' of the definition. This component of the definition, however, also highlights that it is important for firms to know and understand clients' needs and to know and understand the functioning of different market segments.

'... while connecting with and drawing resources from the business environment ...'

This phrase acknowledges that there are factors that are partially outside of the firm's control, but which greatly influence its competitiveness. Collectively, these represent the business environment.

Under ITC's approach to measuring SME competitiveness, the business environment is split into two: the immediate business environment and the national environment. The former captures the sectoral and local environment the firm is in direct contact with, which it may or may not be in a position to influence. The latter captures the more traditional understanding of competitiveness, namely national macroeconomic aspects such as the regulatory framework, school life expectancy and interest rate spread. Both are essential, which is why they are included here.

'... achieving a sustainable return to the resources employed.'

This phrase reflects the dynamic aspect of competitiveness (the time dimension). What is sufficient today to achieve adequate returns on the resources employed, may not be sufficient tomorrow if the competitive environment changes. Firms operating in a local, national or global environment are constantly exposed to change. Adequate returns can only be achieved if resources are exploited in a sustainable way, and if the firm is willing to entertain, and able to embrace change in all areas of its business.

While this definition does not make an explicit reference to the terms international or internationalization, it applies to firms operating in a global context. In an open economy, foreign firms are likely to serve the domestic market. Competitiveness therefore implies generating sustainable returns in the light of foreign competition. For exporting firms, the relevant market segment is 'the global market'.

The SME Competitiveness Grid: An overview

An assessment of SME competitiveness ideally offers responses to these questions:

- To what extent do firm level capabilities (i.e. application of best practices) differ between SMEs and large companies?
- Are SMEs constrained by their business environment (national, local and sectoral)?
- Which aspects of competitiveness are constrained by firm level capabilities or weaknesses in the national, local or sectoral business environment?

The SME Competitiveness Grid is intended as a tool to classify determinants of firm competitiveness according to how they affect competitiveness (three pillars of competitiveness) and according to the layer of the economy at which they intervene (three layers of competitiveness). While the grid was designed with a focus on SME competitiveness, it is scale-independent and can therefore be used to assess the competitiveness of larger firms.

The main motivation behind the SME Competitiveness Grid is to bridge a gap in existing composite indicators that focus on macroeconomic determinants of competitiveness rather than microeconomic determinants. The importance of macroeconomic determinants is, however, fully recognized and reflected in the competiveness grid.

The SME Competitiveness Grid has two core dimensions (Figure 42):

- **The components of competitiveness, identified as the three pillars**: Compete, connect and change. These three pillars reflect traditional static and dynamic notions of competitiveness. They emphasize the importance of connectivity for competitiveness in modern economies. The pillars are reflected in the vertical axis of the grid.
- **The layer of the economy at which this determinant intervenes**: Firm capabilities, the immediate business environment and the national environment. These layers are in line with those identified in related work on competitiveness, but put an explicit focus on the micro, or firm level, dimension. The layers are reflected in the horizontal axis of the grid.

Together, this arrangement produces nine cells, in which it is possible to place any indicator related to firm competitiveness. The following gives an in-depth

FIGURE 42 The SME Competitiveness Grid

		Pillars		
		Capacity to Compete	Capacity to Connect	Capacity to Change
Layers	FIRM LEVEL CAPABILITIES			
	IMMEDIATE BUSINESS ENVIRONMENT			
	NATIONAL ENVIRONMENT			

Source: ITC.

description of the layers and pillars of competitiveness, to provide a better understanding of logic behind the grid.

Three layers of SME competitiveness

The SME Competitiveness Grid is composed of three layers of determinants for firm competitiveness: firm level capabilities, the immediate business environment, and the national environment.

Firm level capabilities

This firm level refers to determinants that are internal to the firm and thus in principle under its control. WEF (2008) views this layer in terms of the sophistication of companies' operations and strategies. This layer also reflects the strength of the firm's management.

The immediate business environment

This refers to factors that are external to the firm but within its micro-environment. While many external factors affecting firms' capacity to compete are determined at the national level and affect the overall economy, conventional wisdom is that a firm's level competitiveness is also shaped by its micro-environment. As Porter put it: 'It is hard to concoct a logic in which the nature of the arena in which firms compete would not be important to performance outcomes' (Porter, 1998). The immediate business environment includes local or industry-related factors that are external to the firm. The distinction between local and national factors reflects the fact that pockets of wealth exist within countries, infrastructures vary with location, clusters usually have a regional dimension, federal states have different state regulations, etc.

The important role of international value chains in global trade reflects the importance of the immediate business environment for firms. The lead firm largely determines the business environment faced by participants in an IVC. Lead firms often set value-chain specific standards and facilitate access to machinery, training and even trade finance. The immediate business environment of SME participants in the chain thus becomes conducive for internationalization.

For SMEs, the immediate business environment is particularly crucial, because it is mainly determined by external factors. In contrast, large firms are often in a position to shape their immediate environment.

The choice to highlight the immediate business environment has largely been driven by this report's focus on SME competitiveness.

The national environment

The third layer is the national dimension. National factors are important, as they establish the fundamentals for the functioning of markets; government action in particular determines whether or not firm activities are facilitated. A range of existing competitiveness-related indices capture many national factors well. These include the WEF Global Competitiveness Index (WEF, 2013), and the World Bank's Doing Business Survey (World Bank, 2014a) and Logistics Performance Index (World Bank, 2014b).

The national environment encompasses all structural factors that exist at the national level, such as policies on entrepreneurship and ease of doing business, trade-related policies, governance, infrastructure and resource endowments.

Layers align with SWOT analysis

From the business perspective, the three layers align well with the standard Strength, Weakness, Opportunity and Threats (SWOT) analysis. Firm capabilities refer to internal factors – the strengths and weaknesses of the firm. The immediate business environment and the national environment are factors external to the firm; together they provide a context of opportunities and threats (or challenges) the firm faces in its daily operations.

The three layers of determinants of competitiveness are concentric to the business and are not entirely dissociated; frontiers between them are blurred. Firm level capabilities are often dictated at the industry level (for example through technology standards). Specific governmental policies might constitute threats for some industries and opportunities for others (such as grants in favour of clean energies). A single firm might impact its local environment. While it may not always be easy to distinguish clearly the three layers, they will together determine the capacity of SMEs to compete today, to connect and to be ready for change.

In a given country, national factors establish a base level for SME competitiveness. Jointly with the performance of national firms, they govern the overall competitiveness of the nation. The competitiveness of a nation is an altogether different concept from that of firm competitiveness (Hatzichronoglou, 1996); it is often characterized by a single metric, productivity, i.e. the real value of output produced by a unit of labour during a certain time (Porter, 1990), but it certainly goes beyond this.

Three pillars of SME competitiveness

The SME Competitiveness Grid is also composed of three pillars, which capture the time-sensitive nature of competitiveness: capacity to compete, to connect and to change. The quick pace of innovation, the rise of IVCs and the dynamic nature of many markets require a high level of adjustability and flexibility from firms, and SMEs in particular. Firms that are competitive today need to connect effectively to information channels and world markets to sustain their competitiveness, while retaining the capability adapt to the new market conditions of tomorrow.

Capacity to Compete

This first pillar centres on present operations of firms and their efficiency in terms of cost, time, quality and quantity. It refers to the static dimension of competitiveness. Examples of potential thematic areas covered by this pillar include the capacity to meet quality and time requirements, and to maintain uninterrupted operations. Examples of determinants of capacity to compete along the layers of competitiveness include: application of quality control mechanisms by firm (firm level capability), existence of a commensurate quality certification system accessible to firms and relevant to their offer (immediate

business environment), and smooth customs procedures related to quality certification (macro-environment).

Capacity to Connect

This second pillar centres on the gathering and exploitation of information and knowledge. At the firm level, this refers to efforts to gather information flowing into the firm (e.g. consumer profiles, preferences and demand) and efforts to facilitate information flows from the firm (e.g. marketing and advertising). At the immediate business environment level, this includes links to sector associations, chambers of commerce as well as TISIs. At the national level, capacity to connect is predominantly about the availability of ICT infrastructure. While capacity to connect is not strictly a time-sensitive phenomenon, information gathering and exploitation are so central to current and future competitiveness that they act as an essential link between the two pillars of static competitiveness and dynamic competitiveness.

Capacity to Change

This third pillar centres on the capacity of a firm to execute change in response to, or in anticipation of, dynamic market forces and to innovate through investments in human and financial capital. It incorporates the dynamic dimension of competitiveness. External factors change very rapidly; the only certainty is uncertainty (IDB, 2014). In this context, adaptation and resilience define competitiveness. Industry phases, breakthrough or disruptive innovations, increased competition and exchange-rate fluctuations are all events that require strategy adaptations. The capacity to change, for example, requires interpreting new market trends, the tactics of rivals, opportunities derived from new infrastructures or technologies, and governmental policies.

The enterprise also needs to plan for unexpected events, which can seriously compromise revenue or turnover. These include the unanticipated emergence of a new competitor, change in demand, changes in the cost of supplies, and other developments, such as those linked to climate change.

SMEs are often considered to be at a natural disadvantage when it comes to access to finance, skills or R&D, and thus in their capacity to change. In the policy debate, the emphasis is often put on the need to change the external environment in these three areas, but behaviour at the firm level also influences access to finance, skills and R&D.

CHAPTER 10
SME competitiveness: Using the grid

The SME Competitiveness Grid is a framework for assessing the strengths and weaknesses of firm competitiveness along pillars of competitiveness. It also allows assessments on whether determinants of particular weaknesses or strengths are at the firm level, within the immediate business environment or at the macro level.

The focus is on key determinants of competitiveness discussed earlier in this report. They have been selected from publicly accessible databases which limited their coverage (Box 11). Further data limitations were imposed by the requirements to have timely data with good country coverage and data which follow linear distribution allowing for comparisons.

TABLE 10 The SME Competitiveness Grid, selection of indicators

| Layers | Pillars | | |
	Capacity to Compete	Capacity to Connect	Capacity to Change
FIRM LEVEL CAPABILITIES	• Quality certification • Bank account • Capacity utilization • Manager's experience	• E-mail • Website	• Financial audit • Bank financing • Training • Foreign licences
IMMEDIATE BUSINESS ENVIRONMENT	• Power reliability* • Shipping efficiency* • Dealing with regulation* • Customs clearance*	• Cluster development • Marketing • Supplier quality • R&D collaboration	• Access to finance* • Workforce education* • Licensing and permits*
NATIONAL ENVIRONMENT	• Getting electricity • Ease of trading • Tariff applied* • Tariff faced* • Logistics • ISO 9001 (quality standards) • ISO 14001(environmental standards) • Governance	• ICT access • ICT use • Government online service index	• Getting credit • Interest rate spread* • School life expectancy • Starting a business • Patent applications • Trademark regulations

Note: The values of indicators with an asterisk (*) are transformed to ensure that a higher score indicates a better outcome.
Source: ITC.

The country profiles in this report represent a first attempt at using the grid to assess, with available statistics, firm level competitiveness in 25 countries. The 25 selected countries are those for which ITC has collected NTM survey data, also included in this report. However, the report uses a larger sample of 111 countries to compute reference scores, percentage rankings and summary statistics (ITC, 2015b). It employs simple arithmetic averages and transformations to produce the indicator scores.

Additional ITC proprietary data on NTMs and export potential complement the analysis for each country. Together with the SME competitiveness data, there is information on:

■ The types of economic activity (product lines) in which firms may have particularly strong export potential.
■ The types of impediments – with a focus on NTMs – that firms may encounter at the national level when trying to export.

Box 11: Firm level data sources

Micro level data are expensive to obtain and thus scarce. Several surveys with firm level data exist, but they are not collected on an annual basis or for a sufficiently large number of countries.

■ The World Bank's Enterprise Surveys are the most comprehensive firm level datasets; country averages are freely available online, while firm level datasets are available upon request. Size criteria are homogenous: small firms (5–19 employees); medium (20–99), large (100+). The data cover some 130,000 firms in 145 countries, starting in 2002. Samples are representative of an economy's private sector, except for the surveys undertaken before 2005. They include statistics on a broad range of business environment topics including access to finance, labour skills, infrastructure, corruption, crime, competition and performance measures. In most countries the survey has been conducted only once.

■ The Innovation Surveys of UNESCO follow guidelines set out in the 2005 Oslo Manual (3rd edition). At the time of writing, the data cover the period 2005–2013 for 65 countries, although the UNESCO Institute of Statistics first collected global innovation statistics between July 2013 and July 2014. Only country averages are online, but firm level data are available upon request.

■ The Community Innovation Surveys of the European Union provide firm level data to researchers only, and upon request. The 2012 version covers 21 countries. The country totals are available online; these surveys also follow closely the 2005 Oslo Manual, although they cover a larger range of topics, including innovation activities and expenditures, types of cooperation, strategies, etc.

■ The WEF Executive Opinion Survey (EOS) differs from the above because although partially based on firm level data, it only publishes country totals. It has been computed since 1979, and Gallup audited it twice (in 2008 and 2012). The survey covered 144 economies in 2014, with a total of 140 questions, collecting the opinions of over 14,000 business leaders in 148 economies.

Two other areas are particularly relevant to SMEs: access to finance and access to skills. On these two topics, in addition to firm level data, there are household and/or individual level surveys. The existing databases are usually one-off efforts, however:

■ The World Bank's Global Financial Inclusion Database (Global Findex) provides information on how adults save, borrow, make payments and manage risk in 148 economies. It was conducted in 2011.

■ The World Bank's STEP Skills Measurement Program includes a household survey designed to assess skills in low and middle-income countries. It has data for eight economies in the period 2012–14. These surveys enable a better understanding of skill requirements in the labour market, and how skills and education link to the social environment and the job market.

The Microdata Library, an online platform developed by the World Bank, compiles and provides free access to the most comprehensive collections of micro level data.

Finally, ITC has carried out firm level surveys on NTMs and trade-related obstacles since 2010. The surveys capture at the product and partner country level how businesses perceive NTMs. They document the extent to which importing and exporting companies experience NTMs as regulatory and procedural obstacles to trade, independently of whether this effect is intended by regulatory authorities. The data are available for 25 countries and fieldwork in other countries is ongoing, promising broader data coverage in the future. This data are complementary to the SME Competitiveness Grid and described in detail in the related Annex.

Further information on NTM and Export Potential data presented in the country profiles can be found in the 'How to read' chapter in Part III of this report.

The following presents the rationale for the indicators chosen to assess SME competitiveness and highlights potential limitations and implicit trade-offs. It acts as a simple guide for the interpretation of the indicators used in the 25 country profiles. For more details on the sources and definitions of the indicators highlighted, please refer to the Annexes of this report.

Firm level indicators

For this layer, all indicators come from the World Bank Enterprise Surveys. Other firm level datasets, notably UNESCO Innovation Surveys were considered, but having a lower country coverage, they did not match those of the ITC NTM Surveys. As a result, the 2015 pilot assessment did not use these data series.

Capacity to Compete indicators

At the firm level, a series of factors related to the daily operation of the firm determine the capacity to compete at a given moment in time. Four indicators capture these factors in the country profiles:

- The prevalence of **quality management procedures**, represented by the percentage of firms with an internationally recognized quality certification.
- The capacity to maintain **workflows** in light of financial conditions, represented by the percentage of firms with a checking or savings account.
- The overall performance of firms to **plan** in light of market conditions, represented by capacity utilization.
- **Management skills**, represented by the number of years of managerial experience working in the firm's respective sector.

Capacity to Connect indicators

At the firm level, the use of ICT to gather market information, as well as the ability to connect to other key players in the firm's business environment, determine the capacity to connect. Such players include suppliers, clients, potential academic or corporate partners and public institutions. Two indicators measure these factors:

- The percentage of firms using **e-mail** to interact with clients and suppliers.
- The percentage of firms having their own **website**.

Capacity to Change indicators

At the firm level, several factors critical to growth, adaptation to market trends, and innovation determine the capacity to change. Four indicators capture these factors:

- The capacity to access **funding for investments**, represented by two indicators – the percentage of firms with an annual financial statement reviewed by external auditors and the proportion of investments financed by banks.
- The capability to access and generate **skills**, represented by the percentage of firms offering formal training.
- The capability to access and generate **state-of-the art technologies** for innovation, represented by the percentage of firms using technology licensed from foreign companies.

Immediate business environment indicators

It was challenging to find indicators that measure firms' immediate business environment. These are factors that are external to the firm but are positioned within firms' micro-environment, thus local or sectoral in nature.

Capacity to Compete indicators

In the short term, the immediate business environment to a large extent fosters or constrains the ability to compete. Notable in this environment are infrastructure quality, logistics, bureaucratic efficiency and customs efficiency, as relevant for a firm in a specific location and active in a particular line of activities. Four indicators from the Enterprise Surveys, linked to how individual firms experience their environment, represent these four dimensions:

- **Losses due to electrical outages**, as a percentage of annual sales.
- **The proportion of products lost to breakage or spoilage** during shipping to domestic markets.
- **The percentage of time spent on government regulation** requirements by senior management.
- **The average number of days to clear direct exports and imports from customs**.

Box 12: Sources for composite country performance indicators

There are a number of internationally recognized composite indicators aimed at capturing the performance of countries, rather than firms, in different areas. These global measures rely on macroeconomic variables, opinion surveys and/ or measurements of business regulations. They focus on the overall business environment that influences business performance. These composite indicators usually do not rely on firm level data, except for the perception data collected by the WEF EOS. The following are the most relevant composite indicators:

- The WEF Global Competitiveness Index (GCI), which had its 35th edition in 2014, covers 144 economies based on over 100 indicators. It defines competitiveness as 'the set of institutions, policies and factors that determine the level of productivity of a country'. In 2014, in addition to the regular GCI, the Forum for the first time computed a CGI adjusted for social and environmental sustainability. The GCI is built around 12 pillars, and attributes different weights to these pillars on the basis of five stages of development of countries. The report includes two pages per country profile and data tables. The GCI makes no distinction between small, medium-sized and large firms.

- OECD publishes a series of composite indictors on varied topics, the most relevant being the Small and Medium-Sized Enterprises Policy Index. This is a benchmarking tool designed for emerging economies to assess SME policy frameworks and monitor progress in policy implementation. The framework has been applied to the Western Balkans (2006, 2009 and 2012), Turkey and Eastern Partnership Countries (2012), North-African and Middle East regions (2008 and 2013), and ASEAN. This was in partnership with the European Commission, the European Bank for Reconstruction and Development, the European Training Foundation and the Economic Research Institute for ASEAN and East Asia.

- The World Bank Doing Business Report, published with IFC, also touches upon several business areas of relevance to SME Competitiveness. The focus, however, is usually on a typical business case, with greater emphasis on policies and regulations than on firm behaviour.

- The Global Innovation Index, co-published by Cornell University, INSEAD and WIPO, is in its 6th edition (2014). It covers 143 countries through about 80 indicators. It draws on some 80 metrics compiled globally at the national level, distributed into seven pillars.

- The Enabling Trade Index (WEF) benchmarks the performance of 138 economies in four areas: market access; border administration; transport and communications infrastructure; and regulatory and business environment. The index is part of the Enabling Trade Report, informing policy dialogue and providing a tool to monitor progress on certain aspects of global trade.

- The Global Connectedness Index 2014 by DHL is a composite indicator that ranks 140 economies on more than 1 million data points in a nine-year period since 2005. Global connectedness refers to a country's integration with the rest of the world, as manifested by its participation in 12 types of cross-border international flows grouped into four pillars: trade of goods and services, capital, information, and people. The GCI includes an 'analysis in 3-D': it looks at the depth of interactions (international flows relative to the domestic market size) and their breadth (geographic distribution, concentration and distance); directionality (outward vs inward flows and imbalances) is provided as additional information in the country profiles but not taken into account in computations.

- The Customs Services Index is based on 17 survey questions taken from the Global Express Association (GEA) Customs Capabilities Reports, which evaluate the quality and comprehensiveness of services offered by customs and related agencies. The maximum score an economy can obtain is 1.

- The Customs Transparency Index is based on 7 survey questions taken from the GEA Customs Capabilities Reports, evaluating the overall transparency of the procedures and regulations related to customs clearance. The maximum score an economy can obtain is 1.

- KPMG International and Oxford Economics produce Change Readiness Index, designed to measure how effectively a country's government, private and public enterprises, people and wider civil society anticipate, prepare for, manage and respond to change and cultivate opportunity. Examples of change include: shocks such as financial and social instability and natural disasters, and political and economic opportunities and risks such as technology, competition and changes in government.

Source: KPMG International and Oxford Economics (2015).

Capacity to Connect indicators

The business environment also determines the capacity of the firm to connect to clients and suppliers. For this pillar, the data come from the WEF EOS and the World Bank's Enterprise Surveys. The focus is on the potential to develop linkages to other actors in the economy:

- **Other firms**, represented by the state of cluster development indicator.
- **Customers**, represented by the extent of marketing sophistication.
- **Suppliers**, represented by an indicator that captures the perceived quality of local suppliers.
- **Academia**, including universities, captured by measuring the extent to which firms participate in collaboration between universities and industry in R&D.

Capacity to Change indicators

In the medium and long term, access to finance and skills, along with the ability to purchase business licensing and permits quickly and cheaply, determine the capacity to change. Three indicators capture these components:

- The percentage of firms identifying **access to finance** as a constraint to current operations.
- The percentage of firms identifying an inadequately **educated workforce** as a constraint to current operations.
- The percentage of firms identifying **business and licensing permits** as a constraint to current operations.

National environment indicators

To measure the overall, country-level business environment according to the three pillars of SME competitiveness, indicators used in the analysis have been selected from a range of external sources (Box 12).

Capacity to Compete indicators

At the national level, the availability of quality infrastructure and logistics also affects the capacity to compete. The indicators used here measure quality and availability of infrastructure at the national level, rather than infrastructure quality as perceived and experienced by individual firms.

This pillar contains:

- An assessment of **crucial infrastructure** based on:
- The availability of **electric power,** represented by the ease of getting electricity.
- The quality of **logistics and logistics services**, represented by the logistics performance index.
- **Trade readiness**, captured by three indicators – the ease of trading across borders (trade facilitation), the trade-weighted applied tariff rate (trade openness), and the trade-weighted average tariff faced (foreign market access).

Indicators to measure the overall prevalence of **sustainability and quality standards** are based on the number of certificates of conformity issued, and accompanied by requirements and guidance for use, in a given country, per million of population:

- ISO 9001: 2008 **Quality management systems**.
- ISO 14001:2004 **Environmental management systems.**

Lastly, to measure **governance**:

- The World Bank's six **World Governance Indicators** were combined in a single indicator, through a simple average of six estimates.

Capacity to Connect indicators

Three indicators capture the capacity of the firm to connect at the national level: two composite indicators on **ICT access** and **ICT use**, calculated by the International Telecommunications Union (ITU) on the basis of hard data at household level; and the **government's online service index**, a metric developed by the UN Public Administration Network.

'ICT access' includes five indicators: (1) fixed telephone lines per 100 inhabitants, (2) mobile cellular telephone subscriptions per 100 inhabitants, (3) international Internet bandwidth (bit/s) per Internet user, (4) percentage of households with a computer, and (5) percentage of households with Internet access.

'ICT use' includes three indicators: (1) percentage of individuals using the Internet, (2) fixed (wired-) broadband Internet subscriptions per 100 inhabitants, (3) active subscriptions for mobile broadband subscriptions per 100 inhabitants.

Capacity to Change indicators

Capacity to change includes a number of indicators at the national level:

- Two indicators on **access to finance**, reflecting both access and cost – the ease of getting credit and the interest rate spread.

- The **school life expectancy** in years, to measure the national skills level.

- The '**ease of starting a business**' indicator, from the World Bank's Doing Business survey. This is a good gauge of capacity to change, as it represents the degree of difficulty entrepreneurs must overcome to start a business.

Finding metrics to assess the capacity to innovate at the national level proved difficult. This was due to a lack of a suitable policy indicator, which would have been preferable. Therefore, two performance indicators represent this dimension:

- The number of **patent applications** by residents at the national office (scaled by GDP at purchasing power parity), which captures the overall inventive performance of residents.

- The number of **trademark registrations** by residents at the national office, which captures a multiplicity of business motivations and rationales behind branding, such as marketing sophistication, the development of new products and entrepreneurship.

The focus on national offices helps to show whether these are adequate in channelling and protecting legitimate intellectual property claims.

It is important to emphasize that this is a very preliminary selection of statistics and indicators. In some cases, the indicators chosen only partially capture the concept under discussion. Nevertheless, the presentation of potential indicators for the SME Competiveness Grid will hopefully stimulate feedback and insights through interactions with experts and practitioners. Furthermore, ITC is currently designing a detailed questionnaire to fit within the grid structure. Finally, several datasets and methodologies developed by ITC in other contexts provide strong complementary insights to the key indicators.

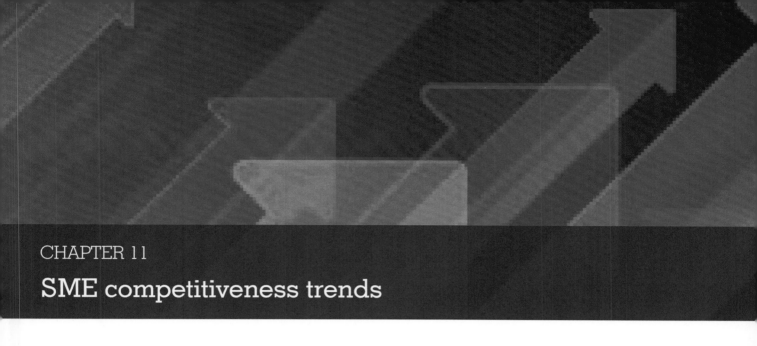

CHAPTER 11

SME competitiveness trends

The SME Competitiveness Grid is structured to provide an overview of the strengths and weaknesses in countries and regions. This chapter presents some of trends and findings resulting from an analysis of 111 countries. To provide a broad overview of the results, the analysis is limited to common development groupings and geographic regions. There is more detailed information on individual countries in the 25 country profiles presented in Part III.

Regional trends

Figures 43 and 44 present scores for the three pillars of competitiveness in countries grouped by development stage and by geographic region. Simple averages of all the indicators within each pillar are taken to generate scores. The developing country group consists of countries that are neither LDCs (UN definition) nor OECD members. The regional definitions follow standard World Bank groupings.

Developing countries are well covered in the datasets used to generate the figures presented here. However, the Europe and Central Asia group, as well as the developed countries group, do not include many prominent developed countries, such as Switzerland, the United Kingdom and the United States.

Figure 43 presents information on all layers of competitiveness and, unsurprisingly, reveals that firms tend to be more competitive in advanced countries than in developing countries. Figure 43 also shows that developed countries score highest and LDCs score lowest along all three pillars of competitiveness.

Pronounced differences in connectivity

LDCs perform particularly poorly in the Capacity to Connect pillar, reflecting low ICT and cluster development scores. The opposite is true for developed countries, where firms perform especially well in connectivity. LLDCs also perform relatively poorly in the connectivity pillar, which includes access to and use of information. It is well known that transportation costs tend to be higher in LLDCs; this seems also to apply to information costs.

Plotting the scores according to geographic region, Europe and Central Asia perform best, while South Asia and sub-Saharan Africa perform worst on the three central pillars of competitiveness (Figure 44). East Asia and the Pacific, and LAC show similar capacity to compete and capacity to change scores. However, LAC performs significantly better regarding connectivity. The MENA region also performs on a par with the LAC region in the Capacity to Compete and connectivity but underperforms somewhat in the Capacity to Change pillar.

Restricting the analysis to the first layer of competitiveness, Firm Level Capabilities, reveals that large firms systematically outperform medium-sized firms and medium-sized firms systematically outperform small firms. This holds for all income groups and for all regional groupings, as reflected in Figures 45 and 46.

Gaps between large and small firm performance widen as economic development levels fall

In the Capacity to Compete pillar, when the score of large firms is used as the baseline, medium-sized firms score 89% and small firms 74% of this baseline

FIGURE 43 Pillars of competitiveness according
to development stage

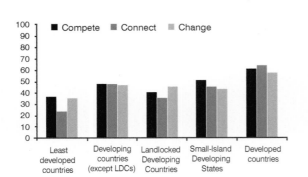

FIGURE 44 Pillars of competitiveness according
to geographic region

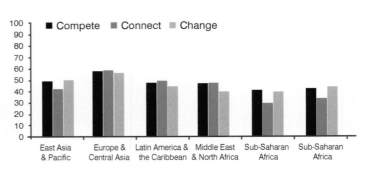

FIGURE 45 Firm level capabilities by pillars of competitiveness and development stage

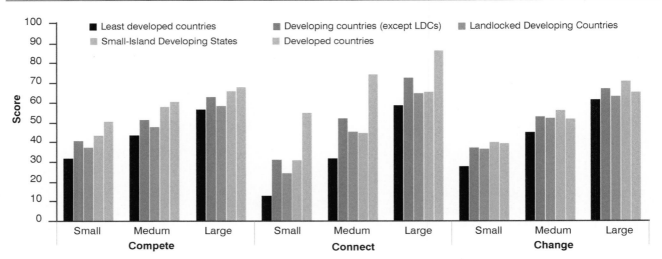

FIGURE 46 Firm level capabilities by pillars of competitiveness and geographic region

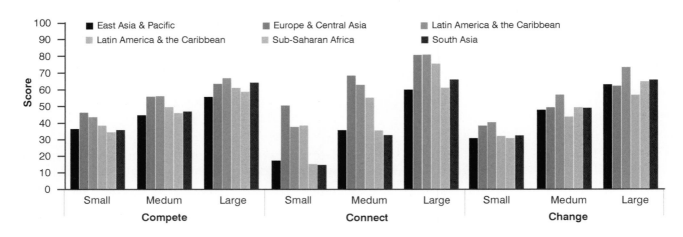

in developed countries. In contrast, in LDCs, the performance gap is much more pronounced. Medium-sized and small firms in LDCs only score 77% and 57% of the score attained by large firms, respectively. Dragging LDCs' scores down are the low rates of firms with bank accounts (25% and 40% for small and medium-sized firms, respectively). In general, firms in developed countries perform best, followed by SIDSs, developing countries, LLDCs and finally LDCs.

As indicated in Figure 45, there are similar findings for the other two pillars – Capacity to Connect and Capacity to Change. Medium-sized and small firms in developed countries score 86% and 64% of the large firm baseline regarding the Capacity to Connect. In the same pillar, medium-sized firms and small firms in LDCs only score 54% and 22% of the score attained by large firms, respectively.

These results suggest that the indicators used in the grid to measure firm level capacity likely are among the core determinants of firms' productivity, as the scores reflect the firm level productivity patterns discussed in Part I of this report, which showed that productivity differences between small and large firms are significantly more pronounced in the developing world than in the developed world.

In LDCs, the largest gap is in connectivity

The Capacity to Connect is of particular interest, because it is the pillar in which small firms in developed countries perform very strongly, whereas small firms in the other country groups perform very poorly. Overall, firms from developed countries perform best, followed by developing countries. SIDS and LLDCs perform similarly while LDCs show the lowest Capacity to Connect scores. Furthermore, small firms in LDCs only attain 22% of the connectivity score of large firms in LDCs, compared to 64% in developed countries.

Developed countries do not always outperform others in change capacity

This pattern differs when it comes to firms' Capacity to Change. Here differences across development groups are much less pronounced and it is not always the case that developed economies in the sample outperform other country groupings. For example, firms in SIDS actually fare best in this pillar.

Regional performances vary

Plotting the scores according to geographic regions, no single region systematically outperforms others, reflecting economic diversity within regions (Figure 46). Large firms from Europe, LAC as well as Central and South Asia perform strongest in the Capacity to Compete. While small and medium-sized firms from Europe, LAC as well as Central Asia also perform strongly in this regard, their counterparts in South Asia, and East Asia and the Pacific perform rather poorly due to low scores on quality certification. Small, medium-sized and large firms from East Asia and the Pacific perform similar to sub-Saharan firms across the three pillars of competitiveness.

In Capacity to Connect, small and medium-sized firms in South Asia are the worst performers, closely followed by sub-Saharan African firms. Their counterparts in Europe and Central Asia perform strongest. Large firms from LAC perform equally well as large firms from Europe and Central Asia. Figure 46 confirms that the differences across firm size are most pronounced in the Capacity to Connect pillar. Taking large firms' score as a baseline, small firms from the sub-Saharan region only score 22% of the baseline score while their counterparts in Europe and Central Asia score 63% of the baseline in their own region.

With regards to the Capacity to Change, there is much less variation across geographic regions and across firm size. Small firms from South Asia score 50% of the baseline attained by large firms, while small firms from Europe and Central Asia score about 60%. Regardless of size, firms from LAC perform strongest, although the regional differences decrease with falling firm size.

Looking at the detail

The country profiles in Part III organize information on SME competitiveness using radar diagrams. This makes it possible to assess competitiveness across the pillars of competitiveness, the layers of competitiveness, and across firm sizes. Here, the report takes a closer look at these groupings and highlights a selection of the most interesting trends and findings.

Comparing firms' strengths and weaknesses

For most indicators, small enterprises perform worse than medium-sized enterprises, and medium-size firms perform worse than large enterprises. Figure 47 reflects this trend, showing Firm level Capability charts for LDCs and developed economies.

IT services exports from Bangladesh

ITC and the Dutch Centre for the Promotion of Imports from developing countries (CBI) are cooperating on a series of programmes called Netherlands Trust Fund (NTF).

The third phase of this programme, NTF III, is deployed in Uganda, Kenya, Myanmar and Bangladesh. It aims to increase the value and volume of exports of the beneficiary companies, and diversify their range of customers by introducing them to new clients and markets.

In Bangladesh, NTF II – which ended in 2013 – arranged approximately 800 meetings between Bangladeshi IT companies and European Union companies, which resulted in the boosting of exports by an average of 20% for 25 of the 40 beneficiary companies. Over the next three years, NTF III will support more IT companies in Bangladesh to export.

As part of this process, a pilot version of the ITC SME Competitiveness Survey was carried out on the 40 beneficiary companies. The aims were to create a baseline and measure the overall firm competitiveness, using competitiveness indicators which measure whether companies follow best practices. Based on the collected data, some of the strengths and weaknesses of the surveyed firms were identified.

Two competitiveness indicators – meeting quality requirements and innovation – are examined below.

Certification often serves as a guarantee of the quality of a company's main product or service. Bangladesh ranks 95 out of 148 countries on 'Local Supplier Quality,' according to WEF. Quality certificates are important to customers seeking to reduce the risk of non-delivery in an unfamiliar market. Therefore, training on quality certification – part of the NTF III Bangladesh project – is crucial to boosting exports. According to Bangladesh's Competitiveness Country Profile, only 14.3% of all Bangladeshi firms have quality certificates, as opposed to 34.6% for large firms. For the firms surveyed, 20 of the 40 beneficiary companies (or 50%) have an internationally recognized quality certificate, highlighting the contribution to development of Bangladesh's IT sector.

On innovation, the beneficiary companies scored highly. All but one reported the development of 'new or improved products, services or processes'. As this is a sample of IT companies, this is perhaps unsurprising. WEF ranks Bangladesh 120 out of 148 countries on 'Innovation Capacity'. This highlights the importance of innovative industries that can help Bangladesh to move up the value chain.

Source: ITC (2015a).

Figure 47 also highlights two trends that emerged earlier in this report:

- Firms of all sizes in developed countries achieve higher scores than their counterparts in LDCs. This is driven by low scores in LDCs for:

  - Connectivity-related indicators.

  - Bank account use by small firms.

  - ISO quality certification by small firms.

- The performance gap between small and large firms is significantly larger in LDCs than in developed countries.

Each layer of the SME Competitiveness Grid (Firm Level Capabilities, the Immediate Business Environment and the National Environment) is given its own radar diagram. The indicators surrounding each diagram reflect the three pillars of competitiveness and are colour-coded.

The indicators in the outer space of the radar chart measure each competitiveness pillar. The indicator scores are transformed so that higher is always better. Thus, the closer the indicator score is to the edge of the plot, the more competitive are a country's firms.

The Firm Level Capabilities radar diagram is unique because it uses firm level data (e.g. Figure 47). This makes it possible to distinguish the performance of

small (dotted lines), medium (solid lines) and large-sized enterprises (dash lines). The white area on the firm level radar diagram reflects the average scores attained by all firms. The grey circular line around the centre reflects the median score of the sample of 111 countries. For firm level capabilities, this corresponds to the median score of all firms, regardless of size. For the immediate and national business environments, where it is not possible to break the data down at firm level, the grey line corresponds to the median country score. Comparing scores against the grey line thus makes it possible to assess how regions and firms within those regions perform in relation to the median.

Medium-sized firms fare far better in developed countries

The firm level radar diagrams also reveal how firms in different country groupings perform when compared with the global sample of firms. Comparing firm size performance with the benchmark (median score of all firms in the sample) in Figure 47 shows that:

- In developed economies, medium-sized firms outperform the global median, while in LDCs such firms do not reach median performance.

- In developed economies, the trade readiness of small firms is close to median performance, while in LDCs it is significantly below the median benchmark.

FIGURE 47   Firm level capabilities for small, medium-sized and large companies – LDCs vs developed countries

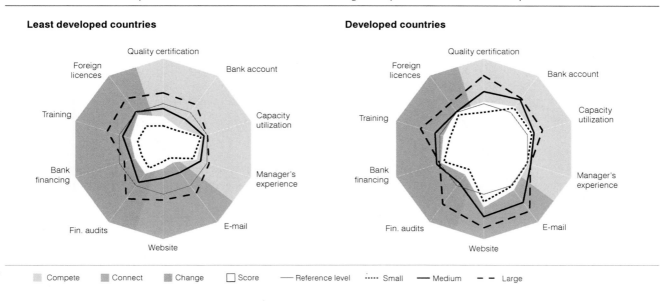

Source: ITC calculation based on data SME Outlook data.

This implies that small firms (defined as 4–19 employees) in developed countries perform on average significantly better than medium-sized firms (defined as 20–99 employees) in LDCs.

Radar diagrams for the next two layers, the Immediate Business Environment and National Environment, are not broken down by firm size, as most of the data do not come from firm level surveys. In these cases, the white area simply represents the headline score. Comparing white areas across layers of competitiveness helps to pinpoint the factors that contribute to SME competitiveness. This comparison reveals that in LLDCs, SMEs' weak performance in the connectivity pillar stems from weaknesses in all three layers of determinants: macro, immediate business environment and weak firm level capacity, notably for small firms (Figure 48). The country group's score remains within the grey comparator line in all three radar diagrams.

Challenges to measure the immediate business environment

It is difficult to make comparisons across layers based on existing datasets. There is hardly any information available on firm level capacity to create linkages with customers, peers, suppliers and technical institutions. Available indicators focus on e-connectivity, admittedly an important aspect of connectivity, but not the only one. These indicators can be compared with macro level information, but not with information for the immediate business environment. ITC is seeking to address this by collecting a larger array of information on SME firm level capacity, notably for the pillar of connectivity.

An additional challenge with the immediate business environment layer is that it currently relies largely on indicators based on opinion surveys. This is particularly the case for the Capacity to Compete and the Capacity to Change, where indicators reflect firms' perceptions of macroeconomic performance rather than objective measures of the immediate business environment's quality. As a result, those indicators may reveal more about respondents' expectations than the actual quality of the immediate business environment.

This could explain why the immediate business environment is near the median line in many of the country groupings, despite significant variations in macro indicators and firm level capacities. Firms used to operating in a weak overall economic environment have lower expectations and are therefore more easily satisfied with the status quo than their counterparts operating in a high quality environment. This is especially visible when comparing LLDCs (Figure 48) and developed economies (Figure 49).

Firms in LLDCs suffer from weak e-connectivity

A reading of the SME competiveness charts across layers can nevertheless offer clues about the sources of identified weaknesses.

The analysis of SME Competitiveness Grid information for LLDCs, for example, reveals opportunities for LLDCs to compensate for their natural disadvantage in logistics by putting a stronger emphasis on e-connectivity and access to finance.

LLDCs' relative weakness in the connectivity pillar stems from a poor performance at the immediate business environment and national levels, compared to SIDS, based on comparing Figures 48 and 50. At the firm level, this weakness is especially reflected in a low e-mail use among small and medium-sized firms.

The financial system appears to be another major difference. Most SIDS firms have their own bank account, including small firms. This is not the case in LLDCs, which likely undermines the capacity of LLDC firms to organize competitive operations. SIDS firms make more use of bank finance, and the interest rate spread is lower. (Firms' perceptions of access to finance are similar to those in LLDCs, possibly reflecting the expectation bias referred to above.)

On average, LLDCs perform below the median line on all indicators in the economic environment, as revealed when using information on sample performance (white area) to analyse SME competitiveness across development groups within one layer (Figure 51).

LLDCs perform better, though, than LDCs.

Not surprisingly, developed countries performed better than other development groupings at the national level.

In LAC, medium-sized firms outperform the global median

Figures 52 to 57 show radar graphs for a selection of geographic regions.

When comparing firm level capabilities across regions, the radar charts reveal that determinants of medium-sized firm performance tend to exceed the median global level in Europe and Central Asia, and in LAC. Small firm performance is also relatively strong in these regions. However, in sub-Saharan Africa and South Asia, small firms fare poorly in the determinants of the trade performance. In South Asia, the wide gap between small and large firms in the use of e-mails for day-to-day operations and the existence of a firm website is particularly striking.

Performance on training and quality certification depends on firm size

Some patterns appear to hold across different geographic regions.

In LAC and MENA, scores for 'training' and the two Capacity to Connect indicators are closely linked to the size of the firm under consideration (Figure 53 and 55). While large firms are relatively strong in these aspects, small firms perform considerably worse than the median in the sample.

These findings are in line with other research suggesting that large firms invest more in training their workforce than smaller firms (e.g. Jansen and Lanz, 2013). In MENA, this pattern is also evident regarding 'quality certification'. In contrast, 'experience' does not appear to be size dependent, with small firms in MENA outperforming the sample median.

When it comes to the National Environment, countries in LAC and MENA hover around the median country performance, while firms in European and Central Asian countries fare better. The National Environment is weakest in sub-Saharan Africa and South Asia. The quality of the Immediate Business Environment follows roughly the same pattern, although differences across regions tend to be smaller. This may reflect that firms adjust their expectations to the national environment they encounter.

The difference in Immediate Business Environment between LAC and MENA is nevertheless interesting, with LAC performing significantly worse when it comes to access to an adequately skilled workforce, the time managers spend dealing with bureaucracy and losses due to time spent in customs.

Firms reveal high levels of entrepreneurship despite their environment

There are other interesting patterns when comparing the layers of determinants of competitiveness across regions. Figure 53 reveals that overall LAC SME competitiveness is lower than SME competitiveness in Europe and Central Asia across all three pillars of competitiveness.

A closer analysis reveals that this is not due to poor firm level capacities. On the contrary, the capacities of small and medium-sized firms are very similar in the two regions, possibly reflecting the strong entrepreneurial culture and tradition in LAC. Large firms in LAC even outperform Europe and Central Asia, yet they have to struggle with a significantly weaker overall economic environment.

However, in MENA, firm level capabilities are lower than in the regions of Europe and Central Asia, LAC, and East Asia and the Pacific. Interestingly, this pattern is present for all three firm size groups. The national environment, instead, is comparable with the one in the LAC and the immediate business environment is stronger.

Large firms compensate for weaknesses in the national environment

Firms in sub-Saharan Africa and South Asia suffer from very weak national environments. In South Asia problems related to logistics and access to finance are, however, somewhat less pronounced. Significantly, in both regions, large firms manage to compensate for those weaknesses, particularly in connectivity. Such firms tend to have their own website and e-mail addresses despite a generally weak ICT environment. In contrast, for medium-sized performance indicators remain below (though close to) the median level.

FIGURE 48 LLDCs: The SME Competitiveness Grid

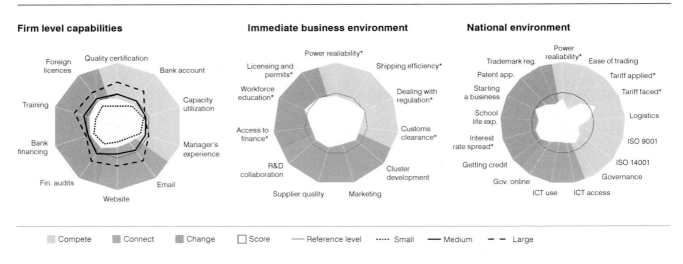

FIGURE 49 Developed countries: The SME Competitiveness Grid

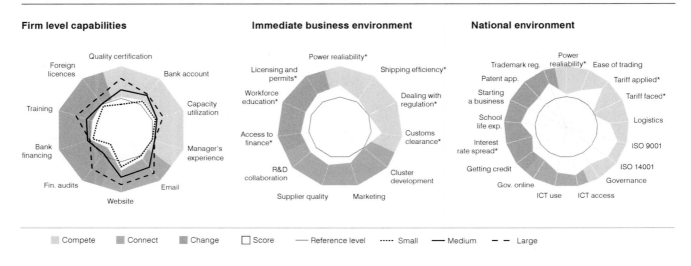

FIGURE 50 SIDS: The SME Competitiveness Grid

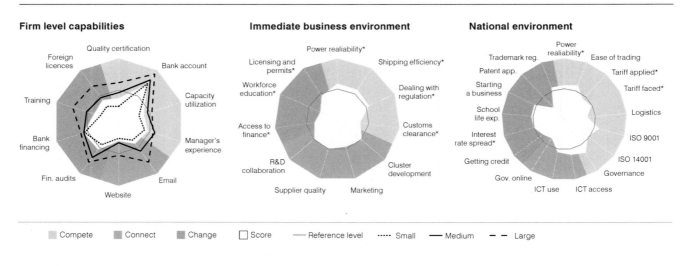

Source: ITC calculation based on data SME Outlook data.

FIGURE 51 The overall economic environment across income groups

High-income countries

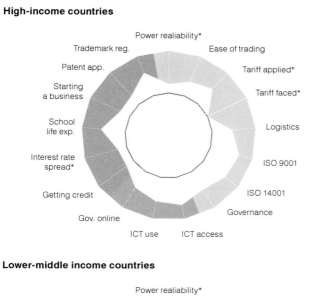

Upper-middle income countries

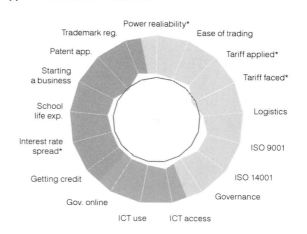

Lower-middle income countries

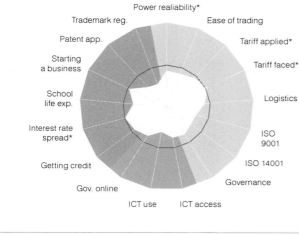

Low-income countries

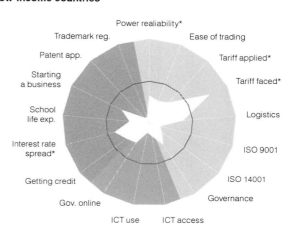

Compete ■ Connect ■ Change □ Score —— Reference level

FIGURE 52 Europe and Central Asia: The SME Competitiveness Grid

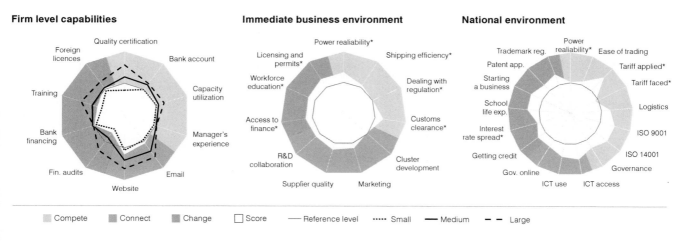

Firm level capabilities

Immediate business environment

National environment

Compete ■ Connect ■ Change □ Score —— Reference level ····· Small —— Medium – – Large

Source: ITC calculation based on data SME Outlook data.

FIGURE 53   LAC: The SME Competitiveness Grid

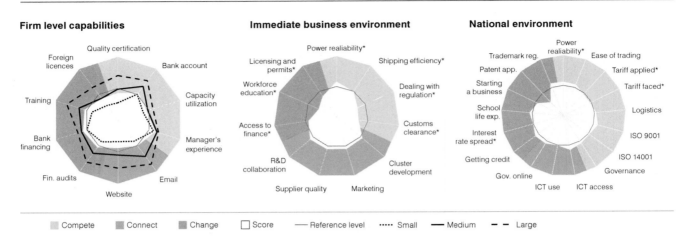

FIGURE 54   East Asia and the Pacific: The SME Competitiveness Grid

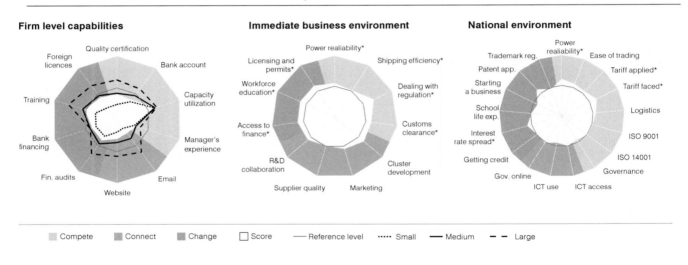

FIGURE 55   MENA: The SME Competitiveness Grid

Source: ITC calculation based on SME Outlook data.

FIGURE 56 Sub-Saharan Africa: The SME Competitiveness Grid

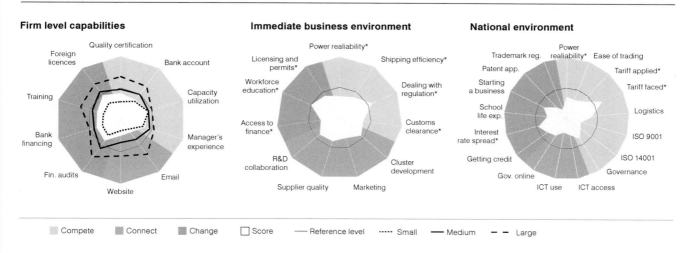

FIGURE 57 South Asia: The SME Competitiveness Grid

Source: ITC calculation based on SME Outlook data.

ENDNOTES

1. See Annex III the composition of country groupings.

2. As previously mentioned, competitiveness scores of developed countries are likely to be lower than would be expected, as due to data restrictions; countries such as Switzerland, the United Kingdom and the United States are not included in the analysis.

3. More information on the methodology described above can be found in Annex I.

4. In country profiles and as explained in Annex I, the grey comparator line is not based on the median performance but is calculated as a benchmark performance depending on individual countries' level of development. The grey line thus helps to assess whether firms perform better or worse than expected based on the GDP per capita in their country.

Summary of findings

Based on three competitiveness pillars – to connect, compete and change – the SME Competitiveness Grid makes it easier to spot strengths and weaknesses of enterprises. It determines whether these are from within the firm, the immediate business environment or the macro level national environment. This helps countries understand their trade potential and address what is stopping them.

The findings suggest that the competitiveness gap between SMEs and large firms is considerably less pronounced in developed countries than in less developed countries. The findings also suggest that, in contrast to SMEs, large firms compensate for weak immediate business and national environments. In a number of cases, large firms perform strongly in providing training, even when there are low 'workforce' and 'school life expectancy' scores. Similarly, large firms achieve respectable scores in 'bank financing' even though the immediate and national environments in which they operate receive low scores for 'access to finance' and 'getting credit'.

When zooming in on individual pillars of competitiveness (Figure 58 and 59), the following picture emerges:

Connect: Focus on e-connectivity for SMEs to succeed in international markets.

- **The biggest gap between small and large firms is in e-connectivity**, with three regions – East Asia and the Pacific, sub-Saharan Africa and South Asia – performing worst.

- **Landlocked countries** have more than just a physical challenge with roads and ports. They also have a virtual challenge: e-connectivity rates are among the world's lowest.

- **Bridge the 'connectivity gap' between small and large firms in LDCs:** Small firms in LDCs only attain 22% of the connectivity score of large firms in LDCs, compared to 64% in developed countries.

Compete: The strongest pillar for SMEs from developing countries is the 'compete' pillar.

- **Compete gap:** As measured by the SME Competitiveness Grid, the 'compete' gap between medium and large firms is only 11% in developed countries, compared to 18% for developing countries (excluding LDCs).

- **In LDCs**, medium and small firms only score 77% and 57% of the score attained by large firms, compared to 89% and 74% in developed countries. Dragging LDCs' scores down are the low rates of firms with bank accounts (25% and 40% for small and medium-sized firms, respectively).

- **South Asia:** Small firms in South Asia, and East Asia and the Pacific score poorly on quality certification.

Change: Firms in developed countries do not systematically outperform firms in other development groupings in the 'change' pillar.

- **Average scores for the firm level capbilities 'change' pillar** follow similar patterns in all country groupings, with small firms scoring between 45% to 60% and medium-sized firms around 70% to 80% of the score attained by large firms. The differences are somewhat larger in LDCs.

- **In LDCs**, the low proportion of investment financed by banks drags the score down.

One salient feature of the analysis is the performance of LAC SMEs. The firm level capacities of medium-sized firms are second only to those from Europe and Central Asia, with small-sized firms actually outscoring Europe and Central Asia. They are strong entrepreneurial performers, on a par with the best developing country SMEs, and outpace countries in other regions ITC assessed, including in Asia and the Pacific.

While the radar diagrams provide valuable explanations for differences in competitiveness across development stages and geographic regions, they also point towards potential data shortcomings. First, existing datasets provide relatively little information about application of best practices by firms. Second, when it comes to assessing the Immediate Business Environment, the analysis presented here suffers from the use of perception-based data, as firms may adjust their expectations to their environment. Future data collection exercises, including those conducted by ITC, could attempt to address these shortcomings.

The analysis suggests there is considerable potential for SMEs to catch up. Moreover, if SMEs in less developed countries can increase their productivity, in relative terms, to levels in developed countries, there would be significant gains from growth, particularly for the vulnerable groups that SMEs employ. The country profiles in this SME Outlook provide a first indication of how this could be accomplished.

FIGURE 58 Gap in firm level capabilities: SMEs vs large enterprises, by development group

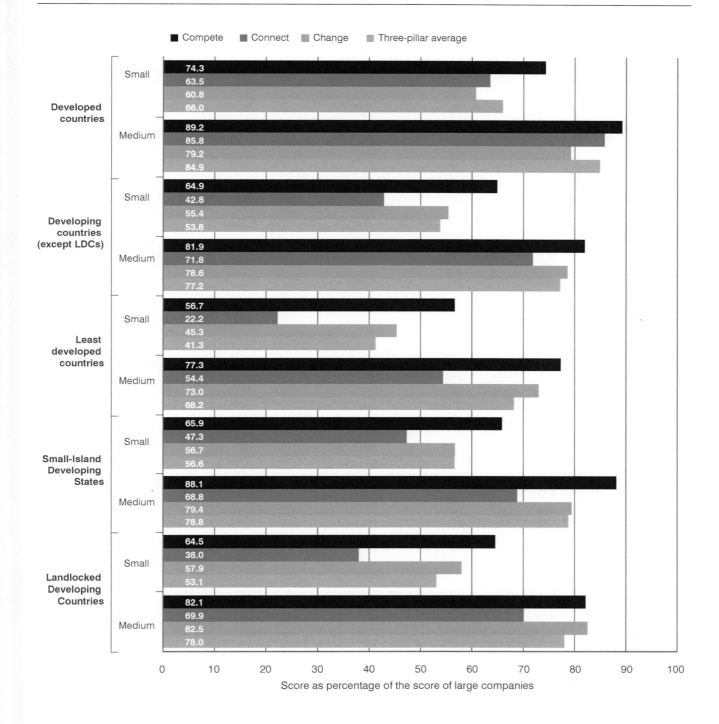

Score as percentage of the score of large companies

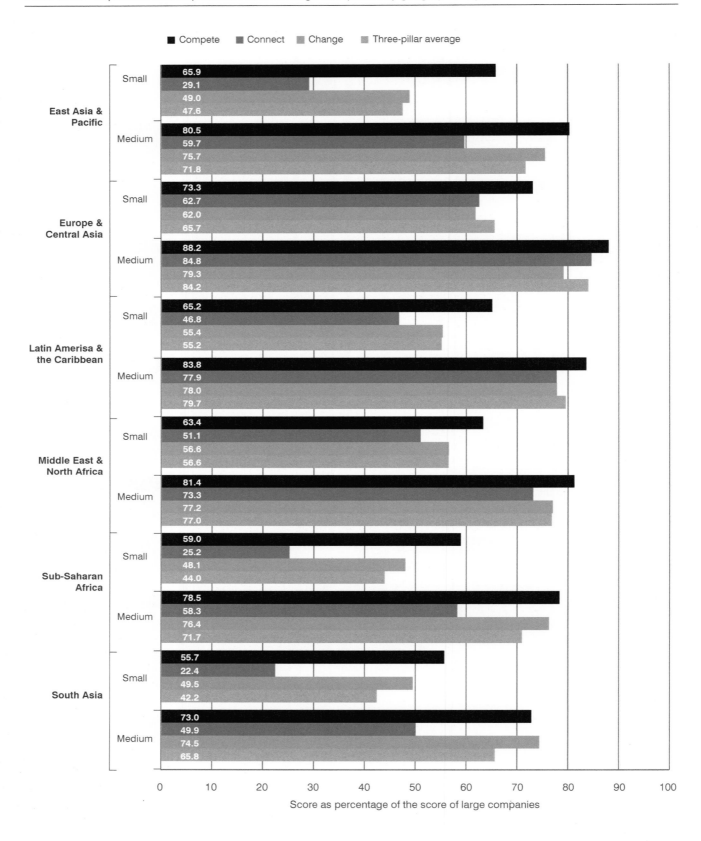

■ Compete ■ Connect ▨ Change ▨ Three-pillar average

East Asia & Pacific

Small
- 65.9
- 29.1
- 49.0
- 47.6

Medium
- 80.5
- 59.7
- 75.7
- 71.8

Europe & Central Asia

Small
- 73.3
- 62.7
- 62.0
- 65.7

Medium
- 88.2
- 84.8
- 79.3
- 84.2

Latin Amerisa & the Caribbean

Small
- 65.2
- 46.8
- 55.4
- 55.2

Medium
- 83.8
- 77.9
- 78.0
- 79.7

Middle East & North Africa

Small
- 63.4
- 51.1
- 56.6
- 56.6

Medium
- 81.4
- 73.3
- 77.2
- 77.0

Sub-Saharan Africa

Small
- 59.0
- 25.2
- 48.1
- 44.0

Medium
- 78.5
- 58.3
- 76.4
- 71.7

South Asia

Small
- 55.7
- 22.4
- 49.5
- 42.2

Medium
- 73.0
- 49.9
- 74.5
- 65.8

Score as percentage of the score of large companies

PART III.

Country Profiles

How to read country profiles

The following country profiles provide information on the SME Competitiveness Grid and complementary indicators for 25 countries. The selection of countries in this edition is driven by the availability of firm level data on companies' experience with NTMs and related barriers to trade, i.e. countries where ITC has completed business surveys on NTMs.[1] Statistics are provided for 25 countries, but computations of reference points (global top performance,

global median performance, reference level in heat map) are based on a larger sample of 111 countries, which are described in the regional analysis provided in Part II.[2]

An example Country Profile is shown in Figure 60. The first page is split into three sections: (A) key indicators, (B) SME Competitiveness Grid, consisting of tables and corresponding radar charts, and (C) SME Competitiveness Grid Summary in the form of a heat map. The second

FIGURE 60   Country Profile example

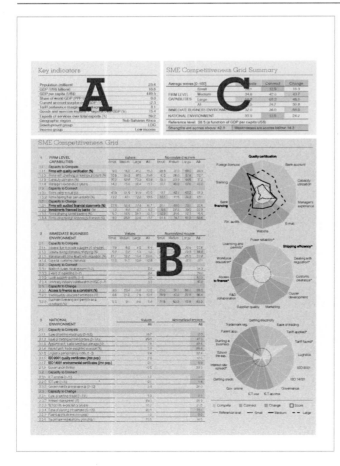

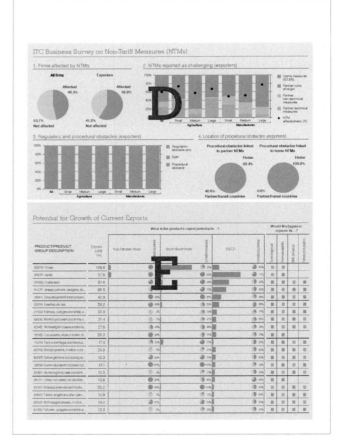

page consists of two sections; (D) ITC Business Survey on NTMs, and (E) product ranking of current exports based on their growth potential.

Section A: Key indicators

At the top left of each Country Profile, eight key indicators are provided to set the context for each economy:

- Population (millions)
- GDP (US$ billions)
- GDP per capita (PPP US$)
- Share of world GDP (PPP US$, %)
- Current account surplus over GDP (%)
- Tariff preference margin (percentage points)
- Goods and services imports + exports over GDP (%)
- Exports of services over total exports (%)
- Geographic region
- Development group
- Income group

Section B: SME Competitiveness Grid (data tables and corresponding radar charts)

Section B of each Country Profile includes a series of statistics compiled according to the SME Competitiveness Grid. The Grid has a matrix format (Chapter 9), here displayed as a list.

There are three layers of determinants of competitiveness (the first digit in each indicator code):

1. Firm level capabilities;
2. Immediate business environment;
3. National environment.

Each layer is divided into the three pillars of competitiveness (the second digit in each indicator code):

1. Capacity to Compete (in blue);
2. Capacity to Connect (in purple);
3. Capacity to Change (in grey).

The third digit in each code represents the particular indicator. For instance, indicator 3.1.2, '*Ease of trading*

across borders', corresponds to the second indicator in the third layer (national environment) and first pillar (Capacity to Compete).

For each indicator, data tables include: the value and corresponding score for each indicator. In case of firm level indicators, details are provided by company size group (small, medium-sized, and large firms). Scores 1.5 times above or 0.5 times below the country-specific reference level are singled out as strengths (in green) and weaknesses (in red) respectively (refer to Annex I).

Each layer is given its own radar chart. Colours indicate pillars (blue for compete, purple for connect, and grey for change). Radar charts are based on scores: values are transformed and normalized, so that for each indicator in a sample of 111 countries, the worst value gets a score of 0, the best value gets a score of 100, with the median set at 50. The plain white area inside the radar charts reflects national statistics or firm level data averages for all firms. The solid grey line in all radar charts is the reference level that reflects the expected performance for individual indicators taking into account the level of development of each country. This reference level makes it therefore possible to identify strengths and weaknesses.

For the first layer on firm level capabilities (upper chart), small firms are indicated with a dotted black line, medium-sized firms are shown using a solid black line, and large firms are indicated with a dashed black line. Indicators for which data are not available appear as '-' in the tables and are not included in the radar charts.

Indicator scores are transformed such that higher is always better. Thus, the closer the indicator score is to the edge of the radar chart, the more competitive is the country. SME performance (dotted and solid lines) can be compared to the performance of large firms (dashed line); the distance between these lines represents the performance gap between small and large companies. All radar charts have a white inside area indicating countries' performance (for firm level data, this is calculated as an average across all firms). This means, the radar charts are comparable across layers, making it easy to analyse whether strengths (or weaknesses) lie in the immediate business environment, national environment or firm performance.

Section C: SME Competitiveness Grid summary (presented as a heat map)

Section C aggregates details of the SME Competitiveness Grid into an easy-to-read summary table where green highlights the country's strengths and red indicates weaknesses for each layer and pillar of competitiveness. Higher numbers indicate better outcomes, while lower numbers signal a room for improvement. For firm level capabilities, indicators are provided by company size, making it possible to single out SME performance and compare it to that of large firms.

The heat map also provides, for each component of the grid, the arithmetic mean of the scores of each indicator. The data is then presented in the format of a heat map; again, scores above or below the 50% reference level (last item in the key indicators) are singled out as strengths (in green) and weaknesses (in red). A note indicates the year of the World Bank Enterprise Survey used for each country (exhaustive data availability tables are provided in Annex III).

Section D: ITC Business Surveys on NTMs

Section D draws from data generated by ITC Business Surveys on NTMs (referred to as NTM Surveys). Each Country Profile includes four figures summarizing the key results by sector and company size whenever data availability allows. The section focuses on exporting companies (further information including dedicated country reports and results for importing companies are available at http://ntmsurvey.intracen.org/).

The NTM Surveys conducted by ITC since 2010 capture perceptions of the private sector of NTMs and related obstacles to trade, including underlying challenges in the immediate business environment and national environment. It was not possible to combine the information from the NTM surveys with the other information on SME competitiveness used in the grid, because of significant differences in country coverage and firm samples per country. Parallels can, nevertheless, easily be drawn between firm perceptions of NTMs on the one hand, and firms' or country performance in specific layers and pillars of the grid on the other hand.

For example, one can link the answers that companies provide on whether their difficulties relate to producing up-to-quality standards or demonstrating conformity to the Capacity to Compete pillar. This applies to different layers: firm level capacity and the immediate business environment (the availability of quality infrastructure in the country). Hence, the NTM Survey data complements the grid – making it possible to cross-check results and obtain additional insights.

ITC has completed the NTM Survey in all 25 countries included in the country profiles section, and the interviews are ongoing in further countries. The survey is large scale. In each country phone screening included 120 to over 1000 interviews, followed by 64 to over 400 in-depth face-to-face interviews with exporting and importing firms in all sectors except arms and minerals. For further details, please see Annex I providing technical notes on survey design and implementation.

This report makes a selective use of the most relevant questions, focusing on the following aspects reported by exporting companies.[3]

The top left figure 'Firms affected by NTMs' indicates the percentage of all phone-screened firms that declared being affected by NTMs and related obstacles to trade. A similar figure is provided for exporting firms (including firms that both import and export).

The top right bar chart 'NTMs reported as challenging (exporters)' specifies types of NTMs that companies find difficult. The information is collected during in-depth face-to-face interviews with those exporting firms that declared being affected by NTMs. The dot in each column indicates the share of affected companies in agriculture and manufacturing sectors (right scale) by company size. The colour of the bars specifies the type of NTM and whether it is applied by the home country of the exporter or by the partner country (importing country or transit country) and consists of the following broad categories:

- All home measures (regulating exports)
- Partner measures (regulating imports or transit)
  - Rules of origin
  - Non-technical (e.g. inspections, quantity control measures)
  - Technical (e.g. SPS measures)

Results are provided in a disaggregated format, because home measures are generally in the direct control of policymakers, while partner measures require bilateral, regional or multilateral coordination. Compliance with technical measures often requires a strong quality infrastructure, while non-technical measures are related to the business environment.

The left bar chart 'Regulatory and procedural obstacles (exporters)' provides further details on what exporting companies perceive as a challenge. For each case reported by companies, respondents were asked to specify reasons making it difficult to comply with NTMs. They fall into three broad categories:

- Regulatory obstacles (RO) (i.e. requirements specified in the regulation are too strict, e.g. pesticide limits),

- Procedural obstacles (PO) (procedures aimed at complying with the particular regulation are problematic, e.g. excessive paper work, discriminatory behaviour of officials),

- Combination of regulatory and procedural obstacles.

The bar chart provides a detailed breakdown on this distinction between regulatory and procedural obstacles, by sector and firm size. The figure specifies the percentage of NTM cases that involve ROs only, POs only, or both ROs and POs. This distinction is available for 15 of the 25 countries, while for the remaining 10 countries one can only distinguish whether a problem described involves a PO or whether the regulations are too strict. In another words, it is not possible to distinguish whether a reported PO is the primary (and only) cause of concern.

The figure 'Location of procedural obstacles (exporters)' provides details on POs that companies experience in their home country versus those experienced abroad. Each PO is associated with an NTM regulation, which can be enacted by either the home country or the partner (or transit) country. This can be demonstrated using two pie charts:

- The left-side pie chart provides information on NTMs enacted by the partner country, with colours indicating the location of POs reported in conjunction with these partner-imposed NTMs.

- The right-side pie chart shows NTMs enacted by the home country, with colours indicating the location of POs reported in conjunction with the NTMs required in the home country.

This approach shows the share of foreign-imposed regulations difficult for companies due to procedural obstacles at home. For example, an importing country requires that fruits are transported in fumigated containers. The exporter may find this requirement difficult – not because of the requirement per se, but because organizing the fumigation needed in the home country is being complicated by procedural obstacles, e.g. long waiting periods. The graph locating the problem provides an important starting point in searching for solutions and helps companies to overcome obstacles to trade and become more competitive.

Section E: Assessing potential for growth of current exports

Section E contains the top 20 products with the highest export potential, which is based on the Export Potential Assessment (EPA) methodology developed by ITC to help countries and TISIs assessing their export opportunities.

The EPA methodology is based on the calculation of composite indices using trade and market access data to identify existing products with high export potential or diversification opportunities, depending on the needs of the country:

- The Export Potential Indicator (EPI) serves countries that want to further exploit well-established export lines. It identifies products in which the exporting country has already proven to be internationally competitive, but for which the potential has not been yet fully exploited in all target markets.

- The Product Diversification Indicator (PDI) serves countries that want to diversify and develop new export sectors with promising demand in target markets. Based on a product-space approach (Hidalgo et al., 2007), it identifies products that the exporting country does not yet export competitively, but which seem feasible to export based on the country's current export basket and the export baskets of similar countries.

The 'Potential for Growth of Current Exports' represented in the country profiles, is based on the EPI by ITC. The PDI ranking is not included in the 25 country profiles, but the methodology for calculating PDI is explained in detail in Annex I, alongside the technical notes for calculating PDI.

In the figure on potential growth of current exports, a larger horizontal bar size indicates higher potential, while the black area of the pie chart indicates how much of this potential has not been utilized yet (unrealized potential). The information is provided for each country's own regional market with a view of promoting regional integration – for the group of developing country (South-South trade) and developed country markets. An empty cell in export potential means that the product was not consistently demanded over five years by any country in the respective region.

The right side of the table provides development indicators, refining the selection of promising products by combining trade policy objectives and social policy objectives. The indicators show the level of technology used in the production of each listed product, the stability of associated export revenues as well as the participation of SMEs and female labour in the sector to which the product belongs. Development markers are relative to the country's current situation, green indicating performance above its trade-weighted median (positive outcome) and red otherwise. This reflects that a given product, e.g. combed wool, may be a step up the value chain for one country, but not for others, or the wool processing sector may employ relatively more women in some countries, but not necessarily in others. Empty cells for development markers mean the data is not available.

Thus, the export potential results of country profiles highlight the product dimension of competitiveness based on revealed comparative advantage. A country's endowments have a strong impact on export potential and corresponding product rankings, while firms can increase their competitiveness by wisely selecting their export product portfolio and by strengthening their firm level capabilities (summarized in the first layer of the SME Competitiveness Grid).

Index of country profiles

Bangladesh

Key indicators

Population (millions)	158.2
GDP (US$ billions)	185.4
GDP per capita (US$)	1,171.9
Share of world GDP (PPP US$, %)	0.5
Current account surplus over GDP (%)	−0.1
Tariff preference margin (percentage points)	8.5
Goods and services imports + exports over GDP (%)	46.3
Exports of services over total exports (%)	10.9
Geographic region	South Asia
Development group	LDC
Income group	Lower-middle income

SME Competitiveness Grid Summary

Average scores [0–100]		Compete	Connect	Change
FIRM LEVEL CAPABILITIES	Small	36.9	3.0	18.0
	Medium	48.2	8.7	30.5
	Large	71.5	57.9	62.2
	All	49.2	16.2	38.3
IMMEDIATE BUSINESS ENVIRONMENT		48.6	40.6	52.4
NATIONAL ENVIRONMENT		29.5	23.7	31.6

Reference level: 36.6 (a function of GDP per capita US$)

Strengths are scores above: 54.9	Weaknesses are scores below: 18.3

SME Competitiveness Grid

1	FIRM LEVEL CAPABILITIES	Values				Normalized scores			
		Small	Medium	Large	All	Small	Medium	Large	All
1.1	Capacity to Compete								
1.1.1	Firms with quality certification (%)	4.9	9.2	34.6	14.3	17.4	28.2	63.2	38.1
1.1.2	Firms with checking or savings account (%)	70.5	93.7	98.8	86.4	18.0	45.2	71.8	31.8
1.1.3	Capacity utilization (%)	79.0	83.2	88.8	84.0	60.0	71.4	90.0	73.8
1.1.4	Manager's experience (years)	18.1	16.9	20.5	18.3	52.2	47.8	60.9	52.9
1.2	Capacity to Connect								
1.2.1	Firms using e-mail (%)	12.0	25.2	86.0	36.6	1.0	5.6	49.9	10.2
1.2.2	Firms having their own website (%)	6.0	14.3	70.8	26.3	4.9	11.8	65.9	22.3
1.3	Capacity to Change								
1.3.1	Firms with audited financial statements (%)	20.6	25.8	75.7	37.2	14.3	18.6	68.1	28.5
1.3.2	Investments financed by banks (%)	10.3	10.4	15.4	12.4	39.5	39.8	51.4	44.8
1.3.3	Firms offering formal training (%)	8.8	15.1	49.3	21.9	11.7	19.6	56.8	27.7
1.3.4	Firms using foreign technology licences (%)	1.0	12.3	33.6	16.7	6.4	43.9	72.6	52.0

2	IMMEDIATE BUSINESS ENVIRONMENT	Values				Normalized scores			
		Small	Medium	Large	All	Small	Medium	Large	All
2.1	Capacity to Compete								
2.1.1	Losses due to power outages (% of sales)	4.8	3.3	2.8	3.7	27.9	33.6	36.0	31.8
2.1.2	Losses during domestic shipping (%)	0.7	0.8	0.4	0.7	51.2	48.8	61.0	51.2
2.1.3	Management time spent with regulation (%)	1.9	3.0	5.5	3.3	76.9	69.0	56.5	67.2
2.1.4	Days for customs clearance	9.8	8.6	8.7	8.8	40.5	44.7	44.4	44.0
2.2	Capacity to Connect								
2.2.1	State of cluster development (1–7)				3.8				60.4
2.2.2	Extent of marketing (1–7)				3.5				33.6
2.2.3	Local supplier quality (1–7)				3.9				44.2
2.2.4	University-industry collaboration in R&D (1–7)				2.6				24.1
2.3	Capacity to Change								
2.3.1	Access to finance as a constraint (%)	26.5	22.7	17.6	22.8	42.6	47.7	55.5	47.5
2.3.2	Inadequately educated workforce (%)	12.9	14.4	21.2	15.7	61.4	58.6	47.9	56.3
2.3.3	Business licensing and permits as a constraint (%)	6.9	9.0	11.9	9.0	59.5	53.4	46.7	53.4

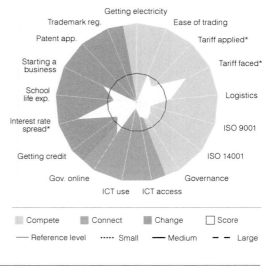

3	NATIONAL ENVIRONMENT	Values	Normalized scores
		All	All
3.1	Capacity to Compete		
3.1.1	Ease of getting electricity (0–100)	17.3	0.5
3.1.2	Ease of trading across borders (0–100)	61.4	38.5
3.1.3	Applied tariff, trade-weighted average (%)	13.6	26.4
3.1.4	Faced tariff, trade-weighted average (%)	2.9	67.5
3.1.5	Logistics performance index (1–5)	2.6	41.5
3.1.6	ISO 9001 quality certificates (/mn pop.)	1.7	16.9
3.1.7	ISO 14001 environmental certificates (/mn pop.)	0.4	20.4
3.1.8	Governance (index)	−0.9	24.5
3.2	Capacity to Connect		
3.2.1	ICT access (0–10)	2.6	18.1
3.2.2	ICT use (0–10)	0.3	7.2
3.2.3	Government's online service (0–10)	3.5	45.8
3.3	Capacity to Change		
3.3.1	Ease of getting credit (0–100)	30.0	29.4
3.3.2	Interest rate spread (%)	1.8	75.8
3.3.3	School life expectancy (years)	10.0	27.9
3.3.4	Ease of starting a business (0–100)	81.4	45.9
3.3.5	Patent applications (/mn pop.)	1.0	0.0
3.3.6	Trademark registrations (/mn pop.)	51.0	10.8

Legend: Compete, Connect, Change, Score, Reference level, Small, Medium, Large

Note: For each indicator, the table includes the values and the corresponding scores. Radar charts are based on scores: values are transformed and normalized so that for each indicator in a sample of 111 countries, the worst value gets a score of 0, the best value gets a score of 100, and the median gets a score of 50. If in the original values higher numbers indicate worse outcomes, the chart labels are marked with an asterisk (*). Series with missing data are indicated as (-) in the tables and omitted from the radar charts.

Source: World Bank Enterprise Survey (2013) for firm level data; for other sources refer to Annex III.

Potential for Growth of Current Exports

PRODUCT/PRODUCT GROUP DESCRIPTION	Exports (US$ mn)	What is the product's export potential in...?						Would Bangladesh improve its...?			
		South Asia	Unrealized potential	South-South trade	Unrealized potential	OECD	Unrealized potential	Technology level	Revenues stability	SME presence	Female participation
620342 Mens/boys trousers and shorts, o...	3379.7		31%		50%		20%				
610910 T-shirts, singlets and other vests...	3809.1		59%		37%		9%				
620462 Womens/girls trousers and shorts...	1647.7		29%		38%		19%				
620520 Mens/boys shirts, of cotton, not k...	1266.7		21%		57%		29%				
611020 Pullovers, cardigans and similar, a...	1567.1		18%		36%		26%				
611030 Pullovers, cardigans and similar ar...	1014.0		54%		31%		13%				
610510 Mens/boys shirts, of cotton, knitted	639.5		37%		55%		24%				
530710 Yarn of jute or of other textile bast...	307.2		77%		60%		68%				
0306Xa Crustaceans	443.7		93%		69%		49%				
610462 Womens/girls trousers and shorts...	367.7		80%		62%		29%				
611120 Babies garments and clothing...	286.0		46%		42%		38%				
530310 Jute and other textile bast fibres...	210.1		62%		52%		46%				
6403XX Footwear, upper of leather	208.0		68%		69%		65%				
620630 Womens/girls blouses and shirts...	276.8		79%		31%		28%				
620920 Babies garments and clothing ac...	220.9		56%		58%		39%				
610990 T-shirts, singlets and other vests, o...	244.1		45%		37%		14%				
620343 Mens/boys trousers and shorts...	227.9		17%		68%		32%				
610610 Womens/girls blouses and shirts...	218.1		81%		41%		29%				
630510 Sacks&bags,for packg of goods...	150.8		46%		39%		59%				
530720 Yarn of jute or of oth textile bast ...	128.3		36%		29%		57%				

Note: Top 20 products listed in decreasing order of their export potential to the world. Development indicators are relative to the country's current situation, green indicating performance above its trade-weighted median and red otherwise; a blank cell indicates data are not available. A blank cell in export potential means that the product was not consistently demanded over five years by any country in the respective region. Exports (US$ mn) corresponds to the yearly average exports to the world over the period 2009-13. Refer to Annexes I, II and III for details.

Source: ITC Export Potential Assessment, additional results are available at ITC Country Pages http://www.intracen.org/country/bangladesh/

Burkina Faso

Key indicators

Population (millions)	17.4
GDP (US$ billions)	12.5
GDP per capita (US$)	717.4
Share of world GDP (PPP US$, %)	0.0
Current account surplus over GDP (%)	−6.1
Tariff preference margin (percentage points)	0.8
Goods and services imports + exports over GDP (%)	60.7
Exports of services over total exports (%)	22.0
Geographic region	Sub-Saharan Africa
Development group	LDC, LLDC
Income group	Low income

SME Competitiveness Grid Summary

Average scores [0–100]		Compete	Connect	Change
FIRM LEVEL CAPABILITIES	Small	43.3	11.8	28.3
	Medium	48.5	31.6	43.0
	Large	63.7	37.9	65.3
	All	45.9	17.8	36.7
IMMEDIATE BUSINESS ENVIRONMENT		37.0	35.4	23.1
NATIONAL ENVIRONMENT		30.3	23.0	28.5

Reference level: 32.5 (a function of GDP per capita US$)

Strengths are scores above: 48.7	Weaknesses are scores below: 16.2

SME Competitiveness Grid

1	FIRM LEVEL CAPABILITIES	Values				Normalized scores			
		Small	Medium	Large	All	Small	Medium	Large	All
1.1	**Capacity to Compete**								
1.1.1	Firms with quality certification (%)	11.7	14.4	35.7	14.4	33.4	38.3	64.2	38.3
1.1.2	Firms with checking or savings account (%)	96.8	95.6	100.0	96.8	56.6	51.3	100.0	56.6
1.1.3	Capacity utilization (%)	71.4	77.7	70.1	72.9	42.8	56.7	40.2	45.9
1.1.4	Manager's experience (years)	14.9	16.9	17.6	15.6	40.3	47.8	50.4	43.0
1.2	**Capacity to Connect**								
1.2.1	Firms using e-mail (%)	48.3	77.1	76.8	57.5	15.9	37.7	37.3	21.3
1.2.2	Firms having their own website (%)	9.3	29.9	43.9	17.2	7.6	25.5	38.5	14.3
1.3	**Capacity to Change**								
1.3.1	Firms with audited financial statements (%)	37.4	54.3	88.0	46.0	28.7	44.8	83.3	36.7
1.3.2	Investments financed by banks (%)	14.6	14.0	24.3	15.6	49.7	48.4	66.9	51.8
1.3.3	Firms offering formal training (%)	17.2	39.8	39.6	24.8	22.1	47.3	47.1	31.0
1.3.4	Firms using foreign technology licences (%)	2.2	7.2	25.2	5.9	12.8	31.5	63.8	27.5

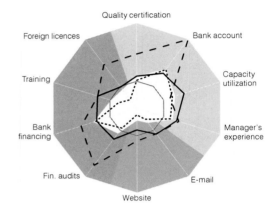

2	IMMEDIATE BUSINESS ENVIRONMENT	Values				Normalized scores			
		Small	Medium	Large	All	Small	Medium	Large	All
2.1	**Capacity to Compete**								
2.1.1	Losses due to power outages (% of sales)	4.0	1.6	1.1	3.2	30.6	44.4	50.0	34.0
2.1.2	Losses during domestic shipping (%)	0.3	1.1	0.9	0.5	65.8	43.0	46.7	57.2
2.1.3	Management time spent with regulation (%)	20.0	29.4	20.0	22.2	24.6	14.3	24.6	21.9
2.1.4	Days for customs clearance	23.3	10.6	5.3	11.7	11.3	37.9	60.0	34.8
2.2	**Capacity to Connect**								
2.2.1	State of cluster development (1–7)				2.9				25.7
2.2.2	Extent of marketing (1–7)				3.1				21.6
2.2.3	Local supplier quality (1–7)				4.1				49.8
2.2.4	University-industry collaboration in R&D (1–7)				3.2				44.3
2.3	**Capacity to Change**								
2.3.1	Access to finance as a constraint (%)	80.2	66.0	59.7	75.0	0.0	8.1	12.2	2.8
2.3.2	Inadequately educated workforce (%)	33.8	43.4	47.5	37.5	33.2	24.8	21.7	29.8
2.3.3	Business licensing and permits as a constraint (%)	19.9	13.8	10.9	17.6	33.5	43.0	48.9	36.8

3	NATIONAL ENVIRONMENT	Values	Normalized scores
		All	All
3.1	**Capacity to Compete**		
3.1.1	Ease of getting electricity (0–100)	40.8	18.5
3.1.2	Ease of trading across borders (0–100)	29.5	13.4
3.1.3	Applied tariff, trade-weighted average (%)	10.4	35.2
3.1.4	Faced tariff, trade-weighted average (%)	3.5	52.3
3.1.5	Logistics performance index (1–5)	2.6	44.8
3.1.6	ISO 9001 quality certificates (/mn pop.)	2.6	21.3
3.1.7	ISO 14001 environmental certificates (/mn pop.)	0.2	14.0
3.1.8	Governance (index)	−0.5	43.1
3.2	**Capacity to Connect**		
3.2.1	ICT access (0–10)	2.5	16.1
3.2.2	ICT use (0–10)	0.5	12.4
3.2.3	Government's online service (0–10)	3.0	40.5
3.3	**Capacity to Change**		
3.3.1	Ease of getting credit (0–100)	30.0	29.4
3.3.2	Interest rate spread (%)	9.0	45.1
3.3.3	School life expectancy (years)	7.8	9.6
3.3.4	Ease of starting a business (0–100)	69.1	30.0
3.3.5	Patent applications (/mn pop.)	-	-
3.3.6	Trademark registrations (/mn pop.)	-	-

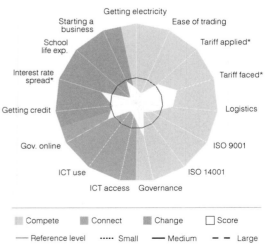

Compete	Connect	Change	☐ Score
— Reference level	····· Small	— Medium	– – Large

Note: For each indicator, the table includes the values and the corresponding scores. Radar charts are based on scores: values are transformed and normalized so that for each indicator in a sample of 111 countries, the worst value gets a score of 0, the best value gets a score of 100, and the median gets a score of 50. If in the original values higher numbers indicate worse outcomes, the chart labels are marked with an asterisk (*). Series with missing data are indicated as (-) in the tables and omitted from the radar charts.

Source: World Bank Enterprise Survey (2009) for firm level data; for other sources refer to Annex III.

ITC Business Survey on Non-Tariff Measures (NTMs)

1. Firms affected by NTMs

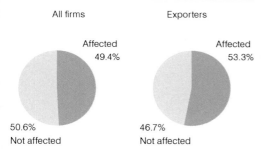

All firms

Affected
49.4%

50.6%
Not affected

Exporters

Affected
53.3%

46.7%
Not affected

2. NTMs reported as challenging (exporters)

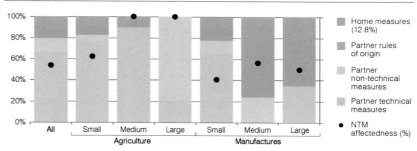

Legend:
- Home measures (12.8%)
- Partner rules of origin
- Partner non-technical measures
- Partner technical measures
- ● NTM affectedness (%)

Categories: All | Small, Medium, Large (Agriculture) | Small, Medium, Large (Manufactures)

3. Regulatory and procedural obstacles (exporters)

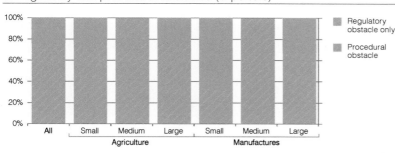

Legend:
- Regulatory obstacle only
- Procedural obstacle

Categories: All | Small, Medium, Large (Agriculture) | Small, Medium, Large (Manufactures)

4. Location of procedural obstacles (exporters)

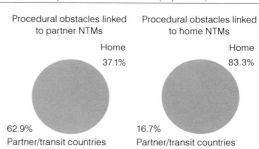

Procedural obstacles linked to partner NTMs

Home 37.1%

62.9%
Partner/transit countries

Procedural obstacles linked to home NTMs

Home 83.3%

16.7%
Partner/transit countries

Source: ITC NTM Survey, additional results are available at http://ntmsurvey.intracen.org/ntm-survey-data/country-analysis/burkina-faso/

Potential for Growth of Current Exports

PRODUCT/PRODUCT GROUP DESCRIPTION	Exports (US$ mn)	Sub-Saharan Africa	Unrealized potential	South-South trade	Unrealized potential	OECD	Unrealized potential	Technology level	Revenues stability	SME presence	Female participation
710813 Gold in oth semi-manufactd form...	633.6		3%		79%		6%	■	■	■	■
520100 Cotton, not carded or combed	313.2		97%		36%		40%	■	■		
120740 Sesamum seeds, whether or not b...	63.6		58%		55%		67%	■	■		
1515XX Veg fats&oils nes&their fractions,r...	5.2		73%		72%		88%	■		■	■
080450 Guavas, mangoes and mangoste...	7.4		87%		88%		80%				
230610 Cotton sed oil-cake&oth solid resi...	2.7		90%		90%		82%	■		■	■
080131 Cashew nuts, in shell, fresh or dried	19.1		68%		46%		73%	■			
080132 Cashew nuts, without shell, fresh...	4.4		99%		86%		74%				
560129 Waddg of oth textile materials&arti...	1.3		86%		87%		100%	■		■	■
1207Xa Oil seeds	12.8		43%		45%		84%	■			
721420 Bars & rods,i/nas,hr,hd or he,cntg...	3.3		51%		56%		100%	■			■
070310 Onions and shallots, fresh or chilled	1.7		64%		65%		100%	■			
0713Xa Dried vegetables, shelled	1.3		66%		68%		100%	■			
970300 Original sculptures and statuary,...	0.3		95%		94%		95%	■			
151229 Cotton-seed and its fractions refin...	0.6		84%		84%		100%	■		■	■
41XXXc Raw hides and skins (other than f...	2.2		97%		94%		88%	■		■	■
1008Xa Buckwheat, millet and canary seed	0.2		96%		96%		100%	■			
100590 Maize (corn) nes	2.9		10%		28%		95%	■		■	
071333 Kidney beans&white pea beans dr...	1.5		95%		95%		89%	■			
070200 Tomatoes, fresh or chilled	2.4		2%		9%		100%	■			

Column group headers: What is the product's export potential in...? | Would Burkina Faso improve its...?

Note: Top 20 products listed in decreasing order of their export potential to the world. Development indicators are relative to the country's current situation, green indicating performance above its trade-weighted median and red otherwise; a blank cell indicates data are not available. A blank cell in export potential means that the product was not consistently demanded over five years by any country in the respective region. Exports (US$ mn) corresponds to the yearly average exports to the world over the period 2009-13. Refer to Annexes I, II and III for details.

Source: ITC Export Potential Assessment, additional results are available at ITC Country Pages http://www.intracen.org/country/burkina_faso/

Cambodia

Key indicators

Population (millions)	15.3
GDP (US$ billions)	16.6
GDP per capita (US$)	1,080.8
Share of world GDP (PPP US$, %)	0.0
Current account surplus over GDP (%)	−12.0
Tariff preference margin (percentage points)	7.6
Goods and services imports + exports over GDP (%)	175.0
Exports of services over total exports (%)	21.7
Geographic region	East Asia & Pacific
Development group	LDC
Income group	Low income

SME Competitiveness Grid Summary

Average scores [0–100]		Compete	Connect	Change
FIRM LEVEL CAPABILITIES	Small	32.0	21.1	37.5
	Medium	28.3	29.3	33.7
	Large	40.0	61.6	49.1
	All	31.5	24.2	38.6
IMMEDIATE BUSINESS ENVIRONMENT		77.7	45.4	54.6
NATIONAL ENVIRONMENT		42.8	25.9	35.1

Reference level: 35.9 (a function of GDP per capita US$)	
Strengths are scores above: 53.9	Weaknesses are scores below: 18.0

SME Competitiveness Grid

1	FIRM LEVEL CAPABILITIES	Values				Normalized scores			
		Small	Medium	Large	All	Small	Medium	Large	All
1.1	Capacity to Compete								
1.1.1	Firms with quality certification (%)	8.6	10.5	17.4	9.5	26.9	31.0	43.1	28.9
1.1.2	Firms with checking or savings account (%)	29.9	41.0	75.2	35.0	2.5	5.6	21.1	3.9
1.1.3	Capacity utilization (%)	81.5	74.0	77.3	79.7	66.6	48.2	55.8	61.8
1.1.4	Manager's experience (years)	-	-	-	-	-	-	-	-
1.2	Capacity to Connect								
1.2.1	Firms using e-mail (%)	42.0	62.7	93.8	49.1	12.7	24.8	67.7	16.3
1.2.2	Firms having their own website (%)	34.4	39.0	61.0	37.1	29.6	33.9	55.5	32.1
1.3	Capacity to Change								
1.3.1	Firms with audited financial statements (%)	14.2	15.6	45.4	16.8	9.2	10.3	36.1	11.3
1.3.2	Investments financed by banks (%)	4.4	3.1	0.9	3.9	20.9	15.6	5.1	18.9
1.3.3	Firms offering formal training (%)	66.0	68.8	85.9	67.9	72.3	74.8	89.1	74.0
1.3.4	Firms using foreign technology licences (%)	14.2	8.2	27.1	15.7	47.7	34.3	66.0	50.3

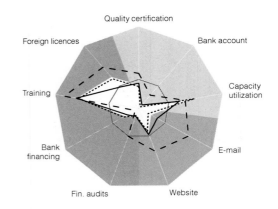

2	IMMEDIATE BUSINESS ENVIRONMENT	Values				Normalized scores			
		Small	Medium	Large	All	Small	Medium	Large	All
2.1	Capacity to Compete								
2.1.1	Losses due to power outages (% of sales)	0.2	0.7	0.8	0.3	73.7	56.6	54.7	68.4
2.1.2	Losses during domestic shipping (%)	-	-	-	-	-	-	-	-
2.1.3	Management time spent with regulation (%)	1.1	1.6	2.0	1.3	84.5	79.6	76.1	82.4
2.1.4	Days for customs clearance	-	2.1	2.5	2.5	-	86.8	81.7	82.2
2.2	Capacity to Connect								
2.2.1	State of cluster development (1–7)				3.9				60.9
2.2.2	Extent of marketing (1–7)				4.0				48.8
2.2.3	Local supplier quality (1–7)				3.5				33.5
2.2.4	University-industry collaboration in R&D (1–7)				3.0				38.4
2.3	Capacity to Change								
2.3.1	Access to finance as a constraint (%)	14.0	16.9	10.5	14.2	61.9	56.7	69.1	61.5
2.3.2	Inadequately educated workforce (%)	25.8	26.3	44.6	27.3	41.9	41.3	23.9	40.1
2.3.3	Business licensing and permits as a constraint (%)	4.3	10.4	15.6	6.1	69.2	50.0	39.9	62.2

3	NATIONAL ENVIRONMENT	Values	Normalized scores
		All	All
3.1	Capacity to Compete		
3.1.1	Ease of getting electricity (0–100)	62.4	39.8
3.1.2	Ease of trading across borders (0–100)	65.9	43.5
3.1.3	Applied tariff, trade-weighted average (%)	9.2	38.9
3.1.4	Faced tariff, trade-weighted average (%)	2.2	100.0
3.1.5	Logistics performance index (1–5)	2.7	49.2
3.1.6	ISO 9001 quality certificates (/mn pop.)	1.2	13.8
3.1.7	ISO 14001 environmental certificates (/mn pop.)	0.5	24.1
3.1.8	Governance (index)	−0.7	33.0
3.2	Capacity to Connect		
3.2.1	ICT access (0–10)	3.7	37.4
3.2.2	ICT use (0–10)	0.6	15.1
3.2.3	Government's online service (0–10)	1.7	25.1
3.3	Capacity to Change		
3.3.1	Ease of getting credit (0–100)	80.0	82.7
3.3.2	Interest rate spread (%)	-	-
3.3.3	School life expectancy (years)	10.9	35.7
3.3.4	Ease of starting a business (0–100)	41.2	9.1
3.3.5	Patent applications (/mn pop.)	-	-
3.3.6	Trademark registrations (/mn pop.)	64.0	13.1

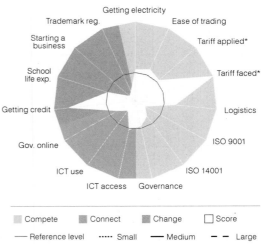

Note: For each indicator, the table includes the values and the corresponding scores. Radar charts are based on scores: values are transformed and normalized so that for each indicator in a sample of 111 countries, the worst value gets a score of 0, the best value gets a score of 100, and the median gets a score of 50. If in the original values higher numbers indicate worse outcomes, the chart labels are marked with an asterisk (*). Series with missing data are indicated as (-) in the tables and omitted from the radar charts.

Source: World Bank Enterprise Survey (2013) for firm level data; for other sources refer to Annex III.

ITC Business Survey on Non-Tariff Measures (NTMs)

1. Firms affected by NTMs

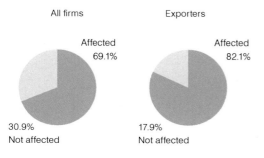

All firms

Affected
69.1%

30.9%
Not affected

Exporters

Affected
82.1%

17.9%
Not affected

2. NTMs reported as challenging (exporters)

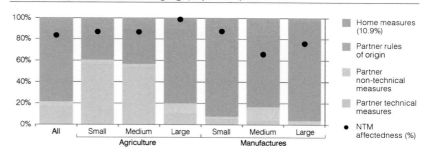

- Home measures (10.9%)
- Partner rules of origin
- Partner non-technical measures
- Partner technical measures
- NTM affectedness (%)

3. Regulatory and procedural obstacles (exporters)

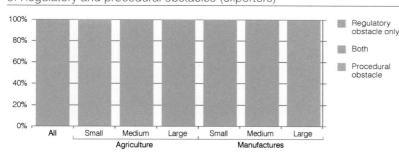

- Regulatory obstacle only
- Both
- Procedural obstacle

4. Location of procedural obstacles (exporters)

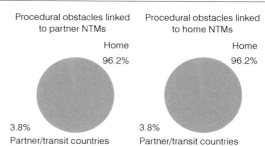

Procedural obstacles linked to partner NTMs

Home
96.2%

3.8%
Partner/transit countries

Procedural obstacles linked to home NTMs

Home
96.2%

3.8%
Partner/transit countries

Source: ITC NTM Survey, additional results are available at http://ntmsurvey.intracen.org/ntm-survey-data/country-analysis/cambodia/

Potential for Growth of Current Exports

PRODUCT/PRODUCT GROUP DESCRIPTION	Exports (US$ mn)	East Asia & Pacific	Unrealized potential	South-South trade	Unrealized potential	OECD	Unrealized potential	Technology level	Revenues stability	SME presence	Female participation
611020 Pullovers, cardigans and similar, a...	724.9		78%		76%		14%				
071410 Manioc (cassava), fresh or dried,...	111.4		77%		77%		100%				
6403XX Footwear, upper of leather	362.8		48%		61%		58%				
611030 Pullovers, cardigans and similar ar...	431.8		78%		69%		11%				
620462 Womens/girls trousers and shorts...	341.8		54%		75%		18%				
610910 T-shirts, singlets and other vests,...	367.9		62%		65%		16%				
610462 Womens/girls trousers and shorts...	245.0		91%		90%		21%				
620342 Mens/boys trousers and shorts, o...	318.6		37%		57%		21%				
400122 Technically specified natural rubb...	175.7		30%		29%		94%				
871200 Bicycles and other cycles (include...	196.3		84%		82%		58%				
611120 Babies garments and clothing acc...	112.4		57%		60%		54%				
610220 Womens/girls overcoats, anoraks...	98.1		92%		83%		43%				
610990 T-shirts, singlets and other vests, o...	147.6		76%		62%		15%				
610510 Mens/boys shirts, of cotton, knitted	101.3		70%		71%		18%				
6402XX Footwear nes, outer soles and up...	110.2		58%		70%		43%				
610832 Womens/girls nightdresses and...	76.9		89%		88%		38%				
610610 Womens/girls blouses and shirts...	78.2		83%		86%		28%				
640419 Footwear o/t sports,w outer soles...	83.7		60%		59%		49%				
710813 Gold in oth semi-manufactd form...	108.9		46%		48%		100%				
610463 Womens/girls trousers and shorts...	89.0		76%		69%		21%				

What is the product's export potential in...?

Would Cambodia improve its...?

Note: Top 20 products listed in decreasing order of their export potential to the world. Development indicators are relative to the country's current situation, green indicating performance above its trade-weighted median and red otherwise; a blank cell indicates data are not available. A blank cell in export potential means that the product was not consistently demanded over five years by any country in the respective region. Exports (US$ mn) corresponds to the yearly average exports to the world over the period 2009-13. Refer to Annexes I, II and III for details.

Source: ITC Export Potential Assessment, additional results are available at ITC Country Pages http://www.intracen.org/country/cambodia/

Colombia

Key indicators

Population (millions)	47.7
GDP (US$ billions)	384.9
GDP per capita (US$)	8,075.6
Share of world GDP (PPP US$, %)	0.6
Current account surplus over GDP (%)	-5.0
Tariff preference margin (percentage points)	2.6
Goods and services imports + exports over GDP (%)	35.2
Exports of services over total exports (%)	8.8
Geographic region	LAC
Development group	DC
Income group	Upper-middle income

SME Competitiveness Grid Summary

Average scores [0–100]		Compete	Connect	Change
FIRM LEVEL CAPABILITIES	Small	47.0	60.4	45.6
	Medium	66.9	85.0	57.8
	Large	84.4	94.4	79.5
	All	54.9	67.6	55.1
IMMEDIATE BUSINESS ENVIRONMENT		41.6	59.6	33.4
NATIONAL ENVIRONMENT		57.7	68.6	57.9

Reference level: 52.9 (a function of GDP per capita US$)	
Strengths are scores above: 79.4	Weaknesses are scores below: 26.5

SME Competitiveness Grid

1 FIRM LEVEL CAPABILITIES

		Values				Normalized scores			
		Small	Medium	Large	All	Small	Medium	Large	All
1.1	Capacity to Compete								
1.1.1	Firms with quality certification (%)	11.8	23.8	77.9	20.8	33.6	51.8	90.9	48.0
1.1.2	Firms with checking or savings account (%)	94.3	99.8	100.0	95.8	46.9	91.2	100.0	52.1
1.1.3	Capacity utilization (%)	64.6	74.8	80.4	71.2	30.1	50.0	63.6	42.4
1.1.4	Manager's experience (years)	25.2	24.4	26.9	25.2	77.3	74.6	83.1	77.3
1.2	Capacity to Connect								
1.2.1	Firms using e-mail (%)	98.7	99.9	100.0	99.1	89.7	99.1	100.0	92.5
1.2.2	Firms having their own website (%)	36.0	75.4	90.9	48.2	31.1	70.9	88.8	42.7
1.3	Capacity to Change								
1.3.1	Firms with audited financial statements (%)	47.3	57.2	90.7	53.5	37.9	47.7	86.9	44.0
1.3.2	Investments financed by banks (%)	9.9	24.9	56.0	21.2	38.5	67.8	100.0	62.0
1.3.3	Firms offering formal training (%)	63.6	53.7	94.2	65.2	70.2	61.0	95.6	71.6
1.3.4	Firms using foreign technology licences (%)	8.8	18.3	8.6	11.8	35.9	54.6	35.4	42.9

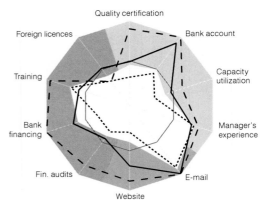

2 IMMEDIATE BUSINESS ENVIRONMENT

		Values				Normalized scores			
		Small	Medium	Large	All	Small	Medium	Large	All
2.1	Capacity to Compete								
2.1.1	Losses due to power outages (% of sales)	0.5	1.0	0.0	0.5	61.4	51.4	100.0	61.4
2.1.2	Losses during domestic shipping (%)	1.2	1.7	0.9	1.3	41.4	34.9	46.7	39.9
2.1.3	Management time spent with regulation (%)	12.4	15.7	12.2	12.9	37.0	31.0	37.4	36.0
2.1.4	Days for customs clearance	16.9	6.4	17.8	13.9	22.4	54.2	20.6	29.0
2.2	Capacity to Connect								
2.2.1	State of cluster development (1–7)				3.7				56.0
2.2.2	Extent of marketing (1–7)				4.0				49.1
2.2.3	Local supplier quality (1–7)				4.8				67.9
2.2.4	University-industry collaboration in R&D (1–7)				3.9				65.4
2.3	Capacity to Change								
2.3.1	Access to finance as a constraint (%)	51.6	15.7	11.6	41.4	18.0	58.8	66.7	26.6
2.3.2	Inadequately educated workforce (%)	50.6	31.1	23.2	44.5	19.5	36.0	45.2	23.9
2.3.3	Business licensing and permits as a constraint (%)	10.2	9.2	15.0	10.5	50.5	52.9	40.9	49.8

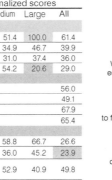

3 NATIONAL ENVIRONMENT

		Values	Normalized scores
		All	All
3.1	Capacity to Compete		
3.1.1	Ease of getting electricity (0–100)	74.2	54.3
3.1.2	Ease of trading across borders (0–100)	72.7	52.3
3.1.3	Applied tariff, trade-weighted average (%)	6.4	50.3
3.1.4	Faced tariff, trade-weighted average (%)	3.5	52.4
3.1.5	Logistics performance index (1–5)	2.6	44.9
3.1.6	ISO 9001 quality certificates (/mn pop.)	284.2	80.8
3.1.7	ISO 14001 environmental certificates (/mn pop.)	59.1	76.6
3.1.8	Governance (index)	-0.3	49.7
3.2	Capacity to Connect		
3.2.1	ICT access (0–10)	5.4	61.0
3.2.2	ICT use (0–10)	3.1	58.5
3.2.3	Government's online service (0–10)	7.9	86.2
3.3	Capacity to Change		
3.3.1	Ease of getting credit (0–100)	95.0	100.0
3.3.2	Interest rate spread (%)	6.8	48.8
3.3.3	School life expectancy (years)	13.5	57.7
3.3.4	Ease of starting a business (0–100)	86.1	54.7
3.3.5	Patent applications (/mn pop.)	5.0	41.6
3.3.6	Trademark registrations (/mn pop.)	399.0	44.7

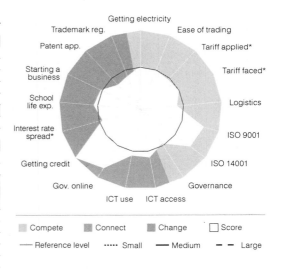

Legend: Compete · Connect · Change · Score · Reference level · Small · Medium · Large

Note: For each indicator, the table includes the values and the corresponding scores. Radar charts are based on scores: values are transformed and normalized so that for each indicator in a sample of 111 countries, the worst value gets a score of 0, the best value gets a score of 100, and the median gets a score of 50. If in the original values higher numbers indicate worse outcomes, the chart labels are marked with an asterisk (*). Series with missing data are indicated as (-) in the tables and omitted from the radar charts.

Source: World Bank Enterprise Survey (2010) for firm level data; for other sources refer to Annex III.

ITC Business Survey on Non-Tariff Measures (NTMs)

1. Firms affected by NTMs

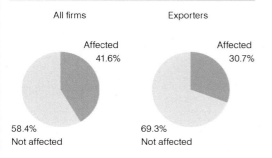

All firms

Affected 41.6%

58.4% Not affected

Exporters

Affected 30.7%

69.3% Not affected

2. NTMs reported as challenging (exporters)

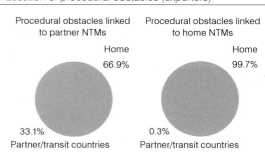

- Home measures (25.2%)
- Partner rules of origin
- Partner non-technical measures
- Partner technical measures
- ● NTM affectedness (%)

(x-axis: All | Small, Medium, Large — Agriculture | Small, Medium, Large — Manufactures)

3. Regulatory and procedural obstacles (exporters)

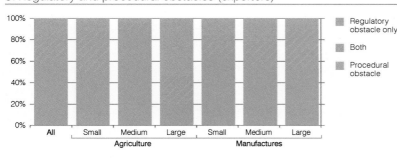

- Regulatory obstacle only
- Both
- Procedural obstacle

(x-axis: All | Small, Medium, Large — Agriculture | Small, Medium, Large — Manufactures)

4. Location of procedural obstacles (exporters)

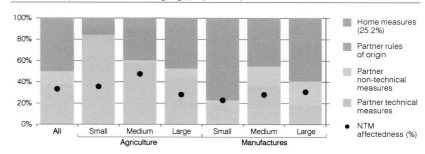

Procedural obstacles linked to partner NTMs

Home 66.9%

33.1% Partner/transit countries

Procedural obstacles linked to home NTMs

Home 99.7%

0.3% Partner/transit countries

Source: ITC NTM Survey, additional results are available at http://ntmsurvey.intracen.org/ntm-survey-data/country-analysis/colombia

Potential for Growth of Current Exports

| PRODUCT/PRODUCT GROUP DESCRIPTION | Exports (US$ mn) | What is the product's export potential in…? | | | | | | Would Colombia improve its…? | | | |
		Latin America and the Caribbean	Unrealized potential	South-South trade	Unrealized potential	OECD	Unrealized potential	Technology level	Revenues stability	SME presence	Female participation
090111 Coffee, not roasted, not decaffein…	2021.5		99%		94%		30%	■	■		
0803XX Bananas and plantains, fresh or…	1287.0		99%		86%		37%	■	■		
0603XX Cut flowers and flower buds for…	1098.9		89%		64%		16%	■			
720260 Ferro-nickel	781.0		23%		2%		22%	■	■	■	■
170199 Refined sugar, in solid form, nes	351.2		49%		60%		22%	■	■	■	■
170490 Sugar confectionery nes (includin…	226.1		54%		54%		65%	■	■	■	■
390410 Polyvinyl chloride, not mixed with…	279.5		69%		69%		65%	■	■	■	■
3808Xb Fungicides	189.2		67%		69%		25%	■	■	■	■
0102XX Live bovine animals	142.1		61%		62%		100%	■	■	■	■
210111 Coffee extracts, essences, concen…	253.4		84%		84%		13%	■	■	■	■
96XXXX Sanitary towels (pads) and tamp…	185.6		47%		50%		60%	■	■	■	■
390210 Polypropylene	211.4		15%		19%		71%	■	■	■	■
340111 Toilet soap & prep, shaped; papers…	63.0		62%		63%		87%	■	■	■	■
330300 Perfumes and toilet waters	104.3		39%		44%		78%	■	■	■	■
170410 Chewing gum containing sugar, e…	48.8		79%		79%		45%	■	■	■	■
3808Xa Insecticides	64.9		57%		55%		88%	■	■	■	■
870323 Automobiles w reciprocatg piston…	204.6		32%		61%		90%	■	■	■	■
300490 Medicaments nes, in dosage	298.9		7%		20%		83%	■	■	■	■
151110 Palm oil, crude	119.4		54%		78%		25%	■	■	■	■
330590 Hair preparations, nes	57.7		49%		49%		79%	■	■	■	■

Note: Top 20 products listed in decreasing order of their export potential to the world. Development indicators are relative to the country's current situation, green indicating performance above its trade-weighted median and red otherwise; a blank cell indicates data are not available. A blank cell in export potential means that the product was not consistently demanded over five years by any country in the respective region. Exports (US$ mn) corresponds to the yearly average exports to the world over the period 2009-13. Refer to Annexes I, II and III for details.

Source: ITC Export Potential Assessment, additional results are available at ITC Country Pages http://www.intracen.org/country/colombia/

Côte d'Ivoire

Key indicators

Population (millions)	22.7
GDP (US$ billions)	34.0
GDP per capita (US$)	1,494.7
Share of world GDP (PPP US$, %)	0.1
Current account surplus over GDP (%)	−3.3
Tariff preference margin (percentage points)	3.1
Goods and services imports + exports over GDP (%)	88.9
Exports of services over total exports (%)	8.7
Geographic region	Sub-Saharan Africa
Development group	DC
Income group	Lower-middle income

SME Competitiveness Grid Summary

Average scores [0–100]		Compete	Connect	Change
FIRM LEVEL CAPABILITIES	Small	23.6	4.4	10.6
	Medium	30.7	18.6	29.1
	Large	52.3	46.6	56.3
	All	25.7	6.6	16.9
IMMEDIATE BUSINESS ENVIRONMENT		41.8	47.6	34.5
NATIONAL ENVIRONMENT		33.4	19.2	39.4

Reference level: 38.7 (a function of GDP per capita US$)	
Strengths are scores above: 58.0	Weaknesses are scores below: 19.3

SME Competitiveness Grid

1	FIRM LEVEL CAPABILITIES	Values				Normalized scores			
		Small	Medium	Large	All	Small	Medium	Large	All
1.1	Capacity to Compete								
1.1.1	Firms with quality certification (%)	4.2	2.5	18.6	4.3	15.3	9.8	44.9	15.6
1.1.2	Firms with checking or savings account (%)	65.3	76.2	95.1	67.4	15.1	21.8	49.5	16.2
1.1.3	Capacity utilization (%)	70.0	75.0	75.8	71.9	40.0	50.4	52.3	43.8
1.1.4	Manager's experience (years)	10.6	15.0	21.0	11.4	23.8	40.7	62.7	26.9
1.2	Capacity to Connect								
1.2.1	Firms using e-mail (%)	16.2	53.8	82.2	22.1	2.4	19.0	44.0	4.5
1.2.2	Firms having their own website (%)	7.9	21.8	54.7	10.7	6.5	18.3	49.1	8.8
1.3	Capacity to Change								
1.3.1	Firms with audited financial statements (%)	5.3	30.8	80.8	10.1	2.4	22.9	74.2	6.0
1.3.2	Investments financed by banks (%)	3.3	4.4	7.2	3.7	16.4	20.9	30.6	18.1
1.3.3	Firms offering formal training (%)	13.6	28.7	65.2	19.1	17.7	35.4	71.6	24.4
1.3.4	Firms using foreign technology licences (%)	0.9	9.3	14.8	3.6	5.8	37.2	48.8	19.1

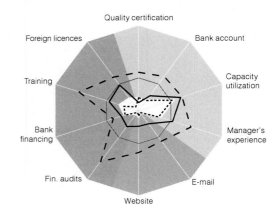

2	IMMEDIATE BUSINESS ENVIRONMENT	Values				Normalized scores			
		Small	Medium	Large	All	Small	Medium	Large	All
2.1	Capacity to Compete								
2.1.1	Losses due to power outages (% of sales)	2.2	2.1	2.8	2.2	39.7	40.4	36.0	39.7
2.1.2	Losses during domestic shipping (%)	1.9	0.3	1.0	1.4	32.7	65.8	44.8	38.5
2.1.3	Management time spent with regulation (%)	1.4	1.9	8.6	1.6	81.4	76.9	46.1	79.6
2.1.4	Days for customs clearance	-	30.0	14.2	24.6	-	2.6	28.1	9.5
2.2	Capacity to Connect								
2.2.1	State of cluster development (1–7)				3.3				40.4
2.2.2	Extent of marketing (1–7)				4.0				48.7
2.2.3	Local supplier quality (1–7)				4.2				52.0
2.2.4	University-industry collaboration in R&D (1–7)				3.3				49.4
2.3	Capacity to Change								
2.3.1	Access to finance as a constraint (%)	66.4	73.3	45.4	66.6	7.9	3.8	23.0	7.7
2.3.2	Inadequately educated workforce (%)	24.4	38.9	47.2	26.7	43.6	28.6	21.9	40.8
2.3.3	Business licensing and permits as a constraint (%)	7.7	13.1	14.1	8.4	57.0	44.3	42.5	55.0

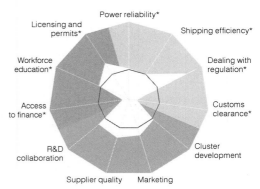

3	NATIONAL ENVIRONMENT	Values	Normalized scores
		All	All
3.1	Capacity to Compete		
3.1.1	Ease of getting electricity (0–100)	55.2	32.0
3.1.2	Ease of trading across borders (0–100)	50.5	28.3
3.1.3	Applied tariff, trade-weighted average (%)	10.4	35.2
3.1.4	Faced tariff, trade-weighted average (%)	3.8	46.3
3.1.5	Logistics performance index (1–5)	2.8	50.1
3.1.6	ISO 9001 quality certificates (/mn pop.)	3.1	23.1
3.1.7	ISO 14001 environmental certificates (/mn pop.)	0.6	25.9
3.1.8	Governance (index)	−0.9	26.1
3.2	Capacity to Connect		
3.2.1	ICT access (0–10)	3.2	28.8
3.2.2	ICT use (0–10)	0.2	3.7
3.2.3	Government's online service (0–10)	1.7	25.1
3.3	Capacity to Change		
3.3.1	Ease of getting credit (0–100)	30.0	29.4
3.3.2	Interest rate spread (%)	9.0	45.1
3.3.3	School life expectancy (years)	8.9	19.3
3.3.4	Ease of starting a business (0–100)	91.2	67.7
3.3.5	Patent applications (/mn pop.)	3.0	35.6
3.3.6	Trademark registrations (/mn pop.)	-	-

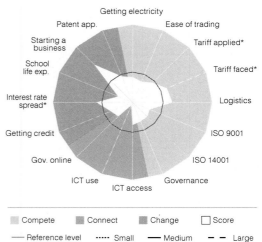

Compete ▮ Connect ▮ Change ▮ Score ☐

— Reference level ····· Small — Medium – – Large

Note: For each indicator, the table includes the values and the corresponding scores. Radar charts are based on scores: values are transformed and normalized so that for each indicator in a sample of 111 countries, the worst value gets a score of 0, the best value gets a score of 100, and the median gets a score of 50. If in the original values higher numbers indicate worse outcomes, the chart labels are marked with an asterisk (*). Series with missing data are indicated as (-) in the tables and omitted from the radar charts.

Source: World Bank Enterprise Survey (2009) for firm level data; for other sources refer to Annex III.

ITC Business Survey on Non-Tariff Measures (NTMs)

1. Firms affected by NTMs

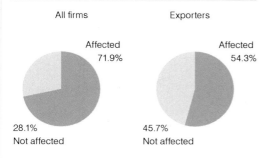

All firms

Affected
71.9%

28.1%
Not affected

Exporters

Affected
54.3%

45.7%
Not affected

2. NTMs reported as challenging (exporters)

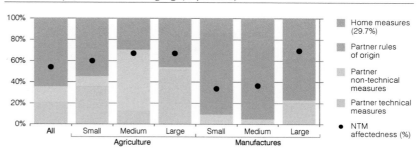

- Home measures (29.7%)
- Partner rules of origin
- Partner non-technical measures
- Partner technical measures
- ● NTM affectedness (%)

3. Regulatory and procedural obstacles (exporters)

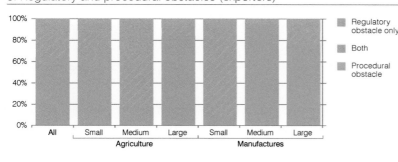

- Regulatory obstacle only
- Both
- Procedural obstacle

4. Location of procedural obstacles (exporters)

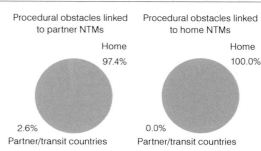

Procedural obstacles linked to partner NTMs

Home
97.4%

2.6%
Partner/transit countries

Procedural obstacles linked to home NTMs

Home
100.0%

0.0%
Partner/transit countries

Source: ITC NTM Survey, additional results are available at http://ntmsurvey.intracen.org/ntm-survey-data/country-analysis/ivory-coast/

Potential for Growth of Current Exports

PRODUCT/PRODUCT GROUP DESCRIPTION	Exports (US$ mn)	What is the product's export potential in…?						Would Côte d'Ivoire improve its…?			
		Sub-Saharan Africa	Unrealized potential	South-South trade	Unrealized potential	OECD	Unrealized potential	Technology level	Revenues stability	SME presence	Female participation
180100 Cocoa beans, whole or broken, ra...	2742.6		100%		61%		29%	■	■		
080131 Cashew nuts, in shell, fresh or dried	299.9		99%		40%		99%	■	■		
180310 Cocoa paste not defatted	596.4		4%		19%		10%	■	■	■	■
400122 Technically specified natural rubb...	602.3		2%		25%		18%	■	■		
090111 Coffee, not roasted, not decaffein...	149.5		97%		33%		84%	■	■		
340119 Soap&orgn surf prep, shapd, nes...	52.7		75%		76%		100%	■	■	■	
180400 Cocoa butter, fat and oil	308.4		80%		58%		19%	■	■	■	■
151190 Palm oil and its fractions refined b...	137.4		23%		41%		85%	■	■		
0803XX Bananas and plantains, fresh or...	191.3		35%		70%		51%	■	■		
520100 Cotton, not carded or combed	175.0		68%		11%		74%	■	■		
210410 Soups and broths and preparation...	39.8		73%		74%		86%	■	■	■	■
400129 Natural rubber in other forms nes	149.8		83%		51%		17%	■	■		
210111 Coffee extracts, essences, concen...	70.4		40%		49%		87%	■	■	■	■
4407Xb Wood sawn/chipped lengthwise,...	108.0		42%		52%		10%	■	■	■	■
180500 Cocoa powder, not containing ad...	118.5		91%		60%		45%	■	■		
252329 Portland cement nes	24.0		68%		69%		100%	■	■		
110100 Wheat or meslin flour	23.9		62%		65%		99%	■	■		
520852 Plain weave cotton fabric,>/=85%...	20.1		62%		63%		100%	■	■		
852610 Radar aparatus	18.4		48%		60%		98%	■	■	■	■
630533 Sacks, bags, packing, of strip pla...	16.3		66%		69%		100%	■	■	■	■

Note: Top 20 products listed in decreasing order of their export potential to the world. Development indicators are relative to the country's current situation, green indicating performance above its trade-weighted median and red otherwise; a blank cell indicates data are not available. A blank cell in export potential means that the product was not consistently demanded over five years by any country in the respective region. Exports (US$ mn) corresponds to the yearly average exports to the world over the period 2009-13. Refer to Annexes I, II and III for details.

Source: ITC Export Potential Assessment, additional results are available at ITC Country Pages http://www.intracen.org/country/ivory-coast/

Egypt

Key indicators

Population (millions)	86.7
GDP (US$ billions)	286.4
GDP per capita (US$)	3,303.8
Share of world GDP (PPP US$, %)	0.9
Current account surplus over GDP (%)	−0.8
Tariff preference margin (percentage points)	3.4
Goods and services imports + exports over GDP (%)	48.3
Exports of services over total exports (%)	36.9
Geographic region	MENA
Development group	DC
Income group	Lower-middle income

SME Competitiveness Grid Summary

Average scores [0–100]		Compete	Connect	Change
FIRM LEVEL CAPABILITIES	Small	27.2	15.8	25.7
	Medium	40.2	29.7	28.4
	Large	57.6	58.9	45.8
	All	34.3	22.1	28.5
IMMEDIATE BUSINESS ENVIRONMENT		46.6	41.4	47.1
NATIONAL ENVIRONMENT		45.8	60.8	53.6

Reference level: 45.4 (a function of GDP per capita US$)	
Strengths are scores above: 68.1	Weaknesses are scores below: 22.7

SME Competitiveness Grid

1	FIRM LEVEL CAPABILITIES	Values				Normalized scores			
		Small	Medium	Large	All	Small	Medium	Large	All
1.1	Capacity to Compete								
1.1.1	Firms with quality certification (%)	3.1	11.3	49.4	8.6	11.8	32.6	75.0	26.9
1.1.2	Firms with checking or savings account (%)	50.2	73.1	85.6	59.6	8.6	19.7	30.8	12.4
1.1.3	Capacity utilization (%)	69.3	76.4	73.7	72.3	38.6	53.6	47.6	44.6
1.1.4	Manager's experience (years)	17.4	18.8	25.1	18.4	49.6	54.7	77.0	53.3
1.2	Capacity to Connect								
1.2.1	Firms using e-mail (%)	35.0	54.6	84.1	44.4	9.5	19.4	46.8	13.9
1.2.2	Firms having their own website (%)	26.0	45.5	75.5	35.3	22.0	40.0	71.0	30.4
1.3	Capacity to Change								
1.3.1	Firms with audited financial statements (%)	65.4	75.0	78.9	69.2	56.4	67.2	71.9	60.6
1.3.2	Investments financed by banks (%)	6.1	2.5	8.3	5.2	27.0	12.9	34.0	23.9
1.3.3	Firms offering formal training (%)	2.4	6.3	26.5	5.2	3.3	8.5	32.9	7.0
1.3.4	Firms using foreign technology licences (%)	2.9	5.1	12.5	4.5	16.1	24.8	44.4	22.6

2	IMMEDIATE BUSINESS ENVIRONMENT	Values				Normalized scores			
		Small	Medium	Large	All	Small	Medium	Large	All
2.1	Capacity to Compete								
2.1.1	Losses due to power outages (% of sales)	5.7	5.5	5.0	5.6	25.3	25.8	27.3	25.5
2.1.2	Losses during domestic shipping (%)	1.1	0.4	1.3	0.9	43.0	61.0	39.9	46.7
2.1.3	Management time spent with regulation (%)	2.4	4.6	3.8	3.1	73.1	60.4	64.4	68.4
2.1.4	Days for customs clearance	5.9	9.7	8.2	8.3	57.0	40.8	46.5	45.9
2.2	Capacity to Connect								
2.2.1	State of cluster development (1–7)				4.3				72.3
2.2.2	Extent of marketing (1–7)				3.5				31.8
2.2.3	Local supplier quality (1–7)				3.9				42.3
2.2.4	University-industry collaboration in R&D (1–7)				2.4				19.3
2.3	Capacity to Change								
2.3.1	Access to finance as a constraint (%)	31.4	23.8	21.9	28.5	36.7	46.1	48.8	40.1
2.3.2	Inadequately educated workforce (%)	13.6	8.9	7.2	11.7	60.1	70.0	74.3	63.8
2.3.3	Business licensing and permits as a constraint (%)	16.8	17.9	17.5	17.2	38.0	36.3	36.9	37.4

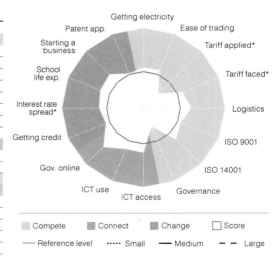

3	NATIONAL ENVIRONMENT	Values	Normalized scores
		All	All
3.1	Capacity to Compete		
3.1.1	Ease of getting electricity (0–100)	71.3	50.5
3.1.2	Ease of trading across borders (0–100)	71.6	50.7
3.1.3	Applied tariff, trade-weighted average (%)	14.0	25.5
3.1.4	Faced tariff, trade-weighted average (%)	3.5	51.5
3.1.5	Logistics performance index (1–5)	3.0	58.4
3.1.6	ISO 9001 quality certificates (/mn pop.)	25.2	48.9
3.1.7	ISO 14001 environmental certificates (/mn pop.)	9.8	56.1
3.1.8	Governance (index)	−0.9	24.9
3.2	Capacity to Connect		
3.2.1	ICT access (0–10)	5.1	56.5
3.2.2	ICT use (0–10)	2.9	56.1
3.2.3	Government's online service (0–10)	5.9	69.8
3.3	Capacity to Change		
3.3.1	Ease of getting credit (0–100)	50.0	50.0
3.3.2	Interest rate spread (%)	4.6	54.5
3.3.3	School life expectancy (years)	13.5	57.6
3.3.4	Ease of starting a business (0–100)	88.1	59.2
3.3.5	Patent applications (/mn pop.)	8.0	46.5
3.3.6	Trademark registrations (/mn pop.)	-	-

Note: For each indicator, the table includes the values and the corresponding scores. Radar charts are based on scores: values are transformed and normalized so that for each indicator in a sample of 111 countries, the worst value gets a score of 0, the best value gets a score of 100, and the median gets a score of 50. If in the original values higher numbers indicate worse outcomes, the chart labels are marked with an asterisk (*). Series with missing data are indicated as (-) in the tables and omitted from the radar charts.

Source: World Bank Enterprise Survey (2013) for firm level data; for other sources refer to Annex III.

ITC Business Survey on Non-Tariff Measures (NTMs)

1. Firms affected by NTMs

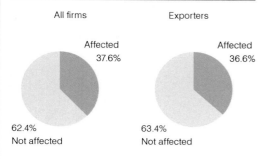

All firms

Affected
37.6%

62.4%
Not affected

Exporters

Affected
36.6%

63.4%
Not affected

2. NTMs reported as challenging (exporters)

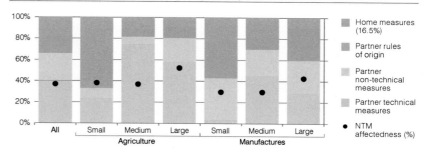

- Home measures (16.5%)
- Partner rules of origin
- Partner non-technical measures
- Partner technical measures
- NTM affectedness (%)

3. Regulatory and procedural obstacles (exporters)

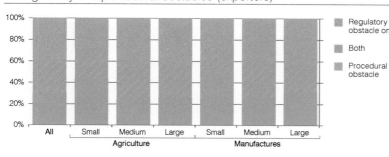

- Regulatory obstacle only
- Both
- Procedural obstacle

4. Location of procedural obstacles (exporters)

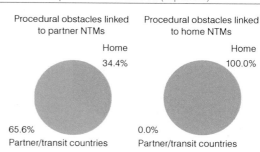

Procedural obstacles linked to partner NTMs

Home
34.4%

65.6%
Partner/transit countries

Procedural obstacles linked to home NTMs

Home
100.0%

0.0%
Partner/transit countries

Source: ITC NTM Survey, additional results are available at http://ntmsurvey.intracen.org/ntm-survey-data/country-analysis/egypt/

Potential for Growth of Current Exports

PRODUCT/PRODUCT GROUP DESCRIPTION	Exports (US$ mn).	Middle East & North Africa	Unrealized potential	South-South trade	Unrealized potential	OECD	Unrealized potential	Technology level	Revenues stability	SME presence	Female participation
310210 Urea,wthr/nt in aqueous solution i...	1097.5		95%		77%		47%				
690810 Tiles, cubes and sim <7 cm rect...	141.2		87%		87%		94%				
080510 Oranges, fresh or dried	549.3		83%		54%		81%				
040630 Cheese processed, not grated or...	193.2		64%		73%		99%				
854420 Co-axial cable and other co-axial...	250.5		57%		50%		63%				
070310 Onions and shallots, fresh or chilled	206.6		66%		54%		52%				
680221 Monumental/buildg stone,cut/sa...	99.3		72%		78%		78%				
620342 Mens/boys trousers and shorts, o...	234.4		97%		84%		56%				
170199 Refined sugar, in solid form, nes	132.8		62%		65%		89%				
854411 Insulated (including enamelled or...	231.7		43%		37%		69%				
3817XX Mixed alkylbenzenes and mixed...	189.7		64%		71%		26%				
100630 Rice, semi-milled or wholly milled...	170.8		65%		85%		59%				
281410 Anhydrous ammonia	194.2		86%		70%		47%				
610910 T-shirts, singlets and other vests,...	208.6		93%		79%		45%				
620462 Womens/girls trousers and shorts...	203.7		90%		73%		43%				
7321Xa Iron & steel toves,ranges,barbecu...	84.5		38%		41%		100%				
740911 Plate,sheet & strip of refined coop...	277.5		3%		7%		72%				
96XXXX Sanitary towels (pads) and tamp...	168.6		47%		45%		92%				
252321 Portland cement, white, whether o...	60.8		82%		76%		75%				
080610 Grapes, fresh	197.3		80%		53%		36%				

What is the product's export potential in...?

Would Egypt improve its...?

Note: Top 20 products listed in decreasing order of their export potential to the world. Development indicators are relative to the country's current situation, green indicating performance above its trade-weighted median and red otherwise; a blank cell indicates data are not available. A blank cell in export potential means that the product was not consistently demanded over five years by any country in the respective region. Exports (US$ mn) corresponds to the yearly average exports to the world over the period 2009-13. Refer to Annexes I, II and III for details.

Source: ITC Export Potential Assessment, additional results are available at ITC Country Pages http://www.intracen.org/country/egypt/

Guinea

Key indicators

Population (millions)	11.4
GDP (US$ billions)	6.5
GDP per capita (US$)	572.5
Share of world GDP (PPP US$, %)	0.0
Current account surplus over GDP (%)	-18.5
Tariff preference margin (percentage points)	0.2
Goods and services imports + exports over GDP (%)	91.2
Exports of services over total exports (%)	5.0
Geographic region	Sub-Saharan Africa
Development group	LDC
Income group	Low income

SME Competitiveness Grid Summary

Average scores [0–100]		Compete	Connect	Change
FIRM LEVEL CAPABILITIES	Small	20.6	4.1	11.6
	Medium	30.8	8.1	19.7
	Large	51.1	35.8	52.9
	All	22.8	5.3	14.9
IMMEDIATE BUSINESS ENVIRONMENT		43.5	17.3	37.2
NATIONAL ENVIRONMENT		31.1	4.2	26.6

Reference level: 30.5 (a function of GDP per capita US$)

Strengths are scores above: 45.8	Weaknesses are scores below: 15.3

SME Competitiveness Grid

1	FIRM LEVEL CAPABILITIES	Values				Normalized scores			
		Small	Medium	Large	All	Small	Medium	Large	All
1.1	Capacity to Compete								
1.1.1	Firms with quality certification (%)	4.4	4.9	26.6	5.2	15.9	17.4	55.1	18.3
1.1.2	Firms with checking or savings account (%)	50.6	73.0	85.4	53.9	8.8	19.6	30.5	10.0
1.1.3	Capacity utilization (%)	67.4	67.8	87.3	68.3	35.1	35.8	84.6	36.8
1.1.4	Manager's experience (years)	10.3	17.6	13.3	11.2	22.6	50.4	34.3	26.2
1.2	Capacity to Connect								
1.2.1	Firms using e-mail (%)	18.4	32.7	26.6	20.0	3.2	8.6	6.1	3.7
1.2.2	Firms having their own website (%)	6.1	9.4	70.4	8.4	5.0	7.7	65.4	6.9
1.3	Capacity to Change								
1.3.1	Firms with audited financial statements (%)	5.5	13.9	41.1	7.4	2.5	9.0	32.1	4.0
1.3.2	Investments financed by banks (%)	0.0	1.8	6.7	0.5	0.0	9.6	29.0	2.9
1.3.3	Firms offering formal training (%)	18.1	13.8	100.0	21.1	23.2	18.0	100.0	26.7
1.3.4	Firms using foreign technology licences (%)	4.0	11.5	15.7	5.5	20.7	42.3	50.3	26.2

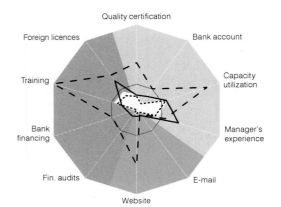

2	IMMEDIATE BUSINESS ENVIRONMENT	Values				Normalized scores			
		Small	Medium	Large	All	Small	Medium	Large	All
2.1	Capacity to Compete								
2.1.1	Losses due to power outages (% of sales)	13.2	11.6	-	13.0	12.5	14.4	-	12.7
2.1.2	Losses during domestic shipping (%)	1.4	0.6	2.1	1.3	38.5	54.0	30.9	39.9
2.1.3	Management time spent with regulation (%)	2.4	3.9	6.1	2.6	73.1	63.9	54.2	71.7
2.1.4	Days for customs clearance	8.4	-	-	7.4	45.7	-	-	49.8
2.2	Capacity to Connect								
2.2.1	State of cluster development (1–7)				3.0				31.2
2.2.2	Extent of marketing (1–7)				2.7				6.1
2.2.3	Local supplier quality (1–7)				3.1				22.3
2.2.4	University-industry collaboration in R&D (1–7)				2.2				9.8
2.3	Capacity to Change								
2.3.1	Access to finance as a constraint (%)	60.4	54.0	13.3	58.3	11.7	16.2	63.3	13.2
2.3.2	Inadequately educated workforce (%)	11.3	9.4	27.9	11.7	64.7	68.8	39.4	63.8
2.3.3	Business licensing and permits as a constraint (%)	17.2	37.6	14.6	19.1	37.4	16.3	41.6	34.6

3	NATIONAL ENVIRONMENT	Values	Normalized scores
		All	All
3.1	Capacity to Compete		
3.1.1	Ease of getting electricity (0–100)	57.6	34.5
3.1.2	Ease of trading across borders (0–100)	60.3	37.3
3.1.3	Applied tariff, trade-weighted average (%)	11.3	32.5
3.1.4	Faced tariff, trade-weighted average (%)	2.7	71.8
3.1.5	Logistics performance index (1–5)	2.5	37.1
3.1.6	ISO 9001 quality certificates (/mn pop.)	0.5	8.0
3.1.7	ISO 14001 environmental certificates (/mn pop.)	0.3	17.6
3.1.8	Governance (index)	-1.2	9.9
3.2	Capacity to Connect		
3.2.1	ICT access (0–10)	2.3	12.7
3.2.2	ICT use (0–10)	0.1	0.0
3.2.3	Government's online service (0–10)	0.0	0.0
3.3	Capacity to Change		
3.3.1	Ease of getting credit (0–100)	30.0	29.4
3.3.2	Interest rate spread (%)	11.9	41.6
3.3.3	School life expectancy (years)	8.7	17.4
3.3.4	Ease of starting a business (0–100)	55.4	18.2
3.3.5	Patent applications (/mn pop.)	-	-
3.3.6	Trademark registrations (/mn pop.)	-	-

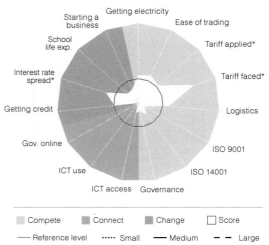

Note: For each indicator, the table includes the values and the corresponding scores. Radar charts are based on scores: values are transformed and normalized so that for each indicator in a sample of 111 countries, the worst value gets a score of 0, the best value gets a score of 100, and the median gets a score of 50. If in the original values higher numbers indicate worse outcomes, the chart labels are marked with an asterisk (*). Series with missing data are indicated as (-) in the tables and omitted from the radar charts.

Source: World Bank Enterprise Survey (2006) for firm level data; for other sources refer to Annex III.

ITC Business Survey on Non-Tariff Measures (NTMs)

1. Firms affected by NTMs

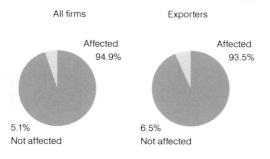

All firms
Affected
94.9%
5.1%
Not affected

Exporters
Affected
93.5%
6.5%
Not affected

2. NTMs reported as challenging (exporters)

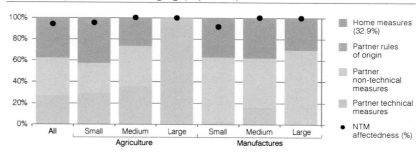

- Home measures (32.9%)
- Partner rules of origin
- Partner non-technical measures
- Partner technical measures
- ● NTM affectedness (%)

3. Regulatory and procedural obstacles (exporters)

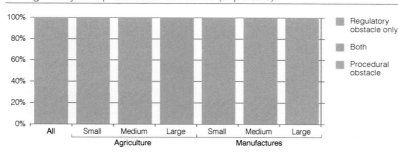

- Regulatory obstacle only
- Both
- Procedural obstacle

4. Location of procedural obstacles (exporters)

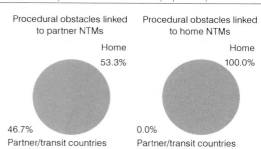

Procedural obstacles linked to partner NTMs
Home 53.3%
46.7% Partner/transit countries

Procedural obstacles linked to home NTMs
Home 100.0%
0.0% Partner/transit countries

Source: ITC NTM Survey, additional results are available at http://ntmsurvey.intracen.org/ntm-survey-data/country-analysis/guinea/

Potential for Growth of Current Exports

PRODUCT/PRODUCT GROUP DESCRIPTION	Exports (US$ mn)	Sub-Saharan Africa	Unrealized potential	South-South trade	Unrealized potential	OECD	Unrealized potential	Technology level	Revenues stability	SME presence	Female participation
090111 Coffee, not roasted, not decaffein...	29.8		100%		12%		73%	■	■		
0303Xa Fish, frozen, whole	20.9		70%		77%		69%	■	■	■	■
180100 Cocoa beans, whole or broken, ra...	15.5		100%		61%		67%	■	■		
0303Xi Frozen Sardines , sardinella, brisli...	6.0		77%		79%		95%	■	■	■	■
080131 Cashew nuts, in shell, fresh or dried	14.5		100%		42%		77%	■	■		
710813 Gold in oth semi-manufactd form...	20.4		100%		53%		83%	■	■	■	■
400122 Technically specified natural rubb...	20.6		3%		65%		33%	■			
392329 Sacks and bags (including cones)...	4.0		46%		61%		100%	■			
400129 Natural rubber in other forms nes	6.8		96%		80%		41%	■			
0305Xb Fish,cured or smoked and fish m...	4.0		98%		67%		99%	■	■	■	■
120740 Sesamum seeds, whether or not b...	1.7		100%		97%		71%	■	■		
4407Xb Wood sawn/chipped lengthwise,...	2.9		99%		60%		78%	■	■	■	■
392490 Household and toilet articles nes...	1.5		57%		68%		100%	■	■	■	■
4403XX Wood in the rough	10.0		92%		29%		95%	■	■		
210410 Soups and broths and preparation...	2.8		42%		43%		96%	■	■		
0303Xe Fish, frozen, whole	1.8		100%		100%		19%	■	■	■	■
392410 Tableware and kitchenware of pla...	1.4		51%		73%		96%	■	■	■	■
0802Xc Nuts nes	0.5		38%		92%		94%	■	■		
080450 Guavas, mangoes and mangoste...	0.7		100%		78%		77%	■	■		
843149 Parts of cranes,work trucks,tovels,...	15.2		14%		39%		43%	■	■	■	■

What is the product's export potential in...?   *Would Guinea improve its...?*

Note: Top 20 products listed in decreasing order of their export potential to the world. Development indicators are relative to the country's current situation, green indicating performance above its trade-weighted median and red otherwise; a blank cell indicates data are not available. A blank cell in export potential means that the product was not consistently demanded over five years by any country in the respective region. Exports (US$ mn) corresponds to the yearly average exports to the world over the period 2009-13. Refer to Annexes I, II and III for details.

Source: ITC Export Potential Assessment, additional results are available at ITC Country Pages http://www.intracen.org/country/guinea/

Indonesia

Key indicators

Population (millions)	251.5
GDP (US$ billions)	888.6
GDP per capita (US$)	3,533.5
Share of world GDP (PPP US$, %)	2.5
Current account surplus over GDP (%)	-3.0
Tariff preference margin (percentage points)	1.5
Goods and services imports + exports over GDP (%)	48.7
Exports of services over total exports (%)	10.2
Geographic region	East Asia & Pacific
Development group	DC
Income group	Lower-middle income

SME Competitiveness Grid Summary

Average scores [0–100]		Compete	Connect	Change
FIRM LEVEL CAPABILITIES	Small	32.2	1.8	10.8
	Medium	40.3	7.7	22.8
	Large	54.0	41.7	49.3
	All	33.5	3.0	13.8
IMMEDIATE BUSINESS ENVIRONMENT		66.8	72.2	69.2
NATIONAL ENVIRONMENT		56.0	44.8	41.5

Reference level: 46.0 (a function of GDP per capita US$)	
Strengths are scores above: 68.9	Weaknesses are scores below: 23.0

SME Competitiveness Grid

1	FIRM LEVEL CAPABILITIES	Values				Normalized scores			
		Small	Medium	Large	All	Small	Medium	Large	All
1.1	Capacity to Compete								
1.1.1	Firms with quality certification (%)	1.6	6.3	40.8	2.9	6.5	21.2	68.6	11.2
1.1.2	Firms with checking or savings account (%)	46.3	89.1	92.5	51.5	7.3	35.7	42.2	9.1
1.1.3	Capacity utilization (%)	86.3	82.8	84.0	85.9	81.1	70.3	73.8	79.8
1.1.4	Manager's experience (years)	13.2	13.2	12.6	13.2	33.9	33.9	31.6	33.9
1.2	Capacity to Connect								
1.2.1	Firms using e-mail (%)	9.4	31.1	81.8	13.2	0.2	7.9	43.5	1.4
1.2.2	Firms having their own website (%)	4.2	9.2	45.3	5.7	3.4	7.5	39.8	4.6
1.3	Capacity to Change								
1.3.1	Firms with audited financial statements (%)	2.1	10.1	51.3	4.0	0.0	6.0	41.8	1.4
1.3.2	Investments financed by banks (%)	5.7	6.5	8.5	6.0	25.6	28.4	34.6	26.7
1.3.3	Firms offering formal training (%)	2.8	13.2	37.5	4.7	3.8	17.2	44.9	6.3
1.3.4	Firms using foreign technology licences (%)	2.4	10.3	37.3	4.0	13.8	39.6	75.9	20.7

2	IMMEDIATE BUSINESS ENVIRONMENT	Values				Normalized scores			
		Small	Medium	Large	All	Small	Medium	Large	All
2.1	Capacity to Compete								
2.1.1	Losses due to power outages (% of sales)	0.5	0.8	0.7	0.6	61.4	54.7	56.6	58.8
2.1.2	Losses during domestic shipping (%)	0.7	1.2	0.3	0.7	51.2	41.4	65.8	51.2
2.1.3	Management time spent with regulation (%)	1.3	3.2	6.9	1.6	82.4	67.8	51.3	79.6
2.1.4	Days for customs clearance	-	2.5	3.5	2.9	-	81.7	72.8	77.6
2.2	Capacity to Connect								
2.2.1	State of cluster development (1–7)				4.5				78.9
2.2.2	Extent of marketing (1–7)				4.9				75.1
2.2.3	Local supplier quality (1–7)				4.3				54.6
2.2.4	University-industry collaboration in R&D (1–7)				4.5				80.3
2.3	Capacity to Change								
2.3.1	Access to finance as a constraint (%)	14.8	12.4	5.7	14.3	60.4	65.1	81.1	61.4
2.3.2	Inadequately educated workforce (%)	4.5	3.7	6.3	4.5	82.2	84.8	76.8	82.2
2.3.3	Business licensing and permits as a constraint (%)	5.6	5.9	6.8	5.6	64.0	62.9	59.8	64.0

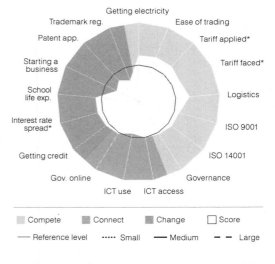

3	NATIONAL ENVIRONMENT	Values	Normalized scores
		All	All
3.1	Capacity to Compete		
3.1.1	Ease of getting electricity (0–100)	76.9	58.0
3.1.2	Ease of trading across borders (0–100)	77.5	59.6
3.1.3	Applied tariff, trade-weighted average (%)	4.7	59.8
3.1.4	Faced tariff, trade-weighted average (%)	3.3	56.4
3.1.5	Logistics performance index (1–5)	3.1	63.0
3.1.6	ISO 9001 quality certificates (/mn pop.)	31.8	51.9
3.1.7	ISO 14001 environmental certificates (/mn pop.)	6.3	51.0
3.1.8	Governance (index)	-0.4	48.1
3.2	Capacity to Connect		
3.2.1	ICT access (0–10)	4.3	46.1
3.2.2	ICT use (0–10)	1.8	40.9
3.2.3	Government's online service (0–10)	3.6	47.5
3.3	Capacity to Change		
3.3.1	Ease of getting credit (0–100)	50.0	50.0
3.3.2	Interest rate spread (%)	5.4	52.1
3.3.3	School life expectancy (years)	13.0	53.1
3.3.4	Ease of starting a business (0–100)	68.8	29.8
3.3.5	Patent applications (/mn pop.)	3.0	35.6
3.3.6	Trademark registrations (/mn pop.)	182.0	28.2

Note: For each indicator, the table includes the values and the corresponding scores. Radar charts are based on scores: values are transformed and normalized so that for each indicator in a sample of 111 countries, the worst value gets a score of 0, the best value gets a score of 100, and the median gets a score of 50. If in the original values higher numbers indicate worse outcomes, the chart labels are marked with an asterisk (*). Series with missing data are indicated as (-) in the tables and omitted from the radar charts.

Source: World Bank Enterprise Survey (2009) for firm level data; for other sources refer to Annex III.

ITC Business Survey on Non-Tariff Measures (NTMs)

1. Firms affected by NTMs

All firms

Affected
36.8%

63.2%
Not affected

Exporters

Affected
29.8%

70.2%
Not affected

2. NTMs reported as challenging (exporters)

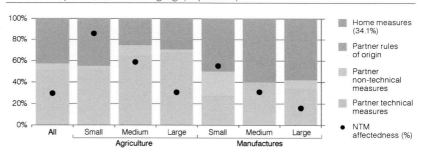

- Home measures (34.1%)
- Partner rules of origin
- Partner non-technical measures
- Partner technical measures
- ● NTM affectedness (%)

3. Regulatory and procedural obstacles (exporters)

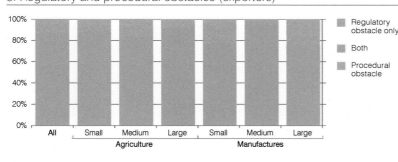

- Regulatory obstacle only
- Both
- Procedural obstacle

4. Location of procedural obstacles (exporters)

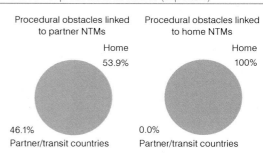

Procedural obstacles linked to partner NTMs

Home
53.9%

46.1%
Partner/transit countries

Procedural obstacles linked to home NTMs

Home
100%

0.0%
Partner/transit countries

Source: ITC NTM Survey, additional results are available at http://ntmsurvey.intracen.org/ntm-survey-data/country-analysis/indonesia/

Potential for Growth of Current Exports

PRODUCT/PRODUCT GROUP DESCRIPTION	Exports (US$ mn)	East Asia & Pacific	Unrealized potential	South-South trade	Unrealized potential	OECD	Unrealized potential	Technology level	Revenues stability	SME presence	Female participation
151190 Palm oil and its fractions refined b...	7671.5		63%		47%		72%				
151110 Palm oil, crude	7400.8		69%		50%		48%				
400122 Technically specified natural rubb...	7002.1		59%		60%		38%				
800110 Tin not alloyed unwrought	2094.8		72%		73%		67%				
48XXXa Paper and paperboard, articles o...	3132.1		12%		11%		22%				
151321 Palm kernel or babassu oil, crude	1051.1		66%		61%		24%				
44XXXX Wood and articles of wood, woo...	1659.0		33%		50%		24%				
84XXXd Machinery, nuclear reactors, boil...	1377.5		27%		39%		28%				
151329 Palm kernel/babassu oil their frac...	556.0		72%		53%		79%				
0306Xa Crustaceans	1009.8		42%		78%		29%				
090111 Coffee, not roasted, not decaffein...	1068.6		13%		24%		44%				
470329 Chemical wood pulp,soda/sulpha...	1497.2		2%		3%		71%				
38XXXX Miscellaneous chemical products	1017.0		81%		82%		62%				
041000 Edible products of animal origin nes	317.8		77%		77%		75%				
382319 Industrial fatty acids, acid oils nes	716.3		53%		43%		58%				
6403XX Footwear, upper of leather	1416.9		55%		39%		30%				
401110 Pneumatic tire new of rubber f mot...	1211.4		21%		34%		10%				
180100 Cocoa beans, whole or broken, ra...	784.2		7%		10%		76%				
8528Xa Television receivers (incl video m...	1007.6		28%		37%		25%				
750110 Nickel mattes	1035.8		1%		100%		21%				

Note: Top 20 products listed in decreasing order of their export potential to the world. Development indicators are relative to the country's current situation, green indicating performance above its trade-weighted median and red otherwise; a blank cell indicates data are not available. A blank cell in export potential means that the product was not consistently demanded over five years by any country in the respective region. Exports (US$ mn) corresponds to the yearly average exports to the world over the period 2009-13. Refer to Annexes I, II and III for details.

Source: ITC Export Potential Assessment, additional results are available at ITC Country Pages http://www.intracen.org/country/indonesia/

Jamaica

Key indicators

Population (millions)	2.8
GDP (US$ billions)	13.8
GDP per capita (US$)	4,925.8
Share of world GDP (PPP US$, %)	0.0
Current account surplus over GDP (%)	-6.4
Tariff preference margin (percentage points)	6.5
Goods and services imports + exports over GDP (%)	84.4
Exports of services over total exports (%)	65.5
Geographic region	LAC
Development group	SIDS
Income group	Upper-middle income

SME Competitiveness Grid Summary

Average scores [0–100]		Compete	Connect	Change
FIRM LEVEL CAPABILITIES	Small	55.0	29.2	39.2
	Medium	62.5	37.1	63.4
	Large	71.2	73.5	74.4
	All	58.1	32.2	51.0
IMMEDIATE BUSINESS ENVIRONMENT		67.8	57.1	40.0
NATIONAL ENVIRONMENT		47.3	48.3	58.6

Reference level: 48.8 (a function of GDP per capita US$)

Strengths are scores above: 73.1	Weaknesses are scores below: 24.4

SME Competitiveness Grid

1	FIRM LEVEL CAPABILITIES	Values				Normalized scores			
		Small	Medium	Large	All	Small	Medium	Large	All
1.1	Capacity to Compete								
1.1.1	Firms with quality certification (%)	15.3	14.2	57.9	16.5	39.8	37.9	80.4	41.7
1.1.2	Firms with checking or savings account (%)	99.7	100.0	98.9	99.8	88.0	100.0	73.0	91.2
1.1.3	Capacity utilization (%)	76.5	77.2	77.6	76.9	53.9	55.5	56.5	54.8
1.1.4	Manager's experience (years)	14.4	19.3	24.5	16.1	38.5	56.6	74.9	44.8
1.2	Capacity to Connect								
1.2.1	Firms using e-mail (%)	66.5	83.7	95.5	72.6	27.7	46.2	73.7	33.0
1.2.2	Firms having their own website (%)	35.7	32.7	77.6	36.4	30.8	28.0	73.4	31.4
1.3	Capacity to Change								
1.3.1	Firms with audited financial statements (%)	59.5	88.2	95.3	68.9	50.1	83.6	93.2	60.3
1.3.2	Investments financed by banks (%)	20.8	25.9	14.3	21.8	61.4	69.2	49.0	63.0
1.3.3	Firms offering formal training (%)	20.4	32.1	69.3	25.9	25.9	39.1	75.2	32.3
1.3.4	Firms using foreign technology licences (%)	3.7	23.3	42.3	14.6	19.5	61.5	79.9	48.4

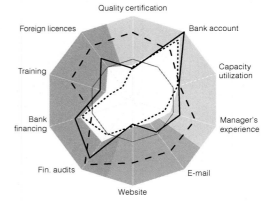

2	IMMEDIATE BUSINESS ENVIRONMENT	Values				Normalized scores			
		Small	Medium	Large	All	Small	Medium	Large	All
2.1	Capacity to Compete								
2.1.1	Losses due to power outages (% of sales)	0.1	0.2	0.0	0.1	81.8	73.7	100.0	81.8
2.1.2	Losses during domestic shipping (%)	0.1	0.4	0.3	0.2	81.4	61.0	65.8	72.1
2.1.3	Management time spent with regulation (%)	1.3	2.6	2.3	1.7	82.4	71.7	73.8	78.7
2.1.4	Days for customs clearance	24.6	6.4	12.0	10.3	9.4	54.4	33.8	38.8
2.2	Capacity to Connect								
2.2.1	State of cluster development (1–7)				3.7				54.7
2.2.2	Extent of marketing (1–7)				4.2				56.2
2.2.3	Local supplier quality (1–7)				4.4				55.6
2.2.4	University-industry collaboration in R&D (1–7)				3.8				62.0
2.3	Capacity to Change								
2.3.1	Access to finance as a constraint (%)	47.1	28.8	10.9	40.5	21.6	39.7	68.2	27.4
2.3.2	Inadequately educated workforce (%)	20.2	18.3	26.3	19.9	49.3	52.1	41.3	49.7
2.3.3	Business licensing and permits as a constraint (%)	14.3	13.2	10.8	13.8	42.1	44.1	49.1	43.0

3	NATIONAL ENVIRONMENT	Values	Normalized scores
		All	All
3.1	Capacity to Compete		
3.1.1	Ease of getting electricity (0–100)	70.4	49.2
3.1.2	Ease of trading across borders (0–100)	68.2	46.3
3.1.3	Applied tariff, trade-weighted average (%)	9.0	39.7
3.1.4	Faced tariff, trade-weighted average (%)	3.8	47.1
3.1.5	Logistics performance index (1–5)	2.8	53.4
3.1.6	ISO 9001 quality certificates (/mn pop.)	9.3	36.2
3.1.7	ISO 14001 environmental certificates (/mn pop.)	4.0	45.8
3.1.8	Governance (index)	0.0	60.3
3.2	Capacity to Connect		
3.2.1	ICT access (0–10)	4.6	49.7
3.2.2	ICT use (0–10)	2.6	52.9
3.2.3	Government's online service (0–10)	3.1	42.3
3.3	Capacity to Change		
3.3.1	Ease of getting credit (0–100)	80.0	82.7
3.3.2	Interest rate spread (%)	14.1	39.5
3.3.3	School life expectancy (years)	12.4	47.8
3.3.4	Ease of starting a business (0–100)	94.1	77.9
3.3.5	Patent applications (/mn pop.)	8.0	46.5
3.3.6	Trademark registrations (/mn pop.)	663.0	57.1

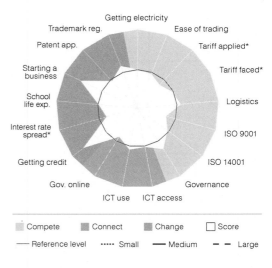

Legend: Compete | Connect | Change | Score | Reference level | Small | Medium | Large

Note: For each indicator, the table includes the values and the corresponding scores. Radar charts are based on scores: values are transformed and normalized so that for each indicator in a sample of 111 countries, the worst value gets a score of 0, the best value gets a score of 100, and the median gets a score of 50. If in the original values higher numbers indicate worse outcomes, the chart labels are marked with an asterisk (*). Series with missing data are indicated as (-) in the tables and omitted from the radar charts.

Source: World Bank Enterprise Survey (2010) for firm level data; for other sources refer to Annex III.

ITC Business Survey on Non-Tariff Measures (NTMs)

1. Firms affected by NTMs

All firms

Affected
34.5%

65.5%
Not affected

Exporters

Affected
41.0%

59.0%
Not affected

2. NTMs reported as challenging (exporters)

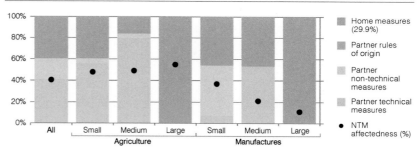

- Home measures (29.9%)
- Partner rules of origin
- Partner non-technical measures
- Partner technical measures
- ● NTM affectedness (%)

3. Regulatory and procedural obstacles (exporters)

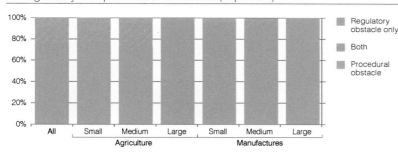

- Regulatory obstacle only
- Both
- Procedural obstacle

4. Location of procedural obstacles (exporters)

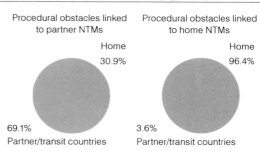

Procedural obstacles linked to partner NTMs

Home
30.9%

69.1%
Partner/transit countries

Procedural obstacles linked to home NTMs

Home
96.4%

3.6%
Partner/transit countries

Source: ITC NTM Survey, additional results are available at http://ntmsurvey.intracen.org/ntm-survey-data/country-analysis/jamaica/

Potential for Growth of Current Exports

PRODUCT/PRODUCT GROUP DESCRIPTION	Exports (US$ mn)	Latin America & the Caribbean	Unrealized potential	South-South trade	Unrealized potential	OECD	Unrealized potential	Technology level	Revenues stability	SME presence	Female participation
281820 Aluminium oxide nes	494.4		68%		8%		8%				
220840 Rum and tafia	53.0		90%		89%		53%				
1701XX Cane or beet sugar and chemica...	65.9		100%		87%		31%				
220710 Undenaturd ethyl alcohol of an al...	110.5		95%		96%		29%				
220300 Beer made from malt	31.3		78%		83%		59%				
0714XX Manioc, arrowroot salem (yams) etc	22.5		94%		95%		64%				
090111 Coffee, not roasted, not decaffein...	22.3		100%		94%		81%				
2008Xb Preserved fruits nes	11.4		93%		94%		57%				
210390 Sauces and preparations nes and...	12.5		90%		92%		26%				
080720 Papaws (papayas), fresh	3.5		100%		100%		79%				
190590 Communion wafers,empty cache...	9.1		87%		86%		35%				
071420 Sweet potatoes, fresh or dried, wh...	3.3		81%		82%		73%				
230990 Animal feed preparations nes	7.7		70%		75%		99%				
281830 Aluminium hydroxide	5.6		66%		80%		48%				
220870 Liqueurs and cordials	3.0		28%		45%		82%				
080450 Guavas, mangoes and mangoste...	1.3		100%		98%		82%				
110100 Wheat or meslin flour	4.4		64%		66%		86%				
220290 Non-alcoholic beverages nes, exc...	6.8		39%		46%		18%				
0904XX Pepper, peppers and capsicum	2.7		92%		91%		58%				
220510 Vermouth&oth grape wines flav w...	3.5		24%		54%		67%				

Column group header: What is the product's export potential in...? / Would Jamaica improve its...?

Note: Top 20 products listed in decreasing order of their export potential to the world. Development indicators are relative to the country's current situation, green indicating performance above its trade-weighted median and red otherwise; a blank cell indicates data are not available. A blank cell in export potential means that the product was not consistently demanded over five years by any country in the respective region. Exports (US$ mn) corresponds to the yearly average exports to the world over the period 2009-13. Refer to Annexes I, II and III for details.

Source: ITC Export Potential Assessment, additional results are available at ITC Country Pages http://www.intracen.org/country/jamaica/

Kazakhstan

Key indicators

Population (millions)	17.4
GDP (US$ billions)	212.3
GDP per capita (US$)	12,183.5
Share of world GDP (PPP US$, %)	0.4
Current account surplus over GDP (%)	1.6
Tariff preference margin (percentage points)	1.3
Goods and services imports + exports over GDP (%)	61.1
Exports of services over total exports (%)	6.6
Geographic region	Europe & Central Asia
Development group	LLDC
Income group	Upper-middle income

SME Competitiveness Grid Summary

Average scores [0–100]		Compete	Connect	Change
FIRM LEVEL CAPABILITIES	Small	36.4	40.4	22.2
	Medium	45.1	51.0	31.9
	Large	61.3	74.5	47.3
	All	41.7	46.2	29.5
IMMEDIATE BUSINESS ENVIRONMENT		52.3	46.1	67.2
NATIONAL ENVIRONMENT		41.4	77.3	60.1

Reference level: 56.4 (a function of GDP per capita US$)	
Strengths are scores above: 84.6	Weaknesses are scores below: 28.2

SME Competitiveness Grid

1 FIRM LEVEL CAPABILITIES

		Values				Normalized scores			
		Small	Medium	Large	All	Small	Medium	Large	All
1.1	Capacity to Compete								
1.1.1	Firms with quality certification (%)	10.1	15.0	48.2	15.0	30.1	39.3	74.1	39.3
1.1.2	Firms with checking or savings account (%)	89.8	94.1	98.8	92.2	36.8	46.3	71.8	41.5
1.1.3	Capacity utilization (%)	75.5	75.7	73.6	75.3	51.6	52.0	47.4	51.1
1.1.4	Manager's experience (years)	11.4	15.6	18.0	13.5	26.9	43.0	51.8	35.0
1.2	Capacity to Connect								
1.2.1	Firms using e-mail (%)	84.8	91.1	98.1	88.2	47.9	60.3	85.9	53.9
1.2.2	Firms having their own website (%)	38.0	47.3	68.1	43.9	32.9	41.8	63.0	38.5
1.3	Capacity to Change								
1.3.1	Firms with audited financial statements (%)	8.5	18.2	22.2	13.3	4.8	12.4	15.7	8.5
1.3.2	Investments financed by banks (%)	6.8	8.8	14.0	8.8	29.3	35.4	48.4	35.4
1.3.3	Firms offering formal training (%)	20.8	32.1	61.1	28.4	26.4	39.1	67.9	35.1
1.3.4	Firms using foreign technology licences (%)	6.1	10.7	20.2	10.0	28.1	40.5	57.4	38.9

2 IMMEDIATE BUSINESS ENVIRONMENT

		Values				Normalized scores			
		Small	Medium	Large	All	Small	Medium	Large	All
2.1	Capacity to Compete								
2.1.1	Losses due to power outages (% of sales)	0.4	0.4	0.5	0.4	64.5	64.5	61.4	64.5
2.1.2	Losses during domestic shipping (%)	0.7	1.1	0.6	0.9	51.2	43.0	54.0	46.7
2.1.3	Management time spent with regulation (%)	4.8	6.6	6.1	5.5	59.5	52.4	54.2	56.5
2.1.4	Days for customs clearance	15.9	7.8	7.1	9.5	24.3	47.9	50.9	41.5
2.2	Capacity to Connect								
2.2.1	State of cluster development (1–7)				3.2				37.2
2.2.2	Extent of marketing (1–7)				4.3				57.1
2.2.3	Local supplier quality (1–7)				3.9				42.2
2.2.4	University-industry collaboration in R&D (1–7)				3.3				48.1
2.3	Capacity to Change								
2.3.1	Access to finance as a constraint (%)	9.0	8.2	10.5	8.8	72.5	74.5	69.1	73.0
2.3.2	Inadequately educated workforce (%)	10.8	14.8	20.5	13.1	65.7	57.9	48.8	61.0
2.3.3	Business licensing and permits as a constraint (%)	1.9	8.6	5.4	4.7	82.5	54.5	64.7	67.5

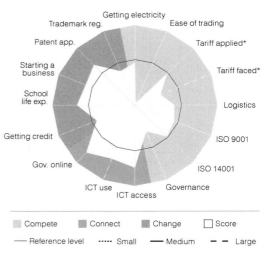

3 NATIONAL ENVIRONMENT

		Values	Normalized scores
		All	All
3.1	Capacity to Compete		
3.1.1	Ease of getting electricity (0–100)	73.0	52.6
3.1.2	Ease of trading across borders (0–100)	7.9	1.9
3.1.3	Applied tariff, trade-weighted average (%)	5.5	54.7
3.1.4	Faced tariff, trade-weighted average (%)	4.8	33.2
3.1.5	Logistics performance index (1–5)	2.7	47.4
3.1.6	ISO 9001 quality certificates (/mn pop.)	30.7	51.4
3.1.7	ISO 14001 environmental certificates (/mn pop.)	8.8	54.9
3.1.8	Governance (index)	-0.7	35.3
3.2	Capacity to Connect		
3.2.1	ICT access (0–10)	6.8	77.1
3.2.2	ICT use (0–10)	4.3	71.8
3.2.3	Government's online service (0–10)	7.5	83.1
3.3	Capacity to Change		
3.3.1	Ease of getting credit (0–100)	50.0	50.0
3.3.2	Interest rate spread (%)	-	-
3.3.3	School life expectancy (years)	15.0	70.1
3.3.4	Ease of starting a business (0–100)	90.2	64.6
3.3.5	Patent applications (/mn pop.)	111.0	70.5
3.3.6	Trademark registrations (/mn pop.)	413.0	45.5

Legend: Compete | Connect | Change | Score | Reference level | ····· Small | —— Medium | – – Large

Note: For each indicator, the table includes the values and the corresponding scores. Radar charts are based on scores: values are transformed and normalized so that for each indicator in a sample of 111 countries, the worst value gets a score of 0, the best value gets a score of 100, and the median gets a score of 50. If in the original values higher numbers indicate worse outcomes, the chart labels are marked with an asterisk (*). Series with missing data are indicated as (-) in the tables and omitted from the radar charts.

Source: World Bank Enterprise Survey (2013) for firm level data; for other sources refer to Annex III.

ITC Business Survey on Non-Tariff Measures (NTMs)

1. Firms affected by NTMs

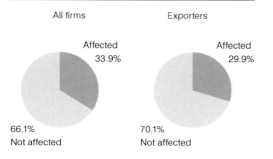

All firms

Exporters

Affected 33.9%

Affected 29.9%

66.1% Not affected

70.1% Not affected

2. NTMs reported as challenging (exporters)

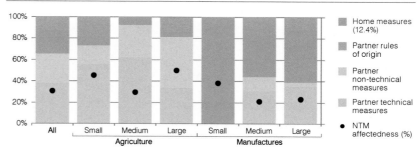

- Home measures (12.4%)
- Partner rules of origin
- Partner non-technical measures
- Partner technical measures
- NTM affectedness (%)

3. Regulatory and procedural obstacles (exporters)

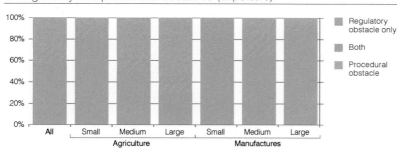

- Regulatory obstacle only
- Both
- Procedural obstacle

4. Location of procedural obstacles (exporters)

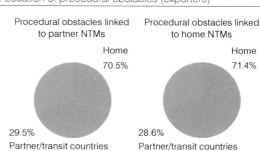

Procedural obstacles linked to partner NTMs

Home 70.5%

29.5% Partner/transit countries

Procedural obstacles linked to home NTMs

Home 71.4%

28.6% Partner/transit countries

Source: ITC NTM Survey, additional results are available at http://ntmsurvey.intracen.org/ntm-survey-data/country-analysis/kazakhstan/

Potential for Growth of Current Exports

PRODUCT/PRODUCT GROUP DESCRIPTION	Exports (US$ mn)	Europe & Central Asia	Unrealized potential	South-South trade	Unrealized potential	OECD	Unrealized potential	Technology level	Revenues stability	SME presence	Female participation
284410 Natural uranium&its compounds;...	1967.9		76%		66%		31%				
740311 Copper cathodes and sections of...	2326.6		27%		5%		33%				
720241 Ferro-chromium containing by we...	1595.4		28%		31%		15%				
110100 Wheat or meslin flour	569.9		57%		54%		100%				
1001Xb Wheat and meslin	913.2		18%		23%		54%				
760110 Aluminium unwrought, not alloyed	370.0		56%		24%		67%				
790111 Zinc not alloyed unwrought contai...	544.1		22%		9%		30%				
710691 Silver in unwrought forms	433.5		46%		58%		48%				
151221 Cotton-seed oil crude, whether or...	15.5		96%		96%		100%				
720230 Ferro-silico-manganese	191.9		55%		48%		65%				
720250 Ferro-silico-chromium	131.0		83%		87%		12%				
8108XX Unwrought titanium; titanium pow...	159.5		85%		97%		48%				
720839 Hot roll iron/steel nes, coil >600m...	216.0		80%		9%		89%				
280470 Phosphorus	121.0		32%		91%		41%				
721049 Flat rolled prod.i/nas,plated or co...	230.6		50%		25%		100%				
281820 Aluminium oxide nes	245.1		18%		29%		100%				
721012 Flat rolld prod.i/nas,platd or coatd...	131.3		48%		19%		98%				
520100 Cotton, not carded or combed	79.3		77%		84%		92%				
0304Xb Fish fillets and pieces, fresh, chill...	76.9		39%		46%		63%				
780110 Lead refined unwrought	183.2		36%		30%		41%				

What is the product's export potential in...?

Would Kazakhstan improve its...?

Note: Top 20 products listed in decreasing order of their export potential to the world. Development indicators are relative to the country's current situation, green indicating performance above its trade-weighted median and red otherwise; a blank cell indicates data are not available. A blank cell in export potential means that the product was not consistently demanded over five years by any country in the respective region. Exports (US$ mn) corresponds to the yearly average exports to the world over the period 2009-13. Refer to Annexes I, II and III for details.

Source: ITC Export Potential Assessment, additional results are available at ITC Country Pages http://www.intracen.org/country/kazakhstan/

Kenya

Key indicators

Population (millions)	42.9
GDP (US$ billions)	60.8
GDP per capita (US$)	1,415.7
Share of world GDP (PPP US$, %)	0.1
Current account surplus over GDP (%)	-9.2
Tariff preference margin (percentage points)	8.4
Goods and services imports + exports over GDP (%)	55.3
Exports of services over total exports (%)	45.2
Geographic region	Sub-Saharan Africa
Development group	DC
Income group	Lower-middle income

SME Competitiveness Grid Summary

Average scores [0–100]		Compete	Connect	Change
FIRM LEVEL CAPABILITIES	Small	40.2	25.7	53.7
	Medium	47.9	55.4	66.8
	Large	60.5	64.9	77.0
	All	46.0	37.2	62.2
IMMEDIATE BUSINESS ENVIRONMENT		33.6	66.9	42.9
NATIONAL ENVIRONMENT		39.5	39.5	37.5

Reference level: 38.2 (a function of GDP per capita US$)

Strengths are scores above: 57.3	Weaknesses are scores below: 19.1

SME Competitiveness Grid

1	FIRM LEVEL CAPABILITIES	Values				Normalized scores			
		Small	Medium	Large	All	Small	Medium	Large	All
1.1	Capacity to Compete								
1.1.1	Firms with quality certification (%)	15.5	22.3	55.2	22.3	40.1	49.9	78.8	49.9
1.1.2	Firms with checking or savings account (%)	91.0	94.7	92.9	92.3	39.0	48.1	43.1	41.7
1.1.3	Capacity utilization (%)	69.4	72.0	76.7	72.2	38.8	44.0	54.3	44.4
1.1.4	Manager's experience (years)	15.6	17.4	21.9	16.9	43.0	49.6	65.8	47.8
1.2	Capacity to Connect								
1.2.1	Firms using e-mail (%)	61.1	87.8	91.8	72.9	23.7	53.2	62.0	33.3
1.2.2	Firms having their own website (%)	32.5	63.0	72.5	46.6	27.8	57.6	67.7	41.1
1.3	Capacity to Change								
1.3.1	Firms with audited financial statements (%)	74.2	93.2	96.5	82.7	66.3	90.3	94.9	76.6
1.3.2	Investments financed by banks (%)	22.6	26.1	24.8	24.2	64.3	69.5	67.7	66.8
1.3.3	Firms offering formal training (%)	35.2	40.3	68.7	40.9	42.5	47.8	74.7	48.4
1.3.4	Firms using foreign technology licences (%)	11.2	21.8	31.6	20.1	41.6	59.6	70.7	57.2

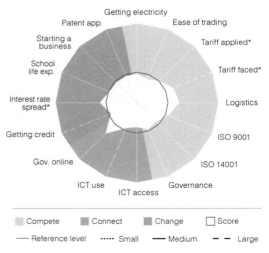

2	IMMEDIATE BUSINESS ENVIRONMENT	Values				Normalized scores			
		Small	Medium	Large	All	Small	Medium	Large	All
2.1	Capacity to Compete								
2.1.1	Losses due to power outages (% of sales)	5.3	5.5	7.1	5.6	26.4	25.8	21.9	25.5
2.1.2	Losses during domestic shipping (%)	2.7	0.9	1.9	1.9	26.1	46.7	32.7	32.7
2.1.3	Management time spent with regulation (%)	6.7	7.9	7.6	7.2	52.0	48.1	49.0	50.3
2.1.4	Days for customs clearance	26.3	14.4	14.9	15.3	7.1	27.7	26.6	25.7
2.2	Capacity to Connect								
2.2.1	State of cluster development (1–7)				4.2				70.3
2.2.2	Extent of marketing (1–7)				4.4				59.9
2.2.3	Local supplier quality (1–7)				4.7				64.7
2.2.4	University-industry collaboration in R&D (1–7)				4.2				72.6
2.3	Capacity to Change								
2.3.1	Access to finance as a constraint (%)	15.3	19.5	22.1	17.4	59.5	52.4	48.5	55.8
2.3.2	Inadequately educated workforce (%)	33.7	20.7	31.0	29.5	33.3	48.6	36.1	37.7
2.3.3	Business licensing and permits as a constraint (%)	18.9	17.5	20.1	18.7	34.9	36.9	33.3	35.2

3	NATIONAL ENVIRONMENT	Values	Normalized scores
		All	All
3.1	Capacity to Compete		
3.1.1	Ease of getting electricity (0–100)	58.8	35.8
3.1.2	Ease of trading across borders (0–100)	54.5	31.8
3.1.3	Applied tariff, trade-weighted average (%)	9.5	38.1
3.1.4	Faced tariff, trade-weighted average (%)	3.7	48.0
3.1.5	Logistics performance index (1–5)	2.8	52.2
3.1.6	ISO 9001 quality certificates (/mn pop.)	14.1	41.4
3.1.7	ISO 14001 environmental certificates (/mn pop.)	1.2	32.8
3.1.8	Governance (index)	-0.7	35.7
3.2	Capacity to Connect		
3.2.1	ICT access (0–10)	3.3	30.5
3.2.2	ICT use (0–10)	1.4	34.0
3.2.3	Government's online service (0–10)	4.3	54.1
3.3	Capacity to Change		
3.3.1	Ease of getting credit (0–100)	35.0	34.4
3.3.2	Interest rate spread (%)	8.7	45.6
3.3.3	School life expectancy (years)	11.0	36.3
3.3.4	Ease of starting a business (0–100)	74.0	35.6
3.3.5	Patent applications (/mn pop.)	3.0	35.6
3.3.6	Trademark registrations (/mn pop.)	-	-

Note: For each indicator, the table includes the values and the corresponding scores. Radar charts are based on scores: values are transformed and normalized so that for each indicator in a sample of 111 countries, the worst value gets a score of 0, the best value gets a score of 100, and the median gets a score of 50. If in the original values higher numbers indicate worse outcomes, the chart labels are marked with an asterisk (*). Series with missing data are indicated as (-) in the tables and omitted from the radar charts.

Source: World Bank Enterprise Survey (2013) for firm level data; for other sources refer to Annex III.

ITC Business Survey on Non-Tariff Measures (NTMs)

1. Firms affected by NTMs

All firms

Affected
70.9%

29.1%
Not affected

Exporters

Affected
51.4%

48.6%
Not affected

2. NTMs reported as challenging (exporters)

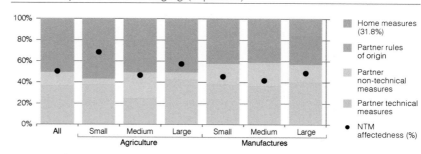

- Home measures (31.8%)
- Partner rules of origin
- Partner non-technical measures
- Partner technical measures
- ● NTM affectedness (%)

3. Regulatory and procedural obstacles (exporters)

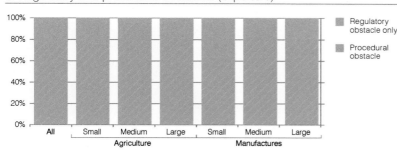

- Regulatory obstacle only
- Procedural obstacle

4. Location of procedural obstacles (exporters)

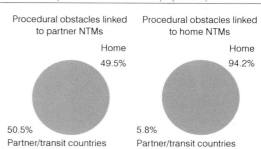

Procedural obstacles linked to partner NTMs

Home
49.5%

50.5%
Partner/transit countries

Procedural obstacles linked to home NTMs

Home
94.2%

5.8%
Partner/transit countries

Source: ITC NTM Survey, additional results are available at http://ntmsurvey.intracen.org/ntm-survey-data/country-analysis/kenya/

Potential for Growth of Current Exports

PRODUCT/PRODUCT GROUP DESCRIPTION	Exports (US$ mn)	Sub-Saharan Africa	Unrealized potential	South-South trade	Unrealized potential	OECD	Unrealized potential	Technology level	Revenues stability	SME presence	Female participation
090240 Black tea (fermented) & partly fer...	1125.6		64%		27%		57%	■	■		
252329 Portland cement nes	80.4		79%		79%		100%	■	■	■	■
0603XX Cut flowers and flower buds for b...	483.6		80%		22%		18%	■	■		
090111 Coffee, not roasted, not decaffein...	236.7		87%		68%		21%	■	■		
170410 Chewing gum containing sugar, e...	26.3		88%		87%		99%	■	■	■	■
830910 Corks, crown, of base metal	14.5		90%		90%		100%	■	■	■	■
721041 Flat rolled prod,i/nas,pltd or ctd w...	17.4		87%		87%		100%	■	■	■	■
070820 Beans, shelled or unshelled, fresh...	118.8		99%		95%		23%	■	■		
060210 Cuttings and slips, unrooted	52.6		92%		90%		56%	■	■		
14XXXX Vegetable products nes	50.2		28%		36%		79%	■	■		
0709Xa Vegetables nes, fresh or chilled	55.2		95%		93%		29%	■	■		
200820 Pineapples nes,o/w prep or unsh...	60.5		74%		61%		53%				
151710 Margarine, excluding liquid marga...	22.4		68%		70%		99%	■	■	■	■
340119 Soap&orgn surf prep, shapd, nes...	15.2		80%		80%		100%	■	■	■	■
210230 Baking powders, prepared	6.1		89%		89%		100%	■	■	■	■
340120 Soap nes	21.5		61%		65%		98%	■	■	■	■
340111 Toilet soap & prep, shaped; papers...	21.3		57%		61%		100%	■	■	■	■
340510 Polishes, creams & similar prepar...	10.1		74%		75%		100%	■	■	■	■
151190 Palm oil and its fractions refined b...	49.1		17%		67%		100%	■	■	■	■
482020 Exercise books of paper	8.9		77%		78%		100%	■	■	■	■

Header: What is the product's export potential in…? / Would Kenya improve its…?

Note: Top 20 products listed in decreasing order of their export potential to the world. Development indicators are relative to the country's current situation, green indicating performance above its trade-weighted median and red otherwise; a blank cell indicates data are not available. A blank cell in export potential means that the product was not consistently demanded over five years by any country in the respective region. Exports (US$ mn) corresponds to the yearly average exports to the world over the period 2009-13. Refer to Annexes I, II and III for details.

Source: ITC Export Potential Assessment, additional results are available at ITC Country Pages http://www.intracen.org/country/kenya/

Madagascar

Key indicators

Population (millions)	23.6
GDP (US$ billions)	10.6
GDP per capita (US$)	449.5
Share of world GDP (PPP US$, %)	0.0
Current account surplus over GDP (%)	-2.3
Tariff preference margin (percentage points)	8.1
Goods and services imports + exports over GDP (%)	73.4
Exports of services over total exports (%)	39.2
Geographic region	Sub-Saharan Africa
Development group	LDC
Income group	Low income

SME Competitiveness Grid Summary

Average scores [0–100]		Compete	Connect	Change
FIRM LEVEL CAPABILITIES	Small	26.1	12.9	15.3
	Medium	34.8	42.3	43.7
	Large	59.8	68.2	48.5
	All	33.5	24.7	30.8
IMMEDIATE BUSINESS ENVIRONMENT		32.0	36.0	65.0
NATIONAL ENVIRONMENT		33.9	12.0	24.2

Reference level: 28.5 (a function of GDP per capita US$)

Strengths are scores above: 42.8	Weaknesses are scores below: 14.3

SME Competitiveness Grid

1	FIRM LEVEL CAPABILITIES	Values				Normalized scores			
		Small	Medium	Large	All	Small	Medium	Large	All
1.1	Capacity to Compete								
1.1.1	Firms with quality certification (%)	9.8	14.2	41.7	15.3	29.5	37.9	69.3	39.8
1.1.2	Firms with checking or savings account (%)	70.5	89.3	97.0	78.6	18.0	36.0	57.6	23.7
1.1.3	Capacity utilization (%)	57.8	59.9	72.3	62.9	19.3	22.5	44.6	27.3
1.1.4	Manager's experience (years)	14.2	15.6	22.4	15.7	37.7	43.0	67.6	43.3
1.2	Capacity to Connect								
1.2.1	Firms using e-mail (%)	47.9	81.5	91.9	62.0	15.7	43.1	62.3	24.3
1.2.2	Firms having their own website (%)	12.3	47.1	78.3	29.5	10.1	41.6	74.2	25.1
1.3	Capacity to Change								
1.3.1	Firms with audited financial statements (%)	27.5	58.4	77.4	41.7	20.1	49.0	70.1	32.6
1.3.2	Investments financed by banks (%)	1.0	6.8	6.7	4.3	5.6	29.3	29.0	20.5
1.3.3	Firms offering formal training (%)	8.2	16.8	26.7	12.7	10.9	21.6	33.2	16.6
1.3.4	Firms using foreign technology licences (%)	5.0	35.9	23.5	17.7	24.4	74.7	61.8	53.6

2	IMMEDIATE BUSINESS ENVIRONMENT	Values				Normalized scores			
		Small	Medium	Large	All	Small	Medium	Large	All
2.1	Capacity to Compete								
2.1.1	Losses due to power outages (% of sales)	7.9	5.8	4.0	6.8	20.3	25.0	30.6	22.6
2.1.2	Losses during domestic shipping (%)	0.9	0.9	1.3	1.0	46.7	46.7	39.9	44.8
2.1.3	Management time spent with regulation (%)	21.1	23.0	13.4	20.8	23.2	20.9	35.0	23.6
2.1.4	Days for customs clearance	11.2	11.7	10.9	10.9	36.1	34.8	37.0	37.1
2.2	Capacity to Connect								
2.2.1	State of cluster development (1–7)				2.9				24.3
2.2.2	Extent of marketing (1–7)				3.4				29.0
2.2.3	Local supplier quality (1–7)				3.9				43.9
2.2.4	University-industry collaboration in R&D (1–7)				3.3				47.0
2.3	Capacity to Change								
2.3.1	Access to finance as a constraint (%)	8.0	20.4	11.8	12.3	75.0	51.1	66.3	65.3
2.3.2	Inadequately educated workforce (%)	6.6	21.2	7.5	10.5	75.9	47.9	73.5	66.4
2.3.3	Business licensing and permits as a constraint (%)	3.8	9.1	8.6	5.8	71.5	53.2	54.5	63.2

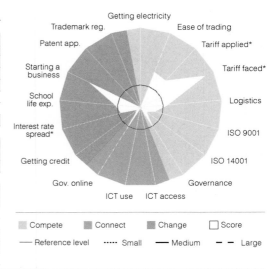

3	NATIONAL ENVIRONMENT	Values	Normalized scores
		All	All
3.1	Capacity to Compete		
3.1.1	Ease of getting electricity (0–100)	16.7	0.0
3.1.2	Ease of trading across borders (0–100)	69.0	47.3
3.1.3	Applied tariff, trade-weighted average (%)	7.5	45.4
3.1.4	Faced tariff, trade-weighted average (%)	2.4	88.4
3.1.5	Logistics performance index (1–5)	2.4	33.4
3.1.6	ISO 9001 quality certificates (/mn pop.)	2.0	18.6
3.1.7	ISO 14001 environmental certificates (/mn pop.)	0.1	8.9
3.1.8	Governance (index)	-0.8	29.5
3.2	Capacity to Connect		
3.2.1	ICT access (0–10)	1.7	0.6
3.2.2	ICT use (0–10)	0.1	1.4
3.2.3	Government's online service (0–10)	2.4	34.0
3.3	Capacity to Change		
3.3.1	Ease of getting credit (0–100)	5.0	4.8
3.3.2	Interest rate spread (%)	49.3	24.9
3.3.3	School life expectancy (years)	10.3	31.0
3.3.4	Ease of starting a business (0–100)	92.0	70.1
3.3.5	Patent applications (/mn pop.)	1.0	0.0
3.3.6	Trademark registrations (/mn pop.)	73.0	14.5

Legend: Compete | Connect | Change | Score | Reference level | ..... Small | — Medium | – – Large

Note: For each indicator, the table includes the values and the corresponding scores. Radar charts are based on scores: values are transformed and normalized so that for each indicator in a sample of 111 countries, the worst value gets a score of 0, the best value gets a score of 100, and the median gets a score of 50. If in the original values higher numbers indicate worse outcomes, the chart labels are marked with an asterisk (*). Series with missing data are indicated as (-) in the tables and omitted from the radar charts.

Source: World Bank Enterprise Survey (2013) for firm level data; for other sources refer to Annex III.

ITC Business Survey on Non-Tariff Measures (NTMs)

1. Firms affected by NTMs

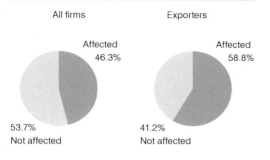

All firms

Affected
46.3%

53.7%
Not affected

Exporters

Affected
58.8%

41.2%
Not affected

2. NTMs reported as challenging (exporters)

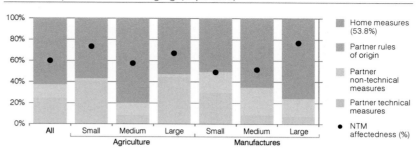

- Home measures (53.8%)
- Partner rules of origin
- Partner non-technical measures
- Partner technical measures
- ● NTM affectedness (%)

3. Regulatory and procedural obstacles (exporters)

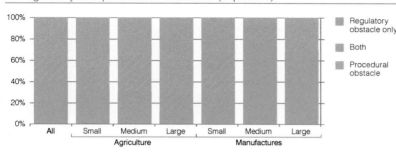

- Regulatory obstacle only
- Both
- Procedural obstacle

4. Location of procedural obstacles (exporters)

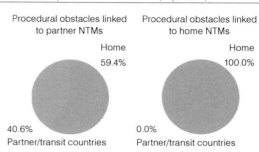

Procedural obstacles linked to partner NTMs

Home
59.4%

40.6%
Partner/transit countries

Procedural obstacles linked to home NTMs

Home
100.0%

0.0%
Partner/transit countries

Source: ITC NTM Survey, additional results are available at http://ntmsurvey.intracen.org/ntm-survey-data/country-analysis/madagascar/

Potential for Growth of Current Exports

PRODUCT/PRODUCT GROUP DESCRIPTION	Exports (US$ mn)	What is the product's export potential in…?						Would Madagascar improve its…?			
		Sub-Saharan Africa	Unrealized potential	South-South trade	Unrealized potential	OECD	Unrealized potential	Technology level	Revenues stability	SME presence	Female participation
0907XX Cloves	139.6		94%		31%		66%				
0905XX Vanilla	57.6		94%		90%		71%				
0306Xa Crustaceans	91.8		78%		84%		47%				
6110XX Jerseys, pullovers, cardigans, etc,...	98.8		50%		73%		49%				
160414 Tunas,skipjack&Atl bonito,prepard...	42.9		99%		96%		38%				
3301Xb Essential oils, nes	29.2		89%		39%		56%				
611020 Pullovers, cardigans and similar, a...	33.3		2%		32%		31%				
620342 Mens/boys trousers and shorts, o...	31.4		5%		27%		36%				
620462 Womens/girls trousers and shorts...	27.6		43%		48%		34%				
180100 Cocoa beans, whole or broken, ra...	20.3		94%		51%		37%				
1701XX Cane or beet sugar and chemica...	17.4		35%		77%		53%				
620520 Mens/boys shirts, of cotton, not k...	24.8		7%		21%		42%				
620920 Babies garments and clothing ac...	10.3		69%		72%		50%				
200559 Beans nes prepard or preservd,o/...	13.1		100%		100%		34%				
620630 Womens/girls blouses and shirts...	14.5		4%		23%		43%				
090111 Coffee, not roasted, not decaffein...	10.6		99%		49%		68%				
621410 Shawls,scarves,veils and the like....	20.2		99%		100%		46%				
610910 T-shirts, singlets and other vests,...	14.9		5%		21%		44%				
620442 Womens/girls dresses, of cotton,...	10.4		65%		68%		45%				
611030 Pullovers, cardigans and similar ar...	13.3		4%		28%		41%				

Note: Top 20 products listed in decreasing order of their export potential to the world. Development indicators are relative to the country's current situation, green indicating performance above its trade-weighted median and red otherwise; a blank cell indicates data are not available. A blank cell in export potential means that the product was not consistently demanded over five years by any country in the respective region. Exports (US$ mn) corresponds to the yearly average exports to the world over the period 2009-13. Refer to Annexes I, II and III for details.

Source: ITC Export Potential Assessment, additional results are available at ITC Country Pages http://www.intracen.org/country/madagascar/

Malawi

Key indicators

Population (millions)	17.6
GDP (US$ billions)	4.3
GDP per capita (US$)	242.2
Share of world GDP (PPP US$, %)	0.0
Current account surplus over GDP (%)	-5.1
Tariff preference margin (percentage points)	11.6
Goods and services imports + exports over GDP (%)	106.8
Exports of services over total exports (%)	8.8
Geographic region	Sub-Saharan Africa
Development group	LDC, LLDC
Income group	Low income

SME Competitiveness Grid Summary

Average scores [0–100]		Compete	Connect	Change
FIRM LEVEL CAPABILITIES	Small	35.1	27.4	35.2
	Medium	43.7	58.6	55.4
	Large	47.8	75.4	60.3
	All	38.7	40.0	47.2
IMMEDIATE BUSINESS ENVIRONMENT		37.3	39.1	48.2
NATIONAL ENVIRONMENT		36.5	12.8	24.7

Reference level: 23.3 (a function of GDP per capita US$)

Strengths are scores above: 34.9	Weaknesses are scores below: 11.6

SME Competitiveness Grid

1	FIRM LEVEL CAPABILITIES	Values				Normalized scores			
		Small	Medium	Large	All	Small	Medium	Large	All
1.1	Capacity to Compete								
1.1.1	Firms with quality certification (%)	5.3	28.5	53.0	18.8	18.5	57.2	77.4	45.2
1.1.2	Firms with checking or savings account (%)	77.0	85.1	93.2	81.9	22.5	30.2	43.9	26.7
1.1.3	Capacity utilization (%)	79.1	73.1	56.3	70.5	60.2	46.3	17.1	41.0
1.1.4	Manager's experience (years)	14.6	15.1	18.3	15.3	39.2	41.1	52.9	41.8
1.2	Capacity to Connect								
1.2.1	Firms using e-mail (%)	69.5	91.3	97.1	79.6	30.2	60.8	80.6	40.6
1.2.2	Firms having their own website (%)	28.9	61.9	74.8	44.9	24.6	56.4	70.3	39.5
1.3	Capacity to Change								
1.3.1	Firms with audited financial statements (%)	35.8	66.1	56.0	47.0	27.3	57.2	46.5	37.6
1.3.2	Investments financed by banks (%)	10.3	19.5	15.3	13.8	39.5	59.1	51.2	47.9
1.3.3	Firms offering formal training (%)	24.4	38.5	53.4	32.9	30.6	45.9	60.8	40.0
1.3.4	Firms using foreign technology licences (%)	12.1	21.6	46.0	24.6	43.5	59.3	82.6	63.1

2	IMMEDIATE BUSINESS ENVIRONMENT	Values				Normalized scores			
		Small	Medium	Large	All	Small	Medium	Large	All
2.1	Capacity to Compete								
2.1.1	Losses due to power outages (% of sales)	4.6	7.3	3.2	5.1	28.5	21.5	34.0	27.0
2.1.2	Losses during domestic shipping (%)	0.6	0.8	5.6	1.6	54.0	48.8	12.0	36.0
2.1.3	Management time spent with regulation (%)	4.0	6.8	5.8	5.0	63.3	51.7	55.3	58.6
2.1.4	Days for customs clearance	-	29.6	10.9	14.5	-	3.0	37.0	27.6
2.2	Capacity to Connect								
2.2.1	State of cluster development (1–7)				3.7				55.4
2.2.2	Extent of marketing (1–7)				3.4				29.1
2.2.3	Local supplier quality (1–7)				3.7				37.9
2.2.4	University-industry collaboration in R&D (1–7)				2.8				33.9
2.3	Capacity to Change								
2.3.1	Access to finance as a constraint (%)	40.0	33.4	19.4	34.9	27.9	34.5	52.6	32.9
2.3.2	Inadequately educated workforce (%)	12.3	13.0	8.9	11.9	62.6	61.2	70.0	63.4
2.3.3	Business licensing and permits as a constraint (%)	13.0	9.1	8.2	11.2	44.5	53.2	55.6	48.2

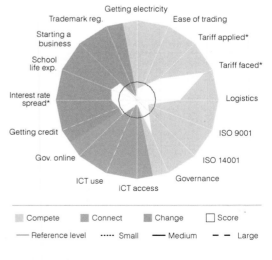

3	NATIONAL ENVIRONMENT	Values	Normalized scores
		All	All
3.1	Capacity to Compete		
3.1.1	Ease of getting electricity (0–100)	35.8	14.3
3.1.2	Ease of trading across borders (0–100)	37.4	18.4
3.1.3	Applied tariff, trade-weighted average (%)	9.7	37.4
3.1.4	Faced tariff, trade-weighted average (%)	2.4	89.0
3.1.5	Logistics performance index (1–5)	2.8	52.2
3.1.6	ISO 9001 quality certificates (/mn pop.)	1.3	14.4
3.1.7	ISO 14001 environmental certificates (/mn pop.)	0.4	20.0
3.1.8	Governance (index)	-0.4	45.9
3.2	Capacity to Connect		
3.2.1	ICT access (0–10)	1.9	5.0
3.2.2	ICT use (0–10)	0.3	8.4
3.2.3	Government's online service (0–10)	1.7	25.1
3.3	Capacity to Change		
3.3.1	Ease of getting credit (0–100)	25.0	24.3
3.3.2	Interest rate spread (%)	27.6	31.5
3.3.3	School life expectancy (years)	10.8	34.4
3.3.4	Ease of starting a business (0–100)	68.5	29.5
3.3.5	Patent applications (/mn pop.)	-	-
3.3.6	Trademark registrations (/mn pop.)	17.0	3.9

Compete · Connect · Change · Score
— Reference level ···· Small — Medium – – Large

Note: For each indicator, the table includes the values and the corresponding scores. Radar charts are based on scores: values are transformed and normalized so that for each indicator in a sample of 111 countries, the worst value gets a score of 0, the best value gets a score of 100, and the median gets a score of 50. If in the original values higher numbers indicate worse outcomes, the chart labels are marked with an asterisk (*). Series with missing data are indicated as (-) in the tables and omitted from the radar charts.

Source: World Bank Enterprise Survey (2014) for firm level data; for other sources refer to Annex III.

ITC Business Survey on Non-Tariff Measures (NTMs)

1. Firms affected by NTMs

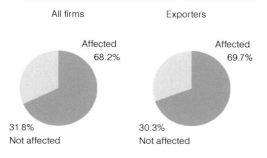

All firms

Affected
68.2%

31.8%
Not affected

Exporters

Affected
69.7%

30.3%
Not affected

2. NTMs reported as challenging (exporters)

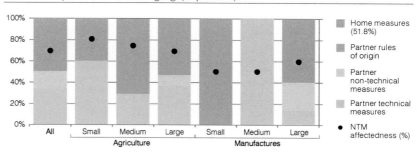

- Home measures (51.8%)
- Partner rules of origin
- Partner non-technical measures
- Partner technical measures
- NTM affectedness (%)

3. Regulatory and procedural obstacles (exporters)

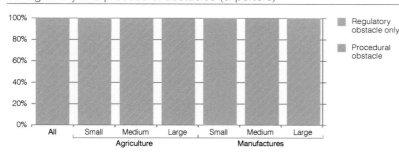

- Regulatory obstacle only
- Procedural obstacle

4. Location of procedural obstacles (exporters)

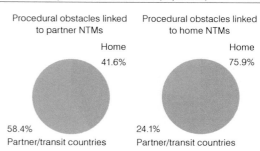

Procedural obstacles linked to partner NTMs

Home
41.6%

58.4%
Partner/transit countries

Procedural obstacles linked to home NTMs

Home
75.9%

24.1%
Partner/transit countries

Source: ITC NTM Survey, additional results are available at http://ntmsurvey.intracen.org/ntm-survey-data/country-analysis/malawi/

Potential for Growth of Current Exports

PRODUCT/PRODUCT GROUP DESCRIPTION	Exports (US$ mn)	Sub-Saharan Africa	Unrealized potential	South-South trade	Unrealized potential	OECD	Unrealized potential	Technology level	Revenues stability	SME presence	Female participation
090240 Black tea (fermented) & partly fer...	76.8		57%		54%		29%				
1701XX Cane or beet sugar and chemicall...	82.1		63%		72%		5%				
1202XX Ground-nuts, not roasted	26.5		59%		61%		100%				
520100 Cotton, not carded or combed	32.0		15%		20%		80%				
100590 Maize (corn) nes	16.6		49%		53%		96%				
0713Xb Dried vegetables, shelled	19.9		69%		5%		73%				
0802Xc Nuts nes	12.9		74%		86%		29%				
230610 Cotton sed oil-cake&oth solid resi...	1.9		88%		88%		100%				
400129 Natural rubber in other forms nes	8.2		26%		43%		100%				
071310 Peas dried, shelled, whether or no...	8.1		30%		49%		75%				
4407Xb Wood sawn/chipped lengthwise,...	5.5		31%		62%		100%				
100510 Maize (corn) seed	3.1		54%		55%		100%				
090111 Coffee, not roasted, not decaffein...	4.0		19%		49%		68%				
170199 Refined sugar, in solid form, nes	4.8		54%		61%		21%				
392490 Household and toilet articles nes,...	3.8		31%		40%		99%				
071320 Chickpeas, dried, shelled, wheth...	3.0		5%		40%		94%				
44XXXX Wood and articles of wood, woo...	4.5		15%		64%		100%				
140420 Cotton linters	3.5		100%		76%		99%				
120810 Soya bean flour and meals	3.9		55%		56%		100%				
520300 Cotton, carded or combed	3.9		84%		81%		96%				

What is the product's export potential in…?

Would Malawi improve its…?

Note: Top 20 products listed in decreasing order of their export potential to the world. Development indicators are relative to the country's current situation, green indicating performance above its trade-weighted median and red otherwise; a blank cell indicates data are not available. A blank cell in export potential means that the product was not consistently demanded over five years by any country in the respective region. Exports (US$ mn) corresponds to the yearly average exports to the world over the period 2009-13. Refer to Annexes I, II and III for details.

Source: ITC Export Potential Assessment, additional results are available at ITC Country Pages http://www.intracen.org/country/malawi/

Mauritius

Key indicators

Population (millions)	1.3
GDP (US$ billions)	13.2
GDP per capita (US$)	10,516.5
Share of world GDP (PPP US$, %)	0.0
Current account surplus over GDP (%)	-7.2
Tariff preference margin (percentage points)	17.9
Goods and services imports + exports over GDP (%)	114.6
Exports of services over total exports (%)	56.6
Geographic region	Sub-Saharan Africa
Development group	SIDS
Income group	Upper-middle income

SME Competitiveness Grid Summary

Average scores [0–100]		Compete	Connect	Change
FIRM LEVEL CAPABILITIES	Small	32.2	23.2	41.1
	Medium	54.1	46.3	61.0
	Large	60.0	73.5	80.1
	All	40.9	30.5	51.6
IMMEDIATE BUSINESS ENVIRONMENT		47.9	61.7	26.9
NATIONAL ENVIRONMENT		68.8	62.5	62.7

Reference level: 55.2 (a function of GDP per capita US$)	
Strengths are scores above: 82.8	Weaknesses are scores below: 27.6

SME Competitiveness Grid

1	FIRM LEVEL CAPABILITIES	Values				Normalized scores			
		Small	Medium	Large	All	Small	Medium	Large	All
1.1	Capacity to Compete								
1.1.1	Firms with quality certification (%)	6.8	16.0	29.4	11.1	22.5	40.9	58.1	32.2
1.1.2	Firms with checking or savings account (%)	96.5	99.0	97.7	97.2	55.1	74.3	61.9	58.8
1.1.3	Capacity utilization (%)	50.1	69.0	76.8	60.3	8.6	38.1	54.6	23.1
1.1.4	Manager's experience (years)	15.5	21.1	21.8	17.4	42.6	63.0	65.5	49.6
1.2	Capacity to Connect								
1.2.1	Firms using e-mail (%)	59.6	86.0	98.5	69.3	22.6	49.9	88.4	30.0
1.2.2	Firms having their own website (%)	27.9	48.3	64.0	35.9	23.7	42.8	58.6	31.0
1.3	Capacity to Change								
1.3.1	Firms with audited financial statements (%)	46.5	79.3	92.8	59.5	37.1	72.4	89.8	50.1
1.3.2	Investments financed by banks (%)	33.9	25.1	30.2	30.8	79.5	68.1	75.0	75.8
1.3.3	Firms offering formal training (%)	15.1	39.4	76.3	25.6	19.6	46.9	81.2	31.9
1.3.4	Firms using foreign technology licences (%)	6.1	19.6	35.6	14.6	28.1	56.5	74.4	48.4

2	IMMEDIATE BUSINESS ENVIRONMENT	Values				Normalized scores			
		Small	Medium	Large	All	Small	Medium	Large	All
2.1	Capacity to Compete								
2.1.1	Losses due to power outages (% of sales)	0.4	0.9	0.2	0.5	64.5	52.9	73.7	61.4
2.1.2	Losses during domestic shipping (%)	0.3	1.8	0.8	0.9	65.8	33.8	48.8	46.7
2.1.3	Management time spent with regulation (%)	9.4	9.7	7.5	9.4	43.9	43.2	49.4	43.9
2.1.4	Days for customs clearance	9.7	9.1	13.2	10.1	40.8	42.9	30.7	39.6
2.2	Capacity to Connect								
2.2.1	State of cluster development (1–7)				4.3				72.8
2.2.2	Extent of marketing (1–7)				4.6				66.2
2.2.3	Local supplier quality (1–7)				4.6				62.6
2.2.4	University-industry collaboration in R&D (1–7)				3.2				45.0
2.3	Capacity to Change								
2.3.1	Access to finance as a constraint (%)	52.2	40.3	22.5	46.3	17.6	27.6	48.0	22.3
2.3.2	Inadequately educated workforce (%)	37.8	67.3	48.6	45.7	29.5	9.2	20.9	23.0
2.3.3	Business licensing and permits as a constraint (%)	17.5	25.9	9.5	18.6	36.9	26.5	52.2	35.3

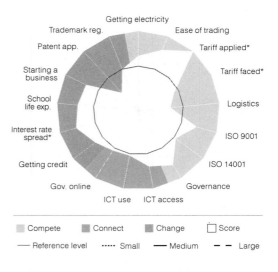

3	NATIONAL ENVIRONMENT	Values	Normalized scores
		All	All
3.1	Capacity to Compete		
3.1.1	Ease of getting electricity (0–100)	83.7	68.4
3.1.2	Ease of trading across borders (0–100)	87.7	81.2
3.1.3	Applied tariff, trade-weighted average (%)	0.7	100.0
3.1.4	Faced tariff, trade-weighted average (%)	3.7	48.8
3.1.5	Logistics performance index (1–5)	2.5	39.4
3.1.6	ISO 9001 quality certificates (/mn pop.)	177.9	74.6
3.1.7	ISO 14001 environmental certificates (/mn pop.)	11.1	57.5
3.1.8	Governance (index)	0.8	80.6
3.2	Capacity to Connect		
3.2.1	ICT access (0–10)	6.3	71.4
3.2.2	ICT use (0–10)	3.0	57.3
3.2.3	Government's online service (0–10)	4.7	58.8
3.3	Capacity to Change		
3.3.1	Ease of getting credit (0–100)	65.0	66.1
3.3.2	Interest rate spread (%)	1.7	79.2
3.3.3	School life expectancy (years)	15.6	74.8
3.3.4	Ease of starting a business (0–100)	92.5	71.7
3.3.5	Patent applications (/mn pop.)	2.0	29.7
3.3.6	Trademark registrations (/mn pop.)	607.0	54.8

Note: For each indicator, the table includes the values and the corresponding scores. Radar charts are based on scores: values are transformed and normalized so that for each indicator in a sample of 111 countries, the worst value gets a score of 0, the best value gets a score of 100, and the median gets a score of 50. If in the original values higher numbers indicate worse outcomes, the chart labels are marked with an asterisk (*). Series with missing data are indicated as (-) in the tables and omitted from the radar charts.

Source: World Bank Enterprise Survey (2009) for firm level data; for other sources refer to Annex III.

ITC Business Survey on Non-Tariff Measures (NTMs)

1. Firms affected by NTMs

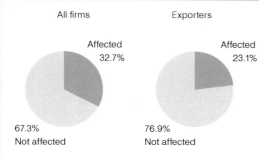

All firms

Affected
32.7%

67.3%
Not affected

Exporters

Affected
23.1%

76.9%
Not affected

2. NTMs reported as challenging (exporters)

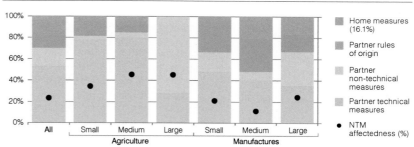

- ■ Home measures (16.1%)
- ■ Partner rules of origin
- ■ Partner non-technical measures
- ■ Partner technical measures
- ● NTM affectedness (%)

Agriculture | Manufactures

3. Regulatory and procedural obstacles (exporters)

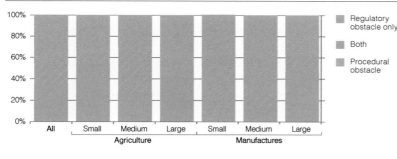

- ■ Regulatory obstacle only
- ■ Both
- ■ Procedural obstacle

Agriculture | Manufactures

4. Location of procedural obstacles (exporters)

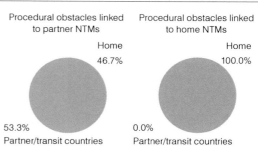

Procedural obstacles linked to partner NTMs

Home
46.7%

53.3%
Partner/transit countries

Procedural obstacles linked to home NTMs

Home
100.0%

0.0%
Partner/transit countries

Source: ITC NTM Survey, additional results are available at http://ntmsurvey.intracen.org/ntm-survey-data/country-analysis/mauritius/

Potential for Growth of Current Exports

PRODUCT/PRODUCT GROUP DESCRIPTION	Exports (US$ mn)	What is the product's export potential in...?						Would Mauritius improve its...?			
		Sub-Saharan Africa	Unrealized potential	South-South trade	Unrealized potential	OECD	Unrealized potential	Technology level	Revenues stability	SME presence	Female participation
160414 Tunas,skipjack&Atl bonito,prepar...	292.7		100%		98%		49%				
610910 T-shirts, singlets and other vests, ...	213.2		21%		26%		33%				
620520 Mens/boys shirts, of cotton, not k...	139.9		65%		64%		64%				
1701XX Cane or beet sugar and chemica...	135.2		92%		82%		11%				
620342 Mens/boys trousers and shorts, o...	92.5		9%		17%		53%				
170199 Refined sugar, in solid form, nes	161.6		98%		96%		14%				
610990 T-shirts,singlets and other vests, o...	60.4		36%		42%		31%				
510610 Yarn of carded wool,>/=85% by w...	15.0		84%		84%		45%				
620462 Womens/girls trousers and shorts...	34.1		6%		14%		58%				
610510 Mens/boys shirts, of cotton, knitted	34.1		25%		30%		33%				
611020 Pullovers, cardigans and similar, a...	35.5		5%		29%		43%				
711319 Articles of jewellry&pt therof of/o pr...	35.9		86%		94%		54%				
520849 Woven fabrics of cotton,>/=85%,...	6.6		73%		73%		84%				
6110XX Jerseys, pullovers, cardigans, etc,...	21.2		22%		44%		36%				
0303Xa Fish, frozen, whole	33.0		96%		67%		47%				
110100 Wheat or meslin flour	11.6		42%		45%		71%				
170310 Cane molasses	12.0		84%		86%		56%				
610462 Womens/girls trousers and shorts...	11.9		7%		29%		44%				
610442 Womens/girls dresses, of cotton,...	12.8		14%		37%		49%				
911430 Clock or watch dials	8.7		99%		99%		40%				

Note: Top 20 products listed in decreasing order of their export potential to the world. Development indicators are relative to the country's current situation, green indicating performance above its trade-weighted median and red otherwise; a blank cell indicates data are not available. A blank cell in export potential means that the product was not consistently demanded over five years by any country in the respective region. Exports (US$ mn) corresponds to the yearly average exports to the world over the period 2009-13. Refer to Annexes I, II and III for details.

Source: ITC Export Potential Assessment, additional results are available at ITC Country Pages http://www.intracen.org/country/mauritius/

Morocco

Key indicators

Population (millions)	33.2
GDP (US$ billions)	109.2
GDP per capita (US$)	3,291.3
Share of world GDP (PPP US$, %)	0.2
Current account surplus over GDP (%)	-5.8
Tariff preference margin (percentage points)	4.9
Goods and services imports + exports over GDP (%)	83.2
Exports of services over total exports (%)	36.9
Geographic region	MENA
Development group	DC
Income group	Lower-middle income

SME Competitiveness Grid Summary

Average scores [0–100]		Compete	Connect	Change
FIRM LEVEL CAPABILITIES	Small	49.4	70.4	42.2
	Medium	49.9	75.9	50.1
	Large	55.3	69.5	61.0
	All	50.4	72.2	48.1
IMMEDIATE BUSINESS ENVIRONMENT		58.0	50.6	39.7
NATIONAL ENVIRONMENT		51.9	64.4	47.6

Reference level: 45.4 (a function of GDP per capita US$)

Strengths are scores above: 68.0	Weaknesses are scores below: 22.7

SME Competitiveness Grid

1	FIRM LEVEL CAPABILITIES	Values				Normalized scores			
		Small	Medium	Large	All	Small	Medium	Large	All
1.1	Capacity to Compete								
1.1.1	Firms with quality certification (%)	6.2	23.1	49.8	18.2	21.0	50.9	75.2	44.3
1.1.2	Firms with checking or savings account (%)	97.5	96.5	96.4	97.0	60.6	55.1	54.6	57.6
1.1.3	Capacity utilization (%)	73.6	63.9	62.6	66.4	47.4	28.9	26.8	33.3
1.1.4	Manager's experience (years)	22.7	21.6	21.5	22.1	68.7	64.8	64.4	66.5
1.2	Capacity to Connect								
1.2.1	Firms using e-mail (%)	96.8	98.0	94.4	97.0	79.2	85.4	69.7	80.1
1.2.2	Firms having their own website (%)	66.8	71.4	74.0	69.4	61.6	66.5	69.4	64.4
1.3	Capacity to Change								
1.3.1	Firms with audited financial statements (%)	42.5	55.3	55.3	48.9	33.4	45.8	45.8	39.5
1.3.2	Investments financed by banks (%)	23.4	20.6	34.9	23.4	65.5	61.0	80.6	65.5
1.3.3	Firms offering formal training (%)	19.1	27.2	52.7	26.3	24.4	33.7	60.1	32.7
1.3.4	Firms using foreign technology licences (%)	13.0	21.9	20.3	18.5	45.4	59.7	57.5	54.9

2	IMMEDIATE BUSINESS ENVIRONMENT	Values				Normalized scores			
		Small	Medium	Large	All	Small	Medium	Large	All
2.1	Capacity to Compete								
2.1.1	Losses due to power outages (% of sales)	0.2	0.3	0.3	0.3	73.7	68.4	68.4	68.4
2.1.2	Losses during domestic shipping (%)	1.5	0.7	0.5	1.0	37.2	51.2	57.2	44.8
2.1.3	Management time spent with regulation (%)	4.0	5.5	4.3	4.6	63.3	56.5	61.8	60.4
2.1.4	Days for customs clearance	6.2	5.8	5.5	5.6	55.2	57.5	58.9	58.6
2.2	Capacity to Connect								
2.2.1	State of cluster development (1–7)				3.8				58.1
2.2.2	Extent of marketing (1–7)				3.8				41.5
2.2.3	Local supplier quality (1–7)				4.4				56.7
2.2.4	University-industry collaboration in R&D (1–7)				3.2				46.3
2.3	Capacity to Change								
2.3.1	Access to finance as a constraint (%)	30.1	25.3	25.2	27.7	38.2	44.1	44.3	41.1
2.3.2	Inadequately educated workforce (%)	37.8	26.2	24.6	31.8	29.5	41.4	43.4	35.2
2.3.3	Business licensing and permits as a constraint (%)	17.9	10.2	9.9	14.0	36.3	50.5	51.2	42.7

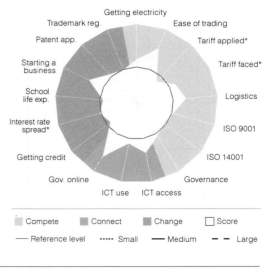

3	NATIONAL ENVIRONMENT	Values	Normalized scores
		All	All
3.1	Capacity to Compete		
3.1.1	Ease of getting electricity (0–100)	74.4	54.5
3.1.2	Ease of trading across borders (0–100)	84.6	73.6
3.1.3	Applied tariff, trade-weighted average (%)	10.0	36.3
3.1.4	Faced tariff, trade-weighted average (%)	3.5	53.0
3.1.5	Logistics performance index (1–5)	3.0	61.1
3.1.6	ISO 9001 quality certificates (/mn pop.)	21.0	46.5
3.1.7	ISO 14001 environmental certificates (/mn pop.)	2.8	41.9
3.1.8	Governance (index)	-0.3	48.4
3.2	Capacity to Connect		
3.2.1	ICT access (0–10)	5.6	63.3
3.2.2	ICT use (0–10)	2.5	51.3
3.2.3	Government's online service (0–10)	6.9	78.6
3.3	Capacity to Change		
3.3.1	Ease of getting credit (0–100)	40.0	39.6
3.3.2	Interest rate spread (%)	8.0	46.7
3.3.3	School life expectancy (years)	11.6	41.2
3.3.4	Ease of starting a business (0–100)	90.3	65.0
3.3.5	Patent applications (/mn pop.)	10.0	48.7
3.3.6	Trademark registrations (/mn pop.)	400.0	44.7

Note: For each indicator, the table includes the values and the corresponding scores. Radar charts are based on scores: values are transformed and normalized so that for each indicator in a sample of 111 countries, the worst value gets a score of 0, the best value gets a score of 100, and the median gets a score of 50. If in the original values higher numbers indicate worse outcomes, the chart labels are marked with an asterisk (*). Series with missing data are indicated as (-) in the tables and omitted from the radar charts.

Source: World Bank Enterprise Survey (2013) for firm level data; for other sources refer to Annex III.

ITC Business Survey on Non-Tariff Measures (NTMs)

1. Firms affected by NTMs

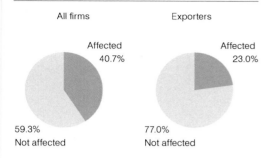

All firms

Affected
40.7%

59.3%
Not affected

Exporters

Affected
23.0%

77.0%
Not affected

2. NTMs reported as challenging (exporters)

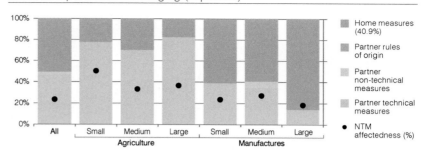

- Home measures (40.9%)
- Partner rules of origin
- Partner non-technical measures
- Partner technical measures
- ● NTM affectedness (%)

Categories along x-axis: All | Small, Medium, Large (Agriculture) | Small, Medium, Large (Manufactures)

3. Regulatory and procedural obstacles (exporters)

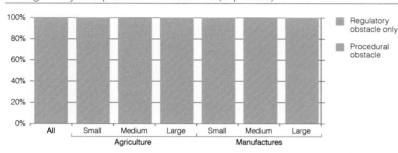

- Regulatory obstacle only
- Procedural obstacle

Categories along x-axis: All | Small, Medium, Large (Agriculture) | Small, Medium, Large (Manufactures)

4. Location of procedural obstacles (exporters)

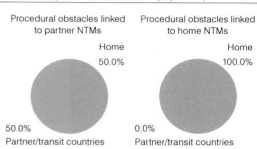

Procedural obstacles linked to partner NTMs

Home 50.0%

50.0% Partner/transit countries

Procedural obstacles linked to home NTMs

Home 100.0%

0.0% Partner/transit countries

Source: Source: ITC NTM Survey, additional results are available at http://ntmsurvey.intracen.org/ntm-survey-data/country-analysis/morocco/

Potential for Growth of Current Exports

PRODUCT/PRODUCT GROUP DESCRIPTION	Exports (US$ mn)	Middle East & North Africa	Unrealized potential	South-South trade	Unrealized potential	OECD	Unrealized potential	Technology level	Revenues stability	SME presence	Female participation
280920 Phosphoric acid and polyphosph...	1540.7		87%		17%		66%	■	■	■	■
854430 Ignition wirg sets&oth wirg sets u...	1143.9		100%		99%		26%	■	■	■	■
310530 Diammonium phosphate, in pack...	849.0		87%		47%		65%	■	■	■	■
310540 Monoammonium phosphate&mx...	592.5		75%		17%		65%	■	■	■	■
160413 Sardines,sardinella&brislg o sprat...	337.2		37%		58%		58%	■	■	■	■
030759 Octopus, frozen, dried, salted or i...	302.8		99%		71%		56%	■	■	■	■
880330 Aircraft parts nes	153.6		94%		98%		66%	■	■		■
070820 Beans, shelled or unshelled, fresh...	173.0		100%		96%		68%	■	■	■	■
870331 Automobiles with diesel engine di...	236.3		87%		86%		58%	■	■	■	■
310310 Superphosphates, in packages w...	321.5		73%		26%		71%	■	■	■	■
070200 Tomatoes, fresh or chilled	463.5		100%		42%		21%	■	■		
080520 Mandarins(tang&sats)clementine...	330.5		99%		25%		67%	■	■		
8544Xa Electric conductors for a voltage...	466.6		30%		74%		43%	■	■	■	■
620462 Womens/girls trousers and shorts...	349.2		68%		63%		23%	■	■	■	■
620342 Mens/boys trousers and shorts, o...	315.0		82%		64%		31%	■	■	■	■
6403XX Footwear, upper of leather	250.9		85%		40%		46%	■	■	■	■
610910 T-shirts, singlets and other vests...	211.8		90%		78%		41%	■	■	■	■
0303Xi Frozen Sardines , sardinella, brisli...	87.0		56%		69%		79%	■	■	■	■
620640 Womens/girls blouses and shirts...	131.8		82%		66%		28%	■	■	■	■
200570 Olives prepard o preservd,oth tha...	137.0		71%		81%		18%	■	■	■	■

What is the product's export potential in...? | Would Morocco improve its...?

Note: Top 20 products listed in decreasing order of their export potential to the world. Development indicators are relative to the country's current situation, green indicating performance above its trade-weighted median and red otherwise; a blank cell indicates data are not available. A blank cell in export potential means that the product was not consistently demanded over five years by any country in the respective region. Exports (US$ mn) corresponds to the yearly average exports to the world over the period 2009-13. Refer to Annexes I, II and III for details.

Source: ITC Export Potential Assessment, additional results are available at ITC Country Pages http://www.intracen.org/country/morocco/

Paraguay

Key indicators

Population (millions)	6.9
GDP (US$ billions)	29.7
GDP per capita (US$)	4,304.6
Share of world GDP (PPP US$, %)	0.1
Current account surplus over GDP (%)	0.1
Tariff preference margin (percentage points)	3.6
Goods and services imports + exports over GDP (%)	75.7
Exports of services over total exports (%)	9.0
Geographic region	LAC
Development group	LLDC
Income group	Upper-middle income

SME Competitiveness Grid Summary

Average scores [0–100]		Compete	Connect	Change
FIRM LEVEL CAPABILITIES	Small	34.6	25.9	30.5
	Medium	54.2	62.7	56.6
	Large	65.8	78.7	80.7
	All	46.3	43.0	50.5
IMMEDIATE BUSINESS ENVIRONMENT		34.3	37.2	33.8
NATIONAL ENVIRONMENT		46.8	38.8	49.3

Reference level: 47.6 (a function of GDP per capita US$)	
Strengths are scores above: 71.4	Weaknesses are scores below: 23.8

SME Competitiveness Grid

1	FIRM LEVEL CAPABILITIES	Values				Normalized scores			
		Small	Medium	Large	All	Small	Medium	Large	All
1.1	Capacity to Compete								
1.1.1	Firms with quality certification (%)	2.3	23.5	42.0	15.0	9.1	51.4	69.5	39.3
1.1.2	Firms with checking or savings account (%)	82.0	95.9	98.8	89.7	26.8	52.5	71.8	36.7
1.1.3	Capacity utilization (%)	74.8	72.4	76.2	74.0	50.0	44.8	53.2	48.2
1.1.4	Manager's experience (years)	18.2	22.5	22.7	20.5	52.6	68.0	68.7	60.9
1.2	Capacity to Connect								
1.2.1	Firms using e-mail (%)	65.4	94.2	96.4	81.0	26.8	69.0	77.3	42.4
1.2.2	Firms having their own website (%)	29.4	61.9	83.5	49.1	25.0	56.4	80.1	43.5
1.3	Capacity to Change								
1.3.1	Firms with audited financial statements (%)	29.1	60.5	89.6	49.0	21.4	51.2	85.5	39.6
1.3.2	Investments financed by banks (%)	21.9	16.8	30.4	20.8	63.2	54.2	75.3	61.4
1.3.3	Firms offering formal training (%)	30.6	72.3	92.1	54.9	37.5	77.8	94.0	62.2
1.3.4	Firms using foreign technology licences (%)	0.0	12.0	28.9	10.0	0.0	43.3	68.0	38.9

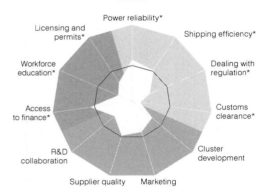

2	IMMEDIATE BUSINESS ENVIRONMENT	Values				Normalized scores			
		Small	Medium	Large	All	Small	Medium	Large	All
2.1	Capacity to Compete								
2.1.1	Losses due to power outages (% of sales)	0.7	0.9	0.9	0.8	56.6	52.9	52.9	54.7
2.1.2	Losses during domestic shipping (%)	0.4	1.2	0.9	0.8	61.0	41.4	46.7	48.8
2.1.3	Management time spent with regulation (%)	19.9	21.1	22.0	20.6	24.8	23.2	22.1	23.8
2.1.4	Days for customs clearance	15.3	30.2	15.5	24.2	25.6	2.4	25.3	10.1
2.2	Capacity to Connect								
2.2.1	State of cluster development (1–7)				3.1				32.7
2.2.2	Extent of marketing (1–7)				3.7				41.2
2.2.3	Local supplier quality (1–7)				4.0				45.9
2.2.4	University-industry collaboration in R&D (1–7)				2.7				29.1
2.3	Capacity to Change								
2.3.1	Access to finance as a constraint (%)	21.1	20.0	10.4	19.5	50.0	51.7	69.3	52.4
2.3.2	Inadequately educated workforce (%)	46.1	57.1	51.5	51.4	22.7	15.2	18.8	18.9
2.3.3	Business licensing and permits as a constraint (%)	22.0	23.9	19.8	22.6	30.9	28.7	33.7	30.2

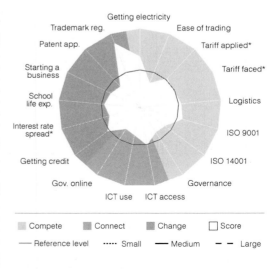

3	NATIONAL ENVIRONMENT	Values	Normalized scores
		All	All
3.1	Capacity to Compete		
3.1.1	Ease of getting electricity (0–100)	81.1	64.3
3.1.2	Ease of trading across borders (0–100)	55.9	33.1
3.1.3	Applied tariff, trade-weighted average (%)	6.6	49.3
3.1.4	Faced tariff, trade-weighted average (%)	3.8	47.0
3.1.5	Logistics performance index (1–5)	2.8	50.8
3.1.6	ISO 9001 quality certificates (/mn pop.)	38.2	54.3
3.1.7	ISO 14001 environmental certificates (/mn pop.)	2.1	38.5
3.1.8	Governance (index)	-0.6	36.9
3.2	Capacity to Connect		
3.2.1	ICT access (0–10)	4.5	48.5
3.2.2	ICT use (0–10)	1.5	35.7
3.2.3	Government's online service (0–10)	2.3	32.1
3.3	Capacity to Change		
3.3.1	Ease of getting credit (0–100)	50.0	50.0
3.3.2	Interest rate spread (%)	15.0	38.7
3.3.3	School life expectancy (years)	11.9	44.1
3.3.4	Ease of starting a business (0–100)	77.5	40.1
3.3.5	Patent applications (/mn pop.)	3.0	35.6
3.3.6	Trademark registrations (/mn pop.)	2,034.0	87.4

Note: For each indicator, the table includes the values and the corresponding scores. Radar charts are based on scores: values are transformed and normalized so that for each indicator in a sample of 111 countries, the worst value gets a score of 0, the best value gets a score of 100, and the median gets a score of 50. If in the original values higher numbers indicate worse outcomes, the chart labels are marked with an asterisk (*). Series with missing data are indicated as (-) in the tables and omitted from the radar charts.

Source: World Bank Enterprise Survey (2010) for firm level data; for other sources refer to Annex III.

ITC Business Survey on Non-Tariff Measures (NTMs)

1. Firms affected by NTMs

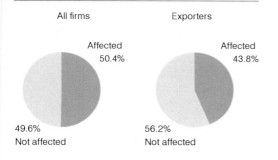

All firms

Affected
50.4%

49.6%
Not affected

Exporters

Affected
43.8%

56.2%
Not affected

2. NTMs reported as challenging (exporters)

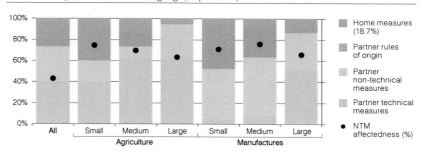

- Home measures (18.7%)
- Partner rules of origin
- Partner non-technical measures
- Partner technical measures
- NTM affectedness (%)

3. Regulatory and procedural obstacles (exporters)

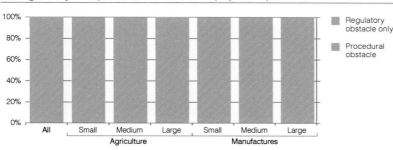

- Regulatory obstacle only
- Procedural obstacle

4. Location of procedural obstacles (exporters)

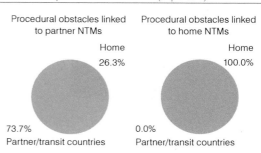

Procedural obstacles linked to partner NTMs

Home
26.3%

73.7%
Partner/transit countries

Procedural obstacles linked to home NTMs

Home
100.0%

0.0%
Partner/transit countries

Source: ITC NTM Survey, additional results are available at http://ntmsurvey.intracen.org/ntm-survey-data/country-analysis/paraguay/

Potential for Growth of Current Exports

PRODUCT/PRODUCT GROUP DESCRIPTION	Exports (US$ mn)	What is the product's export potential in...?						Would Paraguay improve its...?			
		Latin America & the Caribbean	Unrealized potential	South-South trade	Unrealized potential	OECD	Unrealized potential	Technology level	Revenues stability	SME presence	Female participation
1201XX Soya beans, whether or not broken	1813.4		39%		39%		3%	■	■		
020230 Bovine cuts boneless, frozen	478.0		82%		38%		75%	■	■	■	■
230400 Soya-bean oil-cake&oth solid resi...	436.1		20%		48%		60%	■	■	■	■
100590 Maize (corn) nes	379.0		22%		27%		51%	■	■		
020130 Bovine cuts boneless, fresh or chil...	293.7		25%		29%		29%	■	■	■	■
1001Xb Wheat and meslin	212.8		33%		32%		83%	■	■		
150710 Soya-bean oil crude, whether or n...	196.7		66%		47%		66%	■	■	■	■
41XXXa Raw hides and skins (other than f...	101.2		46%		43%		27%	■	■	■	■
392330 Carboys, bottles, flasks and simil...	43.4		31%		32%		100%	■	■		
100620 Rice, husked (brown)	23.0		57%		58%		95%	■	■	■	■
4402XX Wood charcoal (including shell o...	43.8		59%		51%		60%	■	■		
100630 Rice, semi-milled or wholly milled....	55.9		13%		45%		53%	■	■	■	■
1701XX Cane or beet sugar and chemica...	40.1		97%		99%		42%	■	■	■	■
120740 Sesamum seeds, whether or not b...	54.7		51%		83%		62%	■	■		
640610 Uppers and parts thereof, other t...	18.0		57%		64%		100%	■	■	■	
090300 Maté	1.5		99%		99%		91%	■	■		
1207Xa Oil seeds	13.0		71%		66%		71%	■	■		
110812 Maize (corn) starch	9.0		60%		42%		97%	■	■	■	■
050400 Guts, bladders and stomachs of...	19.1		77%		58%		68%	■	■		
151211 Sunflower-seed or safflower oil, cr...	23.8		20%		29%		93%	■	■	■	■

Note: Top 20 products listed in decreasing order of their export potential to the world. Development indicators are relative to the country's current situation, green indicating performance above its trade-weighted median and red otherwise; a blank cell indicates data are not available. A blank cell in export potential means that the product was not consistently demanded over five years by any country in the respective region. Exports (US$ mn) corresponds to the yearly average exports to the world over the period 2009-13. Refer to Annexes I, II and III for details.

Source: ITC Export Potential Assessment, additional results are available at ITC Country Pages http://www.intracen.org/country/paraguay/

Peru

Key indicators

Population (millions)	31.4
GDP (US$ billions)	202.9
GDP per capita (US$)	6,458.3
Share of world GDP (PPP US$, %)	0.3
Current account surplus over GDP (%)	-4.1
Tariff preference margin (percentage points)	2.5
Goods and services imports + exports over GDP (%)	48.0
Exports of services over total exports (%)	12.7
Geographic region	LAC
Development group	DC
Income group	Upper-middle income

SME Competitiveness Grid Summary

Average scores [0–100]		Compete	Connect	Change
FIRM LEVEL CAPABILITIES	Small	39.4	40.4	41.1
	Medium	48.3	49.4	55.8
	Large	70.4	72.3	73.2
	All	45.1	46.4	51.0
IMMEDIATE BUSINESS ENVIRONMENT		40.3	50.5	48.5
NATIONAL ENVIRONMENT		61.5	53.8	51.9

Reference level: 51.1 (a function of GDP per capita US$)	
Strengths are scores above: 76.6	Weaknesses are scores below: 25.5

SME Competitiveness Grid

1	FIRM LEVEL CAPABILITIES	Values				Normalized scores			
		Small	Medium	Large	All	Small	Medium	Large	All
1.1	Capacity to Compete								
1.1.1	Firms with quality certification (%)	9.2	11.7	46.0	14.2	28.2	33.4	72.5	37.9
1.1.2	Firms with checking or savings account (%)	82.4	92.5	99.6	87.4	27.2	42.2	85.3	33.1
1.1.3	Capacity utilization (%)	70.7	70.7	76.0	71.5	41.4	41.4	52.7	43.0
1.1.4	Manager's experience (years)	20.5	24.9	23.4	22.1	60.9	76.3	71.1	66.5
1.2	Capacity to Connect								
1.2.1	Firms using e-mail (%)	81.0	85.8	91.9	83.7	42.4	49.6	62.3	46.2
1.2.2	Firms having their own website (%)	43.7	54.8	85.5	52.2	38.3	49.2	82.4	46.6
1.3	Capacity to Change								
1.3.1	Firms with audited financial statements (%)	23.4	32.2	67.2	31.5	16.6	24.1	58.4	23.5
1.3.2	Investments financed by banks (%)	35.9	34.4	32.0	34.7	81.7	80.1	77.2	80.4
1.3.3	Firms offering formal training (%)	43.3	80.6	94.1	60.1	50.9	84.8	95.5	67.0
1.3.4	Firms using foreign technology licences (%)	2.7	8.2	23.3	7.7	15.2	34.3	61.5	32.9

2	IMMEDIATE BUSINESS ENVIRONMENT	Values				Normalized scores			
		Small	Medium	Large	All	Small	Medium	Large	All
2.1	Capacity to Compete								
2.1.1	Losses due to power outages (% of sales)	0.9	0.4	0.5	0.7	52.9	64.5	61.4	56.6
2.1.2	Losses during domestic shipping (%)	0.6	0.8	0.4	0.7	54.0	48.8	61.0	51.2
2.1.3	Management time spent with regulation (%)	16.7	9.3	11.9	14.1	29.4	44.2	38.1	33.7
2.1.4	Days for customs clearance	18.4	14.2	20.4	18.3	19.5	28.3	15.9	19.7
2.2	Capacity to Connect								
2.2.1	State of cluster development (1–7)				3.3				40.7
2.2.2	Extent of marketing (1–7)				4.3				58.1
2.2.3	Local supplier quality (1–7)				4.6				61.1
2.2.4	University-industry collaboration in R&D (1–7)				3.1				42.2
2.3	Capacity to Change								
2.3.1	Access to finance as a constraint (%)	6.7	14.5	4.5	8.5	78.4	61.0	84.6	73.8
2.3.2	Inadequately educated workforce (%)	23.1	37.5	33.2	28.4	45.3	29.8	33.8	38.9
2.3.3	Business licensing and permits as a constraint (%)	17.2	29.8	15.1	20.4	37.4	22.7	40.7	32.9

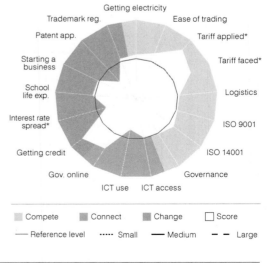

3	NATIONAL ENVIRONMENT	Values	Normalized scores
		All	All
3.1	Capacity to Compete		
3.1.1	Ease of getting electricity (0–100)	75.7	56.3
3.1.2	Ease of trading across borders (0–100)	78.8	62.0
3.1.3	Applied tariff, trade-weighted average (%)	1.8	83.9
3.1.4	Faced tariff, trade-weighted average (%)	2.7	74.9
3.1.5	Logistics performance index (1–5)	2.8	53.3
3.1.6	ISO 9001 quality certificates (/mn pop.)	33.6	52.6
3.1.7	ISO 14001 environmental certificates (/mn pop.)	11.1	57.5
3.1.8	Governance (index)	-0.2	51.8
3.2	Capacity to Connect		
3.2.1	ICT access (0–10)	4.5	49.2
3.2.2	ICT use (0–10)	1.7	39.0
3.2.3	Government's online service (0–10)	6.3	73.3
3.3	Capacity to Change		
3.3.1	Ease of getting credit (0–100)	80.0	82.7
3.3.2	Interest rate spread (%)	15.8	38.1
3.3.3	School life expectancy (years)	13.1	53.7
3.3.4	Ease of starting a business (0–100)	85.1	52.6
3.3.5	Patent applications (/mn pop.)	2.0	29.7
3.3.6	Trademark registrations (/mn pop.)	603.0	54.7

Legend: Compete · Connect · Change · Score · Reference level · Small · Medium · Large

Note: For each indicator, the table includes the values and the corresponding scores. Radar charts are based on scores: values are transformed and normalized so that for each indicator in a sample of 111 countries, the worst value gets a score of 0, the best value gets a score of 100, and the median gets a score of 50. If in the original values higher numbers indicate worse outcomes, the chart labels are marked with an asterisk (*). Series with missing data are indicated as (-) in the tables and omitted from the radar charts.

Source: World Bank Enterprise Survey (2010) for firm level data; for other sources refer to Annex III.

ITC Business Survey on Non-Tariff Measures (NTMs)

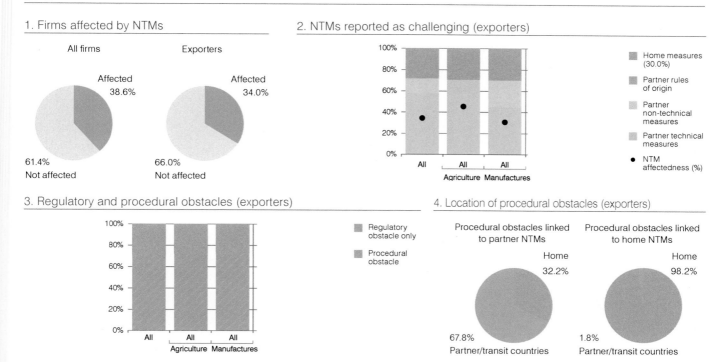

1. Firms affected by NTMs

All firms

Affected
38.6%

61.4%
Not affected

Exporters

Affected
34.0%

66.0%
Not affected

2. NTMs reported as challenging (exporters)

All · All · All
Agriculture · Manufactures

- Home measures (30.0%)
- Partner rules of origin
- Partner non-technical measures
- Partner technical measures
- NTM affectedness (%)

3. Regulatory and procedural obstacles (exporters)

All · All · All
Agriculture · Manufactures

- Regulatory obstacle only
- Procedural obstacle

4. Location of procedural obstacles (exporters)

Procedural obstacles linked to partner NTMs

Home
32.2%

67.8%
Partner/transit countries

Procedural obstacles linked to home NTMs

Home
98.2%

1.8%
Partner/transit countries

Source: ITC NTM Survey, additional results are available at http://ntmsurvey.intracen.org/ntm-survey-data/country-analysis/peru/

Potential for Growth of Current Exports

PRODUCT/PRODUCT GROUP DESCRIPTION	Exports (US$ mn)	What is the product's export potential in...?						Would Peru improve its...?			
		Latin America & the Caribbean	Unrealized potential	South-South trade	Unrealized potential	OECD	Unrealized potential	Technology level	Revenues stability	SME presence	Female participation
230120 Flour,meal&pellet of fish,crust,mo...	1711.9		90%		44%		47%				
740311 Copper cathodes and sections of...	2257.0		17%		30%		24%				
090111 Coffee, not roasted, not decaffein...	979.0		83%		82%		50%				
080610 Grapes, fresh	319.0		88%		57%		56%				
150420 Fish fats&oils&their fractions exc...	391.1		77%		68%		38%				
070920 Asparagus, fresh or chilled	388.9		73%		72%		17%				
610910 T-shirts, singlets and other vests....	345.0		19%		15%		32%				
790111 Zinc not alloyed unwrought contai...	280.2		44%		37%		22%				
800110 Tin not alloyed unwrought	437.1		51%		82%		17%				
200560 Asparagus prepard or preservd....	135.5		80%		78%		45%				
710691 Silver in unwrought forms	315.3		12%		50%		28%				
550630 Staple fibres of acrylic or...	18.8		92%		93%		77%				
610510 Mens/boys shirts, of cotton, knitted	221.7		28%		30%		17%				
740811 Wire of refind copper of which the...	251.0		23%		22%		94%				
080440 Avocados, fresh or dried	157.0		94%		91%		43%				
740200 Copper unrefined, copper anode...	139.0		79%		32%		50%				
790112 Zinc not alloyed unwrought contai...	144.4		79%		80%		23%				
030749 Cuttle fish and squid,shelled or no...	163.4		35%		24%		41%				
030729 Scallops,incl queen scallops,shell...	116.0		72%		93%		35%				
0803XX Bananas and plantains, fresh or d...	110.2		100%		100%		49%				

Note: Top 20 products listed in decreasing order of their export potential to the world. Development indicators are relative to the country's current situation, green indicating performance above its trade-weighted median and red otherwise; a blank cell indicates data are not available. A blank cell in export potential means that the product was not consistently demanded over five years by any country in the respective region. Exports (US$ mn) corresponds to the yearly average exports to the world over the period 2009-13. Refer to Annexes I, II and III for details.

Source: ITC Export Potential Assessment, additional results are available at ITC Country Pages http://www.intracen.org/country/peru/

Rwanda

Key indicators

Population (millions)	11.1
GDP (US$ billions)	8.0
GDP per capita (US$)	722.1
Share of world GDP (PPP US$, %)	0.0
Current account surplus over GDP (%)	-12.0
Tariff preference margin (percentage points)	5.7
Goods and services imports + exports over GDP (%)	41.8
Exports of services over total exports (%)	45.2
Geographic region	Sub-Saharan Africa
Development group	LDC, LLDC
Income group	Low income

SME Competitiveness Grid Summary

Average scores [0–100]		Compete	Connect	Change
FIRM LEVEL CAPABILITIES	Small	25.6	24.5	48.7
	Medium	28.4	47.7	58.7
	Large	40.8	69.2	73.0
	All	27.9	33.2	54.2
IMMEDIATE BUSINESS ENVIRONMENT		47.3	48.5	42.9
NATIONAL ENVIRONMENT		41.0	30.5	42.2

Reference level: 32.5 (a function of GDP per capita US$)

Strengths are scores above: 48.8	Weaknesses are scores below: 16.3

SME Competitiveness Grid

1	FIRM LEVEL CAPABILITIES	Values				Normalized scores			
		Small	Medium	Large	All	Small	Medium	Large	All
1.1	Capacity to Compete								
1.1.1	Firms with quality certification (%)	9.1	13.3	23.9	11.7	28.0	36.3	51.9	33.4
1.1.2	Firms with checking or savings account (%)	69.4	69.9	85.6	71.2	17.4	17.7	30.8	18.4
1.1.3	Capacity utilization (%)	-	-	-	-	-	-	-	-
1.1.4	Manager's experience (years)	12.6	12.5	14.7	12.7	31.6	31.2	39.6	32.0
1.2	Capacity to Connect								
1.2.1	Firms using e-mail (%)	68.0	88.3	97.0	76.5	28.9	54.1	80.1	37.0
1.2.2	Firms having their own website (%)	23.8	46.8	63.6	34.2	20.0	41.3	58.2	29.4
1.3	Capacity to Change								
1.3.1	Firms with audited financial statements (%)	44.9	67.7	78.4	54.4	35.6	58.9	71.3	44.9
1.3.2	Investments financed by banks (%)	8.0	17.3	23.9	13.6	33.1	55.1	66.3	47.5
1.3.3	Firms offering formal training (%)	48.1	62.0	81.5	55.4	55.6	68.7	85.5	62.7
1.3.4	Firms using foreign technology licences (%)	31.3	16.8	29.6	23.5	70.4	52.2	68.7	61.8

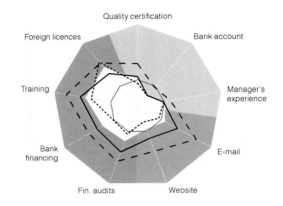

2	IMMEDIATE BUSINESS ENVIRONMENT	Values				Normalized scores			
		Small	Medium	Large	All	Small	Medium	Large	All
2.1	Capacity to Compete								
2.1.1	Losses due to power outages (% of sales)	0.8	1.4	1.6	1.0	54.7	46.4	44.4	51.4
2.1.2	Losses during domestic shipping (%)	-	-	-	-	-	-	-	-
2.1.3	Management time spent with regulation (%)	4.6	5.9	6.7	5.2	60.4	54.9	52.0	57.7
2.1.4	Days for customs clearance	16.6	12.5	10.3	12.4	22.9	32.6	39.0	32.8
2.2	Capacity to Connect								
2.2.1	State of cluster development (1–7)				3.9				62.9
2.2.2	Extent of marketing (1–7)				3.3				27.4
2.2.3	Local supplier quality (1–7)				4.0				45.6
2.2.4	University-industry collaboration in R&D (1–7)				3.7				58.2
2.3	Capacity to Change								
2.3.1	Access to finance as a constraint (%)	37.1	30.8	34.1	35.1	30.7	37.4	33.7	32.7
2.3.2	Inadequately educated workforce (%)	25.6	28.5	45.6	28.4	42.1	38.8	23.1	38.9
2.3.3	Business licensing and permits as a constraint (%)	9.0	4.9	7.3	7.7	53.4	66.7	58.2	57.0

3	NATIONAL ENVIRONMENT	Values	Normalized scores
		All	All
3.1	Capacity to Compete		
3.1.1	Ease of getting electricity (0–100)	79.5	61.8
3.1.2	Ease of trading across borders (0–100)	44.7	23.6
3.1.3	Applied tariff, trade-weighted average (%)	9.7	37.3
3.1.4	Faced tariff, trade-weighted average (%)	2.5	80.4
3.1.5	Logistics performance index (1–5)	2.8	49.9
3.1.6	ISO 9001 quality certificates (/mn pop.)	0.3	4.7
3.1.7	ISO 14001 environmental certificates (/mn pop.)	0.2	14.4
3.1.8	Governance (index)	-0.1	55.9
3.2	Capacity to Connect		
3.2.1	ICT access (0–10)	2.4	15.5
3.2.2	ICT use (0–10)	0.5	13.5
3.2.3	Government's online service (0–10)	5.1	62.6
3.3	Capacity to Change		
3.3.1	Ease of getting credit (0–100)	90.0	94.2
3.3.2	Interest rate spread (%)	9.6	44.3
3.3.3	School life expectancy (years)	10.3	30.4
3.3.4	Ease of starting a business (0–100)	81.7	46.4
3.3.5	Patent applications (/mn pop.)	3.0	35.6
3.3.6	Trademark registrations (/mn pop.)	10.0	2.3

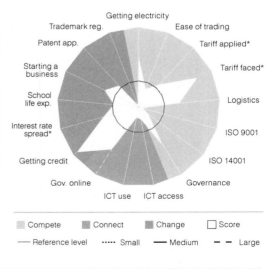

Note: For each indicator, the table includes the values and the corresponding scores. Radar charts are based on scores: values are transformed and normalized so that for each indicator in a sample of 111 countries, the worst value gets a score of 0, the best value gets a score of 100, and the median gets a score of 50. If in the original values higher numbers indicate worse outcomes, the chart labels are marked with an asterisk (*). Series with missing data are indicated as (-) in the tables and omitted from the radar charts.

Source: World Bank Enterprise Survey (2011) for firm level data; for other sources refer to Annex III.

ITC Business Survey on Non-Tariff Measures (NTMs)

1. Firms affected by NTMs

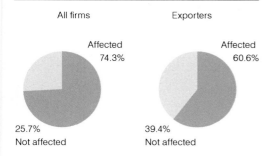

All firms

Affected
74.3%

25.7%
Not affected

Exporters

Affected
60.6%

39.4%
Not affected

2. NTMs reported as challenging (exporters)

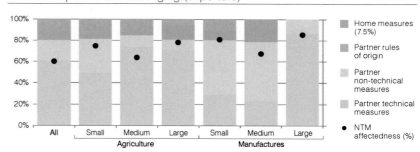

Home measures (7.5%)

Partner rules of origin

Partner non-technical measures

Partner technical measures

● NTM affectedness (%)

Agriculture — Small, Medium, Large
Manufactures — Small, Medium, Large

3. Regulatory and procedural obstacles (exporters)

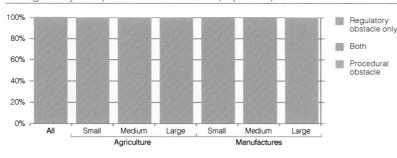

Regulatory obstacle only

Both

Procedural obstacle

Agriculture — All, Small, Medium, Large
Manufactures — Small, Medium, Large

4. Location of procedural obstacles (exporters)

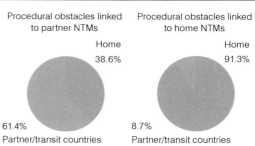

Procedural obstacles linked to partner NTMs

Home
38.6%

61.4%
Partner/transit countries

Procedural obstacles linked to home NTMs

Home
91.3%

8.7%
Partner/transit countries

Source: ITC NTM Survey, additional results are available at http://ntmsurvey.intracen.org/ntm-survey-data/country-analysis/rwanda/

Potential for Growth of Current Exports

PRODUCT/PRODUCT GROUP DESCRIPTION	Exports (US$ mn)	What is the product's export potential in…? Sub-Saharan Africa	Unrealized potential	South-South trade	Unrealized potential	OECD	Unrealized potential	Would Rwanda improve its…? Technology level	Revenues stability	SME presence	Female participation
090240 Black tea (fermented) & partly fer...	47.7		45%		41%		72%	■	■		
090111 Coffee, not roasted, not decaffein...	63.5		33%		30%		5%	■	■		
110100 Wheat or meslin flour	7.4		80%		80%		100%	■	■	■	■
110220 Maize (corn) flour	2.2		90%		90%		99%	■	■	■	■
220300 Beer made from malt	6.6		66%		66%		100%	■	■	■	■
090190 Coffee husks and skins, coffee su...	1.0		88%		88%		58%	■	■	■	■
392310 Boxes, cases, crates & similar arti...	1.3		81%		82%		100%	■	■	■	■
0102XX Live bovine animals	5.2		28%		32%		100%	■	■		
640590 Footwear, nes	1.5		67%		69%		100%	■	■		
220290 Non-alcoholic beverages nes, exc...	2.8		42%		44%		100%	■	■	■	■
1302XX Vegetable saps and extracts nes	2.8		98%		98%		25%	■	■		
1102XX Cereal flour nes	0.7		54%		55%		90%				
41XXXc Raw hides and skins (other than f...	2.7		5%		32%		58%	■	■	■	■
41XXXa Raw hides and skins (other than...	4.6		4%		14%		56%	■	■	■	■
100510 Maize (corn) seed	2.0		54%		55%		100%				
070820 Beans, shelled or unshelled, fresh...	0.7		59%		59%		95%	■	■	■	
870324 Automobiles with reciprocating pi...	4.2		49%		77%		100%	■	■	■	■
0713Xa Dried vegetables, shelled	0.2		69%		71%		100%				
090230 Black tea (fermented)&partly ferm...	3.7		29%		33%		99%	■	■	■	■
110313 Maize (corn) groats and meal	0.2		71%		72%		100%	■	■	■	■

Note: Top 20 products listed in decreasing order of their export potential to the world. Development indicators are relative to the country's current situation, green indicating performance above its trade-weighted median and red otherwise; a blank cell indicates data are not available. A blank cell in export potential means that the product was not consistently demanded over five years by any country in the respective region. Exports (US$ mn) corresponds to the yearly average exports to the world over the period 2009-13. Refer to Annexes I, II and III for details.

Source: ITC Export Potential Assessment, additional results are available at ITC Country Pages http://www.intracen.org/country/rwanda/

Senegal

Key indicators

Population (millions)	14.5
GDP (US$ billions)	15.6
GDP per capita (US$)	1,071.8
Share of world GDP (PPP US$, %)	0.0
Current account surplus over GDP (%)	-10.3
Tariff preference margin (percentage points)	4.6
Goods and services imports + exports over GDP (%)	82.3
Exports of services over total exports (%)	33.7
Geographic region	Sub-Saharan Africa
Development group	LDC
Income group	Lower-middle income

SME Competitiveness Grid Summary

Average scores [0–100]		Compete	Connect	Change
FIRM LEVEL CAPABILITIES	Small	34.6	14.9	22.2
	Medium	46.7	51.5	37.8
	Large	65.1	81.1	46.5
	All	42.3	28.0	31.9
IMMEDIATE BUSINESS ENVIRONMENT		45.5	52.5	48.8
NATIONAL ENVIRONMENT		40.7	33.9	34.5

Reference level: 35.9 (a function of GDP per capita US$)	
Strengths are scores above: 53.8	Weaknesses are scores below: 17.9

SME Competitiveness Grid

1	FIRM LEVEL CAPABILITIES	Values				Normalized scores			
		Small	Medium	Large	All	Small	Medium	Large	All
1.1	Capacity to Compete								
1.1.1	Firms with quality certification (%)	3.3	9.9	39.4	9.3	12.5	29.7	67.4	28.4
1.1.2	Firms with checking or savings account (%)	70.7	90.8	87.4	77.6	18.1	38.6	33.1	22.9
1.1.3	Capacity utilization (%)	78.3	79.4	86.1	79.9	58.2	61.0	80.5	62.3
1.1.4	Manager's experience (years)	17.4	19.5	25.8	19.0	49.6	57.3	79.4	55.5
1.2	Capacity to Connect								
1.2.1	Firms using e-mail (%)	50.2	85.9	97.5	64.7	16.9	49.7	82.6	26.3
1.2.2	Firms having their own website (%)	15.5	58.9	83.0	34.5	12.8	53.4	79.5	29.7
1.3	Capacity to Change								
1.3.1	Firms with audited financial statements (%)	29.9	48.6	53.7	37.3	22.1	39.2	44.2	28.6
1.3.2	Investments financed by banks (%)	1.7	4.4	15.1	6.6	9.1	20.9	50.7	28.7
1.3.3	Firms offering formal training (%)	7.1	35.2	38.0	17.4	9.5	42.5	45.4	22.4
1.3.4	Firms using foreign technology licences (%)	14.5	14.7	13.2	14.4	48.2	48.6	45.8	48.0

2	IMMEDIATE BUSINESS ENVIRONMENT	Values				Normalized scores			
		Small	Medium	Large	All	Small	Medium	Large	All
2.1	Capacity to Compete								
2.1.1	Losses due to power outages (% of sales)	1.5	2.1	1.6	1.6	45.4	40.4	44.4	44.4
2.1.2	Losses during domestic shipping (%)	2.4	1.0	0.1	1.6	28.3	44.8	81.4	36.0
2.1.3	Management time spent with regulation (%)	2.0	5.2	4.3	3.0	76.1	57.7	61.8	69.0
2.1.4	Days for customs clearance	-	11.9	14.3	12.5	-	34.1	27.9	32.4
2.2	Capacity to Connect								
2.2.1	State of cluster development (1–7)				3.3				43.2
2.2.2	Extent of marketing (1–7)				4.1				53.7
2.2.3	Local supplier quality (1–7)				4.4				55.5
2.2.4	University-industry collaboration in R&D (1–7)				3.6				57.8
2.3	Capacity to Change								
2.3.1	Access to finance as a constraint (%)	59.0	42.9	31.1	51.6	12.7	25.2	37.0	18.0
2.3.2	Inadequately educated workforce (%)	6.6	13.3	14.4	9.2	75.9	60.7	58.6	69.3
2.3.3	Business licensing and permits as a constraint (%)	5.8	13.1	2.3	7.0	63.2	44.3	79.8	59.2

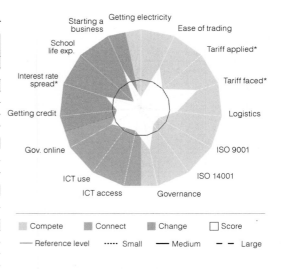

3	NATIONAL ENVIRONMENT	Values	Normalized scores
		All	All
3.1	Capacity to Compete		
3.1.1	Ease of getting electricity (0–100)	34.2	13.0
3.1.2	Ease of trading across borders (0–100)	75.1	55.8
3.1.3	Applied tariff, trade-weighted average (%)	10.4	35.2
3.1.4	Faced tariff, trade-weighted average (%)	2.7	72.9
3.1.5	Logistics performance index (1–5)	2.6	44.1
3.1.6	ISO 9001 quality certificates (/mn pop.)	3.8	25.3
3.1.7	ISO 14001 environmental certificates (/mn pop.)	0.6	25.9
3.1.8	Governance (index)	-0.2	53.7
3.2	Capacity to Connect		
3.2.1	ICT access (0–10)	3.2	29.5
3.2.2	ICT use (0–10)	1.3	31.0
3.2.3	Government's online service (0–10)	3.1	41.4
3.3	Capacity to Change		
3.3.1	Ease of getting credit (0–100)	30.0	29.4
3.3.2	Interest rate spread (%)	9.0	45.1
3.3.3	School life expectancy (years)	7.9	11.1
3.3.4	Ease of starting a business (0–100)	85.0	52.5
3.3.5	Patent applications (/mn pop.)	-	-
3.3.6	Trademark registrations (/mn pop.)	-	-

Note: For each indicator, the table includes the values and the corresponding scores. Radar charts are based on scores: values are transformed and normalized so that for each indicator in a sample of 111 countries, the worst value gets a score of 0, the best value gets a score of 100, and the median gets a score of 50. If in the original values higher numbers indicate worse outcomes, the chart labels are marked with an asterisk (*). Series with missing data are indicated as (-) in the tables and omitted from the radar charts.

Source: World Bank Enterprise Survey (2014) for firm level data; for other sources refer to Annex III.

ITC Business Survey on Non-Tariff Measures (NTMs)

1. Firms affected by NTMs

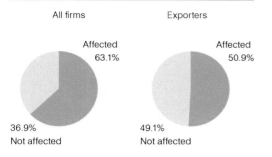

All firms

Affected
63.1%

36.9%
Not affected

Exporters

Affected
50.9%

49.1%
Not affected

2. NTMs reported as challenging (exporters)

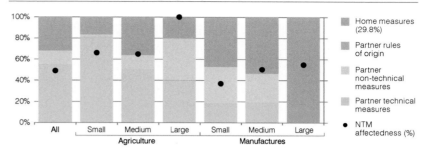

- Home measures (29.8%)
- Partner rules of origin
- Partner non-technical measures
- Partner technical measures
- NTM affectedness (%)

Agriculture: All, Small, Medium, Large
Manufactures: Small, Medium, Large

3. Regulatory and procedural obstacles (exporters)

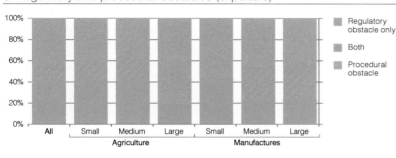

- Regulatory obstacle only
- Both
- Procedural obstacle

Agriculture: All, Small, Medium, Large
Manufactures: Small, Medium, Large

4. Location of procedural obstacles (exporters)

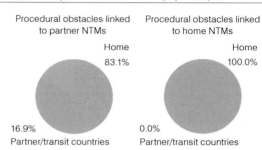

Procedural obstacles linked to partner NTMs

Home
83.1%

16.9%
Partner/transit countries

Procedural obstacles linked to home NTMs

Home
100.0%

0.0%
Partner/transit countries

Source: ITC NTM Survey, additional results are available at http://ntmsurvey.intracen.org/ntm-survey-data/country-analysis/senegal/

Potential for Growth of Current Exports

PRODUCT/PRODUCT GROUP DESCRIPTION	Exports (US$ mn)	Sub-Saharan Africa	Unrealized potential	South-South trade	Unrealized potential	OECD	Unrealized potential	Technology level	Revenues stability	SME presence	Female participation
252329 Portland cement nes	182.8		61%		62%		99%				
280920 Phosphoric acid and polyphosph...	221.9		100%		34%		100%				
210410 Soups and broths and preparation...	60.3		70%		71%		96%				
0303Xa Fish, frozen, whole	91.0		42%		45%		48%				
721590 Bars & rods, i/nas, nes	18.9		74%		75%		99%				
150810 Ground-nut oil, crude	55.1		100%		35%		44%				
030759 Octopus, frozen, dried, salted or i...	42.8		64%		61%		34%				
230500 Ground-nut oil-cake&oth solid res...	8.6		98%		98%		7%				
0302Xe Fish, fresh, whole	60.5		22%		44%		31%				
0303Xi Frozen Sardines , sardinella, brisli...	5.7		74%		75%		82%				
0306Xa Crustaceans	25.9		86%		96%		47%				
030749 Cuttle fish and squid,shelled or no...	20.1		74%		86%		32%				
520100 Cotton, not carded or combed	24.1		100%		15%		73%				
670419 False beard,eyebrows and the like...	8.9		63%		64%		34%				
070820 Beans, shelled or unshelled, fresh...	13.0		96%		96%		45%				
41XXXb Raw hides and skins (other than f...	7.2		37%		74%		47%				
0304Xb Fish fillets and pieces, fresh, chill...	13.2		72%		89%		29%				
160414 Tunas,skipjack&Atl bonito,prepard...	7.3		86%		79%		53%				
330499 Beauty or make-up preparations...	16.6		23%		63%		98%				
080131 Cashew nuts, in shell, fresh or dried	8.8		100%		5%		75%				

What is the product's export potential in...?

Would Senegal improve its...?

Note: Top 20 products listed in decreasing order of their export potential to the world. Development indicators are relative to the country's current situation, green indicating performance above its trade-weighted median and red otherwise; a blank cell indicates data are not available. A blank cell in export potential means that the product was not consistently demanded over five years by any country in the respective region. Exports (US$ mn) corresponds to the yearly average exports to the world over the period 2009-13. Refer to Annexes I, II and III for details.

Source: ITC Export Potential Assessment, additional results are available at ITC Country Pages http://www.intracen.org/country/senegal/

Sri Lanka

Key indicators

Population (millions)	21.0
GDP (US$ billions)	74.6
GDP per capita (US$)	3,557.9
Share of world GDP (PPP US$, %)	0.2
Current account surplus over GDP (%)	-3.7
Tariff preference margin (percentage points)	1.8
Goods and services imports + exports over GDP (%)	54.6
Exports of services over total exports (%)	31.3
Geographic region	South Asia
Development group	DC
Income group	Lower-middle income

SME Competitiveness Grid Summary

Average scores [0–100]		Compete	Connect	Change
FIRM LEVEL CAPABILITIES	Small	37.0	5.6	38.8
	Medium	51.2	27.6	61.3
	Large	65.8	67.3	78.2
	All	42.1	11.6	48.2
IMMEDIATE BUSINESS ENVIRONMENT		52.6	64.2	42.5
NATIONAL ENVIRONMENT		47.9	47.5	51.4

Reference level: 46.0 (a function of GDP per capita US$)	
Strengths are scores above: 69.0	Weaknesses are scores below: 23.0

SME Competitiveness Grid

1	FIRM LEVEL CAPABILITIES	Values				Normalized scores			
		Small	Medium	Large	All	Small	Medium	Large	All
1.1	Capacity to Compete								
1.1.1	Firms with quality certification (%)	4.6	14.7	48.8	9.1	16.5	38.8	74.5	28.0
1.1.2	Firms with checking or savings account (%)	87.2	95.5	98.1	89.4	32.8	50.9	64.9	36.1
1.1.3	Capacity utilization (%)	72.8	80.6	82.8	75.6	45.7	64.1	70.3	51.8
1.1.4	Manager's experience (years)	18.3	17.8	18.5	18.2	52.9	51.1	53.7	52.6
1.2	Capacity to Connect								
1.2.1	Firms using e-mail (%)	19.1	57.5	93.2	30.5	3.4	21.3	65.9	7.7
1.2.2	Firms having their own website (%)	9.4	39.1	73.3	18.6	7.7	34.0	68.6	15.5
1.3	Capacity to Change								
1.3.1	Firms with audited financial statements (%)	54.2	75.2	93.0	60.3	44.7	67.5	90.1	50.9
1.3.2	Investments financed by banks (%)	29.0	53.5	33.8	35.4	73.5	98.1	79.4	81.2
1.3.3	Firms offering formal training (%)	14.3	19.8	66.6	18.4	18.6	25.2	72.9	23.6
1.3.4	Firms using foreign technology licences (%)	3.4	18.1	31.3	9.3	18.3	54.3	70.4	37.2

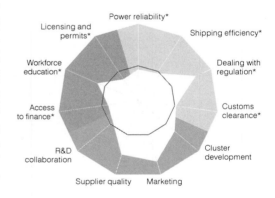

2	IMMEDIATE BUSINESS ENVIRONMENT	Values				Normalized scores			
		Small	Medium	Large	All	Small	Medium	Large	All
2.1	Capacity to Compete								
2.1.1	Losses due to power outages (% of sales)	1.8	3.0	2.1	2.0	42.7	35.0	40.4	41.1
2.1.2	Losses during domestic shipping (%)	1.5	0.5	0.5	1.1	37.2	57.2	57.2	43.0
2.1.3	Management time spent with regulation (%)	1.4	2.6	3.3	1.7	81.4	71.7	67.2	78.7
2.1.4	Days for customs clearance	6.0	8.5	6.5	7.9	56.2	45.1	53.9	47.5
2.2	Capacity to Connect								
2.2.1	State of cluster development (1–7)				3.8				60.0
2.2.2	Extent of marketing (1–7)				5.1				82.4
2.2.3	Local supplier quality (1–7)				5.0				73.0
2.2.4	University-industry collaboration in R&D (1–7)				3.1				41.5
2.3	Capacity to Change								
2.3.1	Access to finance as a constraint (%)	32.8	24.0	17.9	30.3	35.1	45.9	55.0	38.0
2.3.2	Inadequately educated workforce (%)	13.3	21.2	34.7	16.0	60.7	47.9	32.4	55.8
2.3.3	Business licensing and permits as a constraint (%)	20.2	17.6	19.2	19.7	33.2	36.8	34.5	33.8

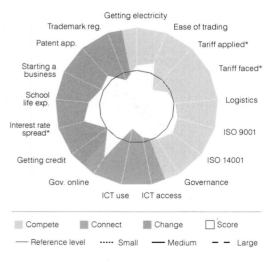

3	NATIONAL ENVIRONMENT	Values	Normalized scores
		All	All
3.1	Capacity to Compete		
3.1.1	Ease of getting electricity (0–100)	72.7	52.3
3.1.2	Ease of trading across borders (0–100)	76.9	58.8
3.1.3	Applied tariff, trade-weighted average (%)	12.7	28.6
3.1.4	Faced tariff, trade-weighted average (%)	4.1	41.5
3.1.5	Logistics performance index (1–5)	2.7	47.2
3.1.6	ISO 9001 quality certificates (/mn pop.)	31.5	51.8
3.1.7	ISO 14001 environmental certificates (/mn pop.)	8.9	55.0
3.1.8	Governance (index)	-0.4	48.1
3.2	Capacity to Connect		
3.2.1	ICT access (0–10)	3.9	39.2
3.2.2	ICT use (0–10)	1.1	27.9
3.2.3	Government's online service (0–10)	6.5	75.3
3.3	Capacity to Change		
3.3.1	Ease of getting credit (0–100)	45.0	44.8
3.3.2	Interest rate spread (%)	2.4	67.0
3.3.3	School life expectancy (years)	13.7	59.1
3.3.4	Ease of starting a business (0–100)	83.0	48.7
3.3.5	Patent applications (/mn pop.)	16.0	53.1
3.3.6	Trademark registrations (/mn pop.)	268.0	35.9

Note: For each indicator, the table includes the values and the corresponding scores. Radar charts are based on scores: values are transformed and noramlized so that for each indicator in a sample of 111 countries, the worst value gets a score of 0, the best value gets a score of 100, and the median gets a score of 50. If in the original values higher numbers indicate worse outcomes, the chart labels are marked with an asterisk (*). Series with missing data are indicated as (-) in the tables and omitted from the radar charts.

Source: World Bank Enterprise Survey (2011) for firm level data; for other sources refer to Annex III.

ITC Business Survey on Non-Tariff Measures (NTMs)

1. Firms affected by NTMs

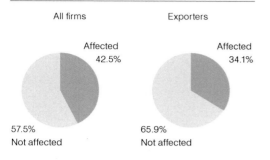

All firms

Affected
42.5%

57.5%
Not affected

Exporters

Affected
34.1%

65.9%
Not affected

2. NTMs reported as challenging (exporters)

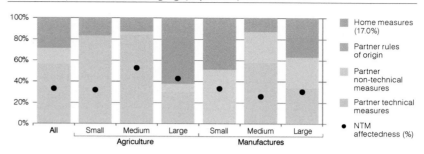

- Home measures (17.0%)
- Partner rules of origin
- Partner non-technical measures
- Partner technical measures
- ● NTM affectedness (%)

Agriculture: All, Small, Medium, Large
Manufactures: Small, Medium, Large

3. Regulatory and procedural obstacles (exporters)

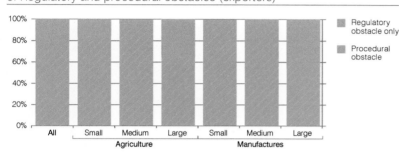

- Regulatory obstacle only
- Procedural obstacle

Agriculture: All, Small, Medium, Large
Manufactures: Small, Medium, Large

4. Location of procedural obstacles (exporters)

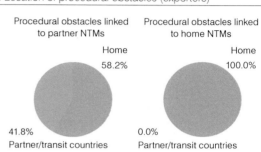

Procedural obstacles linked to partner NTMs

Home 58.2%

41.8%
Partner/transit countries

Procedural obstacles linked to home NTMs

Home 100.0%

0.0%
Partner/transit countries

Source: ITC NTM Survey, additional results are available at http://ntmsurvey.intracen.org/ntm-survey-data/country-analysis/sri-lanka/

Potential for Growth of Current Exports

PRODUCT/PRODUCT GROUP DESCRIPTION	Exports (US$ mn)	South Asia	Unrealized potential	South-South trade	Unrealized potential	OECD	Unrealized potential	Technology level	Revenues stability	SME presence	Female participation
090240 Black tea (fermented) & partly fer...	693.3		91%		22%		82%	■	■		
090230 Black tea (fermented)&partly ferm...	560.7		96%		23%		44%	■	■	■	■
621210 Brassieres and parts thereof, of te...	399.0		71%		71%		34%	■	■	■	■
620342 Mens/boys trousers and shorts, o...	318.7		28%		56%		15%	■	■	■	■
0906XX Cinnamon and cinnamon-tree flo...	102.2		99%		91%		32%	■	■		
090411 Pepper of the genus Piper,ex cube...	53.5		63%		72%		94%				
401290 Solid o cushiond tries,interchange...	277.2		89%		72%		11%	■	■	■	■
611610 Gloves impregnated, coated or co...	180.4		94%		63%		40%	■		■	■
401519 Gloves nes of rubber	117.2		17%		43%		64%	■		■	■
710391 Rubies,sapphires and emeralds f...	108.0		98%		81%		42%	■	■	■	■
620462 Womens/girls trousers and shorts...	230.3		11%		54%		17%	■	■	■	■
620520 Mens/boys shirts, of cotton, not k...	139.8		74%		72%		34%	■	■	■	■
610910 T-shirts, singlets and other vests,...	244.8		47%		52%		26%	■	■	■	■
610821 Womens/girls briefs and panties,...	166.9		77%		55%		23%	■	■	■	■
610462 Womens/girls trousers and shorts...	122.4		94%		88%		28%	■	■	■	■
611120 Babies garments and clothing acc...	89.5		97%		71%		54%	■	■	■	■
610711 Mens/boys underpants and briefs...	102.4		75%		57%		48%	■	■	■	■
611241 Womens/girls swimwear, of synthe...	83.2		78%		83%		43%	■	■	■	■
610990 T-shirts,singlets and other vests, o...	134.6		42%		59%		21%	■	■	■	■
610822 Womens/girls briefs and panties....	109.0		59%		87%		40%	■	■	■	■

What is the product's export potential in…?   Would Sri Lanka improve its…?

Note: Top 20 products listed in decreasing order of their export potential to the world. Development indicators are relative to the country's current situation, green indicating performance above its trade-weighted median and red otherwise; a blank cell indicates data are not available. A blank cell in export potential means that the product was not consistently demanded over five years by any country in the respective region. Exports (US$ mn) corresponds to the yearly average exports to the world over the period 2009-13. Refer to Annexes I, II and III for details.

Source: ITC Export Potential Assessment, additional results are available at ITC Country Pages http://www.intracen.org/country/sri-lanka/

Tanzania, United Rep.

Key indicators

Population (millions)	47.7
GDP (US$ billions)	47.9
GDP per capita (US$)	1,005.6
Share of world GDP (PPP US$, %)	0.1
Current account surplus over GDP (%)	-10.2
Tariff preference margin (percentage points)	5.2
Goods and services imports + exports over GDP (%)	52.7
Exports of services over total exports (%)	41.8
Geographic region	Sub-Saharan Africa
Development group	LDC
Income group	Low income

SME Competitiveness Grid Summary

Average scores [0–100]		Compete	Connect	Change
FIRM LEVEL CAPABILITIES	Small	37.0	9.1	25.8
	Medium	45.9	24.0	47.3
	Large	59.2	74.4	75.5
	All	39.9	13.2	36.2
IMMEDIATE BUSINESS ENVIRONMENT		33.4	42.3	23.4
NATIONAL ENVIRONMENT		42.2	20.4	27.6

Reference level: 35.3 (a function of GDP per capita US$)	
Strengths are scores above: 53.0	Weaknesses are scores below: 17.7

SME Competitiveness Grid

1	FIRM LEVEL CAPABILITIES	Values				Normalized scores			
		Small	Medium	Large	All	Small	Medium	Large	All
1.1	Capacity to Compete								
1.1.1	Firms with quality certification (%)	13.1	25.6	75.4	17.6	36.0	54.0	89.7	43.4
1.1.2	Firms with checking or savings account (%)	69.8	85.2	92.4	73.7	17.6	30.3	41.9	20.1
1.1.3	Capacity utilization (%)	80.9	79.8	82.6	80.8	64.9	62.0	69.7	64.7
1.1.4	Manager's experience (years)	12.1	14.1	13.6	12.6	29.7	37.3	35.4	31.6
1.2	Capacity to Connect								
1.2.1	Firms using e-mail (%)	22.2	49.2	94.1	30.0	4.5	16.4	68.7	7.5
1.2.2	Firms having their own website (%)	16.4	36.6	83.5	22.6	13.6	31.6	80.1	19.0
1.3	Capacity to Change								
1.3.1	Firms with audited financial statements (%)	35.0	52.3	81.7	39.9	26.6	42.8	75.3	31.0
1.3.2	Investments financed by banks (%)	3.5	13.4	37.6	8.8	17.3	47.1	83.6	35.4
1.3.3	Firms offering formal training (%)	27.4	40.0	52.3	30.7	34.0	47.5	59.7	37.6
1.3.4	Firms using foreign technology licences (%)	5.3	16.5	47.4	10.9	25.5	51.7	83.6	40.9

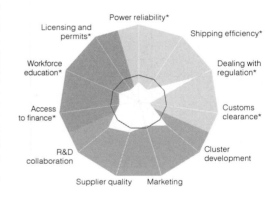

2	IMMEDIATE BUSINESS ENVIRONMENT	Values				Normalized scores			
		Small	Medium	Large	All	Small	Medium	Large	All
2.1	Capacity to Compete								
2.1.1	Losses due to power outages (% of sales)	5.4	6.0	4.9	5.5	26.1	24.5	27.6	25.8
2.1.2	Losses during domestic shipping (%)	4.5	1.7	2.6	4.0	16.2	34.9	26.8	18.5
2.1.3	Management time spent with regulation (%)	1.8	2.6	3.6	2.0	77.8	71.7	65.5	76.1
2.1.4	Days for customs clearance	-	24.6	25.0	22.0	-	9.4	8.9	13.3
2.2	Capacity to Connect								
2.2.1	State of cluster development (1–7)				3.4				46.2
2.2.2	Extent of marketing (1–7)				3.5				32.1
2.2.3	Local supplier quality (1–7)				3.8				40.6
2.2.4	University-industry collaboration in R&D (1–7)				3.4				50.3
2.3	Capacity to Change								
2.3.1	Access to finance as a constraint (%)	43.3	47.0	37.5	43.9	24.9	21.7	30.3	24.3
2.3.2	Inadequately educated workforce (%)	38.8	47.2	48.0	40.8	28.6	21.9	21.3	26.9
2.3.3	Business licensing and permits as a constraint (%)	32.4	42.8	19.9	34.2	20.4	12.6	33.5	18.9

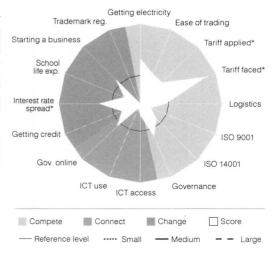

3	NATIONAL ENVIRONMENT	Values	Normalized scores
		All	All
3.1	Capacity to Compete		
3.1.1	Ease of getting electricity (0–100)	75.3	55.8
3.1.2	Ease of trading across borders (0–100)	63.0	40.2
3.1.3	Applied tariff, trade-weighted average (%)	9.8	37.2
3.1.4	Faced tariff, trade-weighted average (%)	2.4	86.7
3.1.5	Logistics performance index (1–5)	2.3	31.1
3.1.6	ISO 9001 quality certificates (/mn pop.)	1.2	13.9
3.1.7	ISO 14001 environmental certificates (/mn pop.)	0.8	28.0
3.1.8	Governance (index)	-0.5	44.4
3.2	Capacity to Connect		
3.2.1	ICT access (0–10)	2.4	14.4
3.2.2	ICT use (0–10)	0.2	6.2
3.2.3	Government's online service (0–10)	3.0	40.5
3.3	Capacity to Change		
3.3.1	Ease of getting credit (0–100)	25.0	24.3
3.3.2	Interest rate spread (%)	6.0	50.5
3.3.3	School life expectancy (years)	9.2	21.3
3.3.4	Ease of starting a business (0–100)	78.9	42.0
3.3.5	Patent applications (/mn pop.)	-	-
3.3.6	Trademark registrations (/mn pop.)	1.0	0.0

Legend: Compete | Connect | Change | Score | Reference level | Small | Medium | Large

Note: For each indicator, the table includes the values and the corresponding scores. Radar charts are based on scores: values are transformed and normalized so that for each indicator in a sample of 111 countries, the worst value gets a score of 0, the best value gets a score of 100, and the median gets a score of 50. If in the original values higher numbers indicate worse outcomes, the chart labels are marked with an asterisk (*). Series with missing data are indicated as (-) in the tables and omitted from the radar charts.

Source: World Bank Enterprise Survey (2013) for firm level data; for other sources refer to Annex III.

ITC Business Survey on Non-Tariff Measures (NTMs)

1. Firms affected by NTMs

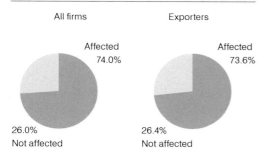

All firms

Affected
74.0%

26.0%
Not affected

Exporters

Affected
73.6%

26.4%
Not affected

2. NTMs reported as challenging (exporters)

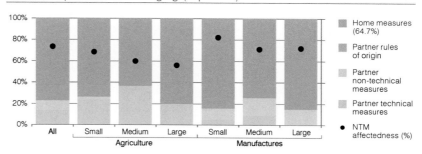

- Home measures (64.7%)
- Partner rules of origin
- Partner non-technical measures
- Partner technical measures
- ● NTM affectedness (%)

Agriculture — Small, Medium, Large
Manufactures — Small, Medium, Large

3. Regulatory and procedural obstacles (exporters)

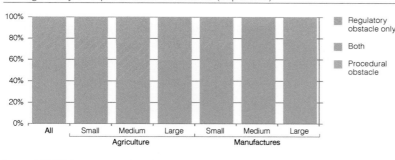

- Regulatory obstacle only
- Both
- Procedural obstacle

All
Agriculture — Small, Medium, Large
Manufactures — Small, Medium, Large

4. Location of procedural obstacles (exporters)

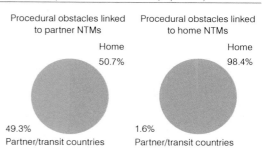

Procedural obstacles linked to partner NTMs

Home
50.7%

49.3%
Partner/transit countries

Procedural obstacles linked to home NTMs

Home
98.4%

1.6%
Partner/transit countries

Source: ITC NTM Survey, additional results are available at http://ntmsurvey.intracen.org/ntm-survey-data/country-analysis/tanzania-united-republic-of/

Potential for Growth of Current Exports

| PRODUCT/PRODUCT GROUP DESCRIPTION | Exports (US$ mn) | What is the product's export potential in…? | | | | | | Would Tanzania improve its…? | | | |
		Sub-Saharan Africa	Unrealized potential	South-South trade	Unrealized potential	OECD	Unrealized potential	Technology level	Revenues stability	SME presence	Female participation
080131 Cashew nuts, in shell, fresh or dried	123.3		87%		56%		98%	■	■		
090111 Coffee, not roasted, not decaffein…	157.0		82%		72%		29%	■	■		
520100 Cotton, not carded or combed	111.8		93%		60%		77%	■	■		
120740 Sesamum seeds, whether or not b…	93.8		100%		45%		49%	■	■		
630491 Furnishing articles nes, of textile…	46.9		71%		71%		96%	■	■	■	■
090240 Black tea (fermented) & partly fer…	44.4		80%		74%		35%	■	■		
230610 Cotton sed oil-cake&oth solid resi…	7.5		94%		93%		100%	■	■	■	■
710813 Gold in oth semi-manufactd form…	311.8		2%		73%		100%	■	■	■	■
110100 Wheat or meslin flour	35.6		55%		59%		100%	■	■	■	■
0907XX Cloves	38.8		100%		53%		94%	■	■		
271210 Petroleum jelly	10.4		87%		87%		100%	■	■	■	■
252329 Portland cement nes	22.1		73%		73%		100%	■	■	■	■
0713Xb Dried vegetables, shelled	35.6		90%		35%		84%	■	■	■	■
0304Xb Fish fillets and pieces, fresh, chill…	62.3		93%		73%		47%	■	■	■	■
340119 Soap&orgn surf prep, shapd, nes…	10.7		76%		76%		100%	■	■	■	■
230630 Sunflower sed oil-cake&oth solid…	16.7		75%		74%		99%	■	■	■	■
630533 Sacks, bags, packing, of strip pla…	8.4		80%		81%		100%	■	■	■	■
7010XX Carboys, bottles, flasks, jars, pots…	18.6		58%		61%		85%	■	■	■	■
721041 Flat rolled prod.i/nas,pltd or ctd w…	7.1		81%		81%		100%	■	■	■	■
252210 Quicklime	6.7		79%		79%		100%	■	■	■	■

Note: Top 20 products listed in decreasing order of their export potential to the world. Development indicators are relative to the country's current situation, green indicating performance above its trade-weighted median and red otherwise; a blank cell indicates data are not available. A blank cell in export potential means that the product was not consistently demanded over five years by any country in the respective region. Exports (US$ mn) corresponds to the yearly average exports to the world over the period 2009-13. Refer to Annexes I, II and III for details.

Source: ITC Export Potential Assessment, additional results are available at ITC Country Pages http://www.intracen.org/country/united-republic-of-tanzania/

Thailand

Key indicators

Population (millions)	68.7
GDP (US$ billions)	373.8
GDP per capita (US$)	5,444.6
Share of world GDP (PPP US$, %)	0.9
Current account surplus over GDP (%)	3.8
Tariff preference margin (percentage points)	3.0
Goods and services imports + exports over GDP (%)	149.6
Exports of services over total exports (%)	20.0
Geographic region	East Asia & Pacific
Development group	DC
Income group	Upper-middle income

SME Competitiveness Grid Summary

Average scores [0–100]		Compete	Connect	Change
FIRM LEVEL CAPABILITIES	Small	31.5	17.1	77.7
	Medium	48.8	32.2	89.3
	Large	54.5	53.4	98.0
	All	51.1	39.4	92.7
IMMEDIATE BUSINESS ENVIRONMENT		95.4	66.1	39.1
NATIONAL ENVIRONMENT		64.4	56.2	53.2

Reference level: 49.6 (a function of GDP per capita US$)	
Strengths are scores above: 74.4	Weaknesses are scores below: 24.8

SME Competitiveness Grid

1	FIRM LEVEL CAPABILITIES	Values				Normalized scores			
		Small	Medium	Large	All	Small	Medium	Large	All
1.1	Capacity to Compete								
1.1.1	Firms with quality certification (%)	6.8	19.6	62.3	39.0	22.5	46.3	83.0	67.1
1.1.2	Firms with checking or savings account (%)	98.6	100.0	99.3	99.6	69.5	100.0	79.0	85.3
1.1.3	Capacity utilization (%)	-	-	-	-	-	-	-	-
1.1.4	Manager's experience (years)	5.3	4.7	5.1	4.9	2.5	0.0	1.7	0.8
1.2	Capacity to Connect								
1.2.1	Firms using e-mail (%)	45.4	67.7	85.4	74.1	14.4	28.6	48.9	34.5
1.2.2	Firms having their own website (%)	23.6	41.0	63.3	50.0	19.9	35.7	57.9	44.4
1.3	Capacity to Change								
1.3.1	Firms with audited financial statements (%)	100.0	100.0	100.0	100.0	100.0	100.0	100.0	100.0
1.3.2	Investments financed by banks (%)	49.9	53.5	53.1	53.0	95.1	98.1	97.8	97.7
1.3.3	Firms offering formal training (%)	30.9	63.3	94.9	75.3	37.8	69.9	96.1	80.4
1.3.4	Firms using foreign technology licences (%)	-	-	-	-	-	-	-	-

2	IMMEDIATE BUSINESS ENVIRONMENT	Values				Normalized scores			
		Small	Medium	Large	All	Small	Medium	Large	All
2.1	Capacity to Compete								
2.1.1	Losses due to power outages (% of sales)	-	-	-	-	-	-	-	-
2.1.2	Losses during domestic shipping (%)	-	-	-	-	-	-	-	-
2.1.3	Management time spent with regulation (%)	0.5	0.4	0.4	0.4	91.9	93.4	93.4	93.4
2.1.4	Days for customs clearance	1.3	1.4	1.3	1.3	97.4	95.8	97.4	97.4
2.2	Capacity to Connect								
2.2.1	State of cluster development (1–7)				4.2				70.3
2.2.2	Extent of marketing (1–7)				4.6				68.4
2.2.3	Local supplier quality (1–7)				4.5				59.6
2.2.4	University-industry collaboration in R&D (1–7)				4.0				66.1
2.3	Capacity to Change								
2.3.1	Access to finance as a constraint (%)	34.9	30.4	21.3	26.4	32.9	37.8	49.7	42.7
2.3.2	Inadequately educated workforce (%)	27.3	37.4	42.3	38.8	40.1	29.9	25.7	28.6
2.3.3	Business licensing and permits as a constraint (%)	15.0	11.6	12.4	12.3	40.9	47.3	45.7	45.9

3	NATIONAL ENVIRONMENT	Values	Normalized scores
		All	All
3.1	Capacity to Compete		
3.1.1	Ease of getting electricity (0–100)	91.7	82.5
3.1.2	Ease of trading across borders (0–100)	83.6	71.2
3.1.3	Applied tariff, trade-weighted average (%)	7.8	44.4
3.1.4	Faced tariff, trade-weighted average (%)	3.8	46.9
3.1.5	Logistics performance index (1–5)	3.4	76.2
3.1.6	ISO 9001 quality certificates (/mn pop.)	130.3	70.5
3.1.7	ISO 14001 environmental certificates (/mn pop.)	46.1	73.8
3.1.8	Governance (index)	-0.3	50.0
3.2	Capacity to Connect		
3.2.1	ICT access (0–10)	4.9	53.8
3.2.2	ICT use (0–10)	3.1	59.1
3.2.3	Government's online service (0–10)	4.4	55.7
3.3	Capacity to Change		
3.3.1	Ease of getting credit (0–100)	45.0	44.8
3.3.2	Interest rate spread (%)	4.1	56.5
3.3.3	School life expectancy (years)	13.5	57.1
3.3.4	Ease of starting a business (0–100)	88.0	58.9
3.3.5	Patent applications (/mn pop.)	23.0	56.5
3.3.6	Trademark registrations (/mn pop.)	416.0	45.6

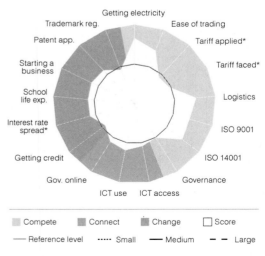

Note: For each indicator, the table includes the values and the corresponding scores. Radar charts are based on scores: values are transformed and normalized so that for each indicator in a sample of 111 countries, the worst value gets a score of 0, the best value gets a score of 100, and the median gets a score of 50. If in the original values higher numbers indicate worse outcomes, the chart labels are marked with an asterisk (*). Series with missing data are indicated as (-) in the tables and omitted from the radar charts.

Source: World Bank Enterprise Survey (2006) for firm level data; for other sources refer to Annex III.

ITC Business Survey on Non-Tariff Measures (NTMs)

1. Firms affected by NTMs

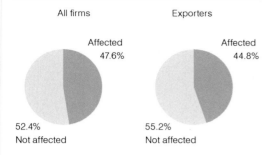

All firms

Affected
47.6%

52.4%
Not affected

Exporters

Affected
44.8%

55.2%
Not affected

2. NTMs reported as challenging (exporters)

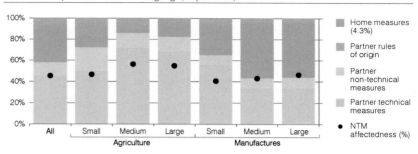

- Home measures (4.3%)
- Partner rules of origin
- Partner non-technical measures
- Partner technical measures
- ● NTM affectedness (%)

3. Regulatory and procedural obstacles (exporters)

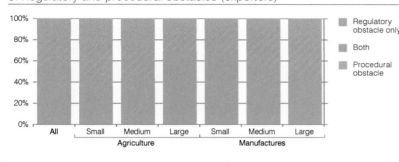

- Regulatory obstacle only
- Both
- Procedural obstacle

4. Location of procedural obstacles (exporters)

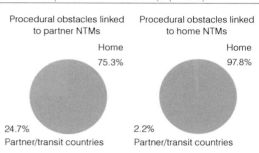

Procedural obstacles linked to partner NTMs

Home
75.3%

24.7%
Partner/transit countries

Procedural obstacles linked to home NTMs

Home
97.8%

2.2%
Partner/transit countries

Source: ITC NTM Survey, additional results are available at http://ntmsurvey.intracen.org/ntm-survey-data/country-analysis/thailand

Potential for Growth of Current Exports

PRODUCT/PRODUCT GROUP DESCRIPTION	Exports (US$ mn)	East Asia & Pacific	Unrealized potential	South-South trade	Unrealized potential	OECD	Unrealized potential	Technology level	Revenues stability	SME presence	Female participation
847170 Computer data storage units	14962.1		32%		30%		32%				
85XXXi Electrical, electronic equipment	10157.4		41%		43%		15%				
400122 Technically specified natural rubb...	3712.8		39%		41%		65%				
870421 Diesel powered trucks with a GV...	6133.0		30%		45%		10%				
100630 Rice, semi-milled or wholly milled,...	4257.7		68%		55%		18%				
400110 Natural rubber latex, whether or n...	1883.7		72%		72%		77%				
400121 Natural rubber in smoked sheets	2413.3		67%		71%		51%				
84XXXe Machinery, nuclear reactors, boil...	4245.6		33%		34%		63%				
8525XX Television cameras, digital camer...	2398.0		68%		72%		21%				
8415XX Air conditioning machines, with m...	2270.9		47%		45%		49%				
160232 Fowl (gallus domesticus) meat, pr...	1900.3		62%		78%		54%				
110814 Manioc (cassava) starch	854.9		74%		75%		53%				
85XXXd Electrical, electronic equipment	2677.3		52%		57%		16%				
160414 Tunas,skipjack&Atl bonito,prepard...	2149.8		50%		16%		43%				
85XXXc Electrical, electronic equipment	2683.3		45%		63%		14%				
1605Xa Crustaceans & molluscs, prepar...	1484.4		61%		78%		41%				
071410 Manioc (cassava), fresh or dried,...	1034.8		58%		58%		67%				
1701XX Cane or beet sugar and chemica...	1649.7		7%		47%		47%				
711311 Articles of jewellery&pts therof of...	1527.2		67%		80%		25%				
0306Xa Crustaceans	1486.4		53%		63%		35%				

What is the product's export potential in...? — Would Thailand improve its...?

Note: Top 20 products listed in decreasing order of their export potential to the world. Development indicators are relative to the country's current situation, green indicating performance above its trade-weighted median and red otherwise; a blank cell indicates data are not available. A blank cell in export potential means that the product was not consistently demanded over five years by any country in the respective region. Exports (US$ mn) corresponds to the yearly average exports to the world over the period 2009-13. Refer to Annexes I, II and III for details.

Source: ITC Export Potential Assessment, additional results are available at ITC Country Pages http://www.intracen.org/country/thailand/

Trinidad and Tobago

Key indicators

Population (millions)	1.4
GDP (US$ billions)	28.8
GDP per capita (US$)	21,310.8
Share of world GDP (PPP US$, %)	0.0
Current account surplus over GDP (%)	8.3
Tariff preference margin (percentage points)	1.7
Goods and services imports + exports over GDP (%)	136.7
Exports of services over total exports (%)	23.4
Geographic region	LAC
Development group	SIDS
Income group	High income

SME Competitiveness Grid Summary

Average scores [0–100]		Compete	Connect	Change
FIRM LEVEL CAPABILITIES	Small	56.4	29.5	37.8
	Medium	62.9	52.9	54.1
	Large	60.5	63.4	63.7
	All	57.7	34.5	44.6
IMMEDIATE BUSINESS ENVIRONMENT		60.1	51.1	40.7
NATIONAL ENVIRONMENT		54.1	60.1	44.7

Reference level: 61.2 (a function of GDP per capita US$)	
Strengths are scores above: 91.7	Weaknesses are scores below: 30.6

SME Competitiveness Grid

1	FIRM LEVEL CAPABILITIES	Values				Normalized scores			
		Small	Medium	Large	All	Small	Medium	Large	All
1.1	Capacity to Compete								
1.1.1	Firms with quality certification (%)	8.9	16.1	17.5	11.0	27.5	41.1	43.3	32.0
1.1.2	Firms with checking or savings account (%)	99.9	100.0	100.0	99.9	95.1	100.0	100.0	95.1
1.1.3	Capacity utilization (%)	73.6	71.2	69.8	72.5	47.4	42.4	39.6	45.0
1.1.4	Manager's experience (years)	19.1	22.5	20.0	19.9	55.8	68.0	59.1	58.7
1.2	Capacity to Connect								
1.2.1	Firms using e-mail (%)	76.1	94.1	98.4	81.2	36.6	68.7	87.8	42.7
1.2.2	Firms having their own website (%)	26.4	42.5	44.5	30.8	22.3	37.2	39.1	26.3
1.3	Capacity to Change								
1.3.1	Firms with audited financial statements (%)	76.0	93.3	77.2	79.5	68.4	90.5	69.8	72.6
1.3.2	Investments financed by banks (%)	15.2	25.9	33.3	19.1	50.9	69.2	78.8	58.4
1.3.3	Firms offering formal training (%)	21.4	42.8	55.6	28.0	27.1	50.4	62.8	34.6
1.3.4	Firms using foreign technology licences (%)	0.7	1.0	12.1	2.2	4.6	6.4	43.5	12.8

2	IMMEDIATE BUSINESS ENVIRONMENT	Values				Normalized scores			
		Small	Medium	Large	All	Small	Medium	Large	All
2.1	Capacity to Compete								
2.1.1	Losses due to power outages (% of sales)	0.1	0.1	0.0	0.1	81.8	81.8	100.0	81.8
2.1.2	Losses during domestic shipping (%)	0.2	0.4	0.7	0.3	72.1	61.0	51.2	65.8
2.1.3	Management time spent with regulation (%)	8.5	5.8	8.3	7.9	46.4	55.3	46.9	48.1
2.1.4	Days for customs clearance	9.0	7.0	9.5	8.7	43.3	51.6	41.5	44.5
2.2	Capacity to Connect								
2.2.1	State of cluster development (1-7)				3.6				51.0
2.2.2	Extent of marketing (1-7)				4.2				55.4
2.2.3	Local supplier quality (1-7)				4.3				54.5
2.2.4	University-industry collaboration in R&D (1-7)				3.1				43.3
2.3	Capacity to Change								
2.3.1	Access to finance as a constraint (%)	31.1	23.9	25.1	29.3	37.0	46.0	44.4	39.1
2.3.2	Inadequately educated workforce (%)	44.2	33.8	26.7	40.9	24.2	33.2	40.8	26.8
2.3.3	Business licensing and permits as a constraint (%)	7.6	11.2	3.8	8.0	57.3	48.2	71.5	56.2

3	NATIONAL ENVIRONMENT	Values	Normalized scores
		All	All
3.1	Capacity to Compete		
3.1.1	Ease of getting electricity (0–100)	88.2	75.9
3.1.2	Ease of trading across borders (0–100)	75.6	56.5
3.1.3	Applied tariff, trade-weighted average (%)	13.0	27.8
3.1.4	Faced tariff, trade-weighted average (%)	3.8	46.6
3.1.5	Logistics performance index (1–5)	-	
3.1.6	ISO 9001 quality certificates (/mn pop.)	39.4	54.7
3.1.7	ISO 14001 environmental certificates (/mn pop.)	8.9	55.0
3.1.8	Governance (index)	0.1	62.4
3.2	Capacity to Connect		
3.2.1	ICT access (0–10)	6.4	71.9
3.2.2	ICT use (0–10)	3.6	64.5
3.2.3	Government's online service (0–10)	3.3	44.0
3.3	Capacity to Change		
3.3.1	Ease of getting credit (0–100)	65.0	66.1
3.3.2	Interest rate spread (%)	6.0	50.6
3.3.3	School life expectancy (years)	12.3	47.1
3.3.4	Ease of starting a business (0–100)	88.3	59.7
3.3.5	Patent applications (/mn pop.)	1.0	0.0
3.3.6	Trademark registrations (/mn pop.)	-	-

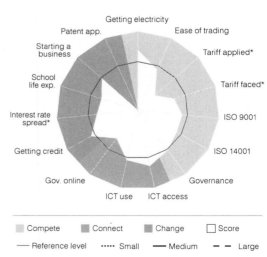

Compete   Connect   Change   Score
— Reference level   ..... Small   — Medium   – – Large

Note: For each indicator, the table includes the values and the corresponding scores. Radar charts are based on scores: values are transformed and normalized so that for each indicator in a sample of 111 countries, the worst value gets a score of 0, the best value gets a score of 100, and the median gets a score of 50. If in the original values higher numbers indicate worse outcomes, the chart labels are marked with an asterisk (*). Series with missing data are indicated as (-) in the tables and omitted from the radar charts.

Source: World Bank Enterprise Survey (2010) for firm level data; for other sources refer to Annex III.

ITC Business Survey on Non-Tariff Measures (NTMs)

1. Firms affected by NTMs

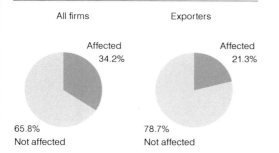

All firms

Affected
34.2%

65.8%
Not affected

Exporters

Affected
21.3%

78.7%
Not affected

2. NTMs reported as challenging (exporters)

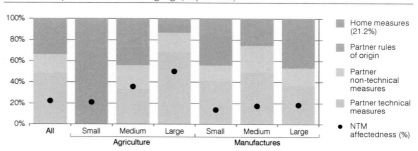

- Home measures (21.2%)
- Partner rules of origin
- Partner non-technical measures
- Partner technical measures
- ● NTM affectedness (%)

Agriculture | Manufactures

3. Regulatory and procedural obstacles (exporters)

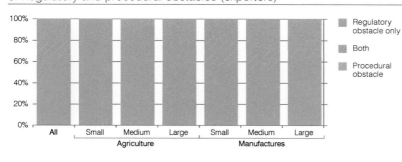

- Regulatory obstacle only
- Both
- Procedural obstacle

Agriculture | Manufactures

4. Location of procedural obstacles (exporters)

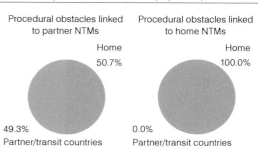

Procedural obstacles linked to partner NTMs

Home
50.7%

49.3%
Partner/transit countries

Procedural obstacles linked to home NTMs

Home
100.0%

0.0%
Partner/transit countries

Source: ITC NTM Survey, additional results are available at http://ntmsurvey.intracen.org/ntm-survey-data/country-analysis/trinidad-and-tobago/

Potential for Growth of Current Exports

PRODUCT/PRODUCT GROUP DESCRIPTION	Exports (US$ mn)	Latin America & the Caribbean	Unrealized potential	South-South trade	Unrealized potential	OECD	Unrealized potential	Technology level	Revenues stability	SME presence	Female participation
281410 Anhydrous ammonia	1952.9		22%		35%		26%				
290511 Methanol (methyl alcohol)	1351.0		52%		53%		1%				
720310 Ferrous products obtained by dire...	737.5		59%		28%		25%				
310280 Urea/ammonium nitrate mx in aqu...	242.8		67%		42%		48%				
310210 Urea,wthr/nt in aqueous solution i...	227.1		54%		56%		25%				
220210 Waters incl mineral&aeratd, conta...	60.3		60%		61%		81%				
220710 Undenaturd ethyl alcohol of an al...	37.6		97%		97%		22%				
721391 Hot rolled bar/rod, irregular coils,...	90.9		8%		14%		92%				
721310 Bars&rods.i/nas,hr,in irreg wound...	21.5		73%		77%		59%				
252329 Portland cement nes	22.7		58%		61%		89%				
220840 Rum and tafia	18.2		91%		90%		69%				
1904XX Breakfast cereals & cereal bars	10.5		69%		69%		100%				
481810 Toilet paper	15.7		57%		56%		99%				
220300 Beer made from malt	16.6		47%		45%		84%				
190410 Prep foods obtaind by the swellg...	14.7		45%		48%		95%				
720720 Semi-fin prod,iron/non-alloy steel...	31.5		59%		60%		92%				
190590 Communion wafers,empty cache...	20.8		26%		28%		66%				
721320 Bars & rods, i/nas, hr, in irreg wou...	14.5		18%		17%		100%				
720610 Ingots, iron or non-alloy steel, of le...	15.1		33%		32%		100%				
480300 Paper,household/sanitary,rolls of...	9.4		66%		65%		98%				

What is the product's export potential in...? | Would Trinidad and Tobago improve its...?

Note: Top 20 products listed in decreasing order of their export potential to the world. Development indicators are relative to the country's current situation, green indicating performance above its trade-weighted median and red otherwise; a blank cell indicates data are not available. A blank cell in export potential means that the product was not consistently demanded over five years by any country in the respective region. Exports (US$ mn) corresponds to the yearly average exports to the world over the period 2009-13. Refer to Annexes I, II and III for details.

Source: ITC Export Potential Assessment, additional results are available at ITC Country Pages http://www.intracen.org/country/trinidad-and-tobago/

Tunisia

Key indicators

Population (millions)	11.0
GDP (US$ billions)	48.6
GDP per capita (US$)	4,414.8
Share of world GDP (PPP US$, %)	0.1
Current account surplus over GDP (%)	-8.9
Tariff preference margin (percentage points)	4.9
Goods and services imports + exports over GDP (%)	106.0
Exports of services over total exports (%)	22.2
Geographic region	MENA
Development group	DC
Income group	Upper-middle income

SME Competitiveness Grid Summary

Average scores [0–100]		Compete	Connect	Change
FIRM LEVEL CAPABILITIES	Small	41.7	56.7	33.9
	Medium	54.1	75.2	54.4
	Large	59.8	76.1	59.0
	All	49.3	64.1	45.6
IMMEDIATE BUSINESS ENVIRONMENT		47.5	44.3	53.6
NATIONAL ENVIRONMENT		56.2	58.6	53.6

Reference level: 47.8 (a function of GDP per capita US$)	
Strengths are scores above: 71.8	Weaknesses are scores below: 23.9

SME Competitiveness Grid

1	FIRM LEVEL CAPABILITIES	Values				Normalized scores			
		Small	Medium	Large	All	Small	Medium	Large	All
1.1	Capacity to Compete								
1.1.1	Firms with quality certification (%)	8.0	21.8	47.1	16.8	25.5	49.3	73.3	42.2
1.1.2	Firms with checking or savings account (%)	95.8	96.7	95.5	96.1	52.1	56.1	50.9	53.3
1.1.3	Capacity utilization (%)	56.3	64.8	70.1	62.3	17.1	30.5	40.2	26.3
1.1.4	Manager's experience (years)	23.7	26.1	24.5	24.6	72.1	80.4	74.9	75.3
1.2	Capacity to Connect								
1.2.1	Firms using e-mail (%)	90.8	97.4	95.9	93.6	59.6	82.1	75.2	67.1
1.2.2	Firms having their own website (%)	59.4	73.0	80.7	66.3	53.9	68.3	76.9	61.1
1.3	Capacity to Change								
1.3.1	Firms with audited financial statements (%)	66.0	87.3	78.9	74.5	57.0	82.4	71.9	66.7
1.3.2	Investments financed by banks (%)	8.1	16.1	19.9	12.9	33.4	52.8	59.8	45.9
1.3.3	Firms offering formal training (%)	20.9	34.8	51.3	28.9	26.5	42.0	58.8	35.6
1.3.4	Firms using foreign technology licences (%)	3.5	10.7	13.0	8.1	18.7	40.5	45.4	34.0

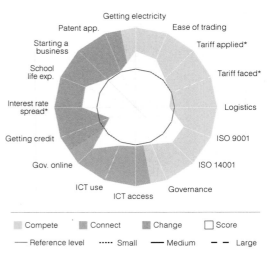

2	IMMEDIATE BUSINESS ENVIRONMENT	Values				Normalized scores			
		Small	Medium	Large	All	Small	Medium	Large	All
2.1	Capacity to Compete								
2.1.1	Losses due to power outages (% of sales)	0.1	0.3	0.0	0.2	81.8	68.4	100.0	73.7
2.1.2	Losses during domestic shipping (%)	0.3	1.0	0.1	0.6	65.8	44.8	81.4	54.0
2.1.3	Management time spent with regulation (%)	44.3	49.6	47.9	46.5	3.1	0.0	1.0	1.8
2.1.4	Days for customs clearance	6.6	4.8	4.1	5.2	53.2	63.0	68.1	60.6
2.2	Capacity to Connect								
2.2.1	State of cluster development (1–7)				3.5				49.4
2.2.2	Extent of marketing (1–7)				3.8				42.4
2.2.3	Local supplier quality (1–7)				4.1				49.0
2.2.4	University-industry collaboration in R&D (1–7)				2.9				36.6
2.3	Capacity to Change								
2.3.1	Access to finance as a constraint (%)	24.1	26.9	14.7	23.9	45.7	42.1	60.6	46.0
2.3.2	Inadequately educated workforce (%)	23.9	36.9	31.1	29.1	44.3	30.3	36.0	38.1
2.3.3	Business licensing and permits as a constraint (%)	1.6	5.5	0.8	2.8	84.6	64.3	91.3	76.8

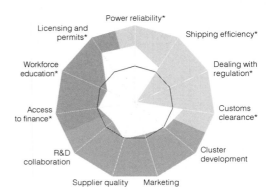

3	NATIONAL ENVIRONMENT	Values	Normalized scores
		All	All
3.1	Capacity to Compete		
3.1.1	Ease of getting electricity (0–100)	84.6	69.8
3.1.2	Ease of trading across borders (0–100)	80.4	64.8
3.1.3	Applied tariff, trade-weighted average (%)	6.5	50.0
3.1.4	Faced tariff, trade-weighted average (%)	3.8	46.6
3.1.5	Logistics performance index (1–5)	2.6	41.0
3.1.6	ISO 9001 quality certificates (/mn pop.)	77.0	63.5
3.1.7	ISO 14001 environmental certificates (/mn pop.)	18.2	63.1
3.1.8	Governance (index)	-0.3	50.4
3.2	Capacity to Connect		
3.2.1	ICT access (0–10)	4.6	49.5
3.2.2	ICT use (0–10)	2.6	52.5
3.2.3	Government's online service (0–10)	6.4	74.0
3.3	Capacity to Change		
3.3.1	Ease of getting credit (0–100)	35.0	34.4
3.3.2	Interest rate spread (%)	2.5	65.9
3.3.3	School life expectancy (years)	14.6	66.8
3.3.4	Ease of starting a business (0–100)	83.6	49.7
3.3.5	Patent applications (/mn pop.)	10.0	48.7
3.3.6	Trademark registrations (/mn pop.)	-	-

Legend: Compete | Connect | Change | Score | Reference level | Small | Medium | Large

Note: For each indicator, the table includes the values and the corresponding scores. Radar charts are based on scores: values are transformed and normalized so that for each indicator in a sample of 111 countries, the worst value gets a score of 0, the best value gets a score of 100, and the median gets a score of 50. If in the original values higher numbers indicate worse outcomes, the chart labels are marked with an asterisk (*). Series with missing data are indicated as (-) in the tables and omitted from the radar charts.

Source: World Bank Enterprise Survey (2013) for firm level data; for other sources refer to Annex III.

ITC Business Survey on Non-Tariff Measures (NTMs)

1. Firms affected by NTMs

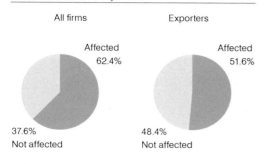

All firms

Affected
62.4%

37.6%
Not affected

Exporters

Affected
51.6%

48.4%
Not affected

2. NTMs reported as challenging (exporters)

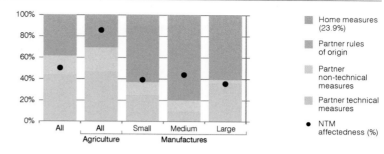

Legend:
- Home measures (23.9%)
- Partner rules of origin
- Partner non-technical measures
- Partner technical measures
- ● NTM affectedness (%)

X-axis: All (Agriculture) | All, Small, Medium, Large (Manufactures)

3. Regulatory and procedural obstacles (exporters)

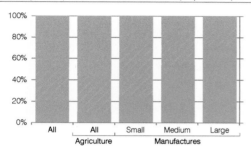

X-axis: All (Agriculture) | All, Small, Medium, Large (Manufactures)

Legend:
- Regulatory obstacle only
- Both
- Procedural obstacle

4. Location of procedural obstacles (exporters)

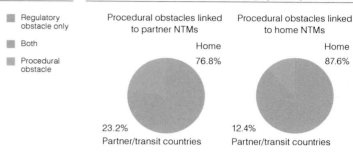

Procedural obstacles linked to partner NTMs

Home
76.8%

23.2%
Partner/transit countries

Procedural obstacles linked to home NTMs

Home
87.6%

12.4%
Partner/transit countries

Source: ITC NTM Survey, additional results are available at http://ntmsurvey.intracen.org/ntm-survey-data/country-analysis/tunisia/

Potential for Growth of Current Exports

| PRODUCT/PRODUCT GROUP DESCRIPTION | Exports (US$ mn) | What is the product's export potential in…? | | | | | | Would Tunisia improve its…? | | | |
		Middle East & North Africa	Unrealized potential	South-South trade	Unrealized potential	OECD	Unrealized potential	Technology level	Revenues stability	SME presence	Female participation
150910 Olive oil, virgin	338.1		68%		75%		69%				
620342 Mens/boys trousers and shorts, o...	644.5		89%		73%		26%				
151529 Maize (corn) oil and its fractions,re...	87.3		85%		85%		98%				
854430 Ignition wirg sets&oth wirg sets us...	652.1		98%		67%		21%				
8544Xa Electric conductors for a voltage...	530.0		92%		81%		16%				
310530 Diammonium phosphate, in pack...	354.3		55%		74%		44%				
080410 Dates, fresh or dried	206.1		62%		64%		66%				
6403XX Footwear, upper of leather	281.7		34%		49%		43%				
310310 Superphosphates, in packages w...	244.9		64%		30%		78%				
8528Xa Television receivers (incl video m...	346.6		90%		87%		57%				
280920 Phosphoric acid and polyphosph...	231.9		89%		38%		58%				
640610 Uppers and parts thereof, other th...	147.1		99%		96%		55%				
8544Xb Electric conductors, for a voltage...	177.8		59%		59%		50%				
880330 Aircraft parts nes	108.1		100%		98%		64%				
620462 Womens/girls trousers and shorts...	349.9		70%		59%		22%				
8708Xb Parts & access of motor vehicles	205.0		50%		68%		32%				
853690 Electrical app for switchg/protec e...	293.2		84%		89%		15%				
610910 T-shirts, singlets and other vests,...	209.1		77%		70%		49%				
840999 Parts for diesel and semi-diesel e...	77.1		93%		97%		69%				
85XXXc Electrical, electronic equipment	274.3		73%		73%		72%				

Note: Top 20 products listed in decreasing order of their export potential to the world. Development indicators are relative to the country's current situation, green indicating performance above its trade-weighted median and red otherwise; a blank cell indicates data are not available. A blank cell in export potential means that the product was not consistently demanded over five years by any country in the respective region. Exports (US$ mn) corresponds to the yearly average exports to the world over the period 2009-13. Refer to Annexes I, II and III for details.

Source: ITC Export Potential Assessment, additional results are available at ITC Country Pages http://www.intracen.org/country/tunisia/

Uruguay

Key indicators

Population (millions)	3.4
GDP (US$ billions)	55.1
GDP per capita (US$)	16,198.5
Share of world GDP (PPP US$, %)	0.1
Current account surplus over GDP (%)	-4.7
Tariff preference margin (percentage points)	5.8
Goods and services imports + exports over GDP (%)	52.2
Exports of services over total exports (%)	24.0
Geographic region	LAC
Development group	DC
Income group	High income

SME Competitiveness Grid Summary

Average scores [0–100]		Compete	Connect	Change
FIRM LEVEL CAPABILITIES	Small	43.7	40.0	30.7
	Medium	53.3	76.3	39.7
	Large	72.6	90.4	67.8
	All	47.0	49.4	37.6
IMMEDIATE BUSINESS ENVIRONMENT		58.4	51.3	49.9
NATIONAL ENVIRONMENT		60.2	81.4	60.6

Reference level: 58.8 (a function of GDP per capita US$)	
Strengths are scores above: 88.3	Weaknesses are scores below: 29.4

SME Competitiveness Grid

1	FIRM LEVEL CAPABILITIES	Values				Normalized scores			
		Small	Medium	Large	All	Small	Medium	Large	All
1.1	Capacity to Compete								
1.1.1	Firms with quality certification (%)	7.9	11.1	38.5	10.8	25.2	32.2	66.7	31.6
1.1.2	Firms with checking or savings account (%)	87.3	98.0	100.0	90.8	33.0	64.1	100.0	38.6
1.1.3	Capacity utilization (%)	71.5	73.9	77.5	72.7	43.0	48.0	56.3	45.5
1.1.4	Manager's experience (years)	24.1	22.8	22.4	23.7	73.5	69.0	67.6	72.1
1.2	Capacity to Connect								
1.2.1	Firms using e-mail (%)	83.3	97.9	99.6	88.0	45.6	84.8	96.4	53.6
1.2.2	Firms having their own website (%)	39.6	72.6	87.2	50.9	34.4	67.8	84.4	45.3
1.3	Capacity to Change								
1.3.1	Firms with audited financial statements (%)	45.0	36.4	80.1	45.5	35.7	27.8	73.3	36.2
1.3.2	Investments financed by banks (%)	6.6	13.3	16.0	9.2	28.7	46.8	52.6	36.5
1.3.3	Firms offering formal training (%)	44.0	51.0	85.5	48.6	51.6	58.5	88.8	56.1
1.3.4	Firms using foreign technology licences (%)	1.1	5.4	19.5	4.2	7.0	25.8	56.4	21.5

2	IMMEDIATE BUSINESS ENVIRONMENT	Values				Normalized scores			
		Small	Medium	Large	All	Small	Medium	Large	All
2.1	Capacity to Compete								
2.1.1	Losses due to power outages (% of sales)	0.0	0.0	0.0	0.0	100.0	100.0	100.0	100.0
2.1.2	Losses during domestic shipping (%)	1.0	1.0	0.4	0.9	44.8	44.8	61.0	46.7
2.1.3	Management time spent with regulation (%)	10.1	15.4	14.2	11.6	42.2	31.5	33.6	38.7
2.1.4	Days for customs clearance	8.9	7.8	5.4	7.7	43.8	47.9	59.7	48.3
2.2	Capacity to Connect								
2.2.1	State of cluster development (1–7)				3.5				48.0
2.2.2	Extent of marketing (1–7)				4.0				49.7
2.2.3	Local supplier quality (1–7)				4.2				50.7
2.2.4	University-industry collaboration in R&D (1–7)				3.6				56.6
2.3	Capacity to Change								
2.3.1	Access to finance as a constraint (%)	16.8	14.2	13.8	16.0	56.9	61.5	62.3	58.3
2.3.2	Inadequately educated workforce (%)	29.5	33.6	34.4	30.8	37.7	33.4	32.7	36.3
2.3.3	Business licensing and permits as a constraint (%)	9.0	7.7	5.2	8.4	53.4	57.0	65.5	55.0

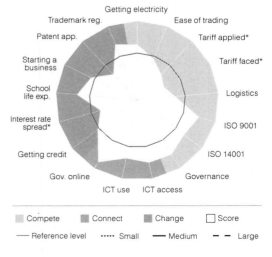

3	NATIONAL ENVIRONMENT	Values	Normalized scores
		All	All
3.1	Capacity to Compete		
3.1.1	Ease of getting electricity (0–100)	84.5	69.6
3.1.2	Ease of trading across borders (0–100)	74.6	55.1
3.1.3	Applied tariff, trade-weighted average (%)	8.1	43.3
3.1.4	Faced tariff, trade-weighted average (%)	4.5	36.3
3.1.5	Logistics performance index (1–5)	2.7	46.5
3.1.6	ISO 9001 quality certificates (/mn pop.)	245.3	78.8
3.1.7	ISO 14001 environmental certificates (/mn pop.)	38.9	71.8
3.1.8	Governance (index)	0.8	79.8
3.2	Capacity to Connect		
3.2.1	ICT access (0–10)	7.1	79.4
3.2.2	ICT use (0–10)	4.6	73.9
3.2.3	Government's online service (0–10)	8.5	91.0
3.3	Capacity to Change		
3.3.1	Ease of getting credit (0–100)	60.0	60.7
3.3.2	Interest rate spread (%)	7.8	47.0
3.3.3	School life expectancy (years)	15.5	74.2
3.3.4	Ease of starting a business (0–100)	89.7	63.2
3.3.5	Patent applications (/mn pop.)	6.0	43.5
3.3.6	Trademark registrations (/mn pop.)	1,306.0	75.0

Legend: Compete | Connect | Change | Score | Reference level | Small | Medium | Large

Note: For each indicator, the table includes the values and the corresponding scores. Radar charts are based on scores: values are transformed and normalized so that for each indicator in a sample of 111 countries, the worst value gets a score of 0, the best value gets a score of 100, and the median gets a score of 50. If in the original values higher numbers indicate worse outcomes, the chart labels are marked with an asterisk (*). Series with missing data are indicated as (-) in the tables and omitted from the radar charts.

Source: World Bank Enterprise Survey (2010) for firm level data; for other sources refer to Annex III.

ITC Business Survey on Non-Tariff Measures (NTMs)

1. Firms affected by NTMs

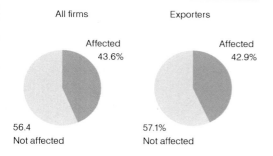

All firms

Affected
43.6%

56.4
Not affected

Exporters

Affected
42.9%

57.1%
Not affected

2. NTMs reported as challenging (exporters)

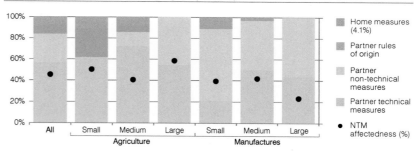

- Home measures (4.1%)
- Partner rules of origin
- Partner non-technical measures
- Partner technical measures
- ● NTM affectedness (%)

(x-axis: All | Small, Medium, Large [Agriculture] | Small, Medium, Large [Manufactures])

3. Regulatory and procedural obstacles (exporters)

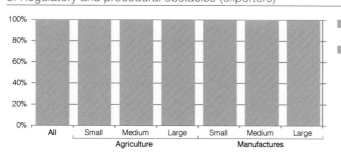

- Regulatory obstacle only
- Procedural obstacle

(x-axis: All | Small, Medium, Large [Agriculture] | Small, Medium, Large [Manufactures])

4. Location of procedural obstacles (exporters)

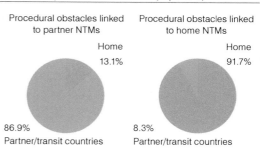

Procedural obstacles linked to partner NTMs

Home
13.1%

86.9%
Partner/transit countries

Procedural obstacles linked to home NTMs

Home
91.7%

8.3%
Partner/transit countries

Source: ITC NTM Survey, additional results are available at http://ntmsurvey.intracen.org/ntm-survey-data/country-analysis/uruguay/

Potential for Growth of Current Exports

PRODUCT/PRODUCT GROUP DESCRIPTION	Exports (US$ mn)	Latin America & the Caribbean	Unrealized potential	South-South trade	Unrealized potential	OECD	Unrealized potential	Technology level	Revenues stability	SME presence	Female participation
1201XX Soya beans, whether or not broken	832.3		95%		52%		78%	■	■		
020230 Bovine cuts boneless, frozen	882.2		56%		41%		8%	■	■	■	
110710 Malt, not roasted	181.3		61%		62%		97%	■	■	■	■
020130 Bovine cuts boneless, fresh or chil...	293.8		75%		82%		55%	■	■	■	■
1001Xb Wheat and meslin	219.9		47%		52%		89%	■	■		
040221 Milk and cream powder unsweete...	196.6		31%		41%		66%	■	■	■	■
100630 Rice, semi-milled or wholly milled...	361.0		13%		31%		52%	■	■	■	■
510529 Wool tops and other combed woo...	142.1		91%		51%		57%	■		■	■
392330 Carboys, bottles, flasks and simil...	152.1		22%		24%		97%	■	■	■	■
41XXXa Raw hides and skins (other than f...	261.5		33%		23%		41%		■	■	■
0102XX Live bovine animals	128.5		94%		80%		57%	■			
100620 Rice, husked (brown)	64.2		73%		75%		27%	■	■	■	■
3808Xb Fungicides	51.6		49%		52%		95%	■	■	■	■
400510 Rubber compounded with carbon...	73.7		49%		50%		98%	■	■	■	■
040690 Cheese nes	182.1		18%		37%		63%	■	■	■	■
1502XX Bovine,sheep&goat fats	48.8		84%		73%		88%	■	■	■	■
340211 Anionic surface-active agents	58.3		44%		48%		82%	■	■	■	■
040210 Milk powder not exceeding 1.5% fat	79.5		24%		41%		63%	■	■	■	■
020443 Sheep cuts, boneless, frozen	27.9		33%		54%		69%	■	■	■	■
940190 Parts of seats other than those of...	77.8		14%		15%		76%	■	■	■	■

Note: Top 20 products listed in decreasing order of their export potential to the world. Development indicators are relative to the country's current situation, green indicating performance above its trade-weighted median and red otherwise; a blank cell indicates data are not available. A blank cell in export potential means that the product was not consistently demanded over five years by any country in the respective region. Exports (US$ mn) corresponds to the yearly average exports to the world over the period 2009-13. Refer to Annexes I, II and III for details.

Source: ITC Export Potential Assessment, additional results are available at ITC Country Pages http://www.intracen.org/country/uruguay/

ENDNOTES

1. The fieldwork for the NTM Survey in Bangladesh has been completed. The results will be available after the validation workshop that will take place in November 2015. The survey in the State of Palestine has been completed, but is not included as it was based on a different questionnaire.

2. See Annexes for details regarding methodological choices, computations, group compositions, sources and definitions.

3. Further information including both exporting and importing companies and a wider range of questions is available at www.ntmsurvey.org.

Annexes

Technical notes

This Annex presents the methodological choices made in the country profiles.

SME Competitiveness Grid

Country and year coverage of country profiles

The country profiles cover 25 countries for which ITC has completed non-tariff measures (NTM) Surveys including each country's last available record (no additional imputation of missing data). Values that are either missing or out of date are indicated with n/a. Nine of the countries are LDCs.

SME Competitiveness Grid

The SME Competitiveness Grid is an analytical framework that relies on three layers of determinants of competitiveness: (1) Firm level capabilities; (2) Immediate business environment; and (3) National environment. Each layer is divided into three pillars: (1) Capacity to Compete; (2) Capacity to Connect; and (3) Capacity to Change.

For the current pilot assessment of the SME Competitiveness Grid, 38 indicators were retained, falling within three categories of data: firm level survey data categorized by firm size (17 indicators) and without size distinction (4 indicators); hard/quantitative/objective data (8 indicators); and index data (9 indicators).

The data comes from a variety of specialized agencies: the International Energy Agency (IEA), ILO, the International Monetary Fund (IMF), ISO, ITU, ITC, UNESCO, the UN Public Administration Network (UNPAN), the World Bank, WEF, and WIPO. Please refer to Annex III: Data availability for complete data tables indicating the year for each data source.

Firm level data

The main limitation of the current analysis is a lack of firm level data suitable for a comprehensive assessment of SME competitiveness. ITC is in the process of carrying out firm level surveys in order to generate the required data.

In the meantime, the potential of the SME Competitiveness Grid is illustrated by firm level data from the World Bank Enterprise Surveys. This is one of the most comprehensive firm level datasets. The data covers some 130,000 firms in 145 countries and addresses a broad range of topics: corruption, crime, finance, firm characteristics, gender, informality, infrastructure, innovation and technology, performance, regulations and taxes, trade, and workforce. Companies are also enquired which of these dimensions represent the largest obstacle to their business. The data collection started in 2002; a revised methodology was adopted in 2005, which has been consistent over time and across countries since then, and which is at the basis of the distinction between 'global' post-2005 surveys and 'not global' pre-2005 surveys. For each country, the last available survey is used.

In the Enterprise Surveys the firm size criteria are homogenous across countries; small firms have between 5 and 19 employees; medium-sized firms between 20 and 99; and large firms more than 100. In the ITC NTM Surveys there are 11 firm size categories that can be grouped into the categories almost equivalent to those used by the World Bank, namely small (1 to 20 employees), medium-sized (21 to 100 employees) and large (101 employees or more). The 'SME presence' indicator in the table 'Potential for Growth of Current Exports' is calculated based on the share of enterprises with 5 to 99 employees in the respective sector.

The additional firm-based metrics come from the WEF Executive Opinion Survey.

ITC firm level surveys on NTMs are complementary to the SME Competitiveness Grid. The responses provided by exporting companies are presented on the second page of the country profiles, and the survey methodology is summarized at the end of this section.

Country level data

In addition to firm level data, the SME Competitiveness Grid encompasses hard data, based on the measurement of observable characteristics (as opposed to surveys measuring perception data), and composite indices.

A total of eight series are hard data series. Half of these indicators do not require scaling or are scaled at the source; ISO indicators 3.1.6 and 3.1.7, and WIPO indicators 3.3.5 and 3.3.6 were scaled by million of population.

Indices capture multi-dimensional phenomena that cannot be captured by a single indicator. The risk of duplicating variables has been avoided by selecting mutually exclusive indices with a narrow focus. Some indicators were also compounded into a single indicator (details are provided in Annex II).

Country coverage for scores and percentage ranks

Each statistical series was normalized within a subsample of countries that includes the 111 countries for which both Enterprise Survey data (World Bank) and Executive Opinion Survey data (WEF) were available. Of these, 27 are LDCs and 17 are OECD countries. The full sample of countries is provided at the end of Annex III: Data availability, including the composition of groups by region and the development stage.

Transformation and normalization

To allow for valid comparisons between indicators and to solve potentially skewed distributions and outliers, all indicators were transformed following the same two-step process. Indicators were first normalized by a linear transformation into a [0–100] range, with the score 100 representing the best score:

$$Y = 100 \ \frac{X - min}{max - min}$$ for cases in which higher values represent better outcomes; and

$$Y = 100 \ \frac{max - X}{max - min}$$ for cases in which higher values represent worse outcomes (such time series are indicated with an asterisk in the text and in the radar charts),

where min and max are the indicator sample minimum and maximum values.

A non-linear transformation was then applied within the same [0, 100] range, aimed at bringing the sample median to 50:

$$Z = 100 \ \frac{\log(1 + aY)}{\log(1 + 100a)}$$

Where a is chosen so that $Z(M) = 50$, M being the median of the sample. Thus:

$$a = \frac{100 - 2M}{M^2}$$

The formula is not defined in the unlikely event that the median would already be equal to 50; but the second step then becomes redundant.

For firm level statistics, the minimum and maximum values are defined with respect to three categories of data for which the World Bank calculates means (small, medium-sized, and large firms).

Strengths and weaknesses: An estimation

The country profiles include an indication of strengths (in green) and weaknesses (in red) according to thresholds that are country-specific. These thresholds take into account the country's stage in development (represented by its GDP per capita in US$) and its performance in competitiveness relative to the full sample of countries (111 countries).

The methodology employed is as follows: scores included in the grid are averaged for each country (in the case of firm level data, only the average of all firms is considered) and plotted against the natural log of GDP per capita (US$); a linear regression line then defines the equation used for computations:

average score = 8.46 ln(GDP per capita) – 23.19.

This equation provides an expected average score for each country; strengths are then specified as all scores that are 50% higher than the expected average score (in other words, above the expected average score multiplied by 1.5); weaknesses are all scores that are 50% lower than the expected average score (in other words, below the expected average score multiplied by 0.5).

At the country level, these thresholds are used for all normalized scores, including the grid scores and the grid heat map. This approach has two advantages: firstly, it highlights indicators/layers/pillars in which each country performs above or below par, and second, it provides an overall picture of dimensions that are either pushing up or pulling down the country's overall performance. A country with a balanced profile with average progress in all dimensions could potentially have no specific strength and/or weakness, and that is an expected result. At the regional level, reference is set equal to 50 to ensure comparability of the analysis across regions.

Complementary firm level data: ITC Business Surveys on NTMs

Each NTM Survey is national and demand-driven; it is conducted by local companies specialized in field interviews on trade topics. As of 2015, the survey has been concluded in 26 countries, including ten LDCs. All surveyed countries are covered in the country profiles except for the State of Palestine (due to a difference in the questionnaire) and Bangladesh (at the moment of publication the field work was finished, but the data had not been verified, validated or analysed).

ITC is responsible for the sampling, training of interviewers, monitoring of interviews, and analysis of results. The NTM survey covers legally registered companies only, of all sizes and types of ownership, in sectors cumulatively accounting for at least 90% of the total export value of each country (excluding minerals and arms). Country-specific adjustments are done if needed, for example niche sectors can be covered because of their potential for development. Goods are covered (not services) in 13 sectors based on the Standard International Trade Classification (SITC) Rev. 3:

Agriculture:
1. Fresh food and raw agro-based products
2. Processed food and agro-based products

Manufactures:
3. Wood, wood products and paper
4. Yarn, fabrics and textiles
5. Chemicals
6. Leather and leather products
7. Metal and other basic manufacturing
8. Non-electric machinery
9. Computer, telecommunications; consumer electronics
10. Electronic components
11. Transport equipment
12. Clothing
13. Miscellaneous manufacturing

The fieldwork is conducted in two stages: a brief phone interview detects companies facing NTM-

TABLE 11 Import- and export-related measures

Import-related measures	Export-related measures
Technical measures:	**P. Export-related:**
A. Technical requirements	PA1. Export inspection
B. Conformity assessment	PA2. Certification required by the exporting country
Non-technical measures:	PA9. Other export technical measures
C. Pre-shipment inspection and other entry formalities	PB1. Export prohibitions
D. Charges, taxes and other para-tariff measures	PB2. Export quotas
E. Quantity control measures	PB3. Licensing or permit to export
F. Finance measures	PB4. Export registration
G. Price control measures	PB9. Other export quantitative restrictions
H. Anti-competitive measures	PC0. Export taxes and charges
I. TRIMS	PD0. Export price control measures
J. Distribution restrictions	PE0. Measures on re-export
K. Restriction of post-sales services	PF0. Export subsidies
L. Subsidies	PZ0. Other export-related measure
M. Government procurement restrictions	
N. Intellectual property	
O. Rules of origin and related certificate of origin	

FIGURE 61   ITC NTM Surveys: Distinction between regulatory and procedural obstacles (focus on exporters)

Stage 1: **Phone screen** **interviews**	Exporters affected				
Stage 2: **Face-to-face** **interviews**	Partner-imposed NTM			NTM regulations imposed by the home country	
	Partner regulatory obstacle	Partner procedural obstacle	Home procedural obstacle	Home procedural obstacle	Home regulatory obstacle

POs that take place
in home country

related obstacles. A detailed face-to-face interview then follows with firms reporting they are affected by NTMs and related procedural obstacles (Table 11). A trained interviewer collects information about the firm (size, age, ownership) and its trading relations (exported and imported products, partner and transit countries), as well as problematic regulations (both government-mandated requirements and voluntary standards are covered), specific reasons making the regulation difficult and the location of the problem (including agencies involved).

Reported measures are classified according to the NTM classification adapted for surveys, which consists of 16 chapters and 120 measures. NTMs can be applied by the importing country or the exporting country. For an exporter, 'import-related measures' (Chapters A to O) are applied by the partner or transit country; while 'export-related measures' (Chapter P) are applied by the home country. For the ease of exposure, the country profiles show aggregated results, with measures grouped into 'technical measures', "non-technical measures' and 'rules of origin' (in bold, Table 11).

Each NTM case reported by the company could either represent a regulatory obstacle (regulation requirements are too strict per se), one or more procedural obstacles (obstacle makes compliance with regulations difficult), or a combination of one regulatory obstacle and one or more procedural obstacles. During the face-to-face interview, each company would typically report a minimum of one burdensome NTM regulation.

Procedural obstacles are categorized into nine groups:
A. Administrative burdens related to regulation
B. Information / transparency issues
C. Inconsistent or discriminatory behaviour of officials

D. Time constraints
E. Payments (informal or unusually high)
F. Infrastructural challenges (lack of sector-specific facilities)
G. Security
H. Legal constraints (e.g. lack of recognition / accreditation)
I. Others

A regulation (for example safety requirements) may not be considered a regulatory obstacle, but can be nonetheless associated to one or more procedural obstacles, for example one at home (e.g. a delay in obtaining certification by a national authority), and one in the partner country (e.g. the inconsistent behaviour of customs officials).

An 'NTM case' is the most disaggregated data unit of the survey. Each 'NTM case' is multi-dimensional, taking into account the reporting company, the product or products affected, the type of NTM, the partner country and, if relevant, related POs, counted separately. For example:

■ Three products affected by the same NTM, applied by the same partner country, and reported by the same company count as three 'NTM cases'.

■ Two companies reporting the same measure applied on the same product, by the same destination country, count as two 'NTM cases'.

■ One product exported to three different countries and affected by the same NTM, applied by the home country, and reported by the same company, count as one 'NTM case' since it is the consequence of a single national policy.

A summary of the NTM survey process, the distinction between ROs and POs and their location are presented in Figure 61.[1]

Complementary product ranking: ITC Export Potential Assessments

The Export Potential Assessment (EPA) is a quantitative approach to identify promising export sectors and markets on a global scale, based on trade and market access data.

This section provides a summary of the methodology; detailed description is available in a dedicated ITC Working Paper (Decreux and Spies, 2015). The approach allows for the identification of existing products with high export potential and of products presenting diversification opportunities:

- The **Export Potential Indicator** (EPI) serves countries that aim to support established export sectors in increasing their exports to new or existing target markets. Inspired by a gravity-type framework, the EPI identifies products in which the exporting country has already proven to be internationally competitive and that have good prospects of export success in specific target market(s) (intensive product margin). The results for 25 economies are presented in the 'Country Profiles' of this report. Results for other countries can be accessed online, on the Country/Territory section of ITC website www.intracen.org.

- The **Product Diversification Indicator** (PDI) serves countries that aim to diversify and develop new export sectors that face promising demand conditions in new or existing target markets. It identifies products which the exporting country does not yet export competitively, but which seem feasible based on the country's current export basket and the export baskets of similar countries (extensive product margin). A hypothetical example is presented in this section.

Conceptually, EPAs are based on a decomposition of a product's share in a country's total exports into a supply and a world demand component. World demand decomposed by target market. While a country's capacity to supply existing products (EPI) is captured through a measure of revealed comparative advantage, its capacity to diversify into new products (PDI) relies on Hausmann and Hidalgo's concept of the product space (Hausmann and Klinger, 2007, Hausmann et al., 2007, and Hidalgo et al., 2007) that establishes links between products through an assessment of how frequently they are found together in the export baskets of countries.

The first approach – the EPI – is based on a structural model that (i) identifies potential shares of products from supply and demand capacities and (ii) converts them into potential values using a projection of bilateral exports. This corresponds to an empirical specification with exporter × product, importer × product and exporter × importer fixed effects, but avoids computational constraints when working at a detailed product level. Any gap between what countries could export and what they actually do export is then argued to result from factors that trade advisers may address together with local companies, such as lacking information on rules and regulations of the target market, difficulties in complying with them or in meeting the (quality) preferences of its consumers.

The second approach – the PDI – is based on the concept of the product space. Export potential assessments improve the purely outcome-based measure of linkages to new products by accounting for natural endowments that are pivotal for the capacity of a country to produce certain products. They also respond to recent criticisms of an entirely supply-side driven approach (see e.g. Harrison and Rodriguez-Clare, 2011, or Lederman and Maloney, 2012) by combining demand and market access information.

Very few attempts to give data-based guidance to developing countries on export opportunities exist. One of them is the Decision Support Model (DSM) that starts with macroeconomic conditions of potential target markets and then continuously filters out product-market combinations according to criteria such as import growth, size or accessibility until a set of opportunities deemed realistic remains (Cuyvers et al., 2012). DSMs differ from ITC EPAs due to their reliance on filters and their implicit assumption that a country's supply capacities can be expanded indefinitely with the only upper boundary being the size of the market. By using bilateral exports to derive potential values from shares, EPAs provide a more conservative estimate of potential future export revenues.

The DSM focuses on existing export products. With the recent advances of the product space, a number of institutions including UNCTAD (Fortunato, P., Razo, C., Vrolijk, K.,2015, and the World Bank (Lederman, D., Maloney, W., 2012) have started advising on diversification opportunities based on supply-side linkages between products. Unlike the ITC PDI, these approaches disregard important demand and market access factors that impact a country's export decisions. Further detail on the ITC EPA methodology can be found in Decreux and Spies (2015).

PDI country tables are still under development by ITC and will soon be made available under the country/ territory section of ITC website at www.intracen.org. Since the descriptive nature of the product space does not allow for any meaningful estimate of potential trade values, export potential assessments will present more cautious rankings of diversification opportunities in a given country or regional market as in the hypothetical example reflected in Table 12.

Limitations of automated export potential assessments

In addition to the measurable components of export potential, there are other, often intangible, factors to consider when selecting sectors and products for targeted trade development programmes. These include for example, the willingness and possibility to attract FDI, the possibilities of marketing and branding, and the existence of synergic development plans or sector strategies. EPAs also abstract from the costs related to export promotion activities. All of these factors may however influence the 'feasibility' of exporting (more of) certain products. Trade advisers should therefore look at results with a critical eye and engage in further investigations, notably in regard to the suggested options for diversification.

A few measurable indicators reflected in the country profiles shed additional light upon the 'desirability' of the identified products (e.g. does the product allow stabilizing export revenues? Does it support the participation of women?), but many developmental, environmental or social aspects cannot be captured with quantitative trade data. Often, they depend more on production practices than on the choice of products.

TABLE 12 Hypothetical example of Product Diversification Indicator of ITC Export Potential Assessment

PRODUCT/PRODUCT GROUP DESCRIPTION	What is the product's diversification potential rank in...?				Would this product help Country X improving its...?			
	World	Own region of country X	South-South trade	OECD	Technology level	Revenues stability	SME presence	Female participation
180100 Cocoa beans, whole or broken, raw or roasted	1	1	1	1	▪	▪		
4407Xa Wood sawn/chipped lengthwise, sliced/peeled	2	2	6	2	▪	▪	▪	▪
151311 Coconut (copra) oil crude	3	5	3	3	▪	▪	▪	▪
151190 Palm oil and its fractions refined but not chemically modified	4	6	2	20	▪	▪	▪	▪
85 44 20 Co-axial cable and other co-axial electric conductors	5	9	4	8	▪	▪	▪	▪
071410 Manioc (cassava), fresh or dried, whether or not sliced or pelleted	6	12	5	12	▪	▪		
230650 Coconut/copra oil-cake&oth solid residues,whether/not ground/pellet	7	3	10	4	▪	▪		▪
440726 Lumber, Meranti nes, Lauan, Seraya, alan sawn >6mm	8	4	7	10	▪	▪	▪	
080111 Coconuts, dessicated	9	25	8	9	▪	▪		
200820 Pineapples nes,o/w prep or presvd,sugared,sweetened,spirited or not	10	23	9	17	▪	▪		▪
080131 Cashew nuts, in shell, fresh or dried	11	7	11	18	▪	▪		
720310 Ferrous products obtained by direct reduction of iron ore, nes	12	10	15	7	▪	▪	▪	▪
750110 Nickel mattes	13	11	64	5	▪	▪	▪	▪
160413 Sardines,sardinella&brislg o sprats prep o presvd,whole o pce ex mincd	14	19	12	23	▪	▪		▪
440725 Lumber, Meranti (red, bakau) sawn lengthwise >6mm	15	18	13	13	▪	▪	▪	▪
450310 Corks and stoppers, natural cork	16	8	21	6	▪	▪	▪	▪
151321 Palm kernel or babassu oil, crude	17	35	17	16	▪	▪	▪	▪
750120 Nickel oxide sinters&oth intermediate products of nickel metallurgy	18	65	19	11	▪	▪	▪	▪
190219 Uncooked pasta, not stuffed or otherwise prepared, nes	19	21	14	40	▪	▪	▪	▪
230660 Palm nut/kernel oil-cake&oth solid residues,whether/not ground/pellet	20	20	16	21	▪	▪	▪	▪

Note: Example of PDI calculations is for 20 products with the highest diversification potential in a hypothetical Contry X. It can be calculated for any country and number of products. Development indicators are relative to the country's current situation, green indicating performance above its trade-weighted median and red otherwise; a blank cell indicates data are not available.

Notwithstanding these limitations, EPAs can represent a very useful starting point in an export promotion decision-making process that needs to be followed by further desk research and consultations including with public and private sector stakeholders in the country.

ANNEX II:
Sources and definitions

This Annex contains the title, description, definition, and source of all the indicators presented in the SME Competitiveness Grid. The most recent data was used for each indicator. Furthermore, the period of data points is provided under parenthesis next to the source. Where appropriate, indicators were scaled or combined into a single indicator. Indicators with higher values indicating worse outcomes are marked with an asterisk. Whenever the indicator is generated through survey data, the exact question is provided.

Key indicators

The following data sources and definitions were used in the section 'Key Indicators' of Chapter 'Country Profiles'.

All trade statistics and customs tariff data derive from the ITC Market Analysis Tools. Preference margin (percentage points) is calculated as the trade-weighted average difference between the Most Favourite Nation (MFN) duty and the most advantageous preferential duty. Tariff lines where either MFN or preferential duties cannot be expressed in ad valorem terms are excluded.

Population, GDP and current account data are from IMF, World Economic Outlook (2014 edition, data for 2014).

The regional group is based on the World Bank classification (July 1, 2015), including North America, LAC, Europe and Central Asia, South Asia, East Asia and the Pacific, MENA, and sub-Saharan Africa.

In addition, developing countries, LDC, LLDCs, and SIDS are singled out (UN classification 31 October, 2013: http://unstats.un.org/unsd/methods/m49/m49regin.htm).

The income group is based on the World Bank classification (July 1, 2015), including low income, lower-middle income, upper-middle income, and high income (http://data.worldbank.org/news/2015-country-classifications).

SME Competitiveness Grid indicators

In what follows, an asterisk is added to single out indicators with higher values implying worst outcomes. The asterisk has the same meaning in the radar charts of the country profiles (Part III of this report).

Firm level capabilities

1. **Capacity to Compete**

   ■ **International quality certification**
   Percentage of firms with internationally-recognized quality certification

   Question: Does this establishment have an internationally-recognized quality certification? The question refers exclusively to internationally recognized certifications. Some examples include: the ISO 9000 series (Quality management systems), the ISO 14000 series (Environmental management systems), HACCP (Hazard Analysis and Critical Control Point) for food (especially, but not exclusively, for seafood and juices), and AATCC (American Association of Textiles Chemists and Colorists) for textiles. Certificates granted only nationally not recognized in international markets are not included.

   Source: Enterprise Surveys (http://www.enterprisesurveys.org), The World Bank (2005–2014).

■ **Checking or savings account**
Percent of firms with a checking or savings account

Question: At this time, does this establishment have a checking or savings account?

Source: Enterprise Surveys (http://www.enterprisesurveys.org), The World Bank (2005–2014).

■ **Capacity utilization**
Capacity utilization based on comparison of the current output with the maximum output possible using the current inputs

Question: In the last fiscal year, what was this establishment's output produced as a proportion of the maximum output possible if using all the resources available (capacity utilization)?

Source: Enterprise Surveys (http://www.enterprisesurveys.org), The World Bank (2005–2014).

■ **Management experience**
Years of the top manager's experience working in the firm's sector

Question: How many years of experience working in this sector does the top manager have?

Source: Enterprise Surveys (http://www.enterprisesurveys.org), The World Bank (2005–2014).

2. **Capacity to Connect**

■ **E-mail usage**
Percentage of firms using e-mail to communicate with clients/suppliers

Question: At the present time, does this establishment use e-mail to communicate with clients or suppliers?

Source: Enterprise Surveys (http://www.enterprisesurveys.org), The World Bank (2005–2014).

■ **Firm website**
Percentage of firms having its own website

Question: At the present time, does this establishment use its own website? [Percentage of firms using website for business related activities, i.e. sales, product promotion etc.]

Source: Enterprise Surveys (http://www.enterprisesurveys.org), The World Bank (2005–2014).

3. **Capacity to Change**

■ **Financial audit**
Percentage of firms with their annual financial statement reviewed by an external auditor

Question: In the last fiscal year, did this establishment have its annual financial statements checked and certified by an external auditor?

Source: Enterprise Surveys (http://www.enterprisesurveys.org), The World Bank (2005–2014).

■ **Investments financed by banks**
Estimated proportion of purchases of fixed assets financed from bank loans

Question: Over the last fiscal year, please estimate the proportion of this establishment's total purchase of fixed assets that was financed from each of the following sources:
  ▪ Internal funds or retained earnings;
  ▪ Owners' contribution or issued new equity shares;
  ▪ Borrowed from banks: private and state-owned;
  ▪ Borrowed from non-bank financial institutions;
  ▪ Purchases on credit from suppliers and advances from customers; or
  ▪ Other, moneylenders, friends, relatives, bonds, etc.

Source: Enterprise Surveys (http://www.enterprisesurveys.org), The World Bank (2005–2014).

■ **Formal training**
Percentage of firms offering formal training programs for its permanent, full-time employees

Question: Over the fiscal year, did this establishment have formal training programs for its permanent, full-time employees?

Source: Enterprise Surveys (http://www.enterprisesurveys.org), The World Bank (2005–2014).

■ **Foreign technology licence**
Percentage of firms using technology licensed from foreign companies (%)

Question: Does this establishment at present use technology licensed from a foreign-owned company, excluding office software?

Source: Enterprise Surveys (http://www.enterprisesurveys.org), The World Bank (2005–2014).

Immediate business environment

1. **Capacity to Compete**

■ **Losses due to power outages***
Losses due to electrical outages, as percentage of total annual sales

Question: Please estimate the losses that resulted from power outages either as a percentage of total annual sales or as total annual losses.

Source: Enterprise Surveys (http://www.enterprisesurveys.org), The World Bank (2005–2014).

■ **Spoilage during shipping***
Proportion of products lost to breakage or spoilage during shipping to domestic markets

Question: In the last fiscal year, what percentage of value of products this establishment shipped to supply domestic markets was lost while in transit because of breakage or spoilage?

Source: Enterprise Surveys (http://www.enterprisesurveys.org), The World Bank (2005–2014).

■ **Time dealing with regulation***
Average percentage of senior management time spent in a typical week in dealing with requirements imposed by government regulation

Question: In a typical week over the last year, what percentage of total senior management's time was spent on dealing with requirements imposed by government regulations? [Senior management means managers, directors, and officers above direct supervisors of production or sales workers. Some examples of government regulations are taxes, customs, labour regulations, licensing and registration, including dealings with officials and completing forms].

Source: Enterprise Surveys (http://www.enterprisesurveys.org), The World Bank (2005–2014).

■ **Customs clearance***
This indicator is calculated as the average of two indicators: average number of days to clear direct exports through customs, and average number of days to clear imports from customs.

Average number of days to clear direct exports through customs

Question: When this establishment exported goods directly, how many days did it take on average from the time this establishment's goods arrived at their main point of exit (e.g., port, airport) until the time these goods cleared customs?

Average number of days to clear imports from customs

Question: When this establishment imported material inputs or supplies, how many days did it take on average from the time these goods arrived to their point of entry (e.g. port, airport) until the time these goods could be claimed from customs?

Source: Enterprise Surveys (http://www.enterprisesurveys.org), The World Bank (2005–2014).

2. **Capacity to Connect**

■ **Cluster development**
Average cluster development score

Question: In your country, how widespread are well-developed and deep clusters (geographic concentrations of firms, suppliers, producers of related products and services, and specialized institutions in a particular field)? [1 = non-existent; 7 = widespread in many fields]

Source: World Economic Forum, Executive Opinion Survey, 2013–2014 (http://reports.weforum.org/global-risks-2015/executive-opinion-survey-2014)

■ **Extent of marketing**
Average marketing extent score

Question: In your country, to what extent do companies use sophisticated marketing tools and techniques? [1 = not at all; 7 = to a great extent]

Source: World Economic Forum, Executive Opinion Survey, 2013–2014 (http://reports.weforum.org/global-risks-2015/executive-opinion-survey-2014)

■ **Local supplier quality**
Average local supplier quality score

Question: In your country, how would you assess the quality of local suppliers? [1 = extremely poor quality; 7 = extremely high quality]

Source: World Economic Forum, Executive Opinion Survey, 2013–2014 (http://reports.weforum.org/global-risks-2015/executive-opinion-survey-2014)

■ **University-industry collaboration in R&D**
Averaged country university-industry collaboration in R&D score

Question: In your country, to what extent do business and universities collaborate on research and development (R&D)? [1 = do not collaborate at all; 7 = collaborate extensively]

Source: World Economic Forum, Executive Opinion Survey, 2013–2014 (http://reports.weforum.org/global-risks-2015/executive-opinion-survey-2014)

3. **Capacity to Change**

■ **Access to finance***
Percentage of firms identifying access to finance as an obstacle to the current operations

Question: To what degree is access to finance an obstacle to the current operations of this establishment? Choices range from 0 (no obstacle) to 4 (very severe obstacle)

Source: Enterprise Surveys (http://www.enterprisesurveys.org), The World Bank (2005–2014).

■ **Inadequately educated workforce***
Percentage of firms identifying an inadequately educated workforce as an obstacle to the current operations

Question: To what degree is an inadequately educated workforce an obstacle to the current operations of this establishment? Choices range from 0 (no obstacle) to 4 (very severe obstacle)

Source: Enterprise Surveys (http://www.enterprisesurveys.org), The World Bank (2005–2014).

■ **Business licensing and permits***
Percentage of firms identifying business licensing and permit as an obstacle to the current operations

Question: To what degree are business licensing and permit an obstacle to the current operations of this establishment? Choices range from 0 (no obstacle) to 4 (very severe obstacle)

Source: Enterprise Surveys (http://www.enterprisesurveys.org), The World Bank (2005–2014).

National environment

1. **Capacity to Compete**

■ **Ease of getting electricity**
Doing Business 'Ease of getting electricity' score (0–100)

Doing Business records all procedures required for a business to obtain a permanent electricity connection and supply for a standardized warehouse. These procedures include applications and contracts with electricity utilities, all necessary inspections and clearances from the utility and other agencies, and the external and final connection works. The questionnaire divides the process of getting an electricity connection into distinct procedures and solicits data for calculating the time and cost to complete each procedure. The ranking of economies on the ease of getting electricity is determined by sorting their distance to frontier scores for getting electricity. These scores are the simple average of the distance to frontier scores for each of the component indicators.

Data are collected from the electricity distribution utility, then completed and verified by electricity regulatory agencies and independent professionals such as electrical engineers, electrical contractors and construction companies. The electricity distribution utility consulted is the one serving the area (or areas) where warehouses are located. If there is a choice of distribution utilities, the one serving the largest number of customers is selected.

To make the data comparable across economies, several assumptions about the warehouse and the electricity connection are used. In addition, details are provided regarding procedures, time, cost, and security deposits.

Source: World Bank, International Finance Corporation, Doing Business 2014: Understanding Regulations for Small and Medium-Size Enterprises, http://www.doingbusiness.org/methodologysurveys/

■ **Ease of trading across borders**
Doing Business 'Ease of trading across borders' score (0–100)

Doing Business measures the time and cost (excluding tariffs) associated with exporting and importing a standardized cargo of goods by sea transport. The time and cost necessary to complete four predefined stages (document preparation; customs clearance and inspections; inland transport and handling; and port and terminal handling) for exporting and importing the goods are recorded; however, the time and cost for sea transport are not included. All documents needed by the trader to export or import the goods across the border are also recorded.

The process of exporting goods ranges from packing the goods into the container at the warehouse to their departure from the port of exit. The process of importing goods ranges from the vessel's arrival at the port of entry to the cargo's delivery at the warehouse. For landlocked economies, where the seaport is located in the transit economy, the time, cost and documents associated with the processes at the inland border are also included. It is assumed that the payment is made by letter of credit, and the time, cost and documents required for the issuance or advising of a letter of credit are taken into account.

The ranking of economies on the ease of trading across borders is determined by sorting their distance to frontier scores for trading across borders. These scores are the simple average of the distance to frontier scores for each of the component indicators. Local freight forwarders, shipping lines, customs brokers, port officials and banks provide information on required documents, cost and time to export and import. To make the data comparable across economies, several assumptions about the business and the traded goods are used. In addition, details are provided regarding documents, time, and costs.

Source: World Bank, International Finance Corporation, Doing Business 2014: Understanding Regulations for Small and Medium-Size Enterprises, http://www.doingbusiness.org/methodologysurveys/

■ Tariffs applied*
Applied tariff rate, trade-weighted mean, all products (%)

A tariff is a customs duty that is levied by the destination country on imports of merchandise goods. Trade-weighted average tariff is calculated for each importing country using the trade patterns of the importing country's reference group (based on 2013 trade statistics). To the extent possible, specific rates have been converted to their ad valorem equivalent rates and included in the calculation of weighted mean tariffs. Preferential tariff arrangements (tariff preferences) have been taken into account.

Source: ITC, based on data from ITC Market Analysis Tools, 2006–2015 (www.intracen.org/marketanalysis).

■ Tariffs faced*
Faced tariff rate, trade-weighted mean, all products

Tariff faced is an indicator calculated as the trade-weighted average of the applied tariff rates, including preferential rates that the rest of the world applies to each country. The weights are the trade patterns of the importing country's reference group (based on 2013 trade statistics).

Source: ITC, based on data from ITC Market Analysis Tools, 2015 (www.intracen.org/marketanalysis).

■ Logistics performance index
Logistics Performance Index score

A multidimensional assessment of logistics performance, the Logistics Performance Index (LPI), compares the trade logistics profiles of 160 countries and rates them on a scale of 1 (worst) to 5 (best). The ratings are based on 6,000 individual country assessments by nearly 1,000 international freight forwarders, who rated the eight foreign countries their company serves most frequently.

The LPI's six components include: (1) Customs: the efficiency of the clearance process (speed, simplicity, and predictability of formalities) by border control agencies, including customs; (2) Infrastructure: the quality of trade- and transport-related infrastructure (ports, railroads, roads, IT); (3) International shipments: the ease of arranging competitively priced shipments; (4) Logistics competence: the competence and quality of logistics services (transport operators, customs brokers); (5) Tracking & tracing: the ability to track and trace consignments; and (6) Timeliness: the frequency with which shipments reach the consignee within the scheduled or expected delivery time.

Details of the survey methodology can be found in Arvis et al.'s Connecting to Compete 2014: Trade Logistics in the Global Economy (2014). Scores are averaged across all respondents.

Source: World Bank and Turku School of Economics, Logistics Performance Index 2014, http://lpi.worldbank.org/

■ **ISO 9001 quality certificates**
ISO 9001:2008 Quality management systems: Number of certificates issued (per million people)

Number of certificates of conformity to standard ISO 9001:2008: Quality management systems. Single-site and multiple-site certificates are not distinguished. Certification to the standard is used in global supply chains to provide assurance about suppliers' ability to satisfy quality requirements and to enhance customer satisfaction in supplier-customer relationships.

Source: ISO, The ISO Survey of Management System Standard Certifications, 2013, www.iso.org

■ **ISO 14001 environmental certificates**
ISO 14001:2004 Environmental management systems: Number of certificates issued (per million people)

Number of certificates of conformity to standard ISO 14001:2004: Environmental management systems. Single-site and multiple-site certificates are not distinguished. The standard specifies requirements for an environmental management system to enable an organization to develop and implement a policy and objectives which take into account legal requirements and other requirements to which the organization subscribes, and information about significant environmental aspects. It applies to those environmental aspects that the organization identifies as those which it can control and those which it can influence. It does not itself state specific environmental performance criteria.

Source: ISO, The ISO Survey of Management System Standard Certifications, 2013, www.iso.org

■ **Governance index**
Governance index

Average score over six dimensions of governance: voice and accountability, political stability and absence of violence, government effectiveness, regulatory quality, rule of law, and control of corruption.

Source: World Bank, Worldwide Governance Indicators (2014), http://info.worldbank.org/governance/wgi/index.aspx#home

2. Capacity to Connect

■ **ICT access**
ICT access sub-index score (0–10)

The ICT access sub-index is the first sub-index in ITU's ICT Development Index (IDI). It is a composite index that weights five ICT indicators (20% each): (1) Fixed-telephone subscriptions per 100 inhabitants; (2) Mobile-cellular telephone subscriptions per 100 inhabitants; (3) International Internet bandwidth (bit/s) per Internet user; (4) Percentage of households with a computer; and (5) Percentage of households with Internet access.

Source: ITU, Measuring the Information Society 2014, ICT Development Index 2014 (2013 data except for Tajikistan, 2008),

http://www.itu.int/en/ITU-D/Statistics/Pages/publications/mis2014.aspx

■ **ICT use**
ICT use sub-index score (0–10)

The ICT use sub-index is the second sub-index in ITU's ICT Development Index (IDI). It is a composite index that weights three ICT indicators (33% each): (1) Percentage of individuals using the Internet; (2) Fixed (wired)-broadband subscriptions per 100 inhabitants; and (3) Wireless-broadband subscriptions per 100 inhabitants.

Source: ITU, Measuring the Information Society 2014, ICT Development Index 2014 (2013 data except for Tajikistan, 2008), http://www.itu.int/en/ITU-D/Statistics/Pages/publications/mis2014.aspx

Government's online service
Government's online service index score (1–10)

To arrive at a set of online service index values, research teams assessed each country's national website, including the national central portal, e-services portal, and e-participation portal as well as the websites of the related ministries of education, labour, social services, health, finance, and environment, as applicable. The websites are assessed for content, features, accessibility and uptake.

The survey covers four stages of government's online service development, with points assigned for: (1) an emerging presence, providing limited and basic information; (2) an enhanced presence, providing greater public policy and governance sources of information, such as policies, laws and regulation, downloadable databases, etc.; (3) a transactional presence, allowing two-way interactions between government and citizens (G2C and C2G), including paying taxes and applying for ID cards, birth certificates, passports, licence renewals, etc.; and (4) a connected presence, characterized by G2G, G2C, and C2G interactions; participatory deliberative policy- and decision-making. A citizen-centric approach was followed. It is the first of three components of the E-Government Development Index (EGDI) of UNPAN, together with components on telecommunication infrastructure and human capital.

Source: UNPAN, e-Government Survey 2014, http:// www2.unpan.org/egovkb/

3. Capacity to Change

■ Ease of getting credit
Doing Business 'Ease of getting credit' score (0–100)

Doing Business measures the legal rights of borrowers and lenders with respect to secured transactions through one set of indicators and the sharing of credit information through another. The ranking is the simple average of the percentile rankings on the component indicators of the ease of getting credit index: strength of legal rights index (range 0–10); and depth of credit information index (range 0–6). The first set of indicators measures whether certain features that facilitate lending exist within the applicable collateral and bankruptcy laws. The second set measures the coverage, scope and accessibility of credit information available through credit reporting service providers such as credit bureaus or credit registries. The ranking of economies on the ease of getting credit is determined by sorting their distance to frontier scores for getting credit.

Source: World Bank, Ease of Doing Business Index 2014, Doing Business 2014, http://www.doingbusiness.org/reports/global-reports/doing-business-2014

■ Interest rate spread*
Interest rate spread

The interest rate spread is the interest rate charged by banks on loans to private sector customers minus the interest rate paid by commercial or similar banks for demand, time, or savings deposits. The terms and conditions attached to these rates differ by country, however, limiting their comparability.

Source: The World Bank, on the basis of data from IMF, International Financial Statistics and data files, 1988–2013, http://data.worldbank.org/indicator/FR.INR.LNDP/countries

■ School life expectancy
School life expectancy, primary to tertiary education (years)

Total number of years of schooling that a child of a certain age can expect to receive in the future, assuming that the probability of his or her being enrolled in school at any particular age is equal to the current enrolment ratio for that age.

Source: UNESCO Institute for Statistics (UIS), 2001–2013, http://stats.uis.unesco.org

■ **Ease of starting a business**
Doing Business 'Ease of starting a business' score (0–100)

Doing Business data measures the number of procedures, time and cost for a small and medium-size limited liability company to start up and formally operate. To make the data comparable across economies, Doing Business uses a standardized business that is 100% domestically owned, has start-up capital equivalent to 10 times income per capita, engages in general industrial or commercial activities, and employs between 10 and 50 people within the first month of operations.

Source: World Bank, Ease of Doing Business Index 2014, Doing Business 2014, http://www.doingbusiness.org/methodology/starting-a-business

■ **Patent applications**
Resident patent applications, equivalent count by applicant's origin (per million people)

Patent filings made by applicants at their home office (national or regional), also called domestic applications. Applications at regional offices are equivalent to multiple applications, one in each of the state members of those offices, therefore each application is multiplied by the corresponding number of member states, except for the European patent Office (EPO) and the African Regional Intellectual Property Organization (ARIPO), for which designated countries are not known, in which case each application is counted as one application abroad if the applicant does not reside in a member state; or as one resident and one application abroad if the applicant resides in a member state.

Source: WIPO, 2000–2013, http://www.wipo.int/portal/en/index.html

■ **Trademark registrations**
Resident trademark registrations, equivalent class count by applicant's origin (per million people)

Depending on different legal systems, one trademark application may specify several classes. Technically, that trademark turns into several marks linking to different goods or services. For international comparability, one should look at the count of classes to counter systemic differences between countries.

A trademark is a distinctive sign, which distinguishes certain goods or services of one undertaking from those produced or provided by other undertakings. The holder of a registered trademark has the legal right to exclusive use of the mark in relation to the products or services for which it is registered. The owner can prevent unauthorized use of the trademark, or a confusingly similar mark, used for goods or services that are identical or similar to the goods and services for which the mark is registered.

Unlike patents, trademark registrations can potentially be maintained indefinitely, as long as the trademark holder pays the renewal fees and actually uses the trademark. The procedures for registering trademarks are governed by the rules and regulations of national and regional IP offices. Trademark rights are limited to the jurisdiction of the authority that issues the trademark. Trademarks can be registered by filing an application with the relevant national or regional IP office(s), or by filing an international application through the Madrid system.

Source: WIPO, 2004–2013, http://www.wipo.int/portal/en/index.html

ITC Business Surveys on NTMs

Firms affected by NTMs

The statistics are at the firm level and calculated based on the answers to the following question:

- *Have any of your products faced restrictive and burdensome regulations and related obstacles to trade during the last 12 months?[2]*

When exporting	*1 ☐ Yes*	*2 ☐ No*
When importing	*1 ☐ Yes*	*2 ☐ No*

The full sample of companies is used in the statistics above. For the remaining questions only answers of exporting companies were considered.

NTMs reported as challenging (exporters)

The statistics are based on the 'NTM case', the most disaggregated data unit of the survey. Each 'NTM case' is multi-dimensional, taking into account the reporting company, the product or products affected, the type of NTM, the partner country and, if relevant, related POs, counted separately. The chart on the types of challenging NTMs is generated using responses to the following questions:

- *Can you please describe in detail which type of burdensome regulation you face for this product, and what related challenges/procedural obstacles you experience? Please provide as much detail as you can.*

- *Please specify the official name of this regulation/requirement/document/certificate, if you know it – or describe it in your own words (e.g. 'phytosanitary certificate'):*

- *Who applies the regulation, is it your own country or the partner country?*

    1 ☐ The regulation is applied by the partner country

    2 ☐ The regulation is applied by home country

    3 ☐ The regulation is applied by the transit country

    4 ☐ It's not a government-imposed regulation, but a voluntary standard

The interviewers are trained to map answers to the measures types and categories defined in the International NTM Classification for Surveys. The mapping is verified by the project team at ITC.

Regulatory and procedural obstacles (exporters)

The statistics are based on 'NTM cases' and constructed based on the answers to the following question, distinguishing between regulatory and procedural issues:

- *Is the described regulation burdensome because of:[3]*

    1 ☐ the measure/requirement itself that is too strict or too difficult to comply with

    2 ☐ the related procedural obstacles

    3 ☐ both of the above

Location of procedural obstacles (exporters)

Each reported non-tariff regulation can be applied by the home country, a transit country or a partner country. Furthermore, each regulation may be associated with POs, which in turn can be also located in the home country, transit country or partner country. The statistics on the location of POs aggregates experience in partner and transit countries and compares it to the experience in the exporter's home country.

The statistics are based on the number of POs linked to each reported 'NTM case' and constructed based on the answers to the following questions:

- *Please specify which procedural obstacle you experience with the described measure (in other words WHY the measure is difficult?). You can mention different problems. (Note to interviewer: If applicable, ask for the number of days of delay, number and names of required documents, amount of additional fee, institutions involved etc.)*

- *In which country does the problem occur?*

    ☐ *Partner country*

    ☐ *Home country*

    ☐ *Transit country*

In the country profiles, the NTM survey data related to partner countries and transit countries are presented together. Companies that do not report their size are shown only in the total statistics. The complete dataset and further details are available at http://ntmsurvey.intracen.org.

ITC Export Potential Assessments

Potential for Growth of Current Exports

The potential for growth of current exports is based on the combination of the EPI and development indicators.

EPI identifies exported products with greatest export potential. The approach is inspired by the gravity model. It estimates potential shares the exporting country's products may attain in particular target markets through the use of a composite indicator.[4]

The following development indicators are included:

- Technological advancement is based on the idea that information on the technology used to produce a good is embedded in the observed export patterns of countries (Hausmann and Hidalgo's concept of product complexity, 2009), based on product-level trade statistics from ITC Market Analysis Tools.

- Stability of export revenues is based on the standard deviation in unit values, based on product-level CEPII data on unit values.

- Share of SMEs in the sector, based on data from the World Bank Enterprise Surveys.

- Female employment in the sector, based on data from the World Bank Enterprise Surveys.

Development markers are relative to the country's current situation, green indicating performance above its trade-weighted median and red otherwise. A blank cell indicates the data for development indicators is not available.

Top 20 products with the highest export potential to the world are reported in the country profiles of this report.

ANNEX III:
Data availability

Composition of regions

All 111 countries covered in the calculations of the SME Competitiveness Grid are listed below, grouped by their geographic region, with indication of whether countries belong to developed countries (DCs), LDCs, LLDCs, SIDS, and/or to OECD. The countries reflected in the country profiles provided in Part III of this report are indicated in bold, while regional averages are computed for the 111 countries listed below. South-South trade designates trade relations between developing countries (defined here as those that are not OECD members).

TABLE 13 Country coverage and groups, by geographic region

Africa

Angola	LDC	**Guinea**	LDC	Nigeria	DC
Burundi	LDC, LLDC	Gambia	LDC	**Rwanda**	LDC, LLDC
Burkina Faso	LDC, LLDC	**Kenya**	DC	**Senegal**	LDC
Botswana	LLDC	Lesotho	LDC, LLDC	Sierra Leone	LDC
Côte d'Ivoire	DC	**Madagascar**	LDC	Swaziland	LLDC
Cameroon	DC	Mali	LDC, LLDC	**Tanzania, United Republic of**	LDC
Cabo Verde	SIDS	Mozambique	LDC	Uganda	LDC, LLDC
Chad	LDC, LLDC	**Mauritania**	LDC	South Africa	DC
Ethiopia	LDC, LLDC	**Mauritius**	SIDS	Zambia	LDC, LLDC
Gabon	DC	Malawi	LDC, LLDC	Zimbabwe	LLDC
Ghana	DC	Namibia	DC		

East Asia and Pacific

China	DC	Lao People's Democratic Republic	LDC, LLDC	Philippines	DC
Indonesia	DC	Myanmar	LDC	**Thailand**	DC
Cambodia	LDC	Mongolia	LLDC	Timor-Leste	LDC, SIDS
Korea, Republic of	OECD	Malaysia	DC	Viet Nam	DC

Europe and Central Asia

Albania	DC	Germany	OECD	Croatia	DC
Armenia	LLDC	Spain	OECD	Hungary	OECD
Azerbaijan	LLDC	Estonia	OECD	Ireland	OECD
Bulgaria		Georgia	DC	**Kazakhstan**	LLDC
Czech Republic	OECD	Greece	OECD	Kyrgyzstan	LLDC

Lithuania		Poland	OECD	Slovenia	OECD
Latvia		Portugal	OECD	Sweden	OECD
Moldova, Republic of	LLDC	Romania		Tajikistan	LLDC
Macedonia, the Former Yugoslav Republic of	LLDC	Russian Federation	DC	Turkey	OECD
		Serbia	DC	Ukraine	DC
Montenegro	DC	Slovakia	OECD		

Latin America and the Caribbean

Argentina	DC	Guatemala	DC	**Paraguay**	LLDC
Bolivia	LLDC	Guyana	SIDS	El Salvador	DC
Brazil	DC	Honduras	DC	Suriname	SIDS
Barbados	SIDS	**Jamaica**	SIDS	**Trinidad and Tobago**	SIDS
Chile	OECD	Mexico	OECD	**Uruguay**	DC
Colombia	DC	Nicaragua	DC	Venezuela	DC
Costa Rica	DC	Panama	DC		
Dominican Republic	SIDS	**Peru**	DC		

Middle East and North Africa

Algeria	DC	Jordan	DC	**Tunisia**	DC
Egypt	DC	Lebanon	DC	Yemen	LDC
Israel	OECD	**Morocco**	DC		

South Asia

Bangladesh	LDC	India	DC	Nepal	LDC, LLDC
Bhutan	LDC, LLDC	**Sri Lanka**	DC	Pakistan	DC

Data sources: SME Competitiveness Grid

All data sources and the latest available year used in the calculation of the SME Competitiveness Grid are listed below, by country. 'N/a' indicates that the data is not available. Country profiles are provided for countries indicated in bold.

TABLE 14 Indicators, their sources and time period

Country or territory	Enterprise survey (WB)	Logistics performance index	ICT access and use (ITU)	Tariff applied (ITC)	Interest rate spread (WB)	School life expectancy (UNESCO)	Patent applications (WIPO)	Trademark applications (WIPO)
Albania	2013	2012	2013	2015	2013	2003	2011	2013
Algeria	2007	2014	2013	2015	2013	2011	2013	2012
Angola	2010	2014	2013	2015	2013	2011	n/a	n/a
Argentina	2010	2014	2013	2014	2013	2012	2013	2013
Armenia	2013	2014	2013	2014	2013	2009	2013	2013
Azerbaijan	2013	2014	2013	2015	2013	2012	2013	2013
Bangladesh	2013	2014	2013	2007	2013	2011	2000	2013
Barbados	2010	n/a	2013	2013	2013	2011	2013	2013
Bhutan	2009	2014	2013	2015	2013	2013	2013	2013
Bolivia (Plurinational State of)	2010	2014	2013	2014	2013	2007	n/a	2007
Botswana	2010	2014	2013	2015	2013	2008	2013	n/a
Brazil	2009	2014	2013	2014	2013	2005	2013	2013
Bulgaria	2013	2014	2013	2015	2013	2012	2013	2013
Burkina Faso	2009	2014	2013	2014	1992	2013	n/a	n/a
Burundi	2014	2014	n/a	2015	1988	2010	n/a	n/a
Cabo Verde	2009	n/a	2013	2015	2013	2013	n/a	n/a
Cambodia	2013	2014	2013	2014	n/a	2008	n/a	2013
Cameroon	2009	2014	2013	2014	2007	2011	n/a	n/a
Chad	2009	2014	2013	2011	2007	2011	n/a	n/a
Chile	2010	2014	2013	2008	2013	2012	2013	2013
China	2012	2014	2013	2015	2013	2012	2013	2013
Colombia	2010	2014	2013	2014	2013	2010	2013	2013
Costa Rica	2010	2014	2013	2014	2013	2013	2013	2012
Côte d'Ivoire	2009	2014	2013	2014	1992	2013	2012	n/a
Croatia	2013	2014	2013	2015	2013	2012	2013	2013
Czech Republic	2013	2014	2013	2015	2013	2012	2013	2013
Dominican Republic	2010	2014	2013	2015	2013	2012	2013	2013
Egypt	2013	2014	2013	2015	2013	2012	2013	n/a
El Salvador	2010	2014	2013	2014	2000	2012	n/a	n/a
Estonia	2013	2014	2013	2015	2013	2012	2013	2013
Ethiopia	2011	2014	2013	2015	2008	2005	n/a	n/a

Gabon	2009	2014	2013	2015	2007	2001	n/a	n/a
Gambia	2006	2014	2013	2012	2013	2010	n/a	2013
Georgia	2013	2014	2013	2015	2013	2013	2013	2013
Germany	2005	2014	2013	2015	2002	2012	2013	2013
Ghana	2013	2014	2013	2013	1988	2012	n/a	n/a
Greece	2005	2014	2013	2015	2003	2012	2013	n/a
Guatemala	2010	2014	2013	2014	2013	2007	2009	2010
Guinea	2006	2014	2013	2012	2000	2012	n/a	n/a
Guyana	2010	2014	2013	2015	2013	2012	n/a	n/a
Honduras	2010	2014	2013	2015	2013	2013	2013	2013
Hungary	2013	2014	2013	2015	2013	2012	2013	2013
India	2014	2014	2013	2009	n/a	2011	2013	2013
Indonesia	2009	2014	2013	2013	2013	2012	2013	2013
Ireland	2005	2014	2013	2015	2005	2012	2013	n/a
Israel	2013	2014	2013	2015	2012	2012	2013	2013
Jamaica	2010	2014	2013	2011	2013	2013	2013	2013
Jordan	2013	2014	2013	2014	2013	2012	2013	2013
Kazakhstan	2013	2014	2013	2015	n/a	2012	2013	2013
Kenya	2013	2014	2013	2015	2013	2009	2013	n/a
Korea, Rep.	2005	2014	2013	2015	2013	2012	2013	2013
Kyrgyzstan	2013	2014	2013	2014	2013	2011	2013	2013
Lao People's Democratic Republic, the	2012	2014	2013	2015	2010	2013	n/a	n/a
Latvia	2013	2014	2013	2015	2013	2012	2013	2013
Lebanon	2013	2014	2013	2015	2013	2013	n/a	n/a
Lesotho	2009	2014	2013	2015	2013	2012	n/a	n/a
Lithuania	2013	2014	2013	2015	2010	2012	2013	2013
Macedonia, FYR	2013	2014	2013	2015	2013	2012	2013	2004
Madagascar	2013	2014	2013	2014	2013	2012	2008	2013
Malawi	2014	2014	2013	2015	2013	2011	n/a	2006
Malaysia	2007	2014	2013	2014	2013	2005	2013	2013
Mali	2010	2014	2013	2014	1992	2011	n/a	n/a
Mauritania	2014	2014	2013	2015	2012	2013	n/a	n/a
Mauritius	2009	2014	2013	2015	2013	2012	2013	2013
Mexico	2010	2014	2013	2014	2013	2012	2013	2013
Moldova	2013	2014	2013	2015	2013	2013	2013	2013
Mongolia	2013	2014	2013	2015	2013	2010	2013	2010
Montenegro	2013	2014	2013	2015	2013	2010	2013	n/a
Morocco	2013	2012	2013	2015	2005	2011	2013	2013
Mozambique	2007	2014	2013	2014	2013	2013	2007	2007
Myanmar	2014	2014	2013	2013	2013	2007	n/a	2012

Namibia	2014	2014	2013	2015	2013	2006	n/a	n/a
Nepal	2013	2014	2013	2014	2010	2011	2013	2013
Nicaragua	2010	2014	2013	2015	2013	2002	2012	2013
Nigeria	2014	2014	2013	2014	2013	2005	n/a	2013
Pakistan	2013	2014	2013	2014	2013	2013	2013	2013
Panama	2010	2014	2013	2013	2013	2012	2013	2013
Paraguay	2010	2014	2013	2014	2013	2010	2010	2010
Peru	2010	2014	2013	2014	2013	2010	2013	2012
Philippines	2009	2014	2013	2013	2013	2009	2013	2013
Poland	2013	2014	2013	2015	2006	2012	2013	2013
Portugal	2005	2014	2013	2015	1999	2012	2013	2013
Romania	2013	2014	2013	2015	2013	2011	2013	2013
Russian Federation	2012	2014	2013	2015	2013	2012	2013	2013
Rwanda	2011	2014	2013	2015	2010	2013	2012	2012
Senegal	2014	2014	2013	2014	1992	2010	n/a	n/a
Serbia	2013	2014	2013	2015	2013	2013	2013	2013
Sierra Leone	2009	2012	n/a	2006	2013	2001	n/a	n/a
Slovakia	2013	2014	2013	2015	2008	2012	2013	2013
Slovenia	2013	2014	2013	2015	2009	2012	2011	2010
South Africa	2007	2014	2013	2015	2013	2012	2013	2013
Spain	2005	2014	2013	2015	2002	2012	2013	2013
Sri Lanka	2011	2014	2013	2014	2013	2012	2013	2013
Suriname	2010	n/a	2013	2007	2013	2002	n/a	n/a
Swaziland	2006	n/a	2013	2015	2013	2011	2012	n/a
Sweden	2014	2014	2013	2015	2005	2012	2013	2013
Tajikistan	2013	2014	2008	2015	2013	2012	2012	2013
Tanzania, United Republic	2013	2014	2013	2015	2013	2012	n/a	2007
Thailand	2006	2014	2013	2014	2013	2012	2013	2013
Timor-Leste	2009	2007	n/a	2015	2013	2010	n/a	n/a
Trinidad and Tobago	2010	n/a	2013	2008	2013	2004	2008	n/a
Tunisia	2013	2014	2013	2015	1988	2011	2013	n/a
Turkey	2013	2014	2013	2014	n/a	2012	2013	2013
Uganda	2013	2010	2013	2015	2013	2011	n/a	2013
Ukraine	2013	2014	2013	2014	2013	2013	2013	2013
Uruguay	2010	2014	2013	2014	2013	2010	2012	2013
Venezuela (Bolivarian Republic of)	2010	2014	2013	2014	2013	2009	2011	2011
Viet Nam	2009	2014	2013	2014	2013	n/a	2013	2013
Yemen	2013	2014	2013	2015	2013	2011	2013	2013
Zambia	2013	2014	2013	2013	2013	n/a	2013	2012
Zimbabwe	2011	2014	2013	2015	2007	2012	n/a	n/a

TABLE 15 ITC Business Surveys on NTMs: Interview period

Surveyed country	Interview period
Burkina Faso	Mar 2010 - Aug 2010
Cambodia	Jan 2012 - Jan 2013
Colombia	Feb 2014 - May 2014
Cote d'Ivoire	May 2012 - Oct 2012
Egypt	May 2011 - Nov 2011
Guinea	Jun 2012 - Oct 2012
Indonesia	Sep 2012 - Aug 2013
Jamaica	Aug 2011 - Mar 2012
Kazakhstan	Jan 2012 - Oct 2012
Kenya	Dec 2010 - Sep 2011
Madagascar	Apr 2011 - Jul 2011
Malawi	Oct 2010 - Jun 2011

Surveyed country	Interview period
Mauritius	Feb 2011 - Oct 2011
Morocco	Apr 2010 - Feb 2011
Paraguay	Apr 2010 - Apr 2011
Peru	Jan 2010 - Jul 2010
Rwanda	Nov 2010 - May 2011
Senegal	Oct 2011 - Jun 2012
Sri Lanka	Feb 2010 - Aug 2010
Tanzania, United Republic of	Jul 2012 - May 2013
Thailand	Aug 2013 - July 2014
Trinidad and Tobago	Aug 2011 - May 2012
Tunisia	Jul 2011 - Jul 2012
Uruguay	Aug 2010 - Mar 2011

Data sources: ITC Export Potential Assessments

TABLE 16 Export Potential Assessments: Data used for calculations

Variable	Source	Link
Export and import values	ITC Trade Map	www.trademap.org
Ad-valorem tariffs	ITC Market Access Map	www.macmap.org
Price elasticities	GTAP (Hertel et al., 2004)	https://www.gtap.agecon.purdue.edu/resources/download/2931.pdf
Distances	CEPII GeoDist (Mayer and Zignago, 2011)	www.cepii.fr/CEPII/fr/bdd_modele/presentation.asp?id=6
GDP growth projections	World Economic Outlook database	www.imf.org/external/pubs/ft/weo/2014/02/weodata/index.aspx
Processing stage classification	ITC based on the Multilateral Trade Negotiation (MTN) list of WTO	Available upon request
Trade unit values	CEPII TUV (Berthou and Emlinger, 2011)	www.cepii.fr/cepii/en/bdd_modele/presentation.asp?id=2
SMEs	World Bank Enterprise Survey	www.enterprisesurveys.org
Female employment	World Bank Enterprise Survey	www.enterprisesurveys.org

ENDNOTES

1. For further details on the methodology and survey results please refer to 'The Invisible Barriers to Trade: How businesses experience non-tariff measures' (ITC, 2015).

2. In earlier surveys, the question did not specify the direction of the trade flow, and the statistics were reconstructed based on the data from other questions and an assumption of proportionality.

3. In earlier surveys, it was not possible to distinguish cases where difficulties are stemming exclusively from POs (answer 2 and 3 used to be merged in a single item, referring to the presence/absence of POs).

4. EPI indicates the intensive margin, in other words, the potential for existing export products. The extensive margin, or opportunities for countries to diversify into other products, is another important dimension for export development. ITC has therefore developed the PDI, a statistical method based on product space approach that allows identifying a range of products for export diversification (the methodology is reported in Annex I).

References

Abiola, Boladale Oluyomi (2008). The Nnewi Automotive Components Cluster in Nigeria. In *Knowledge, Technology, and Cluster-Based Growth in Africa*, Douglas Zhihua Zeng. Washington, D.C.: World Bank.

Abor, Joshua and Peter Quartey (2010). Issues in SME Development in Ghana and South Africa. *International Research Journal of Finance and Economics*, vol. 39, pp. 218–228.

Acs, Zoltan J., David B. Audretsch and Maryann P. Feldman (1994). R&D Spillovers and Recipient Firm Size. *Review of Economics and Statistics*, vol. 76, No. 2, pp. 336-340.

Adams, Avril V. (2007). The Role of Youth Skills Development in the Transition to Work: A Global Review. Human Development Network Children and Youth Working Paper, No. 5. Washington, D.C.: World Bank. Available from http://siteresources.worldbank.org/INTCY/Resources/395766-1187899515414/RoleofYouthSkills.pdf.

African Development Bank (2014). *Trade Finance in Africa*. Abidjan. Available from http://www.afdb.org/fileadmin/uploads/afdb/Documents/Publications/Trade_Finance_Report_AfDB_EN_-_12_2014.pdf.

Aguirre, DeAnne and others (2012). Empowering the Third Billion - Women and the World of Work in 2012. Booz&Co. Available from http://www.strategyand.pwc.com/media/file/Strategyand_Empowering-the-Third-Billion_Full-Report.pdf.

Albarran, Pedro, Raquel Carrasco and Adelheid Holl (2013). Domestic transport infrastructure and firms' export market participation. *Small Business Economics*, vol. 40, No. 4, pp. 879-898.

Allen, Franklin and Elena Carletti, Jun Qian and Patricio Valenzuela (2012). Financial Intermediation, Markets, and Alternative Financial Sectors. Working Papers, No. ECO 2012/11. Florence: European University Institute. Available from http://cadmus.eui.eu/bitstream/handle/1814/21455/ECO_2012_11.pdf?sequence=1.

Almeida, Rita, Jere Behrman and David Robalino (2012). The Right Skills for the Job? Rethinking Training Policies for Workers. Human Development Perspectives, No. 70908. Washington, D.C.: World Bank. Available from https://openknowledge.worldbank.org/bitstream/handle/10986/13075/709080PUB0EPI0067869B09780821387146.pdf?sequence=1.

Amiti, Mary and Jozef Konings(2007). Trade Liberalization, Intermediate Inputs, and Productivity: Evidence from Indonesia. *American Economic Review*, vol. 97, No. 5, pp. 1611-1638.

Arend, Richard J. and Joel D. Wisner (2005). Small Business and Supply Chain Management: Is There a Fit? *Journal of Business Venturing*, vol. 20, No. 3, pp. 403-436 .

Arvis, Jean-François, Monica Alina Mustra, John Panzer, Lauri Ojala and Tapio Naula (2007). Connecting to Compete: Trade Logistics in the Global Economy. In Enabling Trade Report 2008, World Economic Forum. Available from http://www.weforum.org/pdf/GETR08/Chap%201.4_Connecting%20to%20Compete.pdf.

Asian Development Bank (ADB) (2013). *Asia SME Finance Monitor 2013*. Manila. Available from http://www.adb.org/publications/asia-sme-finance-monitor-2013.

Asian Development Bank (ADB) (2014). *ADB Trade Finance Gap, Growth, and Jobs Survey*. ADB Briefs, No. 25. Manila. Available from http://www.adb.org/publications/adb-trade-finance-gap-growth-and-jobs-survey.

Aspen Network of Development Entrepreneurs (ANDE) (2012). *Small and Growing Businesses: Investing in the Missing Middle for Poverty Alleviation*. Washington, D.C. Available from http://www.aspeninstitute.org/sites/default/files/content/docs/ande/ANDE%20Literature%20Review%20-%20FINAL.pdf.

Association of Chartered Certified Accountant (ACCA) (2010). *Small Business: A Global Agenda*. Available from www.accaglobal.org.uk/content/dam/acca/global/PDF-technical/small-business/pol-afb-sbaga.pdf

Aterido, Reyes, Mary Hallward-Driemeier and Carmen Pagés (2011). Big Constraints to Small Firms' Growth? Business Environment and Employment Growth across Firms. *Economic Development and Cultural Change*, vol. 59, No. 3, pp. 609-647.

Auboin, Marc (2015). Improving the availability of trade finance in developing countries: an assessment of remaining gaps. Staff Working Paper, No. ERSD-2015-06, Geneva: World Trade Organization. Available from https://www.wto.org/english/res_e/reser_e/ersd201506_e.pdf.

Audretsch, David B. (2002). The Dynamic Role of Small Firms: Evidence from the U.S.. *Small Business Economics*, vol. 18, No. 1-3, pp. 13-40.

Avendaño, Rolando, Christian Daude and José Ramón Perea (2013). SME Internationalization through Value Chains: What Role for Finance? INTAL, vol. 37, No. 17, pp.71-80. Washington, D.C.: Inter-American Development Bank. Available from http://idbdocs.iadb.org/wsdocs/getdocument.aspx?docnum=38634449.

Awazu, Yukika , Peter Baloh, Kevin C. Desouza, Christoph H. Wecht, Jeffrey Kim and Sanjeev Jha (2009). Information-Communication technologies open up innovation. *Research-Technology Management*, vol. 52, No. 1, pp. 51-58.

Ayyagari, Meghana, Asli Demirgüç-Kunt and Vojislav Maksimovic (2011). Small vs. Young Firms across the World. Policy Research Working Paper, No. 5631. Washington, D.C.: World Bank. Available from http://elibrary.worldbank.org/doi/abs/10.1596/1813-9450-5631.

Ayyagari, Meghana, Asli Demirgüç-Kunt and Vojislav Maksimovic (2012). Financing of Firms in Developing Countries: Lessons from Research. Policy Research Working Paper, No. 6036. Washington, D.C.: World Bank. Available from http://documents.worldbank.org/curated/en/2012/04/16222792/financing-firms-developing-countries-lessons-research.

Ayyagari, Meghana, Asli Demirgüç-Kunt and Vojislav Maksimovic (2014). Who creates jobs in developing countries? *Small Business Economics*, vol. 43, pp. 75-99.

B20 (2015a). *B20 SMEs & Entrepreneurship Taskforce Policy Paper*. Ankara. Available from http://b20turkey.org/policy-papers/b20turkey_sme.pdf.

B20 (2015b). *Summary of B20 recommendations to the G20*. Ankara. Available from http://b20turkey.org/policy-papers/b20turkey_key.pdf.

Baghdadi, Leila (2015). Firms, Trade and Employment in Tunisia. ITC Working paper. Geneva: International Trade Centre.

Balassa, Béla (1965). Trade Liberalisation and Revealed Comparative Advantage. *The Manchester School*, vol. 33, No. 2, pp. 99-123.

Baldwin, Richard E. (1994). *Towards an Integrated Europe*. London: Centre for Economic Policy Research.

Baldwin, Richard E. (2006). Globalisation: the great unbundling(s). In *Globalisation challenges for Europe and Finland*. Helsinki: Secretariat of the Economic Council, Finnish Prime Minister's Office. Available from http://appli8.hec.fr/map/files/globalisationthegreatunbundling(s).pdf.

Banco Bilbao Vizcaya Argentaria (BBVA) Research (2015). *Crowdfunding in 360º: alternative financing for the digital era*. Buenos Aires. Available from https://www.bbvaresearch.com/wp-content/uploads/2015/02/Crowdfunding_Watch.pdf.

Banerjee, Abhijit V. and Esther Duflo (2007). The Economic Lives of the Poor. *Journal of Economic Perspectives*, vol. 21, No. 1, pp. 141-168.

Banerji, Angana, Sergejs Saksonovs and Huidan Lin and Rodolphe Blavy (2014). Youth Unemployment in Advanced Economies in Europe: Searching Solutions. Staff Discussion Note, No. 14/11. Washington, D.C.: International Monetary Fund. Available from http://www.imf.org/external/pubs/ft/sdn/2014/sdn1411.pdf.

Bank for International Settlements (BIS) (2010). Internationalisation of Innovative and High Growth SMEs. Economics Paper, No. 5. Basel. Available from http://www.bis.gov.uk/assets/biscore/economics-and-statistics/docs/10-804-bis-economics-paper-05.

Bank for International Settlements (BIS) (2014). *Trade Finance: Developments and Issues*. Committee on the Global Financial System Papers, No. 50, Basel. Available from http://www.bis.org/publ/cgfs50.htm.

Barbero, José A. (2010). Freight Logistics in Latin America and the Caribbean: An Agenda to Improve Performance. Technical Note, No. IDB-TN-103. Washington, D.C.: Inter-American Development Bank. Available from http://www10.iadb.org/intal/intalcdi/PE/2010/05888.pdf.

Bas, Maria (2012). Input-trade liberalization and firm export decisions: evidence from Argentina. *Journal of Development Economics*, vol. 97, No. 2, pp. 481-493.

Beck, Thorsten, Asli Demirgüç-Kunt and Maria S. Martínez Pería (2008). Bank Financing for SMEs around the World: Drivers, Obstacles, Business Models, and Lending Practices. Policy Research Working Paper, No. 4785. Washington, D.C.: World Bank. Available from http://elibrary.worldbank.org/doi/pdf/10.1596/1813-9450-4785.

Beck, Thorsten, Leora F. Klapper and Juan C. Mendoza (2010). The Typology of partial credit guarantee funds around the world. *Journal of Financial Stability*, vol. 6, pp. 10-25.

Bellone, Flora, Patrick Musso, Lionel Nesta and Stefano Schiavo (2010). Financial constraints and firm export behaviour. *World Economy*, vol. 33, No. 3, pp. 347-373.

Berge, Lars Ivar Oppedal, Kjetil Bjorvatn and Bertil Tungodden (2012). Human and financial capital for microenterprise development: Short-term and long-term evidence from a field experiment in Tanzania. Available from https://www.dartmouth.edu/~neudc2012/docs/paper_173.pdf.

Berger, Allen N. and Gregory F. Udell (2006). A More Complete Conceptual Framework for SME Finance. *Journal of Banking and Finance*, vol.30, No. 11, pp. 2945-2966.

Berger, Allen N., W. Scott Frame and Nathan H. Miller (2005). Credit Scoring and the Availability, Price, and Risk of Small Business Credit. *Journal of Money, Credit and Banking*, vol. 37, No. 2, p. 191-222.

Bernard, Andrew B., J. Bradford Jensen, Stephen J. Redding and Peter K. Schott (2007). Firms in International Trade. *Journal of Economic Perspectives*, vol. 21, No. 3, pp. 105-130.

Berthou, A., Emlinger, C. (2011), The Trade Unit Values Database, CEPII Working Paper 2011-10.

Bjorvatn, Kjetil and Bertil Tungodden (2010). Teaching Business in Tanzania: Evaluating Participation and Performance. *Journal of the European Economic Association*, vol. 8, No. 2-3, pp. 561-570.

Blackden, Mark and Mary Hallward-Driemeier (2013). Ready to Bloom? *Finance & Development*, vol. 50, No. 2, pp. 16-19.

Blalock, Garrick and Paul J. Gertler (2008). Welfare Gains from Foreign Direct Investment through Technology Transfer to Local Suppliers. *Journal of International Economics*, vol. 74, No. 2, pp. 402-421.

Bloom, Nicholas and John Van Reenen (2010). Why do Management Practices Differ across Firms and Countries? *Journal of Economic Perspectives*, vol. 24, No. 1, pp. 326–365.

Bloom, Nicholas, Aprajit Mahajan, David McKenzie and John Roberts (2010). Why Do Firms in Developing Countries

Have Low Productivity? *American Economic Review: Papers and Proceedings*, vol. 100, No. 2, pp. 619-23.

Bloom, Nicholas, Benn Eifert, Aprajit Mahajan, David McKenzie and John Roberts (2013). Does Management Matter? Evidence from India. *Quarterly Journal of Economics*, vol. 128, No. 1, pp. 1-51.

Boermans, Martijn Adriaan (2013). Learning-by-exporting and destination effects: Evidence from African SMEs. *Applied Econometrics and International Development*, vol. 13, No.2, pp. 155-173.

Borden, Neil (1964). The Concept of the Marketing Mix. In *Science in Marketing*, George Schwartz ed. Reproduced in Journal of Advertising Research, Classics Volume II, September 1984.

Boschma, Ron and Gianluca Capone (2014). Relatedness and Diversification in the EU-27 and ENP countries. Papers in Evolutionary Economic Geography, No. 14.07. Utrech. Utrecht University. Available from http://econ.geo.uu.nl/peeg/peeg1407.pdf.

Bossuroy, Thomas and others (2013). Shape Up or Ship Out? Gender Constraints to Growth and Exporting in South Africa. In *Women and Trade: Realizing the Potential*, Brenton, P., E. Gamberoni and C. Sear ed. Washington, D.C.: World Bank.

Bosworth, Derek, and Carol Stanfield (2009). Review of employer collective measures: a conceptual review from a public policy perspective. Evidence Report, No. 6. London: UK Commission for Employment and Skills. Available from http://webarchive.nationalarchives.gov.uk/20140108090250/http://www.ukces.org.uk/assets/ukces/docs/publications/evidence-report-6-employer-collective-measures-conceptual-review.pdf.

Brainard, Lael S. (1997). An Empirical Assessment of the Proximity-Concentration Trade-off between Multinational Sales and Trade. *American Economic Review*, vol.87, No. 4, pp. 520-544.

Brenton, Peter and Elisa Gamberoni (2013). Introduction. In *Women and Trade: Realizing the Potential*, Brenton, Peter, Elisa Gamberoni and Catherine Sear ed. Washington, D.C.: World Bank.

Brown, Gregory W., Larry W. Chavis and Leora F. Klapper (2010). A New Lease on Life: Institutions, External Financing, and Business Growth. AFA 2008 New Orleans Meetings Paper. Cambridge, MA: American Finance Association, Harvard University. Available at SSRN: http://ssrn.com/abstract=972385.

Bruhn, Miriam and Bilal Zia (2013). Stimulating managerial capital in emerging markets: the impact of business training for young entrepreneurs. *Journal of Development Effectiveness*, vol. 5, No. 2, pp. 232-266.

Bruhn, Miriam, Dean Karlan and Antoinette Schoar (2010). What Capital Is Missing in Developing Countries? *American Economic Review*, vol. 100, No. 2, pp. 629-633.

Bruhn, Miriam, Dean Karlan and Antoinette Schoar (2013). The Impact of Consulting Services on Small and Medium Enterprises-Evidence from a Randomized Trial in Mexico. Policy Research Paper, No. 6508. Washington, D.C.: World Bank. Available from http://www-wds.worldbank.org/external/default/WDSContentServer/WDSP/IB/2013/06/26/000158349_20130626085837/Rendered/PDF/WPS6508.pdf.

Cadot, Olivier, Ana Fernandes, Julien Gourdon and Aaditya Mattoo (2011). Impact Evaluation of Trade Interventions: Paving the Way. Discussion Paper Series, No. 8638. London. Centre for Economic Policy Research. Available from file:///C:/Users/klotz/Downloads/CEPR-DP8638.pdf.

Cadot, Olivier, Ana M. Fernandes, Julien Gourdon and Aaditya Mattoo (2015). Are the benefits of export support durable? Evidence from Tunisia. *Journal of International Economics*.

Cadot, Olivier, Céline Carrère and Vanessa Strauss-Kahn (2011). Trade Diversification: Drivers and Impacts. In Trade and Employment: From Myths to Facts, Marion Jansen, Ralf Peters, and José Manuel Salazar-Xirinachs, ed. Geneva: International Labour Organization.

Cainelli, Giulio, Rinaldo Evangelista and Maria Savona (2004). The impact of innovation on economic performance in services. *Service Industries Journal*, vol. 24, No. 1, pp. 116-130.

Canadian Chamber of Commerce (2013). *Upskilling the Workforce: Employer-Sponsored Training and Resolving the Skills gap. Available from* http://www.chamber.ca/media/blog/131009_Upskilling-the-Workforce/131009_Upskilling_the_Workforce.pdf.

Carballo, Jerónimo, Christian Volpe Martincus and Ana Cusolito (2013). New roads to export: Insights from the Inca roads. Available at: http://www.voxeu.org/article/new-roads-export-insights-inca-roads.

Cavusgil, Salih Tamer and Gary A. Knight (2009). Born Global Firms: A New International Enterprise. New York: Business Expert Press.

Centre for European Economic Research (ZEW) (2013). *German Innovation Survey 2013*. Mannheim: Centre for European Economic Research (ZEW). Available from http://www.zew.de/en/publikationen/innovationserhebungen/euroinno.php3.

Centre for the Promotion of Imports from developing countries (CBI) (2015). *SMEs and exporting. Business Issues, SMEs, Confederation of British Industries*. Amsterdam. Available from http://www.cbi.org.uk/business-issues/smes/exporting/.

Cernat, Lucian, Ana Norman-López and Ana Duch T-Figueras (2014). SMEs are more important than you think! Challenges and opportunities for EU exporting SMEs. Chief Economist Note, vol 3. Brussels: European Commission. Available from http://trade.ec.europa.eu/doclib/docs/2014/september/tradoc_152792.pdf.

Chang, Han-Hsin and Charles van Marrewijk (2013). Firm heterogeneity and development: Evidence from Latin American countries. *Journal of International Trade & Economic Development*, vol. 22, No. 1, pp. 11-52.

Cheong, David, Marion Jansen and Ralf Peters (2013). Shared Harvests: Agriculture, Trade and Employment. Geneva: International Labour Organization and United Nations Conference on Trade and Development. Available from http://www.ilo.org/employment/areas/trade-and-employment/WCMS_212849/lang--en/index.htm.

Chesbrough, Henry (2006). Open innovation: A new paradigm for understanding industrial innovation. In *Open Innovation: Researching a New Paradigm*, Henry Chesbrough, Wim Vanhaverbeke and Joel West ed. Oxford: University Press.

Chiu, Richard (2012). Entrepreneurship education in the Nordic countries: strategy implementation and good practices. Nordic Innovation Publication 2012:24. Available from http://www.nordicinnovation.org/.

Christensen, Clayton M. (1997). *The Innovator's Dilemma*. Boston, MA: Harvard Business School Press.

Christensen, Poul R. (1991). The small and medium-sized exporters' squeeze: Empirical evidence and model reflections. *Entrepreneurship and Regional Development*, vol. 3, No. 1, pp. 49–65.

Christopherson, Susan, Michael Kitson and Jonathan Michie (2008). Innovation, Networks and Knowledge Exchange. *Cambridge Journal of Regions, Economy and Society*, vol. 2, No. 2, pp. 165-173.

Collins, Daryl and others (2009). *Portfolios of the Poor: How the World's Poor Live on $2 a Day*. Princeton, NJ: Princeton University Press.

Collins, Jim (2001). *Good to Great*. London: Random House Business Books.

Cook, Lisa D. (1999). Trade credit and bank finance: Financing small firms in Russia. *Journal of Business Venturing*, vol. 14, No. 5-6, pp. 493-518.

Copeland, Brian R. (2008). Is there a case for Trade and Investment promotion policies? University of British Columbia, Department of Foreign Affairs and International Trade. Available from http://www.international.gc.ca/economist-economiste/assets/pdfs/research/TPR_2007/Chapter1-Copeland-en.pdf.

Creusen, Harold and Arjan Lejour (2013). Market Entry and Economic Diplomacy. *Applied Economics Letters*, vol. 20, No. 5, pp. 504-507.

Criscuolo, Chiara, Peter N. Gal and Carlo Menon (2014). The Dynamics of Employment Growth: New Evidence from 18 Countries. Science, Technology and Industry Policy Papers, No. 14. Paris: Organization for Economic Co-operation and Development. Available from http://dx.doi.org/10.1787/5jz417hj6hg6-en.

Cruz, Mario and Maurizio Bussolo (2015). Does Input Tariff Reduction Impact Firms' Export in the Presence of Import Exemption Regimes? Policy Research Working Paper, No. 7231. Washington, D.C.: World Bank. Available from http://www-wds.worldbank.org/external/default/WDSContentServer/WDSP/IB/2015/04/07/090224b082d62678/2_0/Rendered/PDF/Does0input0tar00exemption0regimes00.pdf.

Cuyvers, Ludo, Ermie Steenkamp and Wilma Viviers (2012). The methodology of the Decision Support Model (DSM). In *Export Promotion: a Decision Support Model Approach,* Cuyvers, Ludo and Wilma Viviers ed. South Africa: Sun Media Metro.

Damijan, Jože P., Črt Kostevc and Sašo Polanec (2010). From Innovation to Exporting or Vice Versa? *World Economy*, vol. 33, No. 3, pp. 374-398.

De Kok, Jan and others (2011). Do SMEs create more and better jobs? Report prepared by EIM Business & Policy Research with financial support from the European Communities, under the Competitiveness and Innovation Programme 2007-2013. Zoetermeer, November. Available from http://ec.europa.eu/enterprise/policies/sme/facts-figures-analysis/performance-review/files/supporting-documents/2012/do-smes-create-more-and-better-jobs_en.pdf.

De Kok, Jan, Claudia Deijl and Christi Veldhuis-Van Essen (2013). Is Small Still Beautiful? Geneva and Bonn: International Labour Organization and Deutsche Gesellschaft für International Zusammenarbeit. Available from http://www.ilo.org/employment/Whatwedo/Publications/employment-reports/WCMS_216909/lang--en/index.htm.

Decreux, Yvan and Julia Spies (forthcoming). Export Potential Assessments: A methodology to identify (new) export opportunities for developing countries. Working Paper. Geneva. International Trade Centre.

Deloitte (2014). *Supply Chain & Operations: Leverage the backbone of your business as a source of competitive advantage*. Brussels: Deloitte. Available from http://www2.deloitte.com/content/dam/Deloitte/be/Documents/Operations/201411_SupplyChainOperations_2014.pdf.

Deming, W. Edwards (1982). *Out of the Crisis*. Massachusetts Institute of Technology, Cambridge, MA: MIT-CAES.

Demirgüç-Kunt, Asli and Vojislav Maksimovic (2001). Firms as financial intermediaries - evidence from trade credit data. Policy Research Working Paper, No. 2696. Washington, D.C.: World Bank. Available from http://elibrary.worldbank.org/doi/abs/10.1596/1813-9450-2696.

Demirgüç-Kunt, Asli, Thorsten Beck and Patrick Honohan (2008). Finance for all? Policies and pitfalls in expanding access. Policy Research Report. Washington, D.C.: World Bank. Available from http://siteresources.worldbank.org/INTFINFORALL/Resources/4099583-1194373512632/FFA_book.pdf.

Dezsö, Cristian L. and David Gaddis Ross (2012). Does female representation in top management improve firm performance? A panel data investigation. *Strategic Management Journal*, vol. 33, pp. 1072-1089.

DHL (2013). *Internationalization – a driver for business performance*. Available from http://www.dhl.com/content/dam/downloads/g0/press/publication/dhl_research_internationalization_report.pdf.

DHL Express-IHS Global Insight (2013). *Internationalization – a driver for business performance*. Available from http://www.dhl.com/content/dam/downloads/g0/press/publication/sme-competitiveness-study.pdf.

Dinh, Hint T., Dimitris A. Mavridis and Hoa B. Nguyen (2010). The Binding Constraint on Firms' Growth in Developing Countries. Policy Research Working Paper, No. 5485. Washington, D.C.: World Bank. Available from http://dx.doi.org/10.1596/1813-9450-5485.

Djankov, Simeon, Caralee McLiesh and Andrei Shleifer (2007). Private credit in 129 countries. *Journal of Financial Economics*, vol. 84, No. 2, pp. 299-329.

Dominicé, Roland and Julia Minici (2013). Small Enterprise Impact Investing: Exploring the "Missing Middle" beyond Microfinance. Symbiotics. Available from http://smefinanceforum.org/sites/default/files/media/node-files/sy/457628_symbiotics-small-enterprise-impact-investing.pdf.

Donges, Juergen B. and James Riedel (1977). The expansion of manufactured exports in developing countries: An empirical assessment of supply and demand issues. *Review of World Economics*, vol. 113, No. 1, pp. 58-87.

Drexler, Alejandro, Greg Fischer and Antoinette Schoar (2014). Keeping It Simple: Financial Literacy and Rules of Thumb. *American Economic Journal: Applied Economics*, vol. 6, No. 2, pp. 1-31.

Dunne, Timothy, Mark J. Roberts and Larry Samuelson (1988). Patterns of Firm Entry and Exit in U.S. Manufacturing Industries. *RAND Journal of Economics*, vol. 19, No. 4, pp. 495-515.

Economic Research Institute for ASEAN and East Asia (ERIA) (2014). *ASEAN SME Policy Index 2014 - Towards Competitive and Innovative ASEAN SMEs*. ERIA Research Project Report, No. 8. Jakarta: Economic Research Institute for AEAN and East Asia. Available from http://www.eria.org/publications/research_project_reports/FY2012-no.8.html.

Edinburgh Group (2013). *Growing the global economy through SME*. Available from http://www.edinburgh-group.org/media/2776/edinburgh_group_research_-_growing_the_global_economy_through_smes.pdf.

Egger, Peter (2002). An Econometric View of the Estimation of Gravity Models and the Calculation of Trade Potentials. *World Economy*, vol. 25, No. 2, pp. 297-312.

Estache, Antonio (2010). Infrastructure finance in developing countries: an overview. EIB Papers, vol. 15, No. 2, pp. 60–88. Luxembourg: European Investment Bank. Available from http://www.eib.org/attachments/efs/eibpapers/eibpapers_2010_v15_n02_en.pdf.

European Centre for the Development of Vocational Training (CEDEFOP) (2010). *The skill matching challenge: analysing skill mismatch and policy implications*. Luxembourg. European Centre for the Development of Vocational Training. Available from http://www.cedefop.europa.eu/en/news-and-press/news/new-publication-analyses-policy-implications-mismatched-skills.

European Centre for the Development of Vocational Training (CEDEFOP) (2012). *Skill Mismatch: The Role of the Enterprise*. Research Paper, No. 21. Luxembourg. European Centre for the Development of Vocational Training. Available from http://www.cedefop.europa.eu/en/publications-and-resources.

European Commission (EC) (2002). *Regional clusters in Europe*. Observatory of European SMEs, No. 3. Brussels. Available from http://ec.europa.eu/regional_policy/archive/innovation/pdf/library/regional_clusters.pdf.

European Commission (EC) (2007). *Final Report of the expert group on enterprise clusters and networks*. Brussels. Available from http://ec.europa.eu/growth/tools-databases/newsroom/cf/itemdetail.cfm?item_id=867&lang=en&title=Final-report-of-the-expert-group-on-enterprise-clusters-and-networks.

European Commission (EC) (2008). *The European qualifications framework for lifelong learning (EQF)*. Brussels. European Commission. Available from https://ec.europa.eu/ploteus/sites/eac-eqf/files/brochexp_en.pdf.

European Commission (EC) (2012). Using standards to support growth, competitiveness and innovation. *How to support SME Policy from Structural Funds*. Brussels. Available from http://ec.europa.eu/enterprise/policies/sme/regional-sme-policies/documents/no.2_sme_standards_en.pdf.

European Commission (EC) (2013). *Annual Report on European SMEs 2012/2013: A recovery on the Horizon*. Brussels. Available from http://ec.europa.eu/enterprise/policies/sme/facts-figures-analysis/performance-review/files/supporting-documents/2013/annual-report-smes-2013_en.pdf.

European Commission (EC) (2014). *Annual Report on European SMEs 2013/2014: A partial and fragile recovery*. Brussels. Available from http://ec.europa.eu/enterprise/policies/sme/facts-figures-analysis/performance-review/files/supporting-documents/2014/annual-report-smes-2014_en.pdf.

Fawcett, Stanley E., Gregory M. Magnan and Matthew W. McCarter (2008). A three-stage implementation model for supply chain collaboration. *Journal of Business Logistics*, vol. 29, No. 1, pp. 93-112.

Fedderke, Johannes W. and Zeljko Bogetic (2006). Infrastructure and growth in South Africa : direct and indirect productivity impacts of 19 infrastructure measures. Policy Research Working Paper, No. 3989. Washington, D.C.: World Bank. Available from http://dx.doi.org/10.1596/1813-9450-3989.

Feng, Ling, Zhiyuan Li and Deborah L. Swenson (2012). The connection between imported intermediate inputs and exports: evidence from chinese firms. Working Paper Series, No. 18260. Cambridge, MA: National Bureau of Economic

Research. Available from http://www.nber.org/papers/w18260.pdf.

Field, Erica, Seema Jayachandran and Rohini Pande (2010). Do Traditional Institutions Constrain Female Entrepreneurship? A Field Experiment on Business Training in India. *American Economic Review*, vol. 100, No. 2, pp. 125-129.

Figal Garone, Lucas, Allesandro Maffioli, Joao Alberto de Negri, Cesar M. Rodriguez and Gonzalo Vázquez-Baré (2015). Cluster development policy, SME's performance, and spillovers: evidence from Brazil. *Small Business Economics*, vol. 44, No. 4, pp 925-948.

Fleisig, Heywood, Mehnaz Safavian, and Nuria de la Peña (2006). Reforming Collateral Laws to Expand Access to Finance. Washington, D.C.: World Bank and International Finance Corporation. Available from http://elibrary.worldbank.org/doi/pdf/10.1596/978-0-8213-6490-1.

Fliess, Barbara and Carlos Busquets (2006). The Role of Trade Barriers in SME Internationalisation. Trade Policy Working Paper, No. 45. Paris. Organization for Economic Co-Operation and Development. Available from http://www.oecd.org/trade/ntm/37872326.pdf.

Fontagné, Lionel, Gianluca Orefice, Roberta Piermartini, Nadia Rocha (2015). Product standards and margins of trade: Firm-level evidence. Journal of International Economics, forthcoming.

Fontagné, Lionel, Michael Pajot and Jean-Michel Pateels (2002). Potentiels de commerce entre économies hétérogènes : un petit mode d'emploi des modèles de gravité. *Economie internationale*, vol. 1, No. 152-153, pp. 115-139.

Fortunato, Piergiuseppe, Carlos Razo and Kasper Vrolijk (2015). Operationalizing the Product Space: A Road Map to Export Diversification. Discussion Papers, No. 219. Geneva: United Nations Conference on Trade and Development. Available from http://unctad.org/en/PublicationsLibrary/osgdp20151_en.pdf.

Fortwengel, Johann (2011). Upgrading through Integration? The Case of the Central Eastern European Automotive Industry. *Transcience Journal*, vol 2, No 1. pp. 1-25.

G 20 (2015). *Turkish presidency priorities for 2015*. Istanbul. Available from https://g20.org/wp-content/uploads/2014/12/2015-TURKEY-G-20-PRESIDENCY-FINAL.pdf.

Gaulier, Guillaume and Soledad Zignago (2002). La discrimination commerciale révélée comme mesure désagrégée de l'accès aux marchés. *Economie internationale*, vol. 1, No. 89-90, pp. 261-280.

Gelb, Alan, Christian J. Meyer and Vijaya Ramachandran (2014). Development as Diffusion: Manufacturing Productivity and Sub-Saharan Africa's Missing Middle. Center for Global Development Working Paper, No. 357. Washington, D.C.: Center for Global Development. Available from http://www.cgdev.org/publication/development-diffusion-manufacturing-productivity-and-africas-missing-middle-working.

Gerber, Michael E. (1995). *The E-Myth Revisited: Why Most Small Business Don't Work and What to Do about It*. New York: Harper Business.

Gereffi, Gary (1994). The Organization of Buyer-Driven Global Commodity Chains: How US Retailers Shape Overseas Production Networks. In *Commodity Chains and Global Capitalism*, Miguel Korzeniewicz and Gary Gereffi, ed. London: Praeger.

Gereffi, Gary (1999). International trade and industrial upgrading in the apparel commodity chain. *Journal of International Economics*, vol. 48, pp. 37-70.

Gereffi, Gary, John Humphrey and Tim Sturgeon (2005). The governance of global value chains. *Review of International Political Economy*, vol. 12, No. 1, pp. 78–104.

Geroski, P. A., José Mata and Pedro Portugal (2010). Founding conditions and the survival of new firms. *Strategic Management Journal*, vol. 31, No. 5, pp. 510-529.

Gertler, Meric S. and Wolfe, David A. (2008): Spaces of knowledge flows. Clusters in global context. In *Clusters and Regional Development. Critical reflections and explorations*, Bjørn T. Asheim, Philip Cooke, Ron Martin ed. London: Routledge.

Gibson, Tom and Hubertus Jan van der Vaart (2008). Defining SMEs: Less Imperfect Way of Defining Small and Medium Enterprises in Developing Countries. Washington, D.C.: Brooking Global Economic and Development. Available from http://www.brookings.edu/~/media/research/files/papers/2008/9/development%20gibson/09_development_gibson.pdf.

Giovannetti, Giorgia, Enrico Marvasi and Marco Sanfilippo (2014). Supply Chains and the Internalization of SMEs: Evidence from Italy. Working Papers, No. RSCAS 2014/62. Florence: European University Institute. Available from http://cadmus.eui.eu/handle/1814/31454.

Glaeser, Edward L., William R. Kerr and Giacomo A.M. Ponzetto (2010). Clusters of entrepreneurship. *Journal of Urban Economics*, vol. 67, pp. 150–168.

Glavan, Bogdan (2008). Coordination Failures, Cluster Theory, and Entrepreneurship: A Critical View. *Quarterly Journal of Austrian Economics*, vol. 11, pp. 43-59.

Global Entrepreneurship Monitor (2013). *2013 Global Report*. London. Available from http://gemconsortium.org/report.

Global Entrepreneurship Monitor (2015). *2014 Global Report*. London. Available from http://www.gemconsortium.org/report.

Global Entrepreneurship Monitor (GEM) (2008). *2007 Executive Report*. Available from http://www3.imperial.ac.uk/pls/portallive/docs/1/52833696.PDF.

Global Entrepreneurship Monitor (GEM) (2013). *2012 Global Report*. Available from http://gemconsortium.org/report.

Global Entrepreneurship Monitor (GEM) (2015). *2014 Global Report*. Available from http://gemconsortium.org/report.

Goldberg, Pinelopi, Amit Kumar Khandelwal, Nina Pavcnik and Petia Topalova (2015). Imported Intermediate Inputs and Domestic Product Growth: Evidence from India. *Quarterly Journal of Economics*, vol. 125, No. 4, pp. 1727-1767.

Gönenç, Rauf, Oliver Röhn, Vincent Koen and Fethi Öğünç (2014). Fostering Inclusive Growth in Turkey by Promoting Structural Change in the Business Sector. Economics Department Working Papers, No. 1161. Paris: Organization for Economic Co-operation and Development. Available from http://www.oecd-ilibrary.org/economics/fostering-inclusive-growth-in-turkey-by-promoting-structural-change-in-the-business-sector_5jxx0554v07c-en.

Gourio, François and Nicolas Roys (2014). Size-dependent regulations, firm size distribution, and reallocation. *Quantitative Economics*, vol. 5, pp. 377-416.

Grimm, Michael, Renate Hartwig and Jann Lay (2012). How much does utility access matter for the performance of micro and small enterprises? Working Paper, No. 77935. Washington, D.C.: World Bank. Available from http://documents.worldbank.org/curated/en/2012/11/17753012/much-utility-access-matter-performance-micro-small-enterprises.

Gros, Daniel and Andrzej Gonciarz (1996). A note of the Trade Potential of Central and Eastern Europe. *European Journal of Political Economy*, vol 12, No. 4pp. 709-721.

Grover, Aseem and Katie Suominen (2014). 2014 Summary – State of SME Finance in the United States, White Paper, Trade Up. Available from http://www.growadvisors.com/uploads/2/7/9/9/27998715/state_of_sme_finance_in_the_united_states_-tradeup_2014.pdf.

Haltiwanger, John C., Ron S. Jarmin and Javier Miranda (2013). Who creates jobs? Small versus large versus young. *Review of Economics and Statistics*, vol. XCV, No. 2. pp. 347-361.

Hammer, Michael and James Champy (1993). *Reengineering the Corporation: A Manifesto for Business Revolution*. New York: Harper Business.

Hansen, Henrik and John Rand (2014). The Myth of Female Credit Discrimination in African Manufacturing. *Journal of Development Studies*, vol. 50, No. 1, pp. 81-96.

Harrison, Ann and Andrés Rodríguez-Clare (2010). Trade, Foreign Investment, and Industrial Policy for Developing Countries. *Handbook of Development Economics*, vol .5, pp. 4039-4214.

Harvard Center for International Development (CID) (2015). *The Missing Middle*. Boston, MA. Available from http://www.hks.harvard.edu/centers/cid/programs/entrepreneurial-finance-lab-research-initiative/the-missing-middle.

Harvie, Charles (2015). SMEs, Trade and Development in South-east Asia. ITC Working paper. Geneva: International Trade Centre.

Hausmann, Ricardo and Bailey Klinger (2007). Structural Transformation and Patterns of Comparative Advantage in the Product Space. Working Paper, No. 128. Cambridge, MA: Harvard Centre for International Development. Available from http://www.hks.harvard.edu/centers/cid/publications/faculty-working-papers/cid-working-paper-no.-128.

Hausmann, Ricardo and Dani Rodrik (2006). Doomed to choose: Industrial policy as predicament. Center for International Development Blue Sky Conference, September 9 2006, Cambridge, MA. Available from http://www.hks.harvard.edu/index.php/content/download/69495/1250790/version/1/file/hausmann_doomed_0609.pdf.

Hausmann, Ricardo, Dani Rodrik and Charles F. Sabel (2008). Reconfiguring Industrial Policy: A Framework with an Application to South Africa. Working Paper, No. 168. Cambridge, MA: Center for International Development at Harvard University. Available from http://www.hks.harvard.edu/content/download/69285/1249950/version/1/file/168.pdf.

Hausmann, Ricardo, Jason Hwang and Dani Rodrik (2007). What you export matters. *Journal of Economic Growth*, vol. 12, No. 1, pp. 1-25.

Head, Keith and Thierry Mayer (2014). Gravity Equations: Workhorse,Toolkit, and Cookbook. In *Handbook of International Economics*, vol. 4, Gopinath, Gita, Elhanan Helpman and Kenneth Rogoff. Amsterdam: Elsevier.

Helmers, Christian and Jean-Michel Pasteels (2006). Assessing Bilateral Trade Potential at the Commodity Level: An Operational Approach. Working Paper, November 2006. Geneva: International Trade Centre. Available from http://legacy.intracen.org/mas/pdfs/pubs/2006-11-itc-wp-bilateral-trade-potential.pdf.

Helpman, Elhanan, Marc J. Melitz and Stephen R. Yeaple (2003). Export versus FDI. Working Paper Series, No. 9439. Cambridge, MA: National Bureau of Economic Research. Available from http://www.nber.org/papers/w9439.pdf.

Hertel, Thomas, David Hummels, Maros Ivanic and Roman Keeney (2004). How Confident Can We Be in CGE-Based Assessments of Free Trade Agreements? Working Paper Series, No. 10477. Cambridge, MA: National Bureau of Economic Research. Available from http://www.nber.org/papers/w10477.

Hidalgo, César A. and Ricardo Hausmann (2009). The building blocks of economic complexity. *Proceedings of the National Academy of Sciences of the United States of America*, vol. 106, No. 26, pp. 10570-10575.

Hidalgo, César A., Bailey Klinger, Albert-László Barabasi and Ricardo Hausmann (2007). The product space conditions the development of nations. *Science*. vol. 317, No. 5837, pp. 482-487 .

Humphrey, John and Hubert Schmitz (2000). Governance and upgrading: linking industrial cluster and global value chain research. Working Paper, No. 120. Sussex: Institute of Development Studies, University of Sussex. Available from https://www.ids.ac.uk/files/Wp120.pdf.

Humphrey, John and Hubert Schmitz (2002). How Does Insertion in Global Value Chains Affect Upgrading in Industrial Clusters? *Regional Studies*, vol. 36, No. 9, pp. 1017–1027.

Iacovone, Leonardo, Beata Smarzynska Javorcik, Wolfgang Keller and James R. Tybout (2011). Supplier Responses to Wal-Mart's Invasion of Mexico. *Journal of Internatinal Economics*, vol. 95, No. 1, pp. 1-15.

Independent Evaluation Group (IEG) (2013). *Improving Institutional Capability and Financial Viability to Sustain Transport: An Evaluation of World Bank Group Support Since 2002*. Washington, DC: World Bank. Available from http://ieg.worldbankgroup.org/evaluations/improving-institutional-capability-and-financial-viability-sustain-transport.

Inter-American Development Bank (IDB) (2013).Too Far to Export: Domestic Transport Costs and Regional Export Disparities in Latin America and the Caribbean. Washington, D.C. Available from http://publications.iadb.org/handle/11319/3664?locale-attribute=en.

Inter-American Development Bank (IDB) (2014). *Going global: promoting the internationalization of small and midsize enterprises in Latin America and the Caribbean*. Washington, D.C. Available from http://publications.iadb.org/bitstream/handle/11319/6412/Going%20Global.pdf?sequence=4.

International Finance Corporation (IFC) (2010a). *Scaling-Up SME Access to Financial Services in the Developing World*. G20 Seoul Summit. Available from http://www.ifc.org/wps/wcm/connect/bd1b060049585ef29e5abf19583b6d16/ScalingUp.pdf?MOD=AJPERES.

International Finance Corporation (IFC) (2010b). *SME Banking Knowledge Guide*. Second edition. Washington, D.C.. Available from http://www.ifc.org/wps/wcm/connect/industry_ext_content/ifc_external_corporate_site/industries/financial+markets/publications/toolkits/smebknowledge+guide.

International Finance Corporation (IFC) (2011). *Posing the Challenge on SME Finance*. SME Finance DFI Meeting, Paris, March 2011.

International Finance Corporation (IFC) (2012a). *Credit Reporting Knowledge Guide*. Washington, D.C. Available from http://www.ifc.org/wps/wcm/connect/industry_ext_content/ifc_external_corporate_site/industries/financial+markets/publications/toolkits/credit+reporting+knowledge+guide.

International Finance Corporation (IFC) (2012b). *Customer Management in SME Banking: A Best-in-Class Guide*. Washington, D.C. Available from https://openknowledge.worldbank.org/handle/10986/21739.

International Finance Corporation (IFC) (2013). *Closing the credit gap for formal and informal micro, small, and medium enterprises*. Washington, D.C. Available from http://documents.worldbank.org/curated/en/2013/01/24162672/closing-credit-gap-formal-informal-micro-small-medium-enterprises.

International Finance Corporation (IFC) (2014). *Women-Owned SMEs: A Business Opportunity for Financial Institutions*. Washington, D.C.. Available from http://www.ifc.org/wps/wcm/connect/b229bb004322efde9814fc384c61d9f7/WomenOwnedSMes+Report-Final.pdf?MOD=AJPERES.

International Labour Organization (ILO) (2001). Job Creation in Small and Medium-Sized Enterprises: Guide to ILO Recommendation, No. 189, adopted by the ILC 2-18 June 1998. Geneva. Available from http://www.ilo.org/empent/Publications/WCMS_127673/lang--en/index.htm.

International Labour Organization (ILO) (2008). Promotion of Rural Employment for Poverty Reduction. Geneva: International Labour Conference, 97th session.

International Labour Organization (ILO) (2010). A Skilled Workforce for Strong, Sustainable and Balanced Growth: A G20 Training Strategy. Geneva. Available from http://www.skillsforemployment.org/KSP/en/Details/?dn=FM11G_021626.

International Labour Organization (ILO) (2015). *Small and medium-sized enterprises and decent and productive employment creation*. Geneva. Available from http://www.ilo.org/wcmsp5/groups/public/@ed_norm/@relconf/documents/meetingdocument/wcms_358294.pdf.

International Organization for Standardization (ISO), International Trade Centre (ITC) and United Nations Industrial Development Organization (UNIDO) (2015). ISO 50001: A Practical Guide for SMEs. Vernier. International Organization for Standardization. Available from http://www.iso.org/iso/50001_handbook_preview.pdf.

International Trade Centre (2003). The Business Management System: A Guide on Enterprise Competitiveness. Geneva. International Trade Centre. Available from http://www.portaldecomert.ro/Files/BMS_Guide_for_Managers_20092185737328.pdf.

International Trade Centre (ITC) (2013). *How can we help you better? The Role of multi-lateral trade promotion agencies*. Presented to June, 2013. Available from http://www.comcec.org/UserFiles/Files/WG/Trade/1/RobertSkidmore.pdf.

International Trade Centre (ITC) (2014). *ACP Trade: Prospects for Stronger Performance and Cooperation*, ITC Technical Paper. Geneva: International Trade Centre. Available from http://www.intracen.org/uploadedFiles/intracenorg/Content/Publications/ACP%20Study-FINAL%2011-Sept-14%20with%20cover%20-%20low%20res.pdf.

International Trade Centre (ITC) (2015a). *Connecting Markets, Improving Lives*. Geneva. International Trade Centre (ITC). Available from http://www.intracen.org/uploadedFiles/intracen.org/Content/About_ITC/Corporate_Documents/Impact-Stories-web(1).pdf.

International Trade Centre (ITC) (2015b). *The Invisible Barriers to Trade: How Businesses Experience Non-Tariff Measures*. Geneva. Available from http://www.intracen.org/publication/The-Invisible-Barriers-to-Trade---How-Businesses-Experience-Non-Tariff-Measures/.

Intuit Inc. (2012). *Understanding and Overcoming Barriers to Technology Adoption Among India´s Micro, Small and Medium Enterprises: Building a Roadmap to Bridge the Digital Divide*. Available from http://www.intuit.in/images/MSME%20White%20Paper_FINAL.pdf.

Ivarsson, Inge and Claes Göran Alvstam (2005). Technology Transfer from TNCs to Local Suppliers in Developing Countries: A Study of AB Volvo's Truck and Bus Plants in Brazil, China, India and Mexico. *World Development*, vol. 33, No. 8, pp. 1325-1344.

Jain, Sanjay and Swee Leong (2005). Stress testing a supply chain using simulation. Proceedings of the 37th conference on Winter simulation, pp. 1650-1657. Available from http://dl.acm.org/citation.cfm?id=1162995.

Jansen, Marion and Rainer Lanz (2013). Skills and Export Competitiveness for Small and Medium-Sized Enterprises. Geneva. World Trade Organization. Available from https://www.wto.org/english/tratop_e/devel_e/a4t_e/global_review-13prog_e/skills_and_export_competitiveness_e.pdf.

Jappelli, Tullio and Marco Pagano (2002). Information Sharing, Lending and Defaults: CrossCountry Evidence. *Journal of Banking and Finance*, vol. 26, pp. 2017-2045.

Jaud, Mélise and Caroline Freund (2015). Champions Wanted - Promoting Exports in the Middle East and North Africa. Directions in Development - Trade, No. 95681. Washington, D.C.: World Bank: Available from http://www-wds.worldbank.org/external/default/WDSContentServer/WDSP/IB/2015/05/18/090224b082df91b3/1_0/Rendered/PDF/Champions0want0ast0and0North0Africa.pdf.

Johnson, Robert C. and Guillermo Noguera (2012). Accounting for intermediates: Production sharing and trade in value added. *Journal of International Economics*, vol. 86, No. 2, pp. 224-236.

Joumard, Isabelle, Urban Sila and Hermes Morgavi (2015). Challenges and Opportunities of India's Manufacturing Sector. Economics Department Working Papers, No. 1183. Paris: Organization for Economic Co-operation and Development. Available from http://www.oecd-ilibrary.org/economics/challenges-and-opportunities-of-india-s-manufacturing-sector_5js7t9q14m0q-en.

Jung, Andrés, Cecolia Plottier and Heber Francia (2011). Firm growth: Regional, industry and strategy effects in a Latin American economy. Paper presented at ERSA Congress 2011, Barcelona. Available from http://www-sre.wu.ac.at/ersa/ersaconfs/ersa11/e110830aFinal01502.pdf.

Kaplinsky, Raphael and Mike Morris (2001). Handbook for value chain research. Report prepared for International Development Research Centre. Ottawa. Available from http://www.ids.ac.uk/ids/global/pdfs/ValuechainHBRKMMNov2001.pdf.

Karlan, Dean and Martin Valdivia, 2011. Teaching Entrepreneurship: Impact of Business Training on Microfinance Clients and Institutions. Review of Economics and Statistics, vol. 93, No. 2, pp. 510-527.

Kaspar, Lea and Andrew Puddephatt. (2012, March). Benefits of Transparency in Public Procurement for SMEs: General Lessons for Egypt. Global Partners and Associates. Available from http://global-partners.co.uk/wp-content/uploads/Benefits-of-transparency-in-PP-forSMEs.pdf.

Kauffmann, Céline (2005). Financing SMEs in Africa. Policy Insights, No. 7. Paris: Organization for Economic Co-operation and Development (OECD). Available from http://dx.doi.org/10.1787/021052635664.

Kee, Hiau Looi, Alessandro Nicita and Marcelo Olarreaga (2009). Estimating trade restrictiveness indices. *Economic Journal*, vol. 119, pp. 172-199.

Ketels, Christian (2009). Clusters, Cluster Policy, and Swedish Competitiveness in the Global Economy. Expert Report No. 30 to Sweden's Globalisation Council. Stockholm: The Globalisation Council. Available from http://www.hbs.edu/faculty/Publication%20Files/d6e53822_c15a31c1-2998-49d1-bd5e-8ddcb31cccc5.pdf.

Khalifa, Sherif and Evelina Mengova (2012). Offshoring and Wage Inequality in Developing Countries. *Journal of Economic Development*, vol. 35, No. 3, pp. 1-42.

Kirby, Carlos and Nicolau Brosa (2011). Logistics as a Competitiveness Factor for Small and Medium Enterprises in Latin America and the Caribbean. Discussion Paper, No. IDB-DP-191. Washington, D.C.: Inter-American Development Bank. Available from http://idbdocs.iadb.org/wsdocs/getdocument.aspx?docnum=36592936.

Kirby, Eleanor and Shane Worner (2014). Crowfunding: An Infant Industry Growing Fast. Staff Working Paper, No. 3. Madrid: International Organization of Securities Commissions. Available from http://www.csrc.gov.cn/pub/newsite/gjb/gjzjhzz/ioscogkwj/201505/P020150518750893759706.pdf.

Kirubi, Charles, Arne Jacobson, Daniel M. Kammen and Andrew Mills (2009). Community-Based Electric Micro-Grids Can Contribute to Rural Development: Evidence from Kenya. *World Development*, vol. 37, No. 7, pp. 1208–1221.

Kishimoto, Chikashi (2004). Clustering and upgrading in global value chains: The Taiwanese personal computer industry. In *Local Enterprises in the Global Economy: Issues of Governance and Upgrading*, Hubert Schmitz, ed. Cheltenham: Edward Elgar.

Kitching, John, Mark Hart and Nick Wilson (2015). Burden or benefit? Regulation as a dynamic influence on small business performance. *International Small Business Journal*, vol. 33, No. 2, pp. 130–147.

Klapper, Leora (2005). The Role of Factoring for Financing Small and Medium Enterprises. Policy Research Working Paper, No. 3593. Washington, D.C.: World Bank. Available from https://openknowledge.worldbank.org/bitstream/handle/10986/8939/wps3593.pdf?sequence=1.

Klapper, Leora (2006). Export financing for SMEs : the role of factoring. Trade Note, No. 38239. Washington, D.C.: World Bank. Available from http://www-wds.worldbank.org/external/default/WDSContentServer/WDSP/IB/2006/12/21/0000903 41_20061221162155/Rendered/PDF/382390Trade1Note1291Klapper01PUBLIC1.pdf.

Klasen, Stephan (2005). Economic growth and poverty reduction: Measurement and poilicy issues. Development Centre Working Papers, No. 246. Paris: Organization for Economic Co-operation and Development. Available from http://www.oecd.org/dev/35393795.pdf.

Klasen, Stephan and Claudia Wink (2002). A Turning Point in Gender Bias in Mortality? An Update on the Number of Missing Women. *Population and Development Review*, vol. 28, No. 2, pp. 285-312.

Klasen, Stephan and Francesca Lamanna (2008). The Impact of Gender Inequality in Education and Employment on Economic Growth in Developing Countries: Updates and Extensions. Discussion Papers, No. 175. Göttingen: Ibero-America Institute for Economic Research. Available from https://ideas.repec.org/p/got/iaidps/175.html.

Knaup, Amy E. and Merissa C. Piazza (2007). Business Employment Dynamics data: Survival and longevity II. *Monthly Labor Review*, vol. 130, No. 9, pp. 3-10.

Kniahin, Dzmitry (2014). Modeling International Trade Patterns with the Product Space Methodology, Master thesis. Available from http://kniahin.com/KNIAHIN_Modeling_International_Trade_Patterns_Product_Space_2014.pdf.

Knight, Gary A. and Salih Tamer Cavusgil (1996). The Born Global Firm: A Challenge to Traditional Internationalization Theory. *Advances in International Marketing*, vol. 8.

Koltai & Company (2010). *Backgrounder*. Available from *http://koltai.co/wp-content/uploads/2014/04/KolCo-Backgrounder.pdf/*.

KPMG International and Oxford Economics (2015). 2015 Change Readiness Index. June 2015. Available from kpmg.com/changereadiness

Kubitz, Michal (2011). Leveraging Training: Skills Development in SMEs: An Analysis of Zaglebie sub-region, Poland. Local Economic and Employment Development (LEED) Working Paper, No. 2011/06. Paris: Organization for Economic Co-operation and Development (OECD). Available from http://www.oecd-ilibrary.org/docserver/download/5kgchzjsvnf3.pdf?expires=1440059116&id=id&accname=guest&checksum=B33D8B27400EF8919CCF45A60F985C20.

Kushnir, Khrystyna, Melina Laura Mirmulstein and Rita Ramalho (2010). Micro, Small, and Medium Enterprises Around the World: How Many Are There, and What Affects the Count? Washington, D.C.: World Bank/ International Finance Corporation. Available from http://www.ifc.org/wps/wcm/connect/9ae1dd80495860d6a482b519583b6d16/MSME-CI-AnalysisNote.pdf?MOD=AJPERES.

Lall, Sanjaya (2001). *Competitiveness, Technology and Skills*. Cheltenham, UK: Edward Elgar Publishing, Inc.

Lall, Sanjaya and Carlo Pietrobelli (2002). *Failing to Compete: Technology Development and Technology Systems in Africa*. Cheltenham: Edward Elgar.

Lall, Sanjaya and Carlo Pietrobelli (2003). Manufacturing in Sub-Saharan Africa and the Need of a National Technology System. In: *The Making of African Innovation Systems*. Mammo Muchie, Peter Gammeltoft, Bengt-Åke Lundvall, ed. Aalborg: Aalborg University Press.

Lall, Sanjaya and Carlo Pietrobelli (2005). National Technology Systems in Sub-Saharan Africa. *International Journal of Technology and Globalisation*. vol. 1, No. 3/4, pp. 311–342.

Lauterborn, Bob (1990). New Marketing Litany: Four Ps Passé: C-Words Take Over. *Advertising Age*, vol. 61, No. 41, p. 26.

Lawson, Ben and Danny Samson (2001). Developing Innovation Capability In Organisations: A Dynamic Capabilities approach. *International Journal of Innovation Management*, vol. 5, No. 3, pp. 377–400.

Lederman, Daniel and William F. Maloney (2012). Does What You Export Matter? In Search of Empirical Guidance for Industrial Policies. Washington, D.C.: World Bank. Available from https://www.imf.org/external/np/seminars/eng/2013/SPR/pdf/malo2.pdf.

Lederman, Daniel, Marcelo Olarreaga and Lucy Payton (2006). Export Promotion Agences, What Works and what doesn't? Policy Research Working Paper, No. 4044. Washington, D.C.: World Bank. Available from http://elibrary.worldbank.org/doi/abs/10.1596/1813-9450-4044.

Lederman, Daniel, Marcelo Olarreaga and Lucy Payton (2009). Export Promotion Agencies Revisited. Policy Research Working Paper, No. 5125. Washington, D.C.: World Bank. Available from http://elibrary.worldbank.org/doi/abs/10.1596/1813-9450-5125.

Lee, Joonkoo and Gary Gereffi (2013). The Co-Evolution of Concentration in Mobile Phone Value Chains and Its Impact on Social Upgrading in Developing Countries. Capturing the Gains Working Paper, No. 25. Hayang University and Duke University. Available from file:///C:/Users/klotz/Downloads/SSRN-id2237510.pdf.

Leromäin, Elsa and Gianluca Orefice (2014). New revealed comparative advantage index: Dataset and empirical distribution. *International Economics*. vol. 139, pp. 48-70.

Levinson, Jay Conrad (1984, 2007). *Guerrilla Marketing: Easy and Inexpensive Strategies for Making Big Profits from Your Small Business*, Ed. 4 (First published in 1984). London: Piatkus

Levitsky, Jacob (1997). Credit guarantee schemes for SMEs – an international review. *Small Enterprise Development*, vol. 8, No. 2. pp. 4-17.

Li, Yue and Martín Rama (2015). Firm Dynamics, Productivity Growth, and Job Creation. *World Bank Research Observer*, vol. 30, No.1, pp. 3-38.

Liotta, Giacomo (2012). Simulation of Supply-Chain Networks: A Source of Innovation and Competitive Advantage for Small and Medium-Sized Enterprises. Technology Innovation Management Review. November 2012. Available from http://timreview.ca/sites/default/files/article_PDF/Liotta_TIMReview_November2012.pdf.

Lloyd-Jones, Roger and A.A. Le Roux (1980). The Size of Firms in the Cotton Industry: Manchester 1815–41, *Economic History Review*, vol. 33, No. 1, pp. 72 - 82.

Love, Inessa and Nataliya Mylenko (2003). Credit Reporting and Financing Constraints. Policy Research Working Paper, No. 3142. Washington, D.C.: World Bank. Available from http://siteresources.worldbank.org/DEC/Resources/Credit_Reporting_and_Financing_Constraints.pdf.

Love, Inessa, Maria S. Martínez Pería and Sandeep Singh (2013). Collateral registries for movable assets : does their introduction spur firms'access to bank finance? Policy Research Working Paper, No. 6477. Washington, D.C.: World Bank. Available from http://elibrary.worldbank.org/doi/abs/10.1596/1813-9450-6477.

Love, James and Stephen Roper (2013). SME Innovation, Exporting and Growth. White Paper, No. 5. Enterprise Research Centre. Available from http://www.enterpriseresearch.ac.uk/wp-content/uploads/2013/12/ERC-White-Paper-No_5-Innovation-final.pdf.

Lundström, Anders and Lois Stevenson 2005. *Entrepreneurship Policy: Theory and Practice*. New York: Springer Science+Business Media, Inc.

Lundvall, Bengt-Åke (1992). *National Systems of Innovation: Towards a Theory of Innovation and Interactive Learning*. London: Anthem Press.

Madsen, Tage Koed and Per Servais (1997). The Internationalisation of Born Globals: An evolutionary process? *International Business Review*, vol. 6, No. 6, pp. 561–583.

Maertens, Miet, Colen, Liesbeth and Swinnen, Johan F.M. (2011). Globalisation and poverty in Senegal: a worst case scenario? *European Review of Agricultural Economics*, vol. 38, No. 1, pp. 31-54.

Maffioli, Alessandro Carlo Pietrobelli and Rodolfo Stucchi (2015). *The Evaluation of Cluster Development Programs: Methods and Practice*. Washington, D.C.: Inter-American Development Bank.

Mahate, Ashraf (2015). SME Competitiveness: A Development Perspective of GCC Countries. ITC Working paper. Geneva: International Trade Centre.

Maloney, William F. and Felipe Valencia Caicedo (2014). Engineers, Innovative Capacity and Development in the Americas. Policy Research Working Paper, No. 6814. Washington, D.C.: World Bank. Available from http://elibrary.worldbank.org/doi/pdf/10.1596/1813-9450-6814.

Mano, Yukichi, Alhassan Iddrisu, Yutaka Yoshino and Tetsushi Sonobe (2012). How Can Micro and Small Enterprises in Sub-Saharan Africa Become More Productive? *World Development*, vol. 40, No. 3, pp. 458-468.

Martincus, Christian Volpe and Juan Blyde (2013). Shaky roads and trembling exports: Assessing the trade effects of domestic infrastructure using a natural experiment. *Journal of International Economics*, vol. 90, No. 1, pp. 148–161.

Martínez Pería, Maria S. and Sandeep Singh (2014). The Impact of Credit Information Sharing Reforms On Firm Financing. Policy Research Working Paper, No. 7013. Washington, D.C.: The World Bank. Available from http://hdl.handle.net/10986/20348.

Martinez-Fernandez, Cristina and Ian Miles (2011). Knowledge intensive service activities : integrating knowledge for innovation. In *The Knowledge Economy at Work: Skills and Innovation in Knowledge Intensive Service Activities*, Cristina Martinez-Fernandez, Ian Miles and Tamara Weyman,ed. Cheltenham: Edward Elgar

Martinez-Fernandez, Cristina and Samantha Sharpe (2010). Leveraging Training and Skills Development in Small and Medium Enterprises (SMES): Preliminary Cross-country Analysis of the TSME Survey. Paris. Organization for Economic Co-operation and Development (OECD).

Massolution (2015). *2015CF The Crowdfunding Industry report*. Available from http://reports.crowdsourcing.org/?route=product/product&product_id=54.

Mathews, John A. (1996). High Technology Industrialization in East Asia. *Journal of Industry Studies*, vol. 3, No. 2, p. 1-77.

Mayer, Frederick and William Milberg (2013). Aid for Trade in a World of Global Value Chains: Chain Power, the Distribution of Rents and Implications for the Form of Aid. Capturing the Gains Working Paper, No. 34. Duke University and New School for Social Research. Available from http://www.capturingthegains.org/pdf/ctg-wp-2013-34.pdf.

Mayer, Thierry and Soledad Zignago (2011). Notes on CEPII's distances measures: the GeoDist Database, Working Paper, No. 2011-25. Paris: Centre d'Études Prospectives et d'Informations Internationales (CEPII). Available from http://www.cepii.fr/CEPII/en/publications/wp/abstract.asp?NoDoc=3877.

McCarthy, Jerome E. (1960). *Basic Marketing. A Managerial Approach*. Homewood, IL: Richard D. Irwin.

McCormick, Dorothy (1987). Fundis and Formality: Very Small Manufacturers in Nairobi. In *The Political Economy of Kenya*, Michael G. Schatzberg, ed. New York: Praeger Publishers.

McCormick, Dorothy (1993). Risk and Firm Growth: The Dilemma of Nairobi's Small-scale Manufacturers. IDS Discussion Paper, No. 291. Nairobi: University of Nairobi, Institute for Development Studies. Available from http://opendocs.ids.ac.uk/opendocs/handle/123456789/770#.Vcn94_mqpBc.

McDermott, Gerald A. and Carlo Pietrobelli (2015). SMEs, Trade and Development in Latin America: Toward a new approach on Global Value Chain Integration and Capabilities Upgrading. ITC Working paper. Geneva: International Trade Centre.

McKenzie, David and Christopher Woodruff (2014). What Are We Learning from Business Training and Entrepreneurship Evaluations around the Developing World? *World Bank Research Observer*, vol. 29, No. 1, pp. 48–82.

McKinsey & Company (2008). *Women Matter - Female leadership, a competitive edge for the future*. Available from http://www.mckinsey.de/suche/Women_Matter_2_brochure.pdf.

McKinsey Global Institute (2013). *Infrastructure Productivity: How to Save $1 Trillion a Year*. McKinsey Global Institute. Available from http://www.mckinsey.com/insights/engineering_construction/infrastructure_productivity.

McMillan, John and Christopher Woodruff (1999). Interfirm Relationships and Informal Credit in Vietnam. *Quarterly Journal of Economics*, vol. 114, No. 4, pp.1285-1320.

Melchior, Arne, Jinghai Zheng and Åshild Johnsen (2009), Trade barriers and export potential: Gravity estimates for Norway's exports. Paper written for the Ministry of Trade and Industry, Norway. Available from https://www.regjeringen.no/globalassets/upload/nhd/handelsavtaler/trade-barriers-and-export-potential.pdf.

Melitz, Marc J. (2003). The Impact of Trade on Intra-Industry Reallocations and Aggregate Industry Productivity. *Econometrica*, vol. 71, No. 6, pp. 1695-1725.

Miroudot, Sébastien, Rainer Lanz and Alexandros Ragoussis (2009). Trade in Intermediate Goods and Services. Trade Policy Working Paper, No. 93. Paris: Organization for Economic Co-operation and Development. Available from http://www.oecd.org/trade/its/44056524.pdf.

Mokyr, Joel (2001). The rise and fall of the factory system: technology, firms and households since the Industrial Revolution. *Carnegie-Rochester Conference Series on Public Policy*, vol. 55, No 1. pp. 1-45.

Montfort, Philippe, Hylke Vandenbussche and Emanuele Forlani (2008). Chinese Competition and Skill Upgrading in European Textiles: Firm-level Evidence. Discussinon Paper, No. 198. Leuven. LICOS Centre for Institutions and Economic Performance. Available from http://feb.kuleuven.be/drc/licos/publications/dp/dp198.pdf.

Morrison, Andrea and Carlo Pietrobelli and Roberta Rabellotti (2007). Global Value Chains and Technological Capabilities: A Framework to Study Learning and Innovation in Developing Countries. Working Paper, No. 117. SEMEQ Department - Faculty of Economics - University of Eastern Piedmont. Available from https://ideas.repec.org/p/upo/upopwp/117.html.

Moyo, Busani (2012). Do Power Cuts Affect Productivity? A Case Study Of Nigerian Manufacturing Firms. *International Business & Economics Research Journal*, vol. 11, No. 10, pp. 1163-1174.

Musso, Patrick and Stefano Schiavo (2008). The impact of financial constraints on firm survival and growth. *Journal of Evolutionary Economics*, vol. 18, No. 2, pp. 135–149.

Neely, Andy, Roberto Filippini, Cipriano Forza, Andrea Vinelli and Jasper Hii (2001). A framework for analysing business performance, firm innovation and related contextual factors: perceptions of managers and policy makers in two European regions. *Integrated Manufacturing Systems*, vol. 12, No. 2, pp. 114-24.

Nelson, Richard R. (1993). *National Innovation Systems*. New York: University Oxford Press.

Neumark, David, Brandon Wall and Junfu Zhang (2008). Do small business create more jobs? New evidence from the national establishment time series. Working Paper Series, No. 13818. Cambridge, MA: National Bureau of Economic Research. Available from http://www.nber.org/papers/w13818.

Neumark, David, Brandon Wall, Junfu Zhang (2011). Do Small Businesses Create More Jobs? New Evidence for the United States from the National Establishment Time Series. *Review of Economics and Statistics*, vol. 93, No. 1, pp. 16-29.

Niepmann, Friederike and Tim Schmidt-Eisenlohr (2014). International Trade, Risk and the Role of Banks. Working Paper, No. 4761, Munich: CESifo Group. Available from http://papers.ssrn.com/sol3/papers.cfm?abstract_id=2436838.

Nooteboom, Bart and Robert W. Vossen (1995). Firm size and efficiency in R&D spending. *Studies in Industrial Organization*, vol. 20, pp. 69-86.

Ohno, Taiichi (1988). *Toyota Production System: Beyond Large-Scale Production* (English translation ed.). Portland, Oregon: Productivity Press.

Okada, Aya (2004). Skills Development and Interfirm Learning Linkages under Globalization: Lessons from the Indian

Automobile Industry. *World Development*, vol. 32, No. 7, pp. 1265-1288.

Okello-Obura, Constant, Mabel K. Minishi-Majanja, Linda Cloete and J.R. Ikoja-Odongo (2008). Improving information use by SMEs in northern Uganda through ICT. *MOUSAION*, vol. 26, No.1, pp. 126-149.

Ono, Masanori, (2001). Determinants of Trade Credit in the Japanese Manufacturing Sector. *Journal of the Japanese and International Economies*, vol. 15, No. 2, pp. 160-177.

Organisation for Economic Co-operation and Development (OECD) - United Nations Economic Commission for Latin America and the Caribbean (UN-ECLAC) - Development Bank of Latin America (CAF) (2013). *Latin American Economic Outlook 2014: Logistics and Competitiveness for Development*. Paris, Santiago de Chile and Caracas. Available from http://scioteca.caf.com/bitstream/handle/123456789/480/Outlook2014-eng.pdf?sequence=1&isAllowed=y.

Organisation for Economic Co-operation and Development (OECD) - United Nations Economic Commission for Latin America and the Caribbean (UN-ECLAC) (2012). *Latin American Economic Outlook 2012 - Transforming the State for Development*. Paris and Santiago de Chile. Available from http://www.oecd.org/dev/americas/48965859.pdf.

Organisation for Economic Co-operation and Development (OECD) - United Nations Economic Commission for Latin America and the Caribbean (UN-ECLAC) (2013). *Latin American Economic Outlook 2013 - SME Policies for Structural Change*. Paris and Santiago de Chile. Available from http://www.cepal.org/en/publications/latin-american-economic-outlook-2013-smes-policies-structural-change.

Organisation for Economic Co-operation and Development (OECD) (2004a). *The Economic Impact of ICT – Measurement, Evidence and Implications*. Paris. Organization for Economic Co-operation and Development (OECD). Available from http://www.oecd-ilibrary.org/economics/the-economic-impact-of-ict_9789264026780-en.

Organisation for Economic Co-operation and Development (OECD) (2004b). *Networks, partnerships, clusters and intellectual property rights: opportunities and challenges for innovative SMEs in a global economy networks*. 2nd OECD Conference of ministers responsible for SMEs, Istanbul, Turkey 3-5 June 2004.

Organisation for Economic Co-operation and Development (OECD) (2006). *The SME Financing Gap: Theory and Evidence. Financial Market Trends*, vol. 2006, No. 2, pp. 89-97. Paris: Organization for Economic Co-operation and Development (OECD). Available from http://www.oecd-ilibrary.org/docserver/download/2706021ec004.pdf?expires=1439999825&id=id&accname=ocid195767&checksum=11FBBFDB0A45BE0E300E1B8FC479BA0F.

Organisation for Economic Co-operation and Development (OECD) (2007). *The OECD Tokyo Action Statement for Strengthening the Role of SMEs in Global Value Chains*. Paris. Organization for Economic Co-operation and Development. Available from http://www.oecd.org/cfe/smes/38774814.pdf.

Organisation for Economic Co-operation and Development (OECD) (2008). *Enhancing the Role of SMEs in Global Value Chains*. Paris. Available from http://www.oecd-ilibrary.org/industry-and-services/enhancing-the-role-of-smes-in-global-value-chains_9789264051034-en.

Organisation for Economic Co-operation and Development (OECD) (2010a). *Tackling Inequalities in Brazil, China, India and South Africa: The Role of Labour Market and Social Policies*. Paris. Available from http://www.oecd-ilibrary.org/social-issues-migration-health/tackling-inequalities-in-brazil-china-india-and-south-africa-2010_9789264088368-en.

Organisation for Economic Co-operation and Development (OECD) (2010b). *SMEs, Entrepreneurship and Innovation. OECD Studies on SMEs and Entrepreneurship*. Pairs. Organization for Economic Co-Operation and Development. Available from http://www.oecd.org/cfe/smesentrepreneurshipandinnovation.htm.

Organisation for Economic Co-operation and Development (OECD) (2011). *Intellectual Assets and Innovation: The SME Dimension*. OECD Studies on SMEs and Entrepreneurship. Paris. Organisation for Economic Co-Operation and Development. Available from http://www.oecd-ilibrary.org/industry-and-services/intellectual-assets-and-innovation_9789264118263-en.

Organisation for Economic Co-operation and Development (OECD) (2013a). *Skills Development and Training in SMEs*. Local Economic and Employment Development (LEED). Paris: Organization for Economic Co-operation and Development (OECD). Available from http://www.oecd-ilibrary.org/industry-and-services/skills-development-and-training-in-smes_9789264169425-en.

Organisation for Economic Co-operation and Development (OECD) (2013b). *Trade Costs: What have we learned? A synthesis report*. Trade Policy Paper, No. 150. Pairs. Organization for Economic Co-Operation and Development. Available from http://www.oecd.org/officialdocuments/publicdisplaydocumentpdf/?cote=TAD/TC/WP(2013)3/FINAL&docLanguage=En.

Organisation for Economic Co-operation and Development (OECD) (2013c). *OECD-ASEAN Training on Investment Policy Making*. Paris: Organization for Economic Co-operation and Development. Available from http://www.oecd.org/daf/inv/investment-policy/Module3_2013.pdf.

Organisation for Economic Co-operation and Development (OECD) (2015). *New Approaches to SME and Entrepreneurship Financing: Broadening the Range of Instruments*. Paris: Organization for Economic Co-operation and Development (OECD). Available from http://www.oecd.org/cfe/smes/New-Approaches-SME-full-report.pdf.

Organisation for Economic Co-operation and Development (OECD)/European Commission (EC) (2005). *Oslo Manual 3rd edition: Guidelines for collecting and interpreting innovation data*. Statistical Office of the European Communities and OECD. Available from http://ec.europa.eu/eurostat/documents/3859598/5889925/OSLO-EN.PDF/60a5a2f5-577a-4091-9e09-9fa9e741dcf1?version=1.0.

Osterwalder, Alexander and Yves Pigneur (2010). *Business Model Generation: A Handbook for Visionaries, Game changers and Challengers*. Hoboken, New Jersey: John Wiley & Sons.

Osterwalder, Alexander, Yves Pigneur, Gregory Bernarda and Alan Smith (2014). *Value Proposition Design: How to Create Products and Services Customers Want*. Hoboken, New Jersey: John Wiley & Sons.

Oughton, Christine and Geoff Whittam (1997). Competition and cooperation in the small firm sector. *Scottish Journal of Political Economy*, vol. 44 , No. 1, pp. 1-30.

Ouimet, Paige and Rebecca Zarutskie (2013). Who works for startups? The relation between firm age, employee age and growth. Finance and Economics Discussion Series, No. 2013-75. Washington, D.C.: Federal Reserve Board. Available from http://www.federalreserve.gov/pubs/feds/2013/201375/201375pap.pdf.

Page, John and Måns Söderbom (2012). Is Small Beautiful? Small Enterprise, Aid and Employment in Africa. Working Paper, No. 2012/94. Helsinki: United Nations University World Institute for Development Economics Research (UNU-WIDER). Available from http://www.wider.unu.edu/publications/working-papers/2012/en_GB/wp2012-094/.

Palangkaraya, Alfons, Andreas Stierwald and Jongsay Yong (2009). Is Firm Productivity Related to Size and Age? The Case of Large Australian Firms. *Journal of Industry, Competition and Trade*, vol. 9, No.2, pp. 167-195.

Pande, Peter, Robert Neuman and Roland Cavanagh (2000). *The Six Sigma Way: How GE, Motorola and other Top Companies are Honing Their Performance*. New York: McGraw Hill Professional.

Park, Albert, Gaurav Nayyar and Patrick Low (2013). Supply Chain Perspectives and Issues. A Literature Review. Hong Kong and Geneva: Fung Global Institute and World Trade Organization. Available from https://www.wto.org/english/res_e/booksp_e/aid4tradesupplychain13_e.pdf.

Pavlínek, Petr, Boleslaw Domański and Robert Guzik (2009). Industrial upgrading through foreign direct investment in Central European automotive manufacturing. European Urban and Regional Studies, vol. 16, No. 1, pp. 43-63.

Pietrobelli, Carlo (2008). Global value chains in the least developed countries of the world: threats and opportunities for local producers. *International Journal of Technological Learning, Innovation and Development*, vol. 1, No. 4, pp. 459-481.

Pietrobelli, Carlo and Roberta Rabellotti (2006). Supporting Enterprise Upgrading in Clusters and Value Chains in Latin America. In *Upgrading to Compete. Global Value Chains, SMEs and Clusters in Latin America*, Inter-American Development Bank ed. Washington, D.C.: Inter-American Development Bank.

Pietrobelli, Carlo and Roberta Rabellotti (2011). Global Value Chains Meet Innovation Systems. *World Development*, vol. 39, No. 7, pp. 1261–1269.

Plehn-Dujowich, Jose (2007). Innovation, Firm Size, and RDSearch. *Economics Bulletin*, vol. 12, No. 17. pp. 1-8.

Pomfret, Richard and Patricia Sourdin (2010). Trade Facilitation and the Measurement of Trade Costs. *Journal of International Commerce, Economics and Policy*. vol. 1, No. 1, pp. 145-163.

Poon, Teresa Shuk-Ching (2004). Beyond the global production networks: a case of further upgrading of Taiwan's information technology industry. *International Journal of Technology and Globalisation*, vol. 1, No. 1, pp. 130-144.

Porter, Michael E. (1980). *Competitive Strategy: Techniques for Analysing Industries and Competitors*. New York: The Free Press.

Porter, Michael E. (1985). *Competitive Advantage: Creating and Sustaining Superior Performance*. New York: The Free Press.

Porter, Michael E. (1998). *On Competition*. Cambridge, MA: Harvard Business School Press.

Porter, Michael E. (2008). Clusters and Competition: New Agendas for Companies, Governments, and Institutions. In: *On Competition* (new edition), Porter, Michael E.. Boston: Harvard Business School Press.

Porter, Michael E. and Mark R. Kramer (2011). Creating Shared Value. Harvard Business Review, January-February 2011 Issue. Available from https://hbr.org/2011/01/the-big-idea-creating-shared-value.

Powell, David and Joachim Wagner (2014). The Exporter Productivity Premium along the Productivity Distribution: Evidence from Quantile Regression with Nonadditive Firm Fixed Effects. *Review of World Economics*, vol. 150, No. 4, pp. 763-785.

Rammer, Christian, Dirk Czarnitizki, Alfred Spielkamp (2009). Innovation success of non-R&D-performers: substituting technology by management in SMEs. *Small Business Economics*. vol.33, pp. 35-58.

Reid, Stan (1984). Information acquisition and export entry decisions in small firms. *Journal of Business Research*, vol. 12, No. 2, pp. 141–157.

Rijkers, Bob, Hassen Arouri, Caroline Freund and Antonio Nucifora. 2014. Which Firms Create the most jobs in developing countries? Evidence from Tunisia. Policy Research Working Paper, No. 7068. Washington, D.C.: World Bank. Available from http://elibrary.worldbank.org/doi/pdf/10.1596/1813-9450-7068.

Roberts, Mark J. and James R. Tybout (1997). The Decision to Export in Colombia, An Empirical Model of Entry with Sunk Costs. *American Economic Review*, vol. 87, No. 4, pp. 545-564.

Rodríguez-Clare, Andres (2005). Coordination failures, clusters and microeconomic interventions. Working Paper, No. 544. Washington, D.C.: Inter-American Development Bank. Available from http://www.iadb.org/en/research-and-data/

publication-details,3169.html?pub_id=wp-544.

Rose, Andrew K. (2005). The Foreign Service and Foreign Trade, Embassies as Export Promotion. Working Paper Series, No. 11111. Cambridge, MA: National Bureau of Economic Research. Available from http://www.nber.org/papers/w11111.

Ruffier, Jean (2008). China Textile in Global Value Chain. In *Chinese Firms in the Era of Globalisation*, Jean-Francois Huchet and Wang Wei. China Development Press.

Schmitz, Hubert (1995). Collective efficiency: growth path for small-scale industry. *Journal of Development Studies*, vol. 34, No. 4, pp. 529-566.

Schmitz, Hubert (1999). Collective efficiency and increasing returns. *Cambridge Journal of Economics*, vol. 23, No. 4, pp. 465-483.

Schmitz, Hubert (2004). Local upgrading in global chains: recent findings. DRUID Summer Conference 2004 on Industrial Dynamics, Innovation and Development, Elsinore, Denmark June 14-16. Available from http://www.druid.dk/uploads/ tx_picturedb/ds2004-1422.

Schoar, Antoinette (2009). The Divide between Subsistence and Transformational Entrepreneurship. In *Innovation Policy and the Economy*, Joshua Lerner and Scott Stern ed. Chicago: University of Chicago Press.

Schoof, Ulrich (2006): Stimulating Youth Entrepreneurship: Barriers and incentives to enterprise start-ups by young people. Series on Youth and Entrepreneurship Working Paper, No. 76. Geneva: International Labour Organization. Available from http://www.ilo.org/wcmsp5/groups/public/---ed_emp/---emp_ent/documents/publication/wcms_094025.pdf.

Schwartz, Jordan, José Luis Guasch, Gordon Wilmsmeier and Aiga Stokenberga (2009). Logistics, transport and food prices in LAC: policy guidance for improving efficiency and reducing costs. Sustainable Development Occasional Paper, No. 2009/2. Washington, D.C.: World Bank. Available from http://siteresources.worldbank.org/LACEXT/Resources/258553-1252607325125/LCSSD_OcassionalPapers_August.pdf.

Seringhaus, Rolf (1987). The role of information assistance in the small firm's export involvement. *International Small Business Journal*, vol. 5, No. 2, pp. 26-365.

Shaffer, Paul and Trung Dang Le (2014). Pro-Poor Growth and Firm Size: Evidence from Vietnam. *Oxford Development Studies*, vol. 41, No. 1, pp. 1-28.

Shepotylo, Oleksandr (2009). Gravity with Zeros: Estimating Trade Potential of CIS countries. Discussion Paper, No. 16. Kyiv School of Economics. Available from http://papers.ssrn.com/sol3/papers.cfm?abstract_id=1347997.

Shimizu, Koichi (2009). *Advertising Theory and Strategies*. 16th edition, Souseisha Book Company.

Shingal, Anirudh (2015). Labour market effects of integration into GVCs: Review of Literature. R4D Working Paper, No. 2015/10. Bern: World Trade Institute. Available from http://www.r4d-employment.com/wp-content/uploads/2014/09/GVC.pdf.

Shinnar, Rachel S., Olivier Giacomin and Frank Janssen (2012). Entrepreneurial perceptions and intentions: the role of gender and culture. *Entrepreneurship: Theory and Practice*, vol. 36, No. 3, pp. 465-493.

Simon, Mark, Susan M. Houghton and Karl Aquino (2000). Cognitive Biases, Risk Perception, and Venture Formation: How Individuals Decide to Start Companies. *Journal of Business Venturing*, vol. 15, No. 2, pp. 113-134.

Sokoloff, Kenneth Lee (1984). Was the Transition from the Artisanal Shop to the Nonmechanized Factory Associated with Gains in Efficiency? Evidence from the U.S. Manufacturing Censuses of 1820 and 1850. *Explorations in Economic History*, vol. 21, No. 4, pp. 351-382.

Sölvell, Örjan, Göran Lindqvist and Christian Ketels (2003). *The Cluster Initiative Greenbook*. Stockholm: Bromma Tryck AB.

Sonobe, Tetsushi and Keijiro Otsuka (2006). *Cluster-Based Industrial Development: An East Asian Model*. New York: Palgrave Macmillan.

Sonobe, Tetsushi and Keijiro Otsuka (2011). *Cluster-Based Industrial Development: A Comparative Study of Asia and Africa*. New York: Palgrave Macmillan.

Sonobe, Tetsushi, Yuki Higuchi and Keijiro Otsuka (2012). Productivity Growth and Job Creation in the Development Process of Industrial Clusters. Policy Research Working Paper, No. 6280. Washington, D.C.: World Bank. Available from http://elibrary.worldbank.org/doi/pdf/10.1596/1813-9450-6280.

Stiglitz, Joseph E. and Andrew Weiss. (1981). Credit rationing in markets with imperfect information. *American Economic Review*, vol. 71, No. 3, pp. 393-410.

Stone, Ian (2012). Upgrading workforce skills in smallbusinesses: Reviewing international policy and experience. Presented at the OECD LEED international workshop on SkillDevelopment for SMEs and Entrepreneurship, Danish BusinessAuthority – Copenhagen, 28 November 2012. Available from http://www.oecd.org/cfe/leed/Skills%20Workshop%20Background%20report_Stone.pdf.

Sturgeon, Tim and Olga Memedovic (2010). Mapping global value chains: Intermediate goods trade and structural change in the world economy. Development Policy and Strategic Research Working Paper, No. 5. Vienna. United Nations Industrial Development Organization. Available from http://www.unido.org//fileadmin/user_media/Publications/Research_and_statistics/Branch_publications/Research_and_Policy/Files/Working_Papers/2010/WP%2005%20Mapping%20Glocal%20Value%20Chains.pdf.

Syverson, Chad (2011). What determines productivity? *Journal of Economic Literature*, vol. 49, No. 2, pp. 326-365.

Tambunan, Tulus (2009). SMEs in Asian Developing Countries. *Journal of Development and Agricultural Economics*, vol. 1, No. 2, pp. 27-40.

Tanabe, Koji and Chihiro Watanabe (2003). Advancing technological innovation. Strategies for small and medium enterprises in an IT economy. *Asian Pacific Tech Monitor*, vol. 20, No. 4, pp. 47-51.

Teignier, Marc and David Cuberes (2014). Aggregate Costs of Gender Gaps in the Labor Market: A Quantitative Estimate. Economics Working Papers, No. 308. Barcelona: Universitat de Barcelona. Available from http://papers.ssrn.com/sol3/papers.cfm?abstract_id=2405006.

The Boston Consulting Group (2013). *Bridging the Gap: Meeting the Infrastructure Challenge with Public-Private Partnership*. The Boston Consulting Group. Available from http://www.bcg.de/documents/file128534.pdf.

The Economist (2015). Spanish businesses: Supersize me. 21 February 2015. Available from http://www.economist.com/news/business/21644172-lack-larger-firms-means-fewer-jobs-and-less-resilient-economy-supersize-me.

The Huffington Post (2015). Hearts and Minds. 30 March 2015. Available from http://www.huffingtonpost.com/janine-garner/hearts-and-minds_3_b_6963334.html?.

Türk Ekonomi Bankasý (2013). *Annual Report 2013*. Istanbul. Available from http://www.teb.com.tr/Yatirimci/interaktif_2013/en/en-teb2013.pdf.

Uchida, Hirofumi, Gregory F. Udell and Wako Watanabe (2013). Are trade creditors relationship lenders? *Japan and the World Economy*, vol. 25, pp. 24-38.

United Nations Economic and Social Commission for Asia and the Pacific (UN-ESCAP) (2012). *Policy guidebook for SME development in Asia and the Pacific*. Bangkok. Available from http://www.unescap.org/resources/policy-guidebook-sme-development-asia-and-pacific.

United Nations Conference on Trade and Development (UNCTAD) (1998). *Promoting and sustaining SMEs clusters and networks for development*. New York and Geneva: United Nations. http://unctad.org/en/docs/c3em5d2.pdf.

United Nations Conference on Trade and Development (UNCTAD) (2001). Best Practices in Financial Innovations for SMEs. A paper presented at UNCTAD's intergovernemental Expert Meeting on "Improving the competitiveness of SMEs in developing countries: The Role of Finance To Enhance Enterprise Development" held in Geneva on 22-24 October 2001,UNCTAD/ITE/TEB/Misc.3.

United Nations Conference on Trade and Development (UNCTAD) (2005). Improving the Competitiveness of SMEs Through Enhancing Productive Capacity. Proceedings of four expert meetings. New York and Geneva: United Nations. Available from http://unctad.org/en/Docs/iteteb20051_en.pdf.

United States International Trade Commission (USITC) (2014). *Trade Barriers That U.S. Small and Medium-sized Enterprises perceive as affecting exports to the European Union*, Investigation No. 332-541, Publication 4455. Washington, D.C. Available from http://www.usitc.gov/publications/332/pub4455.pdf.

Vaaland, Terje I. and Morten Heide (2007). Can the SME survive the supply chain challenges? *Supply Chain Management: An International Journal*, vol. 12, No. 1, pp. 20-31.

Van Ark, Bart and Erik Monnikhof (1996). Size Distribution of Output and Employment: A Data Set For Manufacturing Industries in Five OECD Countries, 1960s-1990. Economics Department Working Paper, No. 166. Paris: Organization for Economic Co-operation and Development. Available from http://www.oecd.org/eco/outlook/1863515.pdf.

Van Praag, C. Mirkam (2003). Business Survival and Success of Young Small Business Owners. *Small Business Economics*, vol. 21, No. 1, pp. 1-17.

Van Stel, André, Nardo de Vries and Jan de Kok (2014). The effect of SME productivity increases on large firm productivity in the EU-27. Available from http://www.uni-klu.ac.at/sozio/downloads/Van_Stel_De_Vries_De_Kok_Klagenfurt_ECFED_2014.pdf.

Vogel, Alexander and Joachim Wagner (2010). Higher productivity in importing German manufacturing firms: self-selection, learning from importing, or both? *Review of World Economics*, vol. 145, No. 4, pp. 641-665.

Vollrath, Thomas (1991). A Theoretical Evaluation of Alternative Trade Intensity Measures of Revealed Comparative Advantage. *Review of World Economics (Weltwirtschaftliches Archiv)*, vol. 127, vol. 2, pp 265-280.

Volpe Martincus, Christian (2010). Odyssey in International Markets An Assessment of the Effectiveness of Export Promotion in Latin America and the Caribbean. Special Report on Integration and Trade. Washington, D.C.: Inter-American Development Bank. Available from http://www.iadb.org/research/books/IDB-BK-100/summary/summary_english.pdf.

Volpe Martincus, Christian, Antoni Estevadeordal, Andrés Gallo and Jessica Luna (2010). Information Barriers, Export Promotion Institutions, and the Extensive Margin of Trade. Working Paper, No. IDB-WP-200. Washngton, D.C.: Inter-American Development Bank. Available from http://idbdocs.iadb.org/wsdocs/getdocument.aspx?docnum=35340252.

Wacziarg, Romain and Karen Horn Welch (2008). Trade Liberalization and Growth: New Evidence. *World Bank Economic Review*, vol. 22, No. 2, pp. 187-231.

Wagner, Joachim (2005). Exports and Productivity: a survey of the evidence from firm level data. Working Paper Series in Economics, No. 4. Lüneburg: University of Lüneburg. Available from http://www.leuphana.de/fileadmin/user_upload/Forschungseinrichtungen/ifvwl/WorkingPapers/wp_04_Upload.pdf.

Wagner, Joachim (2012). International Trade and Firm Performance: A Survey of Empirical Studies since 2006. *Review of World Economics*, vol. 148, No. 2, pp. 235-267.

Wamalwa, Herbert and Dorothy McCormick (2015). Small and Medium Enterprises (SMEs), Trade and Development in Africa. ITC Working paper. Geneva: International Trade Centre.

Wang, Z. K. and Winters, Alan L. (1992). The Trading Potential of Eastern Europe. *Journal of Economic Integration*, vol. 7, No. 2, pp. 113-136.

Wignaraja, Ganeshan (2015). Factors Affecting Entry into Supply Chain Trade: An Analysis of Firms in Southeast Asia. *Asia & the Pacific Policy Studies*.

Wilkinson, Timothy and Lance Eliot Brouthers (2006). Trade promotion and SME export performance. *International Business Review*, vol. 15, No. 3, pp. 233-252.

Wilson, Karen E. and Marco Testoni (2014). Improving the Role of Equity Crowdfunding in Europe's Capital Markets. Bruegel Policy Contribution, No. 2014/09. Brussels: Bruegel. Available from SSRN: http://ssrn.com/abstract=2502280.

Winch, Graham. W. and Carmine Bianchi (2006). Drivers and Dynamic Processes for SMEs Going Global. *Journal of Small Business and Enterprise Development,* vol. 13, No. 1, pp. 73–88.

Winters, Rob and Erik Stam (2007). Innovation Networks of High-Tech SMEs: Creation of Knowledge But No Creation of Value. Jena Economic Research Papers, No. 2007-042. Friedrich-Schiller University and the Max Planck Institute of Economics. Available from http://zs.thulb.uni-jena.de/servlets/MCRFileNodeServlet/jportal_derivate_00036454/wp_2007_042.pdf.

Woessman, Ludger (2011). Education Policies to Make Globalization More Inclusive. In Making Globalization Socially Sustainable, Marion Jansen and Marc Bacchetta, ed. Geneva: International Labour Organization and World Trade Organization.

World Bank - InfoDev (2013). *Crowdfunding's Potential for the Developing World*. Washington, D.C. Available from http://www.infodev.org/infodev-files/wb_crowdfundingreport-v12.pdf.

World Bank (2006). *Information and Communications for Development: Global Trends and Policies*. Washington, D.C. Available http://documents.worldbank.org/curated/en/2006/01/6739395/global-trends-policies-2006-information-communications-development.

World Bank (2008). *World Development Report 2008: Agriculture for Development*. Washington, D.C. World Bank. Available from http://web.worldbank.org/WBSITE/EXTERNAL/EXTDEC/EXTRESEARCH/EXTWDRS/0,,contentMDK:23062293~pagePK:478093~piPK:477627~theSitePK:477624,00.html.

World Bank (2011a). *Industrial Clusters and Micro and Small Enterprises in Africa: From Survival to Growth*. Directions in Development, No. 58850. Washington, D.C. Available from https://openknowledge.worldbank.org/handle/10986/2546.

World Bank (2011b). *World Development Report 2012: Gender Equality and Development*. Washington, D.C.. Available from https://siteresources.worldbank.org/INTWDR2012/Resources/7778105-1299699968583/7786210-1315936222006/Complete-Report.pdf.

World Bank (2012). *Africa Can Help Feed Africa, Removing barriers to regional trade in food staples*. Washington, D.C. Available from http://siteresources.worldbank.org/INTAFRICA/Resources/Africa-Can-Feed-Africa-Report.pdf.

World Bank (2014a). *Doing Business 2015: Going Beyond Efficiency*. Washington, D.C. Available from DOI: 10.1596/978-1-4648-0351-2.

World Bank (2014b). *Connecting to Compete 2014 -Trade Logistics in the Global Economy. Washington, D.C. Available from http://www.worldbank.org/content/dam/Worldbank/document/Trade/LPI2014.pdf.*

World Bank (2015). *Enterprise Surveys*. Washington, D.C. Available from http://www.enterprisesurveys.org/.

World Bank Group (2014). *Practical Solutions and Models for Addressing Obstacles to Institutional Investment in Infrastructure in Developing Countries*. Prepared by the Staff of the World Bank Group for the G-20 Investment and Infrastructure Working Group, January 2014.

World Bank Group (2015). *Export Competitiveness. Trade and Competitiveness Global Practice*, Viewpoint Note No. 348. Washington, D.C. Available from http://www-wds.worldbank.org/external/default/WDSContentServer/WDSP/IB/2015/07/09/090224b082fe2dab/2_0/Rendered/PDF/Export0competi00Competition0Matters.pdf.

World Economic Forum (WEF) (2008). *The Global Competitiveness Report 2008-2009*. Geneva. World Economic Forum. Available from http://www.weforum.org/reports/global-competitiveness-report-2008-2009.

World Economic Forum (WEF) (2013). The Global Competitiveness Report 2013 - 2014. Geneva. Available from http://www3.weforum.org/docs/WEF_GlobalCompetitivenessReport_2013-14.pdf.

World Economic Forum (WEF) (2015). *The Global Competitiveness Report 2014 - 2015*. Geneva. Available from http://www.weforum.org/reports/global-competitiveness-report-2014-2015.

World Intellectual Property Organization (WIPO) (2012). *The Global Innovation Index 2012 - Stronger Innovation Linkages for Global Growth*. Paris and Geneva. Available from http://www.wipo.int/edocs/pubdocs/en/economics/gii/gii_2012.pdf.

World Trade Organization (WTO) (2012). *World Trade Report 2012: Trade and public policies: A closer look at non-tar-

iff measures in the 21st century. Geneva. Available from https://www.wto.org/english/res_e/booksp_e/anrep_e/world_trade_report12_e.pdf.

World Trade Organization (WTO) (2014). *World Trade Report 2014. Trade and Development: Recent trends and the role of the WTO*. Geneva. Available from http://www.r4d-employment.com/wp-content/uploads/2014/09/GVC.pdf.

World Trade Organization (WTO) (2015). *Background note on Aid For Trade and infrastructure: Financing the gap*. Committee on Trade and Development Aid for Trade, WT/COMTD/AFT/W/56. 13 February 2015. Available from https://www.wto.org/english/tratop_e/devel_e/a4t_e/wkshop_feb15_e/wkshop_feb15_e.htm.

World Trade Organization (WTO) (forthcoming). *World Trade Report 2015: Speeding up trade: benefits and challenges of implementing the Trade Facilitation Agreement*. Geneva.

World Trade Organization (WTO) and Organization for Economic Co-operation and Development (OECD) (2013). *Aid for Trade at a Glance - Connecting to Value Chains*. Geneva and Paris. Available from https://www.wto.org/english/res_e/booksp_e/aid4trade13_e.pdf.

World Trade Organization (WTO) and Organization for Economic Co-operation and Development (OECD) (2015). *Aid for Trade at a Glance - Reducing trade costs for inclusive, sustainable growth*. Geneva and Paris. Available from https://www.wto.org/english/res_e/publications_e/aid4trade15_e.htm.

Yoshino, Yutaka (2011). Industrial Clusters and Micro and Small Enterprises in Africa : From Survival to Growth. Directions in Development, No. 58850. Washington, D.C.: World Bank. Available from https://openknowledge.worldbank.org/handle/10986/2546.

Zahid, Z and M. Mokhtar (2007). Estimating Technical Efficiency of Malaysian Manufacturing Small and Medium Enterprises: A Stochastic Frontier Modelling, The 4th SMEs in a Global Economy Conference, University of Wollongong, 9-10 July.

Zhalilo, Yaroslav A. (2015). SMEs, Trade and Economic Development in Ukraine. ITC Working paper. Geneva: International Trade Centre.

Zhang, Lei and Wei Xia (2014). Integrating small and medium-sized enterprises into global trade flows: the case of China. In *Connecting to global markets*, Marion Jansen, Mustapha Sadni Jallab and Maarten Smeets, ed. Geneva: World Trade Organization (WTO).

Zhang, Lei, Longxiang Shi and Hang Zhang (2015). Explorations of Small and Medium-Sized Enterprises (SMEs) in China. ITC Working paper. Geneva: International Trade Centre.